MEDIA MANAGEMENT
A Casebook Approach

MEDIA MANAGEMENT
A Casebook Approach

Second Edition

Ardyth Broadrick Sohn
Butler University

Jan LeBlanc Wicks
University of Arkansas

Stephen Lacy
Michigan State University

George Sylvie
University of Texas at Austin

Contributing Authors:

Angela Powers
Northern Illinois

Nora J. Rifon
Michigan State University

C. Ann Hollifield
University of Georgia

LAWRENCE ERLBAUM ASSOCIATES, PUBLISHERS
1999   Mahwah, New Jersey   London

Lawrence Erlbaum Associates, Inc., Publishers
10 Industrial Avenue
Mahwah, NJ 07430

Cover design by Kathryn Houghtaling Lacey

Library of Congress Cataloging-in-Publication Data

Media management : a casebook / Ardyth Broadrick Sohn ...
[et al . — 2nd ed.
    p. cm.
Rev. ed. of: Media management / Stephen Lacy. 1st ed. 1993.
Includes bibliographical references and index.
ISBN 0-8058-3026-X (alk. paper)
    1. Mass media—Management—Case studies. I. Sohn, Ardyth
Broadrick, 1946- . II. Lacy, Stephen, 1948- . Media management.
P96.M34M4   1998
302.23'068—dc21

                                                                98-23331
                                                                CIP

Books published by Lawrence Erlbaum Associates are printed on acid-free paper, and their bindings are chosen for strength and durability.

Printed in the United States of America
10 9 8 7 6 5 4 3 2

CONTENTS

5   Technology and the Future   115

6   Media Regulation and Self-Regulation   147

7   Planning   184

8   Market Analysis   230

PREFACE

This volume marks an improved version of the 1993 edition with all previous authors involved with writing and revisions.

Jan LeBlanc Wicks provides regulatory guidance as well as budgetory background for readers. She also establishes a cultural grounding for readers in her extended case that includes original primary data. Her online chapter references guide readers to new sources of information and analysis. Stephen Lacy's decision-making chapter leads the text with its outline of how media companies operate and how managers function within a complex corporate world. Students are provided with a foundation for structural considerations in Chapter 1 that provides a fine introduction to the cases and content that follow. His market analysis chapter introduces important external management considerations.

George Sylvie's attention to motivation, diversity, and technology in his chapters and end case provide grounding for the next decade which will feature demographic work force changes and emerging technologies. Angela Powers and Nora Rifon guide readers through structural and research topics. C. Ann Hollifield brings an international perspective to chapter 7 which includes her original case study developed around an Eastern European market.

Only one presentation change has been made and that involves a reordering of the chapters that facilitates teaching and content cohesion. In the first edition, the chapters were arranged with internal organization issues first and then external concerns or issues. The final chapter was dedicated to technological issues. For this edition, the internal organizational issues are still presented first, but technology (which straddles internal and organizational topics) is the transitional chapter rather than the final chapter. The increased importance of the content and focus of this chapter in the 4 years since the first edition was published justifies its repositioning.

Another reordering of chapters involves the market analysis and marketing and research chapters, which are now positioned together so that readers have a sense of continuity between the two without an overlap of content.

The cases illustrate and provide practice for students in simple analysis as well as complex synthesis. Instructors have several choices for assignments. They provide an opportunity for students to demonstrate their grasp of all chapters with particular emphasis on creativity, choice, and management responsibility.

Case study has become more common within the field of journalism and mass communication in the past 4 years, and most students and instructors are comfortable with this method of learning. It is ideal for students of management because it takes into account flexibility, individuality, and creativity as students face realistic problems and opportunities mirrored in the professional world. It provides practice in role playing, leadership, communication, and decision making with consequences. All are valuable intellectual and professional exercises. Students are encouraged to distinguish among acts, activities, actors, meanings, relationships, and settings of importance. By recognizing the components individually and collectively students can see the options and choices more clearly. Discussion and debate are hard to avoid when examining cases, and as students recognize themselves and their peers as part of the issues surrounding media study, they will become more adept at finding their own place within the media work force.

—*Ardyth Broadrick Sohn*

1

MANAGERIAL DECISION MAKING

Managers usually make decisions the way most people breathe, without thinking about the process. However, decision making is at the heart of the managerial process, just as breathing is central to life. Simon (1960), probably the most noted scholar in the area of decision making, equated the process of decision making to the process of managing.

Making decisions without considering the process works reasonably well on a day-to-day basis. However, decision making is a skill. To improve that skill, managers must think about the process they use to solve problems. The purpose of this chapter is to help students understand how decisions are made so they can benefit from using the cases in this book. The cases following each chapter provide decision-making practice in a number of managerial areas. This practice will be more effective if a person understands the decision-making process.

DEFINING DECISION MAKING

Definitions of decision making abound. For example, Simon (1960) wrote, "Decision making comprises three principle phases: finding occasions for making decisions; finding possible courses of action; and choosing among the courses of action" (p. 1). Harrison (1987) defined a decision as, "a moment, in an ongoing process of evaluating alternatives for meeting an objective, at which expectations about a particular course of action impel the decision maker to select the course of action most likely to result in obtaining the objective" (p. 2).

Many of the traditional definitions of decision making concentrate on the process as a rational one that involves a person or a group with common goals. However, Taylor (1984) emphasized the role of social and political context of organizations and their environments. This approach suggests that decisions are not as deliberate as often assumed, but occur from interaction among people and groups with sometimes conflicting goals.

The range of definitions for decision making suggests that defining this process is somewhat arbitrary. However, some concepts are common to most definitions. Decisions almost always involve resources; they usually address goals or objectives; they always involve people; and the environment in which these people work almost always affects decisions.

With these common concepts in mind, we define *decision making* as the allocation of scarce resources by individuals or groups to achieve goals under conditions of uncertainty and risk.

This definition has six important terms. First, *allocation* means that objects have been distributed among alternatives. Just as a family allocates its income for food, clothing, housing, transportation, and entertainment, media managers must decide how to distribute their resources.

Scarce resources reflect the fact a manager never has all of the resources he or she would like. Available resources are people's time and money. To a degree, these two resources are interchangeable. If you have money, but need time, you can hire others. If you have time, but need money, you can sell that time. Certainly, other forms of resources are available, but all are related to time and money. For example, technology is a way of increasing the effectiveness and efficiency of time and is acquired with money. Other forms of resources are derivative of time and money, or are ways of improving the allocation of time and money.

The word scarce is equally important. If resources were not scarce, decision making would not be central to management. With a limitless supply of money and time, people could try every alternative until they found the one that worked best. Scarce resources limit the time and money spent on a decision.

The third term includes *individuals and groups*. Decisions can be made by one person or by two or more people functioning as a unit. All other things equal, it takes less time for one person to make a decision than it does a group. However, ease of decision is not the same as effectiveness of decision. Groups make some decisions better than individuals do.

Goal is the fourth term. In our definition, goal means a decision has a purpose. The nature of business goals is complex and has been the subject of much debate and research. The cases in this book may or may not state specific goals, but no decision can be made adequately without considering the goals of that decision and the overall goals of the organization.

In pursuing goals, managers act either in a strictly rational way or with bounded rationality. Managers act in a strictly rational way when their goal is to maximize some aspect of business. Simon (1957) defined a *rational decision* as occurring when a decision maker confronted with alternatives selects the one that has the highest return. This definition of rationality is the basis of classical economic theory and has resulted in the idea that business should maximize some goals, whether it be profits, revenues, or sales.

Acceptance of the assumption of rationality began to crumble after World War II, as scholars began to recognize the limits of the "rational man" approach. Cyert and March (1963) said the profit maximization assumption for businesses was not realistic because people within organizations do not have single-minded purposes. People pursue a variety of goals. Cyert and March also added that firms do not have the perfect knowledge necessary to maximize profits. Maximizing profits occurs when the cost of an additional unit of a product equals the price a consumer pays. This maximizing point is a theoretical idea, because such detailed price and cost data are impossible to collect.

In place of this rational assumption for decision making, Simon (1957) suggested the principle of *bounded rationality*. This principle recognizes that humans cannot be rational in the strict, traditional sense, but Simon was not willing to say people act randomly. Rather, he proposed that humans pursue goals in a purposeful manner but this pursuit is limited by nature of people and by the social environment in which they live. As a result, people will seek goals and make decisions that work to satisfy instead of maximize their benefits from the decisions. This *satisficing* approach means people adopt goals and decision outcomes that are acceptable within the constraints faced by the organizations.

Uncertainty is the fifth term of the definition that needs discussion. We define uncertainty as meaning all decisions are probabilistic. No decision outcome is 100% certain. Reducing uncertainty starts with a subjective estimate of the probability that an outcome will occur. A graduating public relations major, for instance, might estimate that he or she has a 50% chance of finding a job within 1 month. Part of the estimate is figuring out the factors that affect outcomes. Once a person has made such an estimate, the reasons behind the estimate can be used to reduce uncertainty.

These estimates of probability may be as crude as a statement that an outcome is more likely than not, or they may be as sophisticated as a derived mathematical statement of probability. For instance, a person might "bet" another person that Michigan State University will beat the University of Illinois in a football game. This is a statement with subjective probability, as is the statement that there is a 60% chance of rain tomorrow.

However, all such subjective estimates share two characteristics: (a) they are based on analysis of information; and (b) they also are based on assumptions about measurement and time that limit their objective nature. The accuracy of the information and the quality of analysis determines how well the subjective statement of probability predicts rain or the football game winner.

Uncertainty then rests on a continuum from 0% to 100% uncertainty about a decision outcome. This is shown in Fig. 1.1. Because perfect knowledge is impossible, 0% uncertain decisions do not exist, and a 100% uncertain decision would be a random solution. As Bass (1983) pointed out, in the absence of other information, people fill in questionable space with their experience or that of their acquaintances. As uncertainty increases, the difficulty of making an effective decision increases.

The word *risk*, the final term in the definition, is used differently here than in traditional decision-making literature. Risk refers to the amount of resources committed to accomplishing a goal and, therefore, the amount of resources that might be lost. Risk also exists on a continuum, shown in Fig. 1.1. The risk runs from small to great. Small means few resources are allocated, whereas great means a large number of resources is involved. As with uncertainty, rarely will organizations operate at the ends of the risk continuum.

Few organizations will allocate a large percentage of their resources to a given project, much less a single decision. Risk is a relative term. Allocating $1 million would be a huge proportion of resources at most weekly newspapers, but a relatively small proportion of resources at a large media corpora-

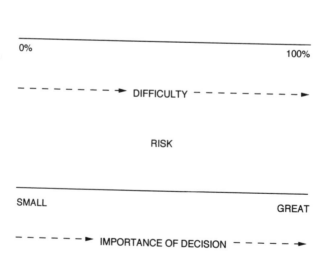

FIG. 1.1. The relationship between uncertainty and risk.

tion, such as CBS or Microsoft. The greater the risk for a company, the more important the decision.

Figure 1.1 can be used to illustrate the importance and difficulty of decisions to a media organization. A decision that concerns a relatively great risk and a high level of uncertainty is important and difficult. In fact, such a venture might not be undertaken. A decision that has little risk and uncertainty would be relatively unimportant and easy to make.

TYPES OF DECISIONS

Decisions fall into two types: *programmed* and *nonprogrammed* (Simon, 1960). A programmed decision sets up a rule that states an action will take place once a certain condition has been reached. A nonprogrammed decision is one that cannot be made by referring to a rule. Programmed decisions tend to be highly structured, with established goals and channels of information. Nonprogrammed decisions have poor structure, vague goals, and ambiguous information. Determining an employee's pay every month is an example of a programmed decision. Publishers at a newspaper do not have to decide how much money to pay their employees at the end of each month. The amount and form have been set up in advance, usually on an annual basis, and larger organizations have computers that will issue the checks.

Nonprogrammed decisions require information and analysis that is specific to a particular decision. Selecting a new news anchor at a local television station is a nonprogrammed decision. The taste viewers have for a news anchor change, and making decisions about new anchors with old data about the audience is likely to lead to lower ratings. Nonprogrammed decisions, such as selecting anchors or hiring journalists, happen too infrequently to develop an effective, programmed policy. Each time, new information and analysis are essential for an effective decision.

The distinction between programmed and nonprogrammed decisions is an important one. If a decision can be programmed effectively, it is wise to do so. The greater the number of programmed decisions, the more time a manager will have to spend on difficult nonprogrammed decisions. Whether or not a decision can be programmed depends on the uncertainty and the risk involved. The lower the uncertainty and risk, the more likely a programmed decision will work.

The two types of decisions often occur in the same process. News selection, for instance, involves both programmed and nonprogrammed decisions. News values are a form of programmed decisions. If an automobile accident kills several people in a city, it will be on the evening television news in that city. It has the news values of proximity (it is local) and impact (extreme consequences). There is little debate because applying the news values to such events has become programmed. The difficulty comes in deciding if an event truly represents certain news values.

Proactive and Reactive Decisions

Another way of categorizing decisions has to do with the impact of external events and trends on an organization. Managers tend to react to changes in the business environment with either *proactive* or *reactive decisions* (Ivancevich, Lorenzi, Skinner, & Crosby, 1994). Proactive decisions are made in anticipation of external changes, and reactive decisions are made as a result of external changes.

Examples of these two types of decisions can be found in the reaction of a newspaper company to web sites that provide information about the newspaper's community. If the newspaper went online in 1995 with a web site about it's community, it is likely that managers made a proactive decision to establish a source of information before other companies did. If the newspaper managers waited until 1998 when competitors had already established a community web site, then they made a reactive decision.

Proactive decisions can work well when they promote solutions to problems before they become particularly burdensome. Reactive decisions often occur after a company's competitor has gained a foothold in the market, which can put the reacting company at a disadvantage. On the other hand, a company can be proactive to an imagined problem and end up wasting money solving a problem that does not exist. Successful proactive decisions require accurate predictions of future external trends and events. Successful reactive decisions require that an organization not wait in responding to changes in the business environment. Timing is crucial.

THE DECISION PROCESS

Despite variation in the names given to the steps in the decision process, most models of decision making are similar. For example, Drucker (1983) gave six steps: classify the problem, define the problem, specify what the decision must do, seek the right decision, build in the action to carry out the decision, and use feedback to test the effectiveness of the decision. Griffin and Moorhead (1986) offered a model that incorporates the difference between programmed and nonprogrammed decisions and that acknowledges the role of information at each step.

The model shown in Fig. 1.2 is called a decision wheel because it represents the cyclical nature of the decision process. It differs from the Griffin and Moorhead (1986) model in two ways. First, it does not include the idea of programmed versus nonprogrammed decisions. Programmed decisions, although important, are not the basis of the case study approach. Although creating a policy may be the solution to a case, this solution results from a nonprogrammed decision process.

A second difference between the decision wheel and other models is the central placement of the collection and analysis of information. Just as a decision making is the heart of management, the collection and appropriate analysis of information are the hub of decision making. All steps of the decision-making process must involve the collection of information and its appropriate evaluation. *Analysis*, which breaks down the information and then examines and classifies it so it can be used, is a key to effective decisions. Correct analysis with little information often is more useful than poor analysis with abundant information.

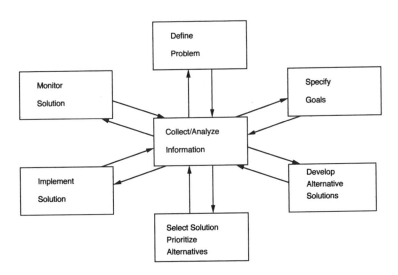

FIG. 1.2. The decision wheel.

Defining the Problem

The first step is defining the problem to be solved. It involves the collection of information about some form of behavior, either inside or outside the organization, that is a problem for the media firm. This information must be analyzed in a way that allows the managers to frame the problem appropriately. For example, a television news department that is losing audience has a problem. To define the problem behind this decline in ratings, management must develop a list of possible causes and collect information about them. Then the information about the potential causes must be analyzed to decide what the cause may be. Perhaps the audience does not like the hard-news focus of the news shows, or they may not like anchors. Each problem holds several possible causes, and in many cases, problems may have more than one cause. The ability to reverse the sliding ratings, however, will depend on management's ability to define the problem in a way that the causes can be identified correctly.

Specifying Goals

After the problem is defined, the next step is specifying the goals of the decision. The goals need to be concrete. Vague statements about reversing a trend will not allow for effective decision making. The goals should be as specific as the problem and available data will allow. Usually the decision process will address multiple goals. All goals should have a time frame for accomplishing them.

In the television news example, the station president and news director may decide that the station should increase its early evening news ratings by 3 points and its late evening news ratings by 2 points within the next 6 months. (A ratings point equals 1% of the TV households in a station's market.) These very specific goals allow for better monitoring and force a manager to use detailed analysis of data. Managers may set up several goals across time. So, the station management may want a 1-point increase in ratings within 3 months and an additional 2-point increase during the following 3 months. The crucial element of goal setting is degree of specificity. To do this, one must collect as a much information as a possible and analyze it effectively.

Developing Solutions

The third step in the decision wheel is developing alternative solutions. This step should yield as a many alternatives as a possible. Inadequate solutions can be rejected, but a solution that has not been considered never can be selected. A weeding-out process follows the listing of the solutions. Here, the obviously unsuitable solution can be dropped, leaving those that have some possibilities for accomplishing the goals.

Just as a with all steps, the narrowing process requires the acquisition of information and its analysis. Two questions for developing this list are: (a) Will the solutions actually accomplish the goals? (b) Will the costs of the solution outweigh the gains to the organization? If the answer to the first question is no, then the solution should be dropped. If the answer to the second question is yes, then the solution should be dropped.

Using the problem of declining ratings, we can list possible solutions to this situation:

1. Hire new anchors.
2. Increase the time devoted to weather.
3. Increase the time devoted to sports.
4. Introduce new segments to the newscast, such as a a health information segment.
5. Use more live coverage.
6. Change the nature of the news by presenting more feature material and fewer hard-news stories.
7. Hire a new sports announcer.
8. Hire a new weather announcer.
9. Create a web site to promote the news.

These are just some of the possible solutions. Only a few of these will get serious consideration, but examining all possible alternatives will help managers identify plausible ones.

The two-question test can be applied to eliminate some of the alternative listed. First, based on a recent viewer survey, the news director might reject solutions 1, 7, and 8 because all of the on-camera talent received good evaluations from the viewers (no answers to question a). Solution 5 can be dropped because the station does not have the money needed to buy technology that would allow more live coverage (yes answer to question b).

Selecting a Solution

With a short list of solutions, a manager moves to the next step, which involves the selection of one solution to the problem. The solution may be a combination of more than one alternative solution, but the next step requires a decision to pursue a specific solution.

The collection and analysis of information are crucial at this point. When one solution is selected, the alternate solutions should not be forgotten. Often the original solution does not work as well as management would like. As a result, managers have to return to the problem and either generate new solutions or choose one of the solutions dropped previously. It is a good idea to prioritize the solutions not used based on information and analysis. This may save time if the chosen solution fails.

Selecting solutions is always a matter of costs and benefits. Often, more than one solution will work, so the correct option involves one that balances costs with benefits. One solution may generate more viewers than another, but the costs would be so high as to consume the entire increase in revenues from getting more viewers. At the same time, a solution may be inexpensive, but the results will not reach the specified goals.

Returning to the television news department, we find the managers considering the five solutions that remain after discarding ineffectual solutions. They reject changing the nature of the news because a recent survey of viewers indicated they generally were pleased with the mix of news being carried. They also reject the web site option because the survey indicated only 18% of the households access the web.

The three remaining solutions all involve the allotment of time. The comparison then becomes one of costs versus expected audience increase. Adding time to weather and sports would not require additional reporters because these two segments already have more material than they use. The potential for increasing audience exists, based on the recent viewer survey, but the survey also revealed a significant segment of the viewers who did not care much for sports.

Considering the potential negative impact of more sports, the managers narrow the solution to either more time for weather or a new daily segment about health. Either solution will require the expense of promotion and advertisements. The costs of the health spot include loss of time for other news and the expense of training a reporter to cover health issues. The potential for an audience increase appears greater for the health spot for three reasons. First, no other station in the market has such a spot, which means it could be promoted and advertised effectively. Second, this type of spot has attracted viewers in other markets. Third, research has indicated a growing awareness of health issues by the general population in the United States. The increase in weather coverage cannot be promoted as well because another station in the market already broadcasts more weather information and cable has a 24-hour weather service.

The managers decide that a daily segment devoted to health issues would be the best way to increase their ratings. As a back-up approach, they decide an increase of about a minute each for sports and weather would be best. However, they delay the decision about the exact content to be included in the new health spot. They want more information about what types of health news other stations have included in their spots.

Implementing the Solution

Once the solution has been selected it must be implemented. This is the fifth step in the decision wheel. The solution means nothing unless it is applied correctly. This requires a detailed plan of action with a timetable for specific actions, a budget, and a breakdown of who has responsibility for carrying out the changes. The details should be as specific as possible.

Again, the collection and analysis of information are important at this stage. Much of the information at this point deals with internal organization issues. The budget, timetable, and delegation of responsibility reflect the resources within the media company. It is important to note that the people with the responsibility for carrying out aspects of the solution must be given the power and budget to do so. Responsibility and power should be connected always.

Our television managers, for example, have selected one of their reporters to be in charge of the daily health spot. This reporter was a science major in college and has an interest in this area. The reporter will work directly with a particular producer. The spot will be introduced in 3 months, following an extensive promotional effort, and will occupy about 2½ minutes every weekday on the early and late evening newscasts. The spots on the two newscasts may or may not cover the same topic, but they should have different angles. The time will be taken mostly from the news hole, but 30 seconds will come from the sports segment. Approximately $5,000 has been set aside to fund workshop attendance by the reporter, and $10,000 has been allocated for researching viewers' responses.

Monitoring the Solution

The final step is monitoring the implementation in the light of the goals. This monitoring should provide feedback on a regular basis to judge progress toward the goals and be part of the implementation plan. For example, the television news managers have decided to evaluate the effectiveness of the spot on a monthly basis, as well as through informal weekly discussions with the producer and reporter. Every month, the managers will have a meeting with those involved to discuss the content and any problems. After 3 months, the managers will have meetings with several small groups of viewers to get their comments on the new segment. Also, after each ratings period, the data will be analyzed to determine if the new spot is having an impact on the ratings.

Crucial to the monitoring system is a timetable. A solution that is not working should be given an adequate test period, but a media organization should not remain committed to a solution once it becomes obvious that it will not work. Times should be established during the implementation process at which the managers must decide to continue or end the plan.

This monitoring process makes the entire decision process cyclical. If the solution is not working, this becomes a problem that starts a new cycle of decision making. The same steps are taken in a new cycle but some may take less time and effort because the previous decision process already provides relevant information. However, managers must be careful not to assume they have all the information they need. An effective manager continues to acquire information until the cost of additional information outweighs the probable benefit from having that information.

CONSTRAINTS ON THE DECISION PROCESS

The decision wheel is an ideal. It is a blueprint that rarely is followed exactly because of practical constraints that fall into two types: who makes the decision and time available for the decision.

Decision Makers

Individuals and groups make decisions. Whether a group or individual makes the decision influences the efficiency and effectiveness of the decision. In some cases, individuals may decide best. In other cases, group decisions work better. Huber (1980) listed three advantages and four disadvantages of group decisions, whereas Harrison (1987) gave nine strengths and four weaknesses. Griffin and Moorhead (1986) presented six advantages of group decision making and three advantages of individual decision making. Table 1.1 summarizes the advantages and disadvantages of group decision making and categorizes them under the headings of timing, uncertainty, and goals.

TABLE 1.1

Advantages and Disadvantages of Group Decision Making

Advantages	Disadvantages
Timing	
Slower decision process	Slower decision process
Division of labor for complex task	Disagreement over goals may result in no decisions
Uncertainty	
Larger amounts of information	Political behavior of group and knowledge generated members reduces acceptance of information from others
Fewer errors in analyzing	Groupthink—tendency of information group members to think the group is infallible
More alternatives generated	
Goals	
Groups can clarify goal understanding	Groups sometimes act in ways inconsistent with goals
Participation increases acceptance of group goals	Groupthink

Interestingly, weaknesses of group decision making can be strengths. For example, one of the advantages and disadvantages of group decision making is its slow process. Group decision making usually increases the time needed for a decision because of problems in organizing meetings and the long process of forming consensus among people with conflicting positions. An individual decision maker does not have these timing problems. Whether the time element is an advantage or a disadvantage depends on the decision. If timing is crucial, individuals make quicker decisions. If timing is not crucial and risk and uncertainty are high, a slower process has advantages.

Deadlines exemplify the timing importance in news departments. News stories do not get used if they are not ready by the printing or broadcast deadlines. So, individuals make most decisions about what stories will run. However, exceptions to this rule involve important stories.

An example of a group decision involving a news story is the case of the Pentagon Papers. The Pentagon Papers were a secret report about the history of the Vietnam War. They were prepared in the late 1960s for Secretary of Defense Robert S. McNamara, who served for President Lyndon Johnson. *The New York Times* obtained the report from Daniel Ellsberg, who helped prepare it. After four installments of the Papers ran in *The New York Times* in June 1971, a federal court issued a restraining order. Meanwhile, *The Washington Post* had obtained a copy of the report. A group of 10 managers of the Post met for 12 hours to discuss whether they should publish parts of the report. They did. (Witcover, 1971)

The inherent lack of speed in group decisions is not the only advantage or disadvantage of groups. When complex tasks are involved, groups have the advantage of division of labor. Dividing tasks among group members can speed up the process because one person does not have to learn the wide range of information required for complex decisions. Buying a new computer system for a newspaper is an example. Because such systems often serve multiple departments, it would make sense to include someone from each department in the decision-making process. It is easier to have people from each department who know the department's computer needs than it is to have one or two people learn about the computer needs of all the departments.

Advantages and disadvantages of group decisions also fall under the heading of uncertainty. Group decision making can reduce uncertainty in three ways. First, having more than one person will increase the amount of information and knowledge brought to the process. Second, it can decrease the number of errors. The cliché "two heads are better than one" applies here. Having more people also can reduce information errors because people can evaluate each other's information and analysis. Third, groups generate more alternative solutions. The ability to compare alternatives with each other can result in better solutions.

Although uncertainty will decline with some groups, it can increase with others. The probabilities that develop from the satisficing approach are subjective. This subjectivity is influenced by the attitudes and perceptions of other group members. Political behavior among group members can create doubt as to appropriate goals and the desirability of solutions. For instance, when a city editor and a sports editor try to persuade other group members that their departments are key to improving quality overall, the very process of persuasion can cast doubt on either department being effective at attracting readers. The result is uncertainty of actions.

Just as dangerous as political behavior, which can divide, is the phenomenon of *groupthink*. Groupthink occurs when group members are so set on sustaining unanimity among themselves that they fail to properly appraise the alternative solutions (Janis, 1982). Although the group feels they have reduced uncertainty because they agree on the best alternative, they actually have decreased the probability that any one solution will work. The solution does not get an adequate evaluation.

The final heading in Table 1.1 is goals. Because of the number of people involved, groups often will develop a better understanding of the organization's and decision group's goals. Reading a statement of goals adopted by an organization does not mean that the employees understand those goals. Hearing others discuss the goals can help clarify them.

Another advantage is that participation in group decision making will increase acceptance of the goals and solutions that are adopted. Increased acceptance can translate into increased effort in accomplishing the goals. People tend to accept more readily those decisions in which they participated.

A disadvantage of group decisions with respect to goals is the tendency of some groups to develop their own goals that may be inconsistent with the organization's goals. For example, a group set up within a media organization to develop ways to cut costs may decide that cost cutting is not a proper goal. The result will be a conflict of goals between management and decision group. Resulting decisions are less likely to accomplish the aims of management.

The advantages and disadvantages of group decisions create problems for deciding when groups or individuals should make decisions. Vroom and Yetton (1973) said that individual managers are likely to make decisions when the problem is well structured, information is plentiful, a previously successful solution to a similar problem is available, and time constraints require a quick decision.

Individual Decision-Making Styles. As with all human skills, managers vary in the style of decision making they use. A decision-making style has to do with common patterns of reaching decisions. Most managers will exhibit more than one style, but often a particular style emerges under pressure.

Driver, Brousseu, and Hunsaker (1993) identified decision style by the way managers use information and how they focus on solutions. *Use of information* involved either satisficing or maximizing. As mentioned earlier, satisficing requires collecting information to reach a "satisfactory" conclusion that may not result in as good a result as possible. *Maximizing* involves collecting information until a decision maker has enough to reach the "best" decision. The difference is related to how long the decision makers will collect information before acting.

Solution focus concerns the use of data to identify possible solutions. *Unifocus* people collect information and identify one solution they think is best, whereas *multifocus* people collect information and provide a variety of solutions to a problem.

These two dimensions were combined to produce the following five decision styles people use:

> **Decisive Style** — This style involves people who are satisficers and are unifocused with respect to solutions. A limited amount of information is collected and acted on quickly. Once solutions are identified, the decision makers are unwavering in their support of the solution.
>
> **Flexible Style** — Flexible decision makers are satisfiers who are multifocused on solutions. Limited information is acted on, but more flexibility is shown in using solutions. If one solution fails to work, another is chosen.
>
> **Hierarchical Style** — This style involves maximizing and unifocus. Large amounts of information are collected in order to select the one best solution, which is pursued using a very detailed plan. People who use this style act slowly, due to the time they spend on getting information.
>
> **Integrative Style** — People using this style are maximizers with multifocus solutions. Collecting and evaluating information takes time, but unlike the hierarchical style, more than one solution to the problem is considered.
>
> **Systemic Style** — This style incorporates both the integrative and the hierarchical styles in a two-step process. The first step involves evaluating large amounts of information and dealing with multiple solutions. The second step is more hierarchical because solutions are prioritized with one or more criteria being considered the "best." This style is more contemplative than the hierarchical style but involves more organized and active solutions than the integrative style.

These types of decision-maker classifications can be useful in understanding decision making, but care must be taken. Often managers will exhibit a combination of these styles with individual decisions and in decisions over time. The usefulness of the classification is its emphasis on types of goals (satisficing and maximizing) and on nature of focus (unifocus or multifocus).

    Types for Group Decisions.   Just as individual decision makers exhibit different styles, so do groups. McEwan (1997) listed 10 ways that groups can reach decisions, which vary by the degree the entire group participates and by the quality (how effectively the decisions result in reaching goals) of the resulting decisions. The group styles are:

Decision by Authority Without Group Discussion — This is not really a group decision, although it may be presented as such because one person makes the decision for the group. It yields a fast decision, but the group does not become involved.

Decision by Default — A group failing to make a decision can be a form of decision. Group inactivity results in either someone else making the decision or the problem going away.

Self-Authorized Decisions — One or more members assume they have the authority to make a decision when they do not. Such decisions have little support from members left out of the process.

Decision by Clique — A few individuals form a subgroup to make decisions and then impose that decision. This breaks the decision-making group into competing factions, which reduces quality of decisions.

Decision by Expert — A person within the group makes the decision, but how the "expert" is selected can create internal disagreements.

Decision by Averaging Individual's Opinions — Members' opinions are asked separately and the results are averaged. Group members have no actual part of the decision because group interaction is missing.

Decision by Authority After Group Discussions — Group members advise the person who has authority to make decision. This can result in competition for authority's attention or telling authority what the group members believe will please him or her.

Decision by Minority — A subgroup is given the authority to make decisions. This makes other members wonder why they were put in the group.

Decision by Majority Vote — The group does as the majority wants. The effectiveness depends on everyone's commitment to this method, whether they are in the majority or the minority.

Decision by Consensus — The group reaches a decision that everyone can support, but it can be very time consuming. This may be the best method if time allows because it results in high quality conclusions.

All of these types of divisions have advantages and disadvantages depending on the goal of the decision. It is helpful for groups to understand how they are making decisions because it will allow them to analyze the weaknesses of these decisions. Suppose a magazine company appoints a committee to plan a long-term strategy for incorporating the World Wide Web (WWW) in its market strategy. Members should represent the various departments in the company, as well as a variety of web experience and technological knowledge. The group might be tempted to let the person with the most technological knowledge (decision by expert) make the decisions, but that person might not know how advertisers and viewers want to interact with the Web. The company's chief executive officer (CEO) might make the decision after hearing all sides (decision by authority after group discussion), but the techies and nontechies might form subgroups and compete for the CEO's support.

The best type of group decision making depends on a variety of factors about the problem and the people involved. One of the most important factors is timing of decisions.

Time and Decision Making

In addition to classifying decisions by type of decision-making style, decisions can be broken down on the basis of time available. Three general timing patterns seem appropriate. Nonprogrammed decisions can be classified as immediate, short-term, or long-term. Immediate decisions must be made quickly. The time that is available between step 1 and step 5 in the decision wheel is measured in hours or even minutes. Story decisions on deadline are the prime examples in media.

As a result of deadlines, it is common to find individuals making content decisions at newspapers, magazines, and television news departments. However, the deadline pressure hides the danger that individuals will begin making all decisions quickly and alone out of habit. No decision should be made before time requires it. If a decision need not be made immediately, participation of others should be sought.

Short-term decisions are ones that need not be made immediately, but they must be made within a reasonable period of time. At a newspaper, the plans for a breakdown of news and advertising space for the coming week would be short-term.

Small groups usually make these decisions, even if one person has that responsibility. For example, the publisher, who has final authority for space in a newspaper, may meet with the advertising manager and editor to determine news holes for a week. Often the publisher has determined a breakdown for the year between news and advertising space. The meetings are monitoring sessions by which the three managers discuss news–editorial needs in light of the year's goal, previous use of space, and the newsroom's space needs for the week.

Long-term decisions are those that affect the organization over a period of years and, therefore, warrant a longer decision-making process. This type of decision includes the television news ratings problem discussed earlier and format changes at a magazine or newspaper. Because of their complexity, these decisions require participation by a large number of people in groups and as individuals. In effect, a long-term decision, such as what next year's budget should be, requires hundreds or thousands of smaller decisions.

Overall, time acts as a constraint on the process shown in the decision wheel by limiting the time available for each of the six steps. These limits determine how much information can be collected, how much analysis can be conducted, and how many people can participate in the decision. Immediate decisions allow very little time for each step and for information collection and analysis. Long-term decisions should include adequate time for each step.

The timing of various types of decisions places a premium on different types of managers. When an immediate decision is needed, a satisfactory solution is more important than an optimal solution. So the person who has command of a great deal of information in an area and who can analyze quickly will perform best. This person need not be as good at working with people as a manager who deals with short- and long-term problems. Decisive and flexible decision styles work well here.

A manager faced with short-term decisions needs both people skills and the ability to reach decisions within a reasonable time. On the other hand, managers who must make long-term decisions are better served by skills that allow them to work with people and that allow them to examine a problem from several angles. This person should be good at analysis, but it is analysis with a different time frame. This manager must be good at developing many alternatives and evaluating them against each other. The variation of needed skills explains why some people make better upper level managers, such as editor, than lower level managers, such as assistant city editor. Long-term decisions that involve high risk and uncertainty work best with integrative or systemic styles for decision makers.

The key to effective decision making is to put people in positions where their abilities will serve them best and then to train them in the areas where they are weakest. The ability to understand and handle time constraints is essential if a person is to be promoted within the media organization.

TOOLS OF MANAGEMENT

Just as decision makers and time constrain decision making, so does the quality of information and analysis, which relate directly to the skills of the decision maker. As with all skills, collecting and analyzing information can be improved through learning. The next section addresses briefly the sources of information and some of the tools of analysis.

Sources of Information

Because information plays an important role in all six steps, it is useful to examine where one gets information. Basically, information comes either from one's own efforts or from the efforts of others. The efforts can take various forms, however, and those forms can affect the quality of information. The two main types of efforts are experience and research. Experience involves participating in events or processes, and research is the application of generally accepted systemic methods of examining events or processes. Someone who works at a news magazine has experience in magazine journalism. Someone who conducts a survey of news magazine reporters is conducting research about magazine journalism. Experience differs from research in that it does not have accepted standards for analyzing data. Experience is inseparable from the person having the experience. But a researcher, if conducting research properly, should have a minimal impact on the events or processes being studied.

Research should be more objective and systematic than experience. Should be are more important words because quality of research depends on the researcher's skills, just as quality of experience depends on the wisdom of the person experiencing the event. Experience can be analyzed systematically and somewhat objectively by a manager, just as a researcher inadvertently can alter the result of research through poor use of methods.

Managers have roughly four sources of information: their own experiences, the experiences of others, their research and the research of others. The tendency among media managers is to depend on their experiences and the experiences of trusted colleagues. Experience has the characteristics of being detailed and specific to a particular situation. This can be an advantage when a decision must be made about a situation similar to previous events. However, using one's experience becomes a liability when that experience is applied to a problem that differs from the original experience. The result in such cases is often a poor decision.

Managers should know the value of all forms of information and seek diverse sources of information, especially in the monitoring step. A successful manager analyzes past decisions so the next decision can be more effective. The results of every decision should become information for future decisions, but the usefulness of this information depends on the ability to use tools of analysis.

Cost–Benefit Analysis

A manager with few analytical skills or with little knowledge and experience will end up depending on others to judge the reliability and validity of information. This can be a problem. Managers who understand analysis are in a better position to select information appropriate for decisions. Analysis involves ways of processing information. Several different types of analysis, which vary in complexity, are available.

Perhaps the most recognized analytical tool is cost–benefit analysis, which is an attempt to estimate the costs and the benefits that result from alternative actions. McKean (1975) listed five steps: (a) identifying benefits to be achieved, (b) identifying the alternatives that will reach the goal, (c) identifying the costs for the alternative methods, (d) developing a model or set of relationships that explain the impact of alternatives on the costs and benefits, and (e) selecting the preferred alternative with a criterion involving both costs and benefits. These steps sound familiar because they correspond to steps of the decision wheel.

The traditional approach to cost–benefit analysis is to place a monetary value on all costs and benefits and compare the resulting differences (Huber, 1980). Because this is difficult to do with many types of costs, cost–benefit analysis may include the "dollar-equivalency technique" (Huber, 1980) which is the development of money equivalents for costs that are difficult to measure in dollars. Obviously, this becomes problematical when costs and benefits involve human behavior.

Two concepts are useful in dealing with the nonmonetary aspects of cost–benefit analysis: *opportunity costs* and *intangibles*. Opportunity costs are the expenses that accrue from giving up alternative actions. It is equivalent to the old saying: "There is no free lunch." For every alternative selected, a person loses what she would have gained from another alternative. For example, a manager is hiring a reporter and must pick from two candidates. The first is stronger at writing and the second at reporting. If the first is hired, an opportunity cost is the reporting ability that will be lost from not hiring the second. If the second is hired, an opportunity cost is the writing skill that will be lost from not hiring the first.

Intangibles are the things that cannot be measured well. This may be leadership in a manager or the ability of some people to raise morale in an organization. Whatever the attribute, a dollar amount cannot be assigned adequately. These intangibles often are ignored in formal tools of analysis because they cannot be measured well.

Opportunity costs and intangibles are the Achilles heel of cost–benefit analysis and most other types of formal analysis. These two concepts relate to all decisions, although sometimes they are more important than at other times. Despite these two problems, cost–benefit analysis can be useful even if it simply allows a manager to think more clearly. The following example demonstrates the potential use of cost–benefit analysis in a situation where quantification is difficult.

The *Times-Leader* recently conducted a readership survey in which 48% of the readers said they would like to have more in-depth local coverage. Managing Editor Jane Smith has been assigned to come up with a plan for doing this. Her first observation is that it can be done either by hiring a new reporter or by using existing staff. She comes up with the benefits and costs presented in Table 1.2.

The monetary benefits f or either alternative are equal in Table 1.2 and amount to $54,000 per year. These benefits are based on retaining 250 readers a year and attracting 250 readers annually as a result of increased in-depth coverage. Two main areas of monetary benefits are saving $4,000 from not having to replace the 250 readers and making $50,000 in advertising revenue that would be lost if the 500 readers were not buying the newspaper.

Both approaches also have intangible benefits in the form of staff morale and promotional advantage of having in-depth coverage that will generate recognition of the newspaper's journalistic efforts. The use of existing staff has added advantage in that it will increase morale of the staff because they will be allowed to spend time on more lengthy projects.

Monetary costs of hiring an additional reporter are about $20,000 more a year because the new reporter would earn $30,000 a year, whereas overtime needed to use existing staff would only amount to $10,000. Both alternatives have opportunity costs. Each alternative would require about the same amount of additional editing, which would have to come from the time spent on editing of day-to-day stories.

Two opportunity costs and two intangible costs stand out as important factors. First, having a new reporter could create dissatisfaction among the

TABLE 1.2

Cost-Benefit Analysis of Increasing In-Depth Reporting at the *Times-Leader*

| | Alternatives | |
Costs	*Hiring a reporter*	*Using existing Staff*
Monetary	$30,000 a year salary	$10,000 a year additional over-time
	$5,000 a year expense for travel & research	$5,000 a year expenses for travel & research
	$13,000 for 26 additional pages at a cost of $500 per page	$13,000 for 26 additional pages at cost of $500 per page
Opportunity	Dissatisfaction among existing staff because they will not be allowed to do in-depth work	Use of staff for in-depth reporting will reduce time for day-to-day reporting
	Editing time lost on day-to-day coverage due to increased editing needs of day-to-day coverage	Editing time lost on day-to-day coverage due to increased editing needs of day-to-day coverage
Intangible	Possible negative impact of new reporter in the newsroom	Added effort needed to balance in-depth coverage
Benefits[a]		
Monetary	Save $4,000 needed to gain 250 lost readers	Save $4,000 needed to gain 250 lost readers
	Save $50,000 in advertising revenue that could be lost with decline of 500 readers	Save $50,000 in advertising revenue that could be lost with decline of 500 readers
Intangible	Increased morale among staff from increased quality of the newspaper	Increased morale among staff from increased quality of the newspaper
	Promotional value of expected recognition from in-depth coverage	Promotional value of expected recognition from in-depth coverage
		Increased staff morale for those who do in-depth reporting

Note: The goal is to increase the amount of in-depth coverage by one page every 2 weeks.
[a]Benefits are based on an estimated retention of 250 readers and attracting 250 new readers as a result of increased in-depth coverage.

existing staff members who would like to pursue in-depth reporting. In-depth work usually is looked on by reporters as reward because it is more satisfying and interesting than most day-to-day coverage. On the other hand, taking time from day-to-day coverage has the opportunity cost of reducing the amount of space and effort spent on everyday reporting. This could negatively affect circulation.

The intangible costs also involve the staff's reaction to a new plan. If a new reporter is hired, he or she may alter the chemistry among people in the newsroom. This impact, combined with the possible resentment, may have negative consequences. On the other hand, a new reporter might add to the newsroom chemistry. Whether this becomes a cost or not would depend on who is hired as the new reporter. The use of existing staff means an added cost for the editors because they must ensure that the in-depth assignments are distributed fairly. Otherwise, staff resentment could develop.

By examining Table 1.2, a manager could see that the question of which approach to take comes down to whether the additional $20,000 cost of a new reporter and the potential newsroom disruption exceeds the impact of reducing the day-to-day coverage in the newspaper. This, in turn, is related to the adequacy of the current staff. If the newsroom is understaffed already, expanding the work required could be disastrous. More readers might drop the paper because of poor day-to-day coverage than would buy the paper because of increased in-depth reporting. In order to make an appropriate selection, a manager needs to have an understanding of the nature of the reporters currently working and an awareness of the informal organizational setting in the newsroom.

An important point of this illustration is that many of the costs and benefits are not quantifiable. But this should not lead to these costs and benefits being ignored. A second point is that the analysis is only as good as the information that goes into it. The monetary costs and benefits should be accurate, but the knowledge of the people in the newsroom needs to be just as reliable and valid.

Social Science Theory

Successful use of cost–benefit analysis depends greatly on the quality of the information used. Poor information will result in poor decisions. However, another analytical tool is available that can improve the quality of information, whether it be from experience or research. This tool is called theory.

Social science theory is a system of abstract statements that describes a set of behaviors. Theories can provide one or more of the following: (a) a method of classifying behavior, called a typology, (b) predictions of future events and behavior, (c) explanations of past events or behaviors, (d) a sense of understanding about what causes events, and (e) the potential to control events or behavior (Reynolds, 1971). The usefulness of a theory depends on how many of and how well these functions are fulfilled by the theory. All of the five possible functions of theory would be useful to a manager in making decisions because they help reduce uncertainty.

Useful theories can be found in sociology, psychology, and economics, and many of these are discussed in this volume. One example of applying theory would be the use of equity theory. Equity theory states that people evaluate how fairly they are being treated by an organization in four steps. First, a person evaluates how he or she is being treated. Second, the person evaluates how a "comparison-other" is being treated. This other is someone the individual considers to be equivalent to himself or herself in some way from the organization's perspective. Third, the individual compares the treatment of himself or herself and the other. Fourth, the individual feels he or she is being treated either equitably or inequitably (Griffin & Moorhead, 1986).

As a result of the comparison, a person who feels equity is motivated to continue the current situation, whereas the person who feels inequity may take several different steps to reduce the inequity feeling. An important implication of this theory is that absolute amount of a pay raise given a person is not as important in many cases as the evaluation of the raise with respect to others in the organization.

Equity theory is one of many behavioral theories that can be used to analyze behavior. If an employee displays lack of motivation or poor performance following a pay raise, for instance, it may be a result of inequity feelings. A manager who explores this possibility may be able to work with the employee by examining the employee's approach to equity. It may be that the person's comparison-other is inappropriate, that the comparison-other got a large raise because of something unusual, or that the inequity feeling was justified. Whatever the case, theory can be useful in classifying and understanding the behavior of people in an organization.

Using theory in decision making involves five steps. First, a person must be familiar enough with theories to identify which are useful in a given situation. Usually, behavior may fit more than one theory. Second, a manager applies several theories and selects the one that might be useful in understanding the given behavior. Third, more information is collected to better fit the behavior to the theories. Fourth, the behavior is examined in light of the appropriate theories. Finally, the resulting information is fed back into the decision wheel process.

Across time, managers will find some theories more useful than others in explaining behavior. However, they should be careful not to apply a theory just because it worked in other cases, and they should make an effort to keep up with theories that develop.

SUMMARY

Decision making is the heart of managing. Decisions are either programmed, which means the solutions take effect under prescribed conditions, or nonprogrammed, which requires attention to the individual problems that must be solved. Nonprogrammed decisions are more difficult to make. All programmed decisions were set up originally by nonprogrammed decisions.

Decisions also can be classified as proactive and reactive. Proactive decisions anticipate changes in the environment that will affect the organization, and reactive decisions are made as a result of environmental changes.

Reaching decisions has an abstract form presented here as a decision wheel. The steps in this wheel occur to some degree in all effective decisions, although the time and effort devoted to the individual steps varies with the conditions surrounding the individual problem.

Just as decision making is at the heart of management, so analysis and information collection are the hub of decisions. Lack of information or poor analysis of information account for a high percentage of decisions that fail to achieve their goals. Several tools are available to improve analysis and information collecting, including social science theories and cost–benefit analysis.

As with the majority of human endeavors, management can be made better with thought and practice. The remainder of this volume is designed to facilitate thought and provide practice through cases. Each chapter also presents background to help explore the cases. The principles, theories, and research presented in the early part of the chapter should be used to analyze the information that either is provided with the case or needs to be collected from outside sources. In all cases, the decision process applies.

CASE 1.1

Looking at Past Decisions

People very often make important decisions without preparing properly or examining fully the decision process. The purpose of this assignment is to have you think about your decision-making process by concentrating on a specific decision. Select some important decision (choosing a college or college major, moving in with someone, etc.) that you made during the past few years that has disappointed you. Think about how you made that decision and why you were disappointed. Now, using the decision wheel try to remember the actions you took that would have fit into the various steps in the wheel.

ASSIGNMENT

Your assignment is to write a brief summary of the decision, and then answer the following questions:

1. Did you take all of the steps in the decision wheel? If not, which ones were not taken and why?
2. Did you complete each step as thoroughly as you should have? If not, which ones were not completed thoroughly and why?
3. If you could make that decision over again, what would you do differently to improve your decision?

CASE 1.2

Using Individual and Group Decision Styles

Dan Smith, publisher of the *Lincoln Daily Chronicle*, sat at his desk thinking about the e-mail he had just received from one of his reporters, Susan Kelley, and from the director of advertising Jane Seymore. Both messages concerned the web site for WZZY, the local CBS-affiliated television station. The web site was not new, but, unlike the other local TV station sites, WZZY had just added a section of classified advertising.

Kelley had e-mailed Smith because she found the site while buying a set of used golf clubs. Seymore had seen an advertisement that WZZY wanted to run in the *Daily Chronicle*. Smith has to make two decisions. First, he has to decide whether the newspaper will run the advertisements for the classified advertising on WZZY's web site. After all, WZZY is now a competitor with the *Daily Chronicle* for classified advertising. Second, he has to decide what to do in response to this new competition for classified advertising. Currently, about 35% of the *Daily Chronicle*'s total revenues came from classified advertising. Before the Web, the cost of delivering classified ads to consumers had kept down competition for this lucrative market.

ASSIGNMENT

Using the material in this chapter answer the following questions.

1. What type of individual decision-making style would work best for deciding whether to run WZZY's advertisement for its classified web page? Why would it be best?
2. Should Smith use group decision making to decide how to react to the threat to the newspaper's classified advertising revenue? Why?
3. Assuming a group will be used to make the decision, which of the 10 group-decision types would work best? Why?

CASE 1.3

Looking to the Future

Technology has created a rapidly changing business environment for the media companies. In such an environment, a company needs to make proactive decisions to keep up with media consumers' demands and with the competition. These decisions are nonprogrammed.

ASSIGNMENT

Using the decision wheel, the types of individual decision styles, and the types of group decision making, suggest a system of identifying and making decisions about new ways a media company can serve its customers. This will require that you pick a type of media company (newspaper, television station, radio stations, magazine, etc.) before developing such a system. You do not need to suggest new ways of service, just a way of identifying new services that might be useful to customers.

Describing this system will require, at minimum, explaining who identifies problems and opportunities and how these problems and opportunities are identified. In addition, discuss who will make the decision about how to solve new problems or pursue opportunities, and how this would happen.

2

LEADERSHIP
AND THE WORK FORCE

Media managers in the next decade will be focused on profit margin, competition, and employee needs, but the internal and external contexts will be driven by two powerful forces: demographics and technology. That is, managers will be dealing with shifting demographics that affect the needs and uses for media products and services in the marketplace. Demographic dynamics also affect the internal operations of media companies adjusting to the changing characteristics of media employees who mirror the larger work force. Emerging technology will affect not only the delivery and production of services and products to consumers but communication options between and among staff members. Managers will have available several tools for hiring, training, and assessing employees. Managerial excellence will be tied to effective and efficient use of the technology available to managers. Something that will not change, however, is the need for managers to be leaders. Although all leaders are good managers, all managers are not good leaders. This chapter identifies the characteristics, behaviors, and theoretical assumptions for positive leadership by media managers. This chapter is related to chap. 3 on motivation and chap. 6 on legal regulations, so readers should feel free to refer to all three chapters when dealing with cases or issues concerning human resources.

GENERAL PROFILE OF MEDIA COMPANIES

In December of 1997, the U.S. Department of Labor (DOL) released a 10-year projection for the U.S. work force. The DOL predicts that by 2006 the overall supply of workers will increase by 15 million with the largest increases for workers in the 45 to 64 age group. On the positive side, this grayer work force will offer a great deal of job experience and stability. These workers understand professional work standards, have faced crises and know how to improvise. They will, however, present some manage-

30

ment challenges. For instance many will require training (particularly with emerging technology). In addition, they may consider themselves semiretired at age 55 and not want to work full time. Salary may not be the key issue for them, but rather benefits (like health insurance) may be most important in recruiting and retaining this group (see chap. 3 for specific information about hiring and motivating employees and chap. 6 for specific laws/regulations affecting personnel). Traditionally, businesses have considered middle-age employees less adaptable, flexible, dynamic, and responsive to new ideas and technological changes than younger workers. However, because there will be fewer young workers and competition for jobs will be intense, media companies will need to move beyond stereotypes. Training sessions and adult education programs will be required for both middle-age workers and younger employees. Middle-aged employees will need training in technological developments and general skill upgrading. In addition, younger workers may need basic educational tools because school reform has not kept pace with the needs of business, and the gap between the education schools provide and the education workers need is widening. According to one researcher, U.S. businesses lose $20 billion each year due to illiteracy in the work force (Pilenzo, 1990).

The newest generation of the work force (born between the mid-1960s and the mid-1970s) also are of interest to managers. Because they realize that companies can no longer guarantee lifetime secure employment they often are described as the generation on a compressed fast-forward professional cycle. Apprenticeship used to be part of the traditional way new employees "learned the job." However, today's work environment includes Generation X workers who may be with a company only a couple of years (or in some instances a few months). In some cases a 23-year-old might even be hired to oversee a staff unfamiliar with a new or developing media product (like a web page). The compelling criteria for hiring this generation is not "who you know" but "what you know." The emphasis on skills and expertise is good news, however this can come packaged in an employee with inflated expectations that put the product and customer last. Management and communication skills as well as judgment and experience may be limited or nonexistent. Vigilant overseeing, explicit instructions, and careful explanation of company values and expectations will be required to help this younger worker fit into the company productively—especially if the employment is short term.

A growing number of women will make up an estimated 47% of the overall work force by 2006. Many of those women will hold college degrees in journalism. Since 1968, close to 60% of all college students majoring in journalism and mass communication have been female. According to Becker and Kosicki (1997), "women made up six of 10 of the bachelor's degree recipients in academic year 1995-96, a ratio that has been virtually unchanged since 1988" (p. 63). Female media managers and employees are expected to increase over the next 10 years. Women's growth in the work force is expected to stimulate support for such innovations as flexi-time, place, and scheduling, shared jobs, alternative career paths, telecommuting, extended leave, and employer-supported day care.

Although Sheppard (1989) concluded that males and females experience organizational life differently, it is difficult to analyze management data on a gender basis because so little of the research has included significant numbers of female managers. Although mid-level media management jobs are held by women, only 4–6% of women hold top-level positions in companies they have not started themselves. Some theorists claim women have a more circular, consensual, and relationship-based style of leadership than men who tend to use linear models. They predict that as female managers increase they will create a new working climate because of their tendency to spend more time with subordinates, listen more carefully, and develop more participative management environments where negotiation and relationships are important tools of decision making.

Asian and Hispanic workers will increase faster in the general work force than any other groups, with predictions calling for Asians to account for 5% of the total work force and Hispanics to hold 12% of all jobs. Black employees also will account for 12% of the work force. However, it is hard to predict growth rates (in the media) for these workers from educational statistics alone. Becker and Kosicki (1997) reported race/ethnicity enrollment records for journalism students have not been carefully or consistently recorded. For instance, although 1996 figures show that White student enrollment decreased from 1995 levels and Black student enrollment increased, data also indicate that overall there is a "persistent gap"between the percentage of students of color enrolled in journalism programs and those who actually graduate (Becker & Kosicki, 1997). This suggests retention and completion problems. It is impossible to know why students abandon journalism or media studies in college, but graduation rates compiled by Becker and Kosicki confirm a very small pool of non-White students hold degrees in the field. They say 9% of all journalism degrees in 1996 were obtained by Black students, 4% were earned by Hispanic students, 3% were earned by Hispanic students, 3% were obtained by Asian students and .9%

were earned by Native Americans. The competition for non-White media professionals with journalism degrees will be intense unless both college enrollments and retention rates increase. The research concerning non-White managers is largely underdeveloped and anecdotal. However, the few media executives who have crossed the color barrier are instructive in their observations. One Hispanic media manager said his supervisors had difficulty when he adopted a style of management that was comfortable for him and his Chicano staff members. He said it was "natural" and effective to develop a working climate built on affiliation rather than authority. He used a model that was closer to a family than a hierarchy. Although the leadership style he used worked well for his staff and took into consideration the ethnic culture from which they emerged, his traditional White male supervisors were uncomfortable and questioned his sense of closeness with the staff because he did not distance himself from his employees. He added that even at a corporate training session on leadership there seemed no understanding of the wisdom of adapting corporate climates to employee needs. He said the management training session was set up to indoctrinate executives into a preconceived management model. There was little room or time for discussion or acceptance of styles that were diverse or that deviated from the White male traditions.

Although growth will not be dynamic for White non-Hispanic workers, they will still hold the largest numbers of jobs with 73% of all workers falling into this category. They also will continue to have the highest levels of educational preparation for media work. Becker and Kosicki (1997), reported that 79% of all 1996 journalism degrees were earned by White students.

Leadership is a dynamic activity, and the next decade will hold even more examples of challenge to the traditional corporate model as diversity within the ranks increases. More women, people of color, and older workers will merge with current employees to create a need for a more complex and encompassing leadership model. In the next decade families and work also will be combined by both women and men. National research suggests leisure time—not money—may become the status symbol.

Managers will be expected to recognize and capitalize on the characteristics of a diverse work force. Cultural and demographic differences will impact training, motivation, production and turnover issues for managers, who will find their jobs challenging. Managers in the next decade may deal with tension, resentment, and conflict among workers who do not share common backgrounds or cultural orientations. Diversity (unlike affirmative action) is not meant to correct past inequity but to ignite dynamic thinking tuned to market demands and service opportunities for the media. Efforts during the 1970s and 1980s to diversify the work force commonly met with hostility, misunderstanding and even backlash. However, development of global markets has contributed to an understanding that a multicultural work force is not just "politically correct" but a smart and necessary business move. However most managers recognize that teams and groups of workers do not bond without help.

It is the job of the manager to initiate and support the process. Managers can lead the effort by first assessing what strengths belong to the group. For instance, if a manager notices that the work force of baby boomers is generally suspicious of authority and perpetually engaged in preserving youthful images then the manager might construct an autonomous rather than authoritarian work climate. He or she might build into technology training the message that technology provides access to and integration with youthful ideas and audiences.

For some employees trust may be the most important determinant of a satisfying work environment. These workers will not invest themselves or become motivated unless they have a working relationship with management that they consider trustworthy. They may define trust as consistency between written/verbal communication and managerial behavior. Or trust may be defined as the ability of management to "let go" of some of its power when employees have expertise, experience, and/or ability to perform without close supervision. However, managers cannot and should not guess at what is important to a particular set of employees. Each employee and work place have their own peculiar characteristics. Educational, professional, experiential, and personal backgrounds will vary, and managers should regularly talk with employees to note changes in expectations and employee needs. Managers also should note abrupt changes in employee behaviors (e.g. a usually prompt employee abruptly becomes tardy on a regular basis). Managers who are alert to cues sent by employees can avert and extinguish many problems before they become general morale or production nightmares.

Most work force experts predict that educational backgrounds may be the most challenging demographic variable to manage in the future. Some staff members will lack basic educational background and require technical training, whereas others will be highly educated professionals who are specialists in their fields. In fact, DOL predicts that jobs for people requiring at least a bachelor's degree will grow by 25%. Studies within the field of journalism support these overall findings with Becker and Kosicki (1997) reporting that an estimated fall 1996 enrollment of 149,256 students in U.S. journalism and mass communication programs was the highest total figure since 1991. They say analyses of the trends over the past several years suggests continued growth for journalism and mass communication college majors. Employment projections for the next 10 years support continued growth in media-related jobs with public relations and management fields ranking third among the top 10 industries. Technical support employees including database administrators, computer support specialists, and other computer scientists will increase by 118% and computer and data processing services will increase by 108% according to DOL projections by Franklin (1997) and by Silvesti (1997). Media managers will be expected to analyze the strengths of each employee and merge talents in a way that benefits company goals.

LEADERSHIP THEORY

A manager who is also a leader may be defined as someone who oversees tasks, is accountable for meeting goals, pays attention to profit objectives, and has a "vision" of where the company is going and why. Decisions reflect an understanding of larger long-term goals.

Early research in the field includes the Michigan Leadership Studies (Likert, 1961), which involved interviews with managers and subordinates to determine effective leadership behaviors. The studies isolated and identified at least two major supervisor orientations. They were job-centered or task-oriented behavior and employee-centered or relations-based managerial behavior. Researchers assumed the two types of managerial orientations were exclusive and represented two ends of a continuum with managers being one or the other but not both. About the same time, researchers at Ohio State University were conducting similar leadership studies. The research, which included data from military and industrial institutions, focused on relations-based decision making. The studies identified at least two typologies that were called consideration behavior and initiating-structure behavior. In the former, the manager considers the needs and ideas of subordinates before making decisions. In the latter, the manager clearly defines the duties of subordinates and communicates their functions to them. These were similar to the Michigan typologies, however the Ohio State researchers suggested that managers were not necessarily one kind of leader. Rather, they concluded that a manager could possess more than one orientation and successful managers could and did alternate styles as circumstances changed. The research described previously was helpful in identifying and confirming certain leadership behaviors. However, it was not complex enough to account for different organizational settings or individual deviations, nor did it explain how employees interpreted apparent inconsistencies when they witnessed managers adopting alternate styles of management as circumstances changed. Fiedler's (1967) contingency theory suggested that leadership effectiveness is related to a leader's personality and the situation. His research proposed that leaders have basic personality preferences that make them task versus relationship motivated, and that these preferences are constant and measurable for leaders. Later research connected job satisfaction and job fit with managerial needs for achievement, affiliation, and power. The research suggested that when a manager's dominant need was matched favorably with those of a company culture then job fit and satisfaction were generally favorable (Sohn & Chusmir, 1985).

All media managers must fit their personalities to an existing culture when they join a company. The cultural context, therefore, bears important consideration in all discussions of leadership behavior. As media companies expand into international arenas, it makes sense to understand the various dimensions for cultural analysis. That is, symbols, language, task definitions, and acceptable behaviors vary between workers, countries and even media. A good manager will balance personal style or preference with complex situational variables. Culture is a construct that underlies behavior and beliefs within a company and the society in which it operates. It guides, explains, and predicts processes and products of a media company. Organizational culture can be "observed" through categorizing and noting patterns of behavior, styles of dress, backgrounds of those hired and promoted, and so forth. Culture also can be defined in terms of shared values or assumptions workers hold about the world and human nature. Such common belief systems result in predictable behaviors and confirming rituals. Hofstede (1980) noted that North American and West European countries stress individualism rather than collectivism. This impacts how workers and managers regard their own relationships as well as those between the company and the individual. If organizational culture is seen as opposed to individualization or as something that impedes or diverts the individual, then supervisor–subordinate conflict is sure to occur in companies where Western values are prevalent. Such conflict affects morale and, in turn, employee production. Early research by Lewin, Lippitt, and White (1939), who studied boys' clubs, found that autocratic leadership produced the largest number of completed tasks, at least while the leader watched, but morale was best under democratic leadership. Interestingly enough, mixed and different results were found when the study was replicated outside the United States within different cultural contexts. For instance, Misumi (1985) found that in Japan the democratic style was effective if the task was easy, but the autocratic style was preferred if the task was difficult. Meade (1967) found in India that the autocratic style was best on all criteria. Other studies have found similar differences between cultures and between types of businesses. For instance, Heller and Wilpert (1981) found that managers in Sweden and France were consistently more participative in their management decision making than were managers in Britain, the United States, West Germany, and Israel, and that participative management styles are more characteristic of the oil and electronics industries than in banking and public transportation fields. Such studies serve to remind us that leadership styles must be considered within the context of worker values and expectations that may be tied to national, professional, and personal cultural orientations. Quite simply, effective leaders are not necessarily interchangeable across international borders, industries or even departments. (An extensive case illustrating media management challenges between countries is provided in chap. 7).

Regarding media news cultures, a shared U.S. value is high regard for competition. The cultural context for this competition includes the notion that being first with the news is being best, and being best translates into more market share and higher profits. Competition can entice managers into considering almost anything short of lying appropriate behavior. Media companies informally monitor one another and through professional groups sometimes even design codes and agreements for themselves that temper the cultural support for such values as competition (see chap. 6 for more discussion). There are also unwritten rules that occasionally have resulted in excommunication of members who violate them. Within large media companies there are several subcultures that reside in departments. They may support or be in conflict with each other as they struggle to maintain a dominant culture that ensures their survival and supports their collective belief systems (e.g. the business department may include norms that are consistent for accountants in general as well as for accountants who work primarily for media companies). However, subcultures will be allowed to exist only if they do not conflict with dominant company philosophy, which may be articulated in a mission statement or through daily work habits.

The Times Mirror Company Mission Statement in the late 1980s included nine separate objectives with, "attract, motivate and retain a high quality work force that reflects the diversity of our society, and provide a positive work environment that allows employees' talents to be developed to the fullest," listed as the seventh objective. The Indianapolis Newspapers, Inc., mission statement also includes diversity among its six objectives and says the company will, "encourage the professional growth of our employees, reward them for their contributions and strive to maintain a staff that reflects the diversity of our community." Both media companies promise commitment to diversity, but the promises vary in specificity and intention. Managers working for the companies would be expected to make daily decisions that are consistent with the mission statement of their company.

All official communication such as employee handbooks (which outline hiring, firing, performance review, and promotion procedures) as well as informal communication concerning daily assignments or even meetings also would be expected to reflect the spirit and purpose of the mission statements.

SOURCES OF POWER

Power is defined in several ways, however within the context of this discussion, it means the ability to accomplish an act or event or to influence an outcome. Media managers are expected to have the authority, ability, and influence to provide expected or desirable outcomes. The bases of leadership influence were identified by Weber (1947) as: (a) rational or resting on legal or normative rules; (b) traditional, resting on the legitimate status of those exercising authority; or (c) charismatic, which could involve leadership arising out of devotion or heroism. In addition, Griffin and Moorhead (1986) suggested a fourth base called (d) expert power, which allows leaders to control via expertise or information they hold that others need. This chapter includes discussion of all four kinds of leadership because they all exist in the modern work force. That is, although (legal authority and traditional authority) leadership types are recognized most easily because they possess titles, fulfill functions on an organizational chart, and have hierarchical recognition, the third type may operate informally and without institutional identification. This type of leader can develop out of positive needs for entrepreneurial development within an organization or out of negative or oppressive situations where workers feel disconnected, unappreciated, and devalued. The fourth leadership power arising out of expertise is dependent on a leader being able to convey, in a subtle, nonthreatening way, his orher possession of information. In addition, sometimes unauthorized leaders emerge out of situational factors that provide platforms for recognition. These types of leaders might be considered "renegades," especially if they threaten traditional, hierarchical corporate authority.

Much of the early leadership work focused on studying "current" leaders, and then identifying the steps on their rise to power. These studies found that people accept or are chosen for legal and traditional leadership positions because they possess certain cultural backgrounds that are acceptable to the current organization. It is still not clear how important personality is in the leadership formula, but it is clearly a variable related to the organizational situation as well as the level of expert competency required for the position. It also is clear that "leaders" who are named through static bureaucratic or institutional edict and are successful within that context may be very different from leaders who "emerge" because of dynamic situational factors growing out of crises or special need.

MEDIA PROFESSIONALS

Communication theorists and historians agree there are significant professional differences between media workers and suggest such differences can be traced to the early origins of each medium. For instance, advertising theory and practice grew out of understanding and adherence to principles tied to profit margins, and the radio and television industry developed from entertainment interests. Research by Powers and Lacy (1992) outlined a model to illustrate how (a) factors within journalists (that is, individual variables), (b) leadership characteristics, (c) organizational settings, and (d) market factors affect a local television newsroom. All four factors affect the perception of goal accomplishment or effectiveness, which in turn affects job satisfaction. Powers and Lacy found that employees are more satisfied with democratic-oriented leadership than with leadership that is autocratic in nature. They suggested that; "this does not mean news directors cannot make their own decisions, but rather that many, if not most, decisions should also include participation by the journalists" (p. 18). If leadership is seen as a dynamic activity, then managers will need to explore intellectually and pragmatically what is effective for the moment as well as for the long-term corporate climate.

Newspapers are the products of historical institutional clashes. Typically newspapers have crusaded against political and government entities, business organizations, religious groups, military structures, and others. Indeed, in the United States the First Amendment is written specifically to protect what U.S.'s founding fathers felt was a crucial voice of future dissent.

Therefore, the conflict between the news department and all other departments of a medium is to be expected and supported, some scholars say. Bagdikian suggested such tension between the news department and all other departments is a necessary ingredient in media companies (personal communication, April 1991). And, according to Bagdikian, the health of the industry depends on corporate support of the uniqueness of the news department in both broadcast and newspaper companies. The tendency for news editorial employees to be skeptical, untrusting, and suspicious of colleagues within their own news organization, may be seen as an historical "condition" sanctioned by professional expectations of those within the field. It is, however, also an obvious and peculiar managerial challenge to provide leadership for employees who routinely are rewarded for their instincts to question and resist authority. Indeed, one editor readily and proudly agrees that the editorial office of a newspaper is a "subculture" within the larger newspaper culture. He believes a newspaper ultimately must be a reflection of personalities who are willing to become identified with and take a stand for what their product is. This notion of personalizing the media company has ample historical reference with Pulitzer, Hearst, Luce, and even more recently Neuharth and Turner providing identity for famous successful media conglomerates.

Personalized Management

Weber (1947) distinguished his concept of *charismatic leadership* by defining it in terms of a psychological need of followers to become committed to a leader who might guide them out of a difficult situation. It is beyond hero worship, Weber said, and has a base in the idea that the charismatic leader should recognize this quality and act on it. He went on to say that this devotion by followers can arise out of enthusiasm, despair, or hope.

It appears then, that charismatic leadership would not occur in a traditional corporate setting unless employees are ripe for deliverance via personality-based leadership. Also, the bond between charismatic leader and follower requires a unidirectional model in that followers are seen to be acted on by a leader. That is, followers tend to see themselves as subordinate to the professional abilities and strategic thinking capabilities of the leader. Charismatic leadership is recognized as a legitimate category that is distinct from more routine definitions of managers or administrators. Charisma is often discussed in terms of *transactional* and *transforming* leadership. The former is as an exchange between leaders and followers that could be built on economic, political, or psychological bonds that continues only as long as leaders and followers find it mutually beneficial. Transforming leadership involves the initiation of a relationship with followers that has each encouraging the other through motivation and morality. Interactive relationships suggest that leaders do not act on followers but that followers somehow agree to the relationship because it is a satisfying one. Yet, it is still clearly the leader who is the definer of what is important. That is, goals are set by the charismatic leader—not by the leader and followers working together. Efforts to quantitatively measure the effectiveness of charismatic leadership have been mixed and generally disappointing (Bass, 1985). However, charisma retains powerful anecdotal meaning within the context of media and other businesses, so it is included here as one of several legitimate recognizable leadership styles. Several media executives have been known as charismatic leaders, including Henry R. Luce, who died in 1967 after forging an enormous publishing empire, Al Neuharth, who gave life and direction to the Gannett organization, and Ted Turner, who as head of CNN was *Time* magazine's 1991 Man of the Year. In summary, the research on leadership has been built upon several theoretical assumptions (Smith and Peterson, 1988):

1. Criteria for measuring leadership vary. They can include but are not limited to: task completion or production quotas, goals set by supervisors and organizations, or they can be subordinate morale.
2. Certain leadership characteristics are thought to be identifiable and measurable and thus capable of being studied and taught.
3. Leadership criteria cannot be assumed to be culturally adaptive, and differences in findings among different cultures are present.
4. Personality factors contribute to leadership.
5. Situational as well as legal, traditional, task, and charismatic leadership are recognized.

EFFECTIVE COMMUNICATION

Everyone agrees that communication is key to the efficient and effective management of a work force. Managers who are adept at communicating can unite, commit, and motivate employees to cooperate successfully for a common goal. Managers who are poor communicators can alienate, distract, and destroy employee momentum and energy. Managers communicate informally and formally with staff and intend for messages to be heard and understood. However, they should be aware that misunderstandings are to be expected, and feedback with quick correction should be built into any corporate communication system.

Traditional theory was built on the assumption that leaders are rule givers who tell employees what to do and when to do it, act as disciplinarians and punish those who do not obey company procedures (Barge, 1994). Although media managers do share some of these responsibilities, they most often supervise employees who are comfortable with autonomy and limited supervision. In addition, the media are change-oriented and technology-driven so that work systems have to be constantly reconfigured to meet customer needs for new and better products, markets, and delivery systems. Clearly leadership requires a productive relationship between managers and employees, but there is not much agreement on the nature of that relationship (see Barge, 1994; Fiedler, 1967; Hersey & Blanchard, 1972).

Leaders, according to Schein (1985), have the ability to communicate organizational messages in at least five different ways: (a) by focusing on and measuring and controlling variables; (b) by reacting to crises or other important events; (c) by coaching and teaching; (d) by rewarding and status conferring; and (e) by promoting, recruiting, and excommunicating. If leaders are consistent in actions supporting these five criteria and if they embellish these actions with stories, myths, and formal statements, the culture can be "managed" and maintained quite effectively. Cultures can be upset by contrary evidence that the criteria in place are wrong or inappropriate, by the emergence of a charismatic leader who readjusts the value system, or by the current culture's failure to meet expectations in some important way. That is, if a media company has as one of its major values community service, and employees have an abiding understanding of that value, the products the employees help develop will reflect that value. However, if for some reason the products become unimportant to the community, or the employees decide because of leadership or self-initiative that the internal value should be social responsibility, which they see as the antithesis of community service, the company culture could change dramatically. Basically, leaders remind staff "who we are" and "what we do." Confusion, and even anarchy, can occur when management delivers unclear or dysfunctional communication. Therefore, it is important that leaders explore all the options they have to communicate.

Written Communication

Typically employee handbooks offer managers the opportunity to communicate with staff in all five ways outlined by Schein (1985). That is, they clarify how staff will be hired, fired, and retired; outline hours of work and attendance policies; identify holidays; explain payroll deductions and set paydays; specify when and how performance will be reviewed and promotions considered; outline how salaries will be determined; list vacation time allowance; define insurance benefits; and outline behavioral and professional expectations. A handbook is generally desirable for five or more employees, essential at 10 and imperative for companies with 15 or more employees because Federal Civil Rights, Americans with Disabilities, and Pregnancy Leave Acts apply to companies with 15 or more employees.

It is important for employees to know what is expected of them and what can be expected in return. Job satisfaction is enhanced for employees when benefits and disciplinary policies are well known, and the company has a measure of assurance that managers will take basically the same course of action in similar circumstances. Because they serve as a contract (see chap. 6), they are written in formal language meant to outline expectations (on the part of both the company and employees) and resolve or mediate future workplace conflicts. They should promise equitable and consistent treatment of all employees.

Expected standards of behavior also should be included in the handbook. An example of this content is the Employment Opportunity Commission's (EEOC) definition of sexual harassment, which is, "unwelcome" sexual attention, whether verbal or physical, that affects an employee's job conditions or creates a 'hostile' working environment" (Adler, 1991, p. B1). The EEOC guidelines were issued in 1980 and unanimously affirmed by the Supreme Court in 1986. Many companies not only have a written statement about harassment but also require training sessions for certain managers to help understand the meaning and spirit of the law. As pointed out later in chap. 6, however, some media companies either do not have employee handbooks or fail to use or refer to the ones they have. This increases their vulnerability to lawsuits or claims from government agencies. For instance, if a manager fires an employee for being late the company may face a lawsuit or a claim from a government agency if there is no carefully spelled out written policy on tardiness—particularly if other employees have suffered no consequences for tardiness (a lack of consistency in enforcing rules can be grounds for discrimination claims). Written job descriptions not only assist in hiring the best possible employees but set the standards for future performance reviews. All job descriptions should state the job title, list the purpose of the job, state the essential duties and responsibilities, outline education and experience expectations, and describe required skills. For instance, a news manager hiring a person to start a web page might advertise for a webmaster (job title); with a journalism or related degree (education); with at least 2 years production experience on a web page (level of experience); who knows HTML, link translations, scanning procedures, and Associated Press (AP) stylebook (skills); who will compose and produce a weekly web page (purpose of job); that will appear every Thursday by 12 pm with rewrites of major local, national, and international news wire stories about lifestyle, sports, and business topics and include movement, color, graphics, and real-time media (essential duties). A detailed description provides guidance for equitable analysis and selection of job applicants, suggests relevant interview questions, provides standards for reward/discipline and assessment, and specifies standards for dismissal.

Verbal Communication

One of the most important conversations managers and employees will hold occurs during the job interview. Media managers should thoroughly discuss not only job expectations but the motivations workers hold (see chap. 3 for a detailed discussion). For instance, it is not unreasonable for managers to ask prospective employees what would cause them to resign and what their overall professional goals are. Such blunt and direct conversations about expectations rarely have occurred outside of mandated or written union understandings. However, it makes sense for managers—and employees—to initiate such conversations before employment commitments are made. One media manager said such a discussion is now a part of all her interview conversations with prospective employees. "I don't want any surprises after I spend the time and money to hire someone."

Discussions should occur on a regularly scheduled formal basis with all employees. This can occur on a monthly, semiannual, or annual basis. These reviews provide managers with the opportunity to discuss problems, recognize outstanding performance, and motivate workers who may need support or encouragement. However, informal encounters are also important and should be scheduled so that managers can observe and notice behaviors and complaints that need minimal, immediate attention before they build into major problems. In the formal setting, employees have the opportunity to self-report about their work-related successes and complaints, and in the informal setting managers have the opportunity to observe how employees are working. Both events should be recorded by the manager. Although the best communication is face to face and all formal performance review sessions are conducted in this way, much can be accomplished by phone, e-mail, or meetings.

Phone and e-mail provide opportunities for discussion as well as debate. If the manager has a good relationship and high trust with the employee, then the informality of the phone and e-mail may work in a positive way. With minimum effort, e-mail as well as voice mail can provide the opportunity for sharing news at the same time with many employees. E-mail also allows employees to ask questions as well as clarify and discuss options even if everyone involved is not in the same office location or same time zone. Meetings, however, are probably the communication mechanism of choice for managers. Mosvick studied meetings from 1981–1995 and found that the average number of meetings jumped from 7 to about 10 a week for all business professionals (Armour, 1997). Unfortunately many meetings are simply a time drain rather than a productive event. A study by 3M Meeting Network, an online resource, says that managers spend between 25% and 60% of their time in meetings but as much as 50% of that time is unproductive (Armour, 1997). Studies even show that meetings can trigger stress in employees unless they foster creativity, reach collective agreement, or gain consensus. All meetings should have an agenda, time limit (20–40 minutes is ideal), and provide follow-up information about decisions made following the meeting.

Team-Building Implications

Work teams are among the business trends that have been integrated into media companies. Emerging technologies, expanding international markets, and the necessity for interdepartmental collaboration have fueled the effort. The purpose of a team is to work efficiently and effectively to identify opportunities and problems, which may seem short-term but in reality have long-term implications. For instance, the decision to "try out" a new media product (e.g. a newspaper zone edition, a "smart" TV, or a web site) requires a team effort to research, develop, produce, distribute, and assess its viability. This kind of team would be task–oriented with a specific product as its goal. Decision teams, on the other hand, might define goals, prepare budgets, or study changing political and economic climates to determine long-term company strategies.

For teams to succeed, the commitment must be strongly supported by management—particularly top levels. This means that mission statements mention teams, and at least one top corporate officer is assigned to develop and provide resources for teams. Secondly, criteria for measuring and rewarding team efforts must be clear. Pay or salary need not be the reward for progress, but something of significant value (to team members) must be offered. Third, resources must be clearly allocated. This is usually time and money. And finally, the purpose of the teamwork should be clear with specific questions and problems identified.

If the team is working well, then the goals are strong and clear to everyone (everyone in the group can independently state objectives that match what others say and think). Everyone in the team understands their role and knows how that role contributes to the results. The work climate is positive, supportive, and trusting. People willingly communicate in open and direct ways sharing data, information, and opinions. When differences occur they are recognized and resolved through negotiation and consensus. Everyone participates in decisions without regard to title or power. Everyone agrees to follow decisions made by the team (Dyer, 1995).

A manager must know how to select and coach a team of employees as well as how to train them to work as a self-directed entity. Team members may have different backgrounds, levels of education, expertise, experience, and company titles. Team members also might have different professional needs for achievement, power, or affiliation. Making a diverse group of employees into a productive team is not an easy task, however it is essential. Teams should spend considerable time agreeing on a common set of goals or a shared vision of what they want to accomplish. Next, they must see diversity as a positive value. That is, they should identify skills, backgrounds, cultures, expertise, and experiences that may impact their collective result. There should be a commitment to using all the resources and strengths of the individuals to help the team.

Leadership of the team can occur several ways. The team can have an appointed leader who has direct influence and control. Or the leader can organize, train, and facilitate the team but not directly influence its work. The team can select its own leader, rotate leadership, or it can even operate without a leader (committee of the whole). The team also has flexibility in terms of how often and how long it meets. For some teams sharing information by e-mail or by phone is satisfactory, but other types of teams might require a high level of interaction. A team working on a new book might meet once to agree on content, time frame and style rules. E-mail or phone conversations would occur as questions arose or changes were ordered by the publisher, but most of the teamwork would be accomplished independently. However, a news team putting out a special edition on a hurricane that just passed through town would work closely conferring every hour about new information, pictures or film that were available, interviews that had been completed, and overall presentation choices.

A team is only as effective as its ability to plan for and deal with predictable problems. One such difficulty is passive behavior by team members. Sometimes artificial agreement occurs when team members are dependent, immature, and have no desire to confront controversial issues. Or team members may have learned over time that conformity is the least stressful option when dealing with a particular leader. Some team members may resist participation if they have little or no trust in the leader and feel they must protect and guard themselves. Other problems may occur between team members if they do not trust one another or they are unwilling or unable to accept differences. However, most problems can be reduced to differences in expectations. If behavior of one person does not meet expectations of another person then negative reactions result. If there is no resolution, the team members can become hostile and the team effort destroyed. Therefore, one of the most important tasks of any team, is to identify not only general expectations for the team, but expectations each individual holds about his or her role and the role of all other members of the team. For instance, if Team Member A "expects" everyone will turn in their work on deadline there must be verbal and written agreement and commitment (from all members of the team) for that expectation to be met successfully.

SUMMARY

Changing demographics and technology will impact the work force for media companies and media managers in the next decade. Training will equalize the experience and education differences of staff, however managers will still need to provide leadership and direction for staffs that will represent several age, gender, ethnic, and national diversities.

Flexibility in styles of management will be of importance as top-down and authoritarian leadership is joined by team and participative management strategies. Leaders who can plan effectively will be as important as leaders who can "act" decisively. The cultural context for leadership including language and communication styles will be important as workers design goals that are significant for their companies, their profession and their personal satisfaction.

CASE 2.1

The Case of Planning Human Resources for WXPT

WXPT is a network affiliate television station in a southern city with a population of 300,000. It is the center of a metro area of 500,000 people and 216,000 households. You are general manager of the station, and your investment in the local television news department during your 3 years has paid off with growing ratings and shares for both the evening and late-night newscasts.

You credit your success to the heavy emphasis of local coverage in your newscast. In your 3 years as station manager the news budget has grown by 50%. Your newsroom now has one director, three producers, six news reporters, two anchors, one sports anchor, one sports reporter, two weather reporters, and 10 camera people.

The 5-year strategic plan calls for expanding the early evening newscast to 1 hour from its current 30-minute format. The local news will run from 5:30–6:30 pm with the network newscast moved to the 6:30 pm slot. In addition, the station is upgrading its equipment and studio, and production training will be required for nearly all staff. The changes are scheduled to take place in 6 months, so it is important that a human resource plan be developed. The current staff include the following:

Jim, a White, 51-year-old man, has been an anchor for 12 years and a reporter for 20 years. He is managing editor and is perceived by viewers as steady and trustworthy. Although Jim is well liked, it is clear he enjoys his status and frequently reminds younger staff members of their lack of experience when he thinks they are acting arrogant.

Sandy is a 25-year-old White woman who has been working as co-anchor with Jim for 2 years. Recent research indicates both men and women in the market think she is beautiful and pleasant. She is not a strong reporter and did not attend college although she has worked as an anchor for two other stations prior to joining this one. Jim frequently corrects her pronunciation and her adlibs, which invariably include factual errors. She has worked hard to achieve her current position and is proud of herself, although she quietly resents Jim's oversight of her work. She thinks she could take over as anchor if Jim were to leave the station.

David is the 57-year-old White weatherperson. He has a college degree in meteorology and is highly respected by viewers, however he has been hinting that he might retire unless the terms of his 5-year-contract (which expires at the end of the year) are favorable. David is very task-oriented and does not appreciate wasted conversation or work time. Although not rude, he is curt and does not socialize with staff members outside the station.

Janice is a 30-year-old African American who was born and raised in the area and has been at the station as a weatherperson for 4 years. She is not a certified meteorologist, but she is a quick learner and has been trained well by David who thinks she does a wonderful job.

She appreciates David's training and help but wishes she had a mentor who was better at communicating. She enjoys relationships, and she would like to be better friends with more of the staff, but she is afraid David will disapprove if he observes her casually talking with coworkers.

The sports anchor is Harve, a 42-year-old White man, who joined the staff 14 months ago after he was recruited from the second-place station in the market. He has fit in well except for a few conflicts with Jim over treatment of sports news. Jim wants him to deal with social issues and sports whereas Harve wants to just give highlights and scores. Harve is well liked by the staff who enjoy his jokes and friendly ways. The staff sense tension between Jim and Harve and hope it never escalates into open warfare.

Susan is the number two sports anchor. She joined the station 1 year ago after she left the local newspaper claiming sexual discrimination. She is currently suing the newspaper publisher for repeated sexual harassment. The station received a large amount of positive mail from viewers when it hired her. She was hired because of her expertise in baseball and car racing, both important sports in the area. In addition to anchoring the weekend sports spot, she also reports during the week. She has received good but not glowing evaluations during her first year on the air. Her weak points have been coordinating film with words, although her evaluations acknowledge her outstanding writing. When Susan first arrived, she was grateful to have a job, but recently she has become disenchanted with the station and wonders if she made the right decision. She does not like editing and cutting news into small pieces, but she is excited by the upcoming changes that will provide more news time. She secretly hopes the station will consider giving her a leadership role in the planning phase because she likes analyzing and coordinating ideas and details. However, she is reluctant to make her desires known because she feels she is too inexperienced and new to offer suggestions.

Leslie is the star reporter. She is a 30-year-old African American who grew up in the area. She joined the station immediately after graduating from the local university with a degree in journalism. She has been named Outstanding Broadcast Journalist for the state for her in-depth reports on problems facing cities. Many people have pointed out she could be working at a network or in a much larger market, and indeed she has turned down such offers because of family commitments in the area. Although she is achievement-oriented, her most striking professional need is affiliation, and she values the relationships she has made at the station and with her sources. The major skill that has contributed to her reporting success is her ability to put people at ease and to build trust. That is the same characteristic that draws people at the station to her. She is the best-liked and most respected member of the staff.

The other reporters are all White males and relatively new to the business although they hold college degrees in journalism.

ASSIGNMENT

In order for the changes to be handled smoothly you will be setting up "teams" to prepare for the changes and to build trust and support for the staff.

1. How will teams be set up?
2. How will team leaders be selected?
3. What promises (from top management) will you make to the teams?
4. Describe the "expectations" top management will have for the teamwork and the time frame for meeting the expectations.
5. Analyze (with support from the chapter) which members of the staff will be most crucial to the success of the station in the future.

CASE 2.2

Shutting Down and Moving On

Nancy is the public relations (PR) vice president for a corporation that is facing a corporate move to another state. Her department is small, but she must figure out a way to complete the department's work with even fewer people because the corporation only will be able to move four people including herself. She has not been able to tell her staff of the move because the president has asked all vice presidents to keep the news to themselves until he makes an official announcement in 2 months. Her task is to cut her staff and to reduce department salary lines.

Her first consideration is expertise and level of production. She needs to retain people who work quickly and efficiently and fire people who are marginal in their performance. She also wants to retain people who can work together well because increased patience and cooperation will be required in the months ahead. And finally, she appreciates staff who are creative and take risks because many times her department is called on to develop campaigns and projects that are unusual, clever and memorable. The president has told her to cut $150,000 in salaries from her budget.

Although Nancy has been in charge of the department, she has not worked closely with the staff because she serves as the personal advisor to the president and delegates direct supervision of the department to 52-year-old Marge, who earns $64,000 per year. Marge is a design expert and has purchased the software and hardware necessary to create most PR packages internally saving thousands of dollars over the years. Nancy hired Marge and considers her a loyal and valuable employee.

Ed is the chief technician and photographer, and his work on the recent annual reports has won national awards for the corporation. His work is creative, professional and always produced on deadline. He has, however, taken many personal leave and sick days, which Marge suspects are spent with his family and Church, because he is very religious. He earns $45.000.

Charlie is 28-years-old and has a background in news. He is a graceful writer who prepares copy for all the corporate publications including the annual report, the brochures, and promotional packages. He is very ambitious and has made friends with several corporate officers. He tends to gossip, and so Marge tells him little about the overall office chores unless he is directly involved. Although she appreciates his talent and performance, she is cautious with him because she believes he is more concerned with his career than with the corporation. He earns $38,000.

Madeline is 22-years-old and started with the corporation as a college intern when she was 20. She is a graphic designer and works with Ed. She is very creative and although she is young and relatively inexperienced she has made several suggestions that have been followed by the department. She is quiet and has not made friends easily, and Marge is not certain she is happy although her performance has been excellent. She earns $29,000.

Paul is 35 and has many of the same skills and background Marge has. He is well respected by the people in the department and is very witty. Many times he has helped Marge with personnel issues because he recognizes problems and is able to diffuse them with a kind or witty word that generally soothes egos. Although he is very respectful of Marge he wonders if she is best suited to manage the unit because her communication skills are sometimes too harsh. He genuinely loves his work, but he wants a raise. He has been reluctant to ask for one because he has heard rumors the corporation is moving and will fire some people. He earns $40,000 and needs his job because his wife has just had a baby and quit her job.

ASSIGNMENT

1. Given Nancy's three goals for retaining people (see second paragraph of Case 2.2) make a case for three employees to be retained (remember that the choices need to represent a $150,000 savings in salary).

2. Write a memo from Nancy to the department that describes the situation and outlines the procedures to be followed. Remember that the memo should ONLY report that a downsizing is necessary and NOT that a move is probable.

3. Write at least five questions that Nancy will ask each member of the department in private interviews to help her decide who will be retained and who will be asked to resign (or be fired if necessary).

3

MOTIVATION

Rose DeLoss is a 27-year-old, 5-year veteran of the newsroom. She is a reporter in the newspaper's suburban bureau, from which she covers everything from the courthouse and city hall to local schools. She says she is happy but Bob, city editor and her immediate boss, thinks Rose is dissatisfied. She never smiles, is frequently ill or late, misses deadline frequently, and consistently protests when assigned a story by the city desk. Her complaints include a low salary. And lately her writing is beginning to suffer—her quotes are matter-of-fact, leads are uninspiring, and her sources are limited to government officials (and frequently the same ones).

Bob wants to be understanding. Her husband is a sports reporter at the paper, which means they work different shifts, seeing each other barely long enough to hand off their 5-month-old infant, and the suburban bureau is not a prime assignment in most reporters' eyes because the newspaper prides itself on its coverage of the central city. But Rose's attitude, like a yawn, is contagious; her younger colleagues in the bureau often take their cue from her on various matters—particularly on coverage issues such as story angles and source selection. Bob is beginning to worry that if he does not do something, he might have more Roses than he can handle. He would like to find a way to motivate her to improve.

Motivation, the way Bob sees it, is being able to manipulate an employee into doing what the manager—in this case, Bob—wants. But Bob does not realize that motivation involves more than action on his part. In fact, motivation may be something that Bob can not control at all. That is because Rose's problem may not even stem from anything Bob is doing or not doing. Media managers supervise creative employees in settings that require enlightened thinking; but motivation's more complicated—managers must understand it in context (Fink, 1993) if they are to successfully deal with employees. The media workplace—because of the rapid, cyclical nature of production—often presents unusual, demanding, and sometimes seemingly chaotic circumstances for managing, thus requiring the media manager to have an objective-based framework for viewing motivation and motivational opportunities. In short, this chapter emphasizes a context for motivation that takes into account the special circumstances of media workplaces. The chapter concludes with a look at some common problems as well as some current trends in the media workplace. Bob's dilemma with Rose requires him to understand why Rose behaves the way she does. The best way to do so is to examine what factors contribute to that behavior.

WORK CONTEXT

Job Mandates

A newspaper requires completion of many tasks by its reporters: writing and reporting, to be sure; but also critical thinking, skepticism (even cynicism); aggression; tenacity; a considerable time commitment; speed; accuracy; fairness; a sense of moral righteousness and civic duty, to name a few. The list gets longer or shorter, depending on the medium and on the position. Whatever the medium, however, employees—particularly those in creative jobs—are required to perform a varying array of tasks. This says nothing of the emotions they go through in executing those tasks. Such feelings may range from the humor or pathos that goes into a creative advertising campaign to an outright lack of caring, which occurs when a reporter must doggedly ask embarrassing questions of incompetent public figures.

For Rose, being a reporter generally means keeping abreast of happenings in suburban government. She has to be aware of various city, county, and state laws and evaluate and monitor the performance of the elected and appointed officials whose duty it is to uphold and execute those laws. She attends countless meetings, reads proposals and budgets, interviews interested and affected parties, and analyzes various kinds of information. Being a good reporter means doing all this well and often.

In essence, then, Rose has *goals* imposed on her by the mere fact of being hired. Organizational goals derive from the organization's needs. Rose, it can be assumed, has adopted the goals of the job as her own. Often, managers can look at motivation simply as a basic process of *needs* producing *drives or motives,* which lead to goals being achieved. Either physical or psychological deficiencies cause needs, which Maslow (1954) classified into a five-tier hierarchy: physiological (food and thirst, sleep, health); safety (shelter, security); social (acceptance, belonging, group membership, love); esteem (recognition and prestige, success); and self-actualization (self-fulfillment of potential). But Maslow theorized only one level of need motivates a person at any given time and that needs are satisfied in order, from lowest (physiological) to highest (self-actualization), as illustrated in Fig. 3.1.

The problem, of course, is that Rose's needs—or anyone else's—may be partially but not completely met or she may be motivated by two or more needs simultaneously (Alderfer, 1972). For example, she may be concerned about her salary (safety) and by her need to grow in the reporting profession (esteem). Alderfer also stipulated that if a person's higher order needs are met—such as Rose's need for journalistic prestige—then the person becomes frustrated and may regress to being motivated by a lower level need. What this might mean in Rose's case we have yet to discover, but Bob would do well to analyze Rose's complaints about her salary.

Because Rose's goal is not reached, it logically follows that there was no drive or motive—a stimulus to action. The drive in this case would have

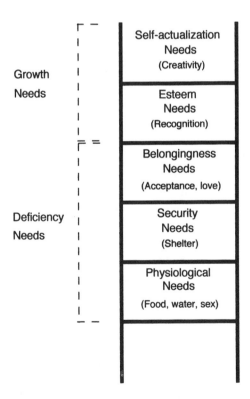

FIG. 3.1. Maslow's hierarchy of needs.

been manifested, for example, in a series of in-depth articles on corruption in suburban government. Bob's goal must be to determine what needs Rose has and which goals she is attempting to meet. Many of these goals can be determined by looking at the mandates of the job. However, other considerations must be made.

Employee Potential

Some management experts (e.g., Straub, 1984) believe that effective employee selection is a prerequisite for successful motivation. In this case, Bob would need to know whether Rose is not only capable of carrying out the tasks required of reporters, but also whether her values match the position and whether she's psychologically capable. In reality, however, Bob and most other media managers have neither the time nor the tools to determine if the person they hire is perfectly suited for the job. So in the absence of the perfect selection method, they must seek to become effective motivators instead.

Most people have a need to achieve, a need for power and a need for affiliation. The need for achievement was discussed in the previous section on goals. The other two needs involve the desire to influence people (power) and the desire to be liked (affiliation). McClelland (1961) developed this typology and suggested most people have a dominant need. Media managers must recognize dominant needs in themselves as well as in employees. Bob sees Rose's need for power in her attempts to guide younger reporters. Her need for affiliation is less clear, although her complaints can be interpreted as evidence of lack of concern for being liked. At the same time Bob probably has a high need for power and achievement, which influences the assumptions he makes about Rose's performance (or, as Bob might say, "lack of achievement").

People share a common level of experiences. For example, people generally repeat behavior that is rewarded or reinforced and avoid behavior that is punished. Such *conditioning* falls into two general categories: classical and operant. The former attempts to generate involuntary, reflexive or quasi-instinctual/physiological behavior through unconditioned stimuli, when a reporter is writing a story and notices she has 10 minutes left before deadline. She experiences a rush of adrenalin and a heightened pulse and other symptoms that indicate heightened anxiety. Operant conditioning (Skinner, 1972) suggests—as illustrated in Fig. 3.2—reinforced behavior will be repeated voluntarily and behavior not reinforced is less likely to be repeated. Reinforcement can be positive (as when Bob rewards Rose for the

desired behavior of producing a good story by placing it on the front page), negative (as when Bob rewards Rose's avoidance of undesired behavior of complaining by increasing her pay), punishing (as when Bob rewards the undesired
behavior of Rose complaining with the negative consequence of firing her) or
extinctive (as when Bob eliminates the unwanted behavior of complaining by
not rewarding it). But regardless of how Bob attempts to condition Rose, the
key point is that he should be aware of options and study what has worked in the
past to determine what might be successful in managing Rose.

Job Performance Issues

Studying this interactive process of job and employee can be approached
from a number of perspectives.

First, there is the process by which people are motivated. Three theories—equity theory, expectancy theory, and goal-setting theory—address
this idea. In equity theory (Adams, 1963), the key assumption is that inequity is a motivator, for example, when employees feel they have been unfairly treated, they will attempt to achieve a sense of equity. If Rose's
unhappiness stems from inequity (she sees reporters with comparable experience earning more), she can become happier by changing how much she
works, by attempting to increase her pay (i.e., asking for a raise), by reas-
sessing how she compares herself, by distorting the comparisons to make
herself compare more favorably, or by quitting. Usually, people who sense
pay inequity reduce their workload to compensate for what they perceive as
missing rewards.

Expectancy theory (Vroom, 1964) asserts that people will do what they
can do when they want to. In other words, the theory says that motivation is
the product of the interaction between expectancy (a person's belief that
working hard will enable various work goals to be achieved), instrumentality (a person's belief that various work-related outcomes will occur as a re-

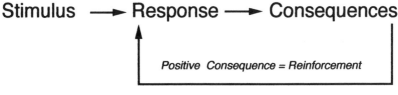

FIG. 3.2. Operant conditioning.

sult of doing the job) and valence (the value the person assigns to those work-related outcomes); see Fig. 3.3. The motivational appeal of a reward (e.g., higher salary) is drastically reduced whenever expectancy, instrumentality, or valence—together or alone—nears zero. In Rose's case, we expect her motivation to earn a pay increase will be low if she feels she can not do the necessary work, if she is not confident that the extra work will result in the pay increase, or if she places little or no value on getting a pay increase.

Finally, goal-setting theory maintains that employees behave the way they do because it helps them reach their goals (Locke, 1968); particularly important are the difficulty and specific nature of the goals. For instance, planning to win an Emmy Award is a sufficient motivator for most television writers to achieve excellence in writing; but if a writer sets such a goal in his or her first year of working, the goal can be too difficult and lead to frustration. But if the writer modifies and specifies the goal (e.g., winning an Emmy in 5 years, or attempting to have a certain number of ideas or scripts produced in a year), then the writer enhances the chance for honest evaluation of the goal and assessment of his or her writing. It is important for the manager to know what goals an employee has set and how that affects behavior. In Rose's case, Bob would do well to familiarize himself with Rose's goals and to determine their difficulty, realistic qualities, and Rose's place on the path to achievement. Doing so will help him to know whether he can help her meet those expectations and, if so, what strategies need to be developed. If Bob thinks the goals are unreachable, he can counsel Rose to help her adjust her expectations.

Another way of looking at job-employee interaction issues is through the prism of job satisfaction. It is widely assumed that a satisfied employee is a productive one; but some might say that satisfaction does not cause performance—that it is the reverse. An employee who performs the job is a satis-

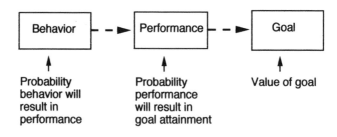

FIG. 3.3.   Expectancy theory.

fied employee (Greene, 1972). So when it comes to motivating employees, it is a good idea for managers to know how satisfaction works in general and—in particular—for their employees.

Alderfer's theory (1972) defines the role of frustration in terms of unmet needs. Recognizing the frustration factor implies that a manager can positively react to the frustrating item and create a more satisfying situation for the employee. But Herzberg and colleagues (Herzberg, Mausner, & Snyderman, 1959) developed the dual-factor theory, which suggests—as illustrated in Fig. 3.4—that satisfaction and dissatisfaction are not related but, rather, affected by different needs and motives.

Herzberg contends that "hygiene," or preventative factors do not produce motivation, but they can prevent motivation from occurring. Such factors—sometimes viewed as environmental influences—include money, status, security, working conditions, work policies, supervision and interpersonal relations. If a manager attends to these items, Herzberg suggests the manager help keep employees from being highly dissatisfied. On the other hand Herzberg predicted that "motivators"—which include job-related factors such as achievement, challenging work, increased responsibility, recognition, advancement, and personal growth—provide true motivation when combined with hygiene factors. Not everyone agrees with Herzberg, however, and this theory has not always been supported (Griffin & Moorhead, 1986).

One major study discovered that journalists differ by medium as to what they consider most important when evaluating their own job satisfaction. Daily newspaper, wire service, and radio journalists cited job security as the major issue, whereas television journalists said the importance of helping people is a primary factor. In addition, although pay was likely to be at the bottom of most journalists' lists (regardless of their employer), wire service and broadcast journalists were more likely than other journalists to cite pay as an issue in job satisfaction (Wilhoit & Weaver, 1994). Additional studies show how elusive managing for satisfaction can be. For instance, in the early 1980s, how often a newspaper journalist received comments from managers was a strong predictor of satisfaction for all journalists except those working at medium-sized newspapers. In addition, the strongest predictor of job satisfaction for journalists at small newspapers was how good a job of informing the public the journalists thought their organization was doing (Bergen & Weaver, 1988). A decade later, the size influence had disappeared. Perceptions about effectiveness in informing the public and about frequency of managerial comments about work were significant pre-

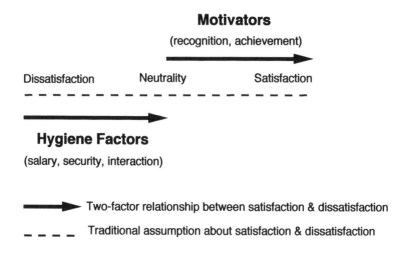

FIG. 3.4. The two-factor theory of motivation.

dictors for journalists working at all newspapers—regardless of size. In addition, older journalists in small and medium-sized papers were most satisfied in the 1980s but by the 1990s the older journalists in small and large papers were most satisfied (Kodrich & Beam, 1997).

Closely linked to satisfaction is the notion of job autonomy. For younger journalists, autonomy has been an important factor in job satisfaction since the 1970s. Size as well as type of ownership determined feelings of autonomy. Journalists who work for smaller media that are independently owned are more likely to report personal discretion at work. Still, the study's authors (Weaver & Wilhoit, 1996) concluded that autonomy was not fully explained by such factors and noted that journalists' sense of autonomy had eroded since the 1980s. Understanding such feelings of powerlessness make Rose's behavior somewhat understandable and suggests managers such as Bob should take a look at the resources they provide their employees and how they deal with job satisfaction in general.

Of course, all this information—although insightful—does not necessarily help the manager in every case. Employees are different and national studies tend to obscure those differences, which can result in a complex dynamic. Sometimes there are other issues that come into play. For example, a growing body of research is beginning to shed light on factors that increasingly diverse workplaces introduce into the satisfaction equation. One school of thought (Pease, 1992) suggests that newspaper journalists of color are less likely than most journalists to accept promises of career advancement and more likely to seek alternative career paths; particularly at risk of newspaper switching are minority females. Supportive studies (Bramlett-Solomon, 1992, 1993) show Black and Latino journalists are twice as likely than their White counterparts to be dissatisfied and to stress job advancement opportunities (over the generally cited "chance to help people") when judging the attractiveness of their jobs.

Managers must recognize what each employee brings to the job. Perceptions are just that—something brought to the job by an individual. It is not surprising Rose and Bob see the situation through different lenses. She would probably say her illness, tardiness, and complaints stem from various things—taking care of an infant, lack of autonomy on assignments, low pay, and lack of time to produce quality reporting. Bob, on the other hand, might say the problems are because of laziness, lack of ambition, and lack of time management. A good manager knows that each perception is selective, in that each person highlights for attention those aspects of a situation that reinforce or appear consistent with that person's beliefs, attitudes, and values. The manager cannot control such defensive posturing by the employee, but to not be able to control his own blinders poses a problem for Bob.

Technology and Performance

In this arena, when management introduces a technology (mechanical or procedural) to employees, the interaction can go in various directions. Consequences of this interaction can be viewed three ways: (a) direct (changes that occur in immediate response) or indirect (changes resulting from immediate responses), (b) desirable (helps the employee or system function more effectively) or undesirable (dysfunctional), and (c) anticipated (changes recognized and intended by management) or unanticipated (changes neither recognized nor intended). From a motivation standpoint, however, the manager needs to ensure there's a good match between the technology and the employee.

Doing so means recognizing employee–technology interactions can be mental or physical, pleasant or unpleasant—but, in any event, fairly quick, partly because of the change such interactions bring in the production process. So how the employees perceive the technology is very important and it is up to the manager to help employees see the technology is better than its predecessor; compatible and consistent with existing values, past experiences, and employee needs; relatively easy to understand and use; experimentally friendly; and capable of an observable job impact (Rogers, 1983).

In Rose's case, Bob might want to introduce improved time management techniques. The key, however, would be whether Bob could show Rose that the techniques would be successful without too great a disruption in her work routines and personal life.

Sometimes the technology itself is a motivator. An obvious example is the Internet's capacity to enhance the information-gathering abilities of reporters. As a result, many reporters have adopted the technology with relish. In some cases, however, the choice is not so obvious. The organizational reward systems must support technology adoption. For instance, the broadcast industry usually pays its salespeople on a straight commission basis—usually 15% of sales. But such a system usually encourages staff members to sell only proven goods because they are easy to sell and constitute a steady income. In addition, a commission-only system fosters competition and conflict in sales departments (usually over who gets the best account list). The challenge to the sales department head is to develop a system—perhaps combining commission methods with salary and incentive plans—that would serve as a more effective motivator and still meet the needs of individual salespeople (Warner, 1997). A final word about pay as a technology: Not every media employee sees money as a primary motivational need. In fact, journalists often rank it below other factors as an influence in their satisfaction level. For a detailed discussion of how a manager should approach this and other technologies, see chapter 5.

GROUPS

Media organizations, like other companies, are composed of groups—committees, task forces, cliques, and entities that help the organization accomplish its objectives. Media managers—if they are to be effective motivators—must become familiar with groups and how they influence the organization's morale, well being, and development. One particular group that media managers must acknowledge is the occupational group, the collection of people who share a set of values, standards, and views that apply to the workplace and beyond. These groups confer, vie, and compromise with each other, thus functioning as significant participants in organizational decisions. Although hiring individuals is a key decision, placing that person in a group adds considerable substance to the action—one which carries with it an implicit obligation of the manager to learn the forces that drive occupational groups. In relationship to Bob and Rose, this means Bob must not only see Rose as an individual affected by personal, task, performance, and technological issues, he also must view her within the context of the groups to which she belongs.

Group Influences

Groups influence people. Group members often get their identities or self-images from their occupational group roles, take other members as their primary reference group, and often socialize with group peers (Van Maanen & Barley, 1984). Understanding groups and their development is essential to managing effectively, especially when the manager views groups as another tool in the motivational arsenal; just as groups offer advantages to their members, they pose great advantage to the manager who understands them. Before using that tool, however, the manager also needs to understand that groups appear in two basic forms: formal and informal.

Managers create formal groups when they formally authorize two or more people to devote time and resources to a task. Such groups garner a variety of names: committees, task forces, project teams, and departments, to name a few. Organizations could not function without these groups and often such groups gain considerable clout and power, depending on their function. They often are temporary but again this depends on function. Managers gain direct control over such groups through selection of members (and, in some cases, leadership), definition of purpose, and performance oversight. Often the group's purpose and status determine the degree to which the group is motivational. For example, selection to prestigious or powerful groups fulfills certain needs for some, whereas omission (or removal) from a nondesirable group also can be a positive motivator—much like it would be if Bob changed Rose's assignment from the suburban bureau to the city/metro department. Formal groups, then, not only provide the media manager with a way to get work done but also with a structural element in the motivation process.

Informal groups, on the other hand, pose a more complex issue. Whereas formal groups are directly linked to the organizational structure, informal groups develop indirectly (and often unintentionally) from the socialization that the formal structure encourages. Creative influences of such groups can range from something as simple as physical proximity of employee workspaces to the common values their jobs (and backgrounds) instill in them. Either way, the manager must realize these groups also serve a function, albeit not necessarily one the manager intended or devised.

As mentioned earlier, groups provide an identity of sorts for their members. Television news anchors, for example, closely identify with each other based on shared experiences and visions of what it is to be a news anchor: a witty, acerbic at times, conversationalist with an eye for news and a sense of how to entertain and accommodate TV viewers on their way to dinner or bed. He or she may become friends with other anchors at the station or at other stations in the community. They may wear similar clothes, speak the same job-related jargon, cut their hair similarly, and carry themselves in public in the same manner. Employees in all departments of media organizations are subject to such mirror behaviors. Chances are their jobs bring them (or many of them) socially together and—in many cases—they begin to identify themselves closely with their jobs.

This is particularly true of journalists, many of whom see themselves as journalists first, human beings second. Journalism encourages a distinct pattern of beliefs, values, norms, and interpretations that many jobs do not. Not only do journalists learn the values of news, they learn to be skeptical, cynical, critical, detached, and analytical. This requires—particularly for younger journalists—the adoption of a particular lifestyle; it is not uncommon, for example, for journalists to feel as if they are always "on," i.e., never able to completely discard their journalistic lens on their environment. Journalists often speak with pride of dangerous experiences (commonly referred to as "war stories") in their careers. Their passion for news also takes a toll on their leisure time and lifestyle, leaving little time for nonjournalistic pursuits and, not surprisingly, fostering close relationships with coworkers.

Managers can guide the development of such groups (often along occupational lines) in how they plan and structure their organizations. For example, organizing work on a functional basis fairly well assures that those performing the functions will form informal groups. Such is the case in most media organizations, although some companies organize or suborganize around certain products (e.g., an organization with a web site will need to develop a staff to maintain it) or markets (such as when Bob's newspaper created the suburban bureau). The key for the manager then becomes recognizing the by-products of informal groups.

One such consequence involves the pressure groups place on their members (Kiesler & Kiesler, 1969). Because they develop shared norms and values, group members become cohesive and begin to form allegiances. The greater the attraction and loyalty to the group, the more likely the members will conform to group norms and values. The group will attempt to dissuade members who violate group norms from doing so; the pressure to make such members conform can be enormous, depending on the stray member's will and attachment to the group. The group exerts such pressure in order to survive and further the group's self-interests. This pressure can be subtle, as when advertising sales staffers attempting to stifle "super performers" jokingly deride their extraordinary peers as "brown-nosers" or when journalists call their investigative brethren "hot shots." In each case, the message is, "you're different," and the group has indicated limits for its members. The media manager—if alert to the group's survival activities—has three decisions to make: What is best for the group? What is best for the threatened employee? What is best for the company?

Sometimes, the same action has positive ramifications for all concerned, albeit not immediately. For example, a Louisiana sports reporter discovered the newspaper's star sports editor/columnist (and his immediate boss) was plagiarizing quotes from a news service. The reporter told the paper's editor, who then *fired the reporter.* At first, it seems as if the columnist—and not the reporter—should have been fired for plagiarism. However, the reporter never confronted the sports editor with the allegation. The paper's editor, realizing proper channels were not followed (the sports reporter also had told several other reporters and staffers), considered the reporter's behavior a bigger threat to internal morale and organizational authority. The sports editor subsequently was disciplined and eventually demoted (but his career was saved) and the rest of the staff was outraged—at first. But they learned what the editor considered a valuable lesson. Follow the chain of command (and keep a tight rein on serious personnel allegations). The sports columnist continued to be one of the paper's stars—albeit with closer editing.

Another informal group phenomenon—and one particularly important in media settings—concerns the innovation that groups foster. Media constantly generate new ideas; the journalistic media do so daily. Media managers facilitate creativity without thinking about it, via the various incentives they normally provide. Bylines (for print), video standups and standard out cues (for broadcasting), and merit pay are some examples. Creative media employees also naturally share the determination, eccentricity, curiosity, and experience required of ingenuity (Straub, 1984). Much innovation depends on the organizational or group culture in place, however, and the degree to which employees feel involved with the organization.

For example, one group of journalists took up a collection to help reunite a family because staffers felt it was in line with the company's tradition of "doing the right thing." (Petersen, 1992). But in addition to involvement, there must be consistently shared meanings, adaptability to the external environment and a shared vision (Denison, 1990). Two Pittsburgh newspapers merged their staffs. Prior to the merger, one paper had a "corporate" management staff whereas the other was described as "freewheeling," "loose," and "breezy." To facilitate the transition, the staff created several committees of reporters and editors from both organizations. But the lack of involvement with the new organization, the lack of a shared culture (inconsistency), and the initial absence of a clear mission (other than to produce a newspaper) helped lead to conflicts in the new, combined newsroom (Jurczak, 1996).

The manager must beware of this final consequence of groups—formal as well as informal—with knowledge that they may (and often do) generate conflict with other groups. As groups become more cohesive and members identify so closely with their own groups, the potential for self-direction (and the desire for autonomy) grows as well (Sherif, 1962). In addition, groups come to see their goals as different from those of other groups—despite being in the same organization (Deutsch, 1949). Various studies have shown media are no different. For example, subdepartments in a television production facility each brought its own agenda to the product (Elliott & Chavez, 1969). Departmental membership was found to affect how a boadcasting station's employees' resolve conflicts and perceived goals (Allen, Seibert, Haas, & Zimmermann, 1988). Finally, one state's newspaper managers' departmental affiliations affected how much cooperation they believed was needed in their individual newspapers.(Sylvie, 1996). Part of the problem lies in the increasing complexity of modern organizations. As a company becomes more complex, it adds more tiers to its hierarchy and lengthens its chain of command. The chances for communication distortion (and thus conflict) increase. This increasing complexity convinces groups they have controlling expertise in the company and, thus, discretion to lead the company (Van Maanen & Barley, 1984).

As a result, if the manager is to be productive, he or she needs to understand groups. Knowledge of in-group communication networks goes far in hastening that understanding (Collins & Guetzkow, 1964). By doing so, managers can get a grasp on the flow of information and the dynamics of how the group reaches decisions. Once the decision-making process is dissected, the manager can better understand the group's motivation and needs.

PROBLEMS AND APPROACHES

Labor-intensive organizations, such as media firms, will run inevitably into motivation-related difficulties. No one knows what specific problems typically beset each media organization, but the following section deals with a few of the more common complications, followed by a discussion of some of the strategies a manager can utilize when faced with these problems.

Turnover

The ultimate motivational problem is turnover—when an employee voluntarily leaves the company. The specific reasons vary but the common theme generally revolves around dissatisfaction with some aspect of the job, the company, or co-workers. Turnover rates vary by company, but in media the incidence can range as high as 50%—in a year's time 50 % of a company's employees will leave the company. Such resignations are costly. Managers and editors must recruit, select, and train replacement employees. In addition, some remaining employees inevitably begin to question the wisdom of their loyalty.

Turnover is an inconsistent foe of media managers. For example, in newspapers, minorities and women make up a disproportionate share of departures. In addition, in some years, certain departments have higher turnover rates than others. For instance, circulation departments lost slightly more than one third of their workforce despite having only one fifth of all newspaper employees in the early 1990s. But even within departments, minority employees are more likely than nonminorities to leave. This should not surprise the media manager, who only has to look at studies that show, for example, that Black and Latino journalists are twice as likely than White journalists to be dissatisfied (Bramlett-Solomon, 1993) or that women sportswriters—despite 75 % of them being satisfied with their jobs—say they receive more sexist comments from their newspaper colleagues than did women in news departments (Miller & Miller, 1995).

Add to that mix the fact that journalists at the beginning of their careers are more likely to defect than veteran journalists (Weaver & Wilhoit, 1996) and much of the problem may center on the race, gender and age differences between managers and those they supervise. Also, managers may have little time to interact with employees on an informal basis, may fear the general 1990s backlash against diversity or see diversity as "weakening" operations. Finally, some experts concede they lack proper methods to evaluate minority employees (Phillips, 1991). Retaining quality employees—in newsrooms as well as other media work environments—remains probably the greatest challenge for media managers.

Stress

Media life is a stressful life. Many ex-journalists, for example, say they left the field because of frustration, low pay, poor management, and bad hours. Newspaper copy editors report a high level of emotional exhaustion and "depersonalization" than reporters (Cook, Banks, & Turner, 1993). Nearly two fifths of editors also say they have a job-related health problem (Giles, 1983). Public relations practitioners say that stress is a constant factor (Butler, Broussard, & Adams, 1987). Managers must realize that stress is an inherent perception and reality for their employees.

Endres and associates (Endres, 1988, 1992; Endres & Wearden, 1991) have studied stress in various journalistic contexts and offer conclusions about stress and its role in journalism's future. First, stress is a matter of perspective. Noting that earlier research (Giles, 1983) reported editors find disagreements with subordinates challenging and stimulating, Endres (1988) also reported that reporters think such incidents are stressful. Second, expectations play a role. For example, there are substantial differences between journalism students' job-related needs and their expectations of achieving those needs. Their major goals include job security, ethical behavior, promotion opportunities, and good pay, but they are not too optimistic about satisfying those needs (Endres & Wearden, 1991). Finally, journalism students are no more or less stress-prone—and the way their stress manifests itself is no different—than professional journalists. Depression, daydreaming, less concern about work quality, and considering a change in major/career constitute common symptoms (Endres, 1992).

Stress can be positive or negative, depending on how an employee reacts to demands placed on him or her by the work setting and its various elements. The media manager must be vigilant in sensing stressful signals; but the problem is that stress can take so many forms as to render it relatively invisible. Generally, these signals tend to stand out by their frequency, intensity, or abnormality; for example, if an employee misses too many deadlines, reacts emotionally or out of character, then the manager should make a mental note of the incident. Managers should seek out the root causes of stress that are within the manager's grasp. For example, stress can be expected when a major change occurs; for example, if there are layoffs or new rules, technology, or increased expectations—as is often the case in change-intensive media workplaces. Media managers must brace for some kind of reaction, depending on the usual employee reactions toward change. In addition, some jobs or environments inherently create stress by design (Aldag & Brief, 1978). In media, such design flaws usually include deadline pressures, the need for creative content and packaging, and the need for continuous production. These major stressors may not be totally within the media manager's control, but awareness of them will go a long way in helping the manager understand employee reaction and, as a result, be prepared to deal with what develops.

Lack of Inspiration, Creativity, and/or Challenge

Perhaps nothing is more important to media employees—and, thus, to their employer—than the employees' ability to create, react constructively, or see the meaning of their work. Nothing is more central to the employee's role and corporate or occupational identity than being able to innovate or fashion something new from what once did not exist, to overcome an obstacle in producing a quality product. For example, a happy journalist—or one contemplating leaving that profession—often is interested in a new challenge (Weaver & Wilhoit, 1996). Creativity is the lifeblood of a media organization, and when it gets strangled, reduced, or obstructed in any way, the media manager faces a difficult task helping the employee relocate his or her inspiration.

Much of the problem stems from insufficient resources, staffing, and space. Other factors might be long hours, inadequate supervision, or an improperly designed job. Many times close inspection reveals burnout as the culprit. Perhaps the primary cause, as all managers are discovering, is the increasing need for self-determination on the job (Braus, 1992), particularly in younger employees. Two of the strongest predictors for job satisfaction in younger journalists are autonomy and "interest or challenge." Likewise journalists who plan to leave the profession cite the need for a new challenge (Weaver & Wilhoit, 1996).

Media managers should be mindful that older workers, with more work experience, often have a different view of those day-to-day problems that seem to threaten autonomy than do younger employees. Like the great professional championship sports teams that dominated certain eras (e.g., the Pittsburgh Steelers, the Boston Celtics, or the Chicago Bulls), veteran employees take a longer view of job pressure, changes, and stress. The opponent—in this case, the tedium and seeming oppression that at times can characterize media work—is simply outlasted by the smarter, more patient, wiser, long-range viewing, older employee. As a result, media managers must themselves be creative and innovative in battling any of these typical motivational maladies.

The wisest course involves planning for these contingencies. Wiser still might be organizing and structuring policies, procedures, and programs that prevent morale problems from arising or, at the least, foster a healthy corporate culture. For example, turnover problems might be approached from a variety of points in the employment process. Let us return to Bob and Rose. If Bob wanted to prevent Rose's situation from ever arising, he might have established a plan for routinely addressing the issues Rose is confronting. Because turnover results in more recruiting—essentially, a duplication of effort—Bob might want to take a closer look at the newspaper's recruiting efforts. He might find, typically, the lack of a plan in this area. Many established companies hire simply because there is a vacancy, without thought as to why no current employee in the company can take over the duties of the vacant position, or to whether the position has a design flaw that encourages turnover. So a recruiting plan might consider the company's strategic staffing needs for an extended period, say 2 or 5 years. Or if Bob has no power over recruiting, he at least can review the interviewing process. Even if a manager examines the peculiarities of the job and the idiosyncrasies of the employee in respect to motivation, the combination of the job and the person brings with it a completely new set of issues for the manager to consider. Bob should carefully reconsider the interviewing process when new employees are hired. Interviews are not just negotiations for salary, benefits and production expectations. They should also reveal how the job fits the person seeking employment.

In the area of creativity and autonomy, media managers frequently complain that managing creative employees is difficult because these employees often want more autonomy than other, perhaps lesser talented peers. It becomes an issue of who will have control—the manager or the employee. This is not uncommon in media organizations in which employees become limited celebrities or "stars" of some kind. Managers must balance pleasing employees and his or her adoring public, behaving fairly (to stars and nonstars), maintaining the indirect revenue stream the star may help generate, and maintaining credibility (and, in some cases, self-respect).

Managers must be patient and realize their job requires pursuing and choosing the best options. One such option may be to establish strong loyalty within stars, because loyalty can stem turnover, which is caused by lack of challenge or autonomy. Many creative employees lack an initial strong commitment to an organization primarily because their creativity—and thus their marketability—and their confidence in that creativity allows them mobility, making job security less of a need. So the media manager needs to establish trust in star performers (after all, as stars they could argue they merit stronger consideration than most employees). Recall the Louisiana newspaper editor who fired the sports reporter. The editor engendered strong loyalty in his staff; he made them feel as if he and they were partners in the paper's news coverage ("Remember: We're David and the competition's Goliath," he often said.). He even informed them of better-paying positions or of more prestigious openings elsewhere. Many reporters declined such opportunities because of the loyalty they felt toward him. More and more media managers are following his lead, particularly on partnering, and participative management—as a style and as a technique—has gained momentum in industry in general.

Teams, team-building and formal work groups have become a large part of the participatory technique, so much that some claim teams are developing into the basic unit of design for organizing work (Kolodny & Stjernberg, 1993). However, the adoption of teams by media firms has been sporadic, probably because of the media's long dependence on individual innovation and creativity. Indeed, to suggest teamwork in some media settings is akin to committing heresy. It is viewed as another managerial attempt at stifling creativity and autonomy. Worse, some particularly resistant employees may view it as a coopting of employees; for example, management appearing to share power when all the while the team is a ruse to squelch complaints and get employees to buy into management's agenda. Despite such concerns, however, teams are beginning to blossom in media. For example, it not uncommon for newspaper reporters, for example, to work together on stories (Russial, 1997) or for media managers facing change or distinct technological challenges to instill a sense of "we-ness" in their staffs, depending on the technology's relative advantage and compatibility with existing methods of operation (Sylvie & Danielson, 1989). More proactive managers see in teams a collective way of managing uncertainties of change that beset media.

For example, *The Nashville Tennessean* instituted "OrgAnalysis," a program which allows the newspaper to focus on work flow issues. In one instance, the program looked at communication throughout the company to identify types and patterns that might be restructured to allow for more effective company-wide communication. It was discovered that the personnel department generally provided senior executives with reports of varying kinds—concerning everything from performance appraisal to applicant tracking. Further inspection revealed that senior executives were not distributing the reports—although nothing prevented them from doing so. This "know-flow" project was unique, however, in that it required all departments to participate and tied participation in the goals and objectives (as well as performance appraisals) of pertinent managers—thus ensuring participation. Managers must create teams including several department heads to develop mission and objective statements that meet the publisher' approval. The process fosters interdepartmental communication as well as enhancing the newspaper's ability to serve its customers. Other OrgAnalysis projects have dealt with specific departmental problems (Lewis, personal communication, Oct.9, 1997). But regardless of the approach, a media manager's style of leadership is crucial to the way he or she motivates or attempts to motivate the staff, depending on the workplace and the situation (McQuarrie, 1992). In television, for instance, a gradual switch in managerial style (from authoritarian to participative) was credited with increasing job satisfaction and productivity (Adams & Fish, 1987), whereas for some newspaper journalists, a manager's style had no effect on their relationships with their editors (Gaziano & Coulson, 1988).

SUMMARY

As the workforce continues to change and as the economy becomes more global in nature, motivation— now more than ever—is crucial to successful media management. Media organizations are too complex and unique for any manager to hope to get by without some understanding of human needs and desires.

An effective first step involves first-hand knowledge of the work context—what employees bring to the job, what the job requires, and how the two interact. That implies not just familiarity with motivation theories and concepts, but also a sensitivity for how those theories play out in the workplace. In other words, for the Roses of the world, the Bobs of the world need to know that for every action Rose takes there is a reason; second-guessing or armchair quarterbacking is unacceptable.

Underlying this approach is the requirement of a deep appreciation for diversity—not just demographically speaking but also for the idiosyncracies and unique traits that each potential employee possesses. Women and people of color bring experiences that most media managers—because they tend to be male and White—do not understand and perhaps, in some odd way, fear. But proper motivation must be a fearless duty. People who are not socially oriented probably should not become managers because dealing with people constitutes the bulk of managerial activity.

Finally, the media are filled with potential psychiatric bombshells in the guise of its workforce. Most people do their jobs and need no external motivation; they are self-driven. But the efficiency orientation of the corporate world mandates that managers know how to solve problems as they arise, which has been the focus of this chapter.

But the media manager or potential manager should look on this information itself as motivation—to not only become a better manager, but as an incentive to help plan and structure systems that properly and adequately recognize and reward media employees. The unspoken wisdom of this chapter is that motivation—because it can be understood and managed—can be planned. The manager has to decide how to structure such a plan—again, according to the needs of the workplace and the people who potentially will work there. Without that perspective, motivation will be viewed as a problem to be solved rather than an inherent opportunity for managing. And media managing will be difficult—to say the least.

CASE 3.1

The Wilting Rose

Rose DeLoss, the 27-year-old, 5 year veteran of the newsroom, and her boss, Bob, were introduced at the beginning of the chapter. Review background information on both.

Rose is the only African-American on the city staff. There have been other African-Americans on the staff over the years, but none in Bob's tenure as city editor. Rose is beginning to feel as if she is being singled out because of her race. Her evaluations over the last 6 months have noted her inconsistency in meeting deadlines and, "an apparent lack of team spirit." But Rose feels these complaints are race-based, primarily because when she started to incorporate nonofficial, Black community sources into some of her education stories, their comments often were buried or cut altogether from the stories. And her ideas for news features about school and city policy impacts on the Black community were ignored by Bob who said there were more pressing deadline pieces. Rose asked Bob for a meeting. She wants to challenge her evaluation and find out if Bob has a problem with Blacks and stories about Blacks. She thinks the problem extends to a salary inequity, too. In preparation for the following questions, review the chapter guidelines.

ASSIGNMENT

1. If you were Bob, how would you prepare for the meeting with Rose?
2. Which factor—job mandates or employee potential—seems to be most influential in this case?
3. Assign one student to play Bob's role, another to play Rose's. Have the two conduct their meeting. Afterward, analyze the discussion to determine which psychological theory—equity, expectancy, or goal-setting—plays a major role in each person's approach to the conversation, and determine Bob's next most logical course of action.
4. How big a factor does the race of each participant play in the meeting? Should Bob consider Rose's race or gender in how he approaches the meeting? In how he devises a solution?

CASE 3.2

Letter to a Mentor

To: Mr. Al Severin, associate media director, JBAds
From: John LaCour, senior planner/buyer
Date: Jan. 1

I've been working with the company 2 years. As you know, I am a liaison between you and clients, a recruiter of new ad accounts, and am in charge of about 30 planner/buyers and coordinators. I like the job, but something has come up that is troubling.

Because of the recent recession (and the subsequent current wage freeze), employees haven't had raises in quite a while. No bonuses have been given and yet the workload has remained constant and even increased in some individual cases.

As a result, I can see some of the staff becoming somewhat disaffected ("unmotivated" might be a better term). Some of them have gone 3 years without a raise. Some are listless and obviously dislike their jobs—which I can tell from looking at their work: It's not as good (nor is there the quantity I'd like to see).

Despite these attitudes, I'm grateful no one has quit because it will mean devoting time I don't have to another job search. Sure, I could fire a few malcontents, but I've seen what they're capable of and it is good; and they're good people to boot. I just don't feel as if the company's doing right by them. In addition, I'm hoping we can do something before turnover *does* become a problem.

This company was built on a vision of excellence, but it's hard for the employees to buy into that vision right now. They see us doing a bang-up job for our clients—sales for Megamart, Transouth Airways and Jaxson Beer are all at record levels—but they don't feel as if they're reaping any of the rewards. That vision seems cloudy, at best, down here on the second floor.

Things are beginning to get out of hand. Theresa Metoyer, one of our better buyers, came in from a recent meeting with a client all red-faced. The client (XYZ Grocers) had complained that they weren't getting their money's worth from JBAds. Their sales are stagnant and that's why they're thinking they might pull their account and go elsewhere. Theresa said she succeeded in changing their minds—for the moment.

But what got Theresa so hot is, ... , well, I'll let her say it, "I work my butt off to keep jokers like that from flying the coop and what do I get? Nothing, nada, zip! It's as if those people upstairs don't know what a rat race it is to just get this company to stay the course with clients. I know times are tough, but what motivation do I have the *next* time XYZ wants to get tough with me? What do I offer them—my first-born child? They probably wouldn't take it anyway."

I pick Theresa not because I think she's a candidate for discipline but just the opposite. Normally, she quietly does her job and maintains her accounts. She's a model buyer; but she's getting close to the edge—where many of them already have gone.

JBAds needs people like Theresa if we are going to weather the storm and increase our billings. So we need to send her and the rest of the staff a message that we care—somehow! But I confess I feel as if my hands are tied. I have been here only two years and most of my experience is as a buyer, not a motivator. I feel inadequate.

That's why I'm writing you. A change is needed in how we reward our staffers. I'm not talking about raises, but I'd like some alternative ideas. If I can offer you any more information, let me know.

ASSIGNMENT

1. Should John send the memo?
2. Using what you learned in this chapter about motivation, what alternative incentives can be developed without raises or bonuses?
3. What group influences might be at work in this motivational scenario? What can John do to guide the planners/buyers into a stronger loyalty toward JBAds?
4. Can the stress inherent in a recession be alleviated by John or by Al? Can creativity or autonomy be factors in the problem presented by John?
5. If you're Al and you receive this memo, what do you do about John, if anything? Would your action concerning John affect John's subordinates? Should you report the memo to your supervisors?

CASE 3.3

In the Dark

The Agton Gazette serves Agton, a 50,000-person city about 2 hours west of Chicago. The morning Gazette has a staff of about 40 full-time writers, editors, and photographers. Most employees feel the paper is a good place to work, but one group has a different opinion.

The photography department consists of five full-time photographers, including photo editor Joe Frame. Joe spends most days scheduling photography assignments, based evenly on the needs of the city/metro desk and the advertising department—in contrast to most daily newspapers, where the photo department is considered part of the news operation. Photographers rarely work with writers as equals on a project and only provide captions for society page prints. "We're a service department," Joe tells a visitor. He—and the other photographers—would rather work with just news and believe taking photos for ads is demeaning. But even that prospect has its drawbacks.

At *The Gazette*, the metro and features newsroom is located in a large space at the east end of the first floor. The main hallway runs the length of the floor, beginning in the newsroom and continuing to the west. At the west end, north of the hallway, is the photo lab. A smaller, north-south hallway separates the photo lab from the copy editing and sports departments, which lie between the photo lab and the metro department. In the metro department, as is common with large open spaces, reporters often shout wisecracks, talk, and interact in unison with the loud background noises of phones, police scanners, and personal computers. But the noise subsides when Joe or any of his staff enters the room.

One day, for example, City Editor Mitch Thomas was hunched over his desk, writing in his appointment book. As Joe entered the room from the hallway, Mitch remained hunched over. Joe stood waiting, hands behind his back, facing Mitch's computer. It took at least 30 seconds for Mitch to notice Joe. When he did, he showed no reaction other than brief eye contact and started to type at his personal computer, which stood between him and Joe. Joe had expected an article (for which there was an accompanying photo) to be printed on that day's front page and questioned Mitch as to why it had not; Mitch brushed him off with a curt explanation that another story had to be printed instead. Mitch continued to type at his computer. The conversation was over. Joe returned to the photo lab.

The lab is home to Joe and his staff. It features the normal equipment and work space allocation, but it also features a 2-year-old strand of Christmas lights, candid staff photos with humorous captions, a "height chart" on the wall indicating each photographer's profile and nickname, and toys. For instance, the plastic, battery-operated space ship that sits on the computer terminal emits missile-launching sounds when staffers push certain buttons. Typical use occurs when someone like Clint, a news editor, comes in. One day Clint dropped in near the 5 pm photo-scanning deadline, looking for a missing assignment form.

"Yo, Mar-TEEN," Clint jokingly said to nearest photographer Martin on entering. The photographers cringed and did not verbally respond. Clint started rooting through some papers on a stool. Joe, after a pause, sighed and noncommittedly asked Clint what he wanted. DeeDee, another photographer, entered the lab with Clint's missing form and began to discuss it with him. At that moment, Martin reached over the computer monitor and began pushing the spaceship's missile-launching buttons.

The animosity between the departments overflows into story budget meetings, where decisions regarding front-page and section-front display are made. Each editor is usually given a chance to "push" or promote a certain work. This means Joe is given time to describe the photos that he would like to have printed in the next day's paper. But often Carl, the managing editor who runs the meetings, attacks Joe's ideas. At a recent meeting (with Carl absent), Joe was moved to comment that it "went well," even though Carl's replacement often forgot to allow Joe to present a story's art before she moved on to the next story. Occasionally, the photographers do stand up for what they believe, as DeeDee—who has the most experience of any *Gazette* photographer—argued for and won bigger and better play for election night photos of losing candidates.

The five are like an extended family, of sorts. They go out for drinks and DeeDee plans other social occasions (such as a trip to a local haunted house). When choosing photos for the next day's paper, often every photographer is queried for advice or opinions. The group also participates in an organized, seasonal game of "warfare" against the copy editors (whom they believe have no talent for page layout) in which they attempt to "kill" the copy editors (and vice-versa) by shooting them with small, relatively harmless balls of paint. They remain cohesive because of their commitment to the community (two recently bought houses), to the paper, and to their profession (three have worked at *The Gazette* for more than 12 years).

But despite this cohesion, Joe knows that his department is outnumbered and can not continue this way forever.

ASSIGNMENT

1. If you were Joe, what would you do to make things better between your department and the other departments? How can cooperation be fostered between the departments?
2. If you were editor of *The Gazette* and you discovered such interdepartmental ill-feelings, what group factors would play a role in attempting to alleviate the animosity? Should the photo department's cohesion be eliminated?
3. Which is more important from a managerial standpoint: the photo group's occupational loyalty or their loyalty to *The Gazette*? Why?
4. Which is a bigger problem: the photo group's cohesion or the way they are treated by other departments? What role does the physical layout play, if any? Would changing the organizational structure of the paper (as it concerns the photo department) be a wise move?

ACKNOWLEDGMENTS

The authors thank ethnographer Sarah VanSickle for the use of materials in the preparation of this case.

CASE 3.4

Going in Circles With The Big Switch

Iris Schultz, office manager and accounts coordinator of the Blackhawk Imaging public relations firm, is not sure what to do.

Blackhawk is a reputable firm, with awards lining the walls and a relatively small turnover rate of 20 % in a town where the norm is 35 %. The account executives (AEs) average about 6 years' experience and accounts run the gamut from institutional to commercial concerns. Net profits went up about 12 % last year, compared to 9 % the year before, so Blackhawk is no sinking ship.

But yesterday, the firm's managing partner, Arthur Daniels, asked Iris to start working on a new performance appraisal system for the firm's eight AEs. There had been problems with the old system, primarily complaints that it was not fair and did not properly function as it should. The major problem, in Iris' eyes, is that Daniels and the AEs in the firm saw different purposes for the evaluations.

The AEs think Daniels uses the system primarily for his own protection—against lawsuits. Daniels has admitted that that is one use, but insists he also wants something that will help him more accurately evaluate everyone's performance so he can determine equitable raises for everyone. The AEs, on the other hand, consider that statement "doublespeak" for management's intent to punish or weed out weak performers. As a result, no one in Blackhawk particularly looks forward to the evaluation process. They essentially see it as an exercise in tree-killing, for example, using reams of paper to justify decisions Daniels will make based on who he likes rather than any rational criteria.

But this is old news to Iris. What bothers her is that Daniels has suggested sharing the decision making on the new instrument with the employees. Iris favors democratic management, but Daniels has given her an additional directive: Create an instrument that not only evaluates employees accurately and fairly, but also one that can motivate employees to perform better between evaluations. In addition, Daniels suggests Iris create a cross-functional task force to develop the instrument.

"Why don't you try one of those quality things—a—whatchamacallit—a quality circle or something?" he said. "You just get some volunteers, about six or eight, get 'em to ID and analyze the problem, meet on a weekly basis and work on it until they come up with something that we can live with."

"But Mr. Daniels," Iris replied, "wouldn't a task force be better? A quality circle can go on forever. If you appoint the task force, give them a set time, make the force smaller—about four or five folks—and make them see this as the long-term issue that it really is, then we might be more effective. If you appoint a quality circle, the employees might see this as a stalling tactic or a way to drag out the process without doing really doing anything."

"Iris," Daniels fumed. "I know the difference between the two. I know quality circles look at an ongoing process instead of at a long-term topic. But that's what I see evaluation as being—or, rather, what it should be here at Blackhawk. Now you've got your orders."

Iris thinks Daniels—not known for his participatory management style—will have problems with any participatory tool, such as the quality circle. She also thinks the other employees' suspicions that Daniels will do what he wants anyway might hold true again. Still, Iris wants to instill faith in Daniels, because she thinks he makes correct decisions 99 % of the time, and he rarely fumes as he did yesterday.

In addition, Iris would like to try the quality circle idea to see if it could work at Blackhawk. Too often the AEs complain about her of Daniels' style; they feel they never have the final say with certain clients and that they have to guess, "What would Arthur want me to say or do?" in too many situations involving even routine decisions. Still, Blackhawk pays well and nobody plans a revolt. And Iris feels the quality circle might be a chance for Daniels to show employees he is a better manager than they give him credit for being. Her worry, however, is that employees are so used to having their autonomy doled out to them that they will not know what do with a free hand and that the result will be either something so idealistic that Daniels will automatically dismiss it or something so conservative it will not solve the problems.

In addition, Iris thinks, the appraisal system *does* need overhauling in certain areas:

- Usually appraisals are done annually, although employees complain that is not often enough.
- There also are criticisms of the process. Normally, Iris and Daniels study each employee individually and develop a written evaluation. In order to receive a raise, the employee must exceed performance standards in the designated areas; but employees criticize what constitutes "exceeding."
- After Iris makes her initial evaluations, she forwards them to Daniels, who then reviews them before discussing them with employees. Here, the main

gripe is that Daniels should not be the one to make the final assessment, because he is not the day-to-day supervisor—Iris is.

ASSIGNMENT

1. Should Iris do as ordered (form a quality circle) or attempt to persuade Daniels toward some other course of action?
2. If she forms a quality circle, what organizational groundwork should she lay before forming the group?
3. What can be done to the evaluation process to make it more effective and to help it become a motivational tool?
4. How would Iris and/or the quality circle go about convincing Daniels to approve a more participatory, democratic evaluative instrument?
5. If you were Daniels, and you knew what Iris knew, would your mind change as to the effectiveness of the quality circle, as compared to a task force or other—perhaps more formal—organizational device?

4

THE STRUCTURE
OF MEDIA ORGANIZATIONS

The structure of media organizations has changed dramatically over the past decade with the globalization of mass media. The term *big media* has been redefined as corporations such as Gannett and Multimedia have combined forces in billion-dollar mergers and buyouts. Within a 2-year period, Walt Disney acquired Capital Cities/ABC Inc. for $19 billion; Time Warner merged with Turner Broadcasting System in a $7.5 billion deal; News Corporation expanded Fox's reach with the $2.5 billion acquisition of New World Communications Group; and NBC merged with Microsoft in a $250 million exchange (Jones, 1996). Such ventures continue to underscore the reality in the world of corporate media that big begets bigger.

Regardless of size of the media organization, many people believe that in the right organizational structure, anyone should be able to perform well. In the 1980s, two assumptions guided behavior in media organizations. One was that a firm's overall success could be achieved through the success of its unrelated parts. The second assumption was that profitability was to be obtained by serving mainly Americans. Today both of these assumptions have been broadly challenged. Non-American audiences have become key, and a firm's success depends on the interrelatedness of its personnel and divisional structures (Turow, 1992).

This chapter integrates a scientific and a humanistic approach to structuring global media organizations. The scientific structure of media organizations defines the tasks, communication, and authority relationships within the organization, with organizational charts illustrating how the parts of an organization fit together. The humanistic structure analyzes ways in which managers and subordinates interact within an organization by looking at leadership behavior, work cultures, and team-building. Taken together, scientific and humanistic organizational structures exist to order and coordinate the actions of employees to achieve key organizational goals.

SCIENTIFIC APPROACH

Classical approaches to studying organizational structure are based on a carefully developed chain of command and efficient division of labor. Although no longer strictly practiced, organizations still adhere to a number of principles drawn from classical literature. Early researchers believed that a firm's overall success was achieved through the success of its unrelated parts. In a formalized structure, positions were specified, roles were defined, and role relationships were prescribed independently of the personal characteristics of members. Organizations were designed to attain specific preset goals and were less concerned with the selection of those goals than with their attainment. Formalization served to make the goals and relationships of an organization appear to be objective. The organizational structure was viewed as a means to an end that could be modified only to improve performance.

Taylor (1947) believed it was possible to scientifically analyze tasks performed by workers and thereby discover procedures that would produce the maximum output with the minimum input of resources. He transformed the role of the manager from arbitrary decision-maker to one who makes decisions based on analytical, scientific procedures. For example, he believed workers would be scientifically selected to perform tasks for which they were best suited. Scientifically determined procedures would allow them to work at optimal efficiency for which they would receive top pay. The following list summarizes four prescribed techniques on ordering the workplace.

1. For each task use a time and motion study to determine the best way of task performance that permits the largest average amount of production over 1 day.
2. Provide the worker with a financial incentive to perform at a good pace in the best way.
3. Use from four to eight specialized experts as functional foremen to instruct and supervise the workers on the different aspects of their work: methods, speeds, tools, task priorities, discipline, quality, and machine maintenance.
4. Adhere absolutely to the principle that the standard production rate must not be arbitrarily changed (Tausky, 1980, pp. 12–13.)

Managers would devise appropriate work arrangements and salaries based on the prescribed techniques and workers would cooperate. Communication was to be formal and hierarchical. Its purpose was to increase productivity and efficiency. Overall, Taylor viewed communication as one-sided (from managers to subordinates) and task-oriented (Taylor, 1947).

Although many managers still adhere to some of Taylor's principles, this approach has many drawbacks. Employers questioned it because it undermined workers' good judgment. They saw the system as an unnecessary interference and an attempt to standardize every aspect of their performance. Workers also rejected incentive systems requiring them to perform continuously at optimal levels (Bendix, 1956).

Another scientific approach was the work of Weber (1947), which has proven to be somewhat more useful for today's organizational structure. Weber developed the bureaucratic model of organizational design. He viewed a bureaucracy as a logical, rational, and efficient form of organization. He developed the model as a normative framework where organizations strive for one best way of administration. A simple list of these administrative characteristics present in bureaucratic forms is listed here.

1. Fixed division of labor among participants—The duties of each office are clearly specified.
2. Hierarchy of offices—Each office is subject to discipline from a superordinate office, but only in regard to the duties of the office. The private life of the official is free from organizational authority.
3. Set of general rules that govern performance—Impersonality, as contrasted to personal relationships, regulates activity. The body of specific and general rules regarding dealings with subordinates, peers, rank and file members and clients are binding.
4. Separation of personal from official property and rights—The officeholder is an employee. The "means of administration" are attached to the office, not the officeholder, and there are no ways whereby to gain personal rights to the office.
5. Selection of personnel on the basis of technical qualifications—Hiring and promotion are governed by competence, as measured by certificated training or performance in office.
6. Employment viewed as a career by participants—Membership in the bureaucracy constitutes a career with distinct ladders of career progression. (Weber, 1947)

The bureaucratic model of organization has several strengths. Elements such as division of labor, reliance on rules, and hierarchy of authority may improve efficiency and are still used in organizations today. The model was also the starting point for later research about organizational design. The bureaucratic model also has several disadvantages. It tends to be rigid and inflexible. The human relations aspects of the organization are neglected. Some of Weber's (1947) assumptions about loyalty and impersonal relations are also unrealistic. However, the bureaucratic model of organization design was an important development of management theory and continues to shape definitions of the central elements of administrative systems. Principles that evolved and are still used today include unity of command, span of control, division of labor, and departmentation.

Unity of Command

The unity of command principle argues that a subordinate should have only one superior to whom he or she is directly responsible. To have more than one superior would create the possibility that subordinates would face conflicting priorities. However, in most newsroom situations, reporters are responsible to several supervisors. For example, television news directors judge overall job performance. Assignment editors evaluate coverage of a news story. Producers are concerned with story visualization and timing. Research suggests when unity of command has to be violated, as is the case in many newsrooms, there should be a clear separation of activities and a supervisor responsible for each. In today's media organizations, strict adherence to the principle of unity of command would create inflexibility and hinder performance; however employees should know to whom they are responsible for different tasks.

Span of Control

Span of control addresses the number of subordinates a manager can efficiently and effectively direct. Early researchers agreed that the number of people who directly report to a manager should become smaller at succeedingly higher levels of the organization (Davis, 1957). For example, the span for top executives should range somewhere between three and nine. The span for middle managers should be between 10 and 30.

The span of control is a major determinant of how many levels an organization has and the number of managers that are needed. Ideally, the wider or larger the span, the more efficient the organizations. For example, as Fig. 4.1 indicates, differing spans result in varying numbers of managers. If one media organization had a span of three and the other a span of nine, the wider span would have three fewer levels and 272 less managers. If the average manager earned $40,000 a year, the wider span would save more than

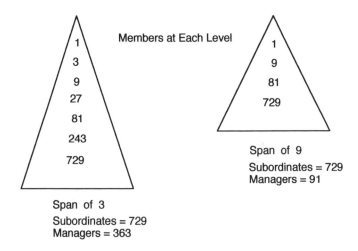

FIG. 4.1.   Contrasting spans of control.

$108 million a year in management salaries. However, questions remain as to whether wider spans are as effective.

Managers can give subordinates more attention when they have narrower spans of control; however, a number of contingency factors that could affect this relationship include the complexity of the work to be done and the amount of time managers spend with subordinates. Also, the degree of similarity of tasks being performed, the degree of standardization of work activities, the training and general capability of subordinates, and the amount of initiative these subordinates demonstrate all affect how the optimum span of control is determined (Mintzberg, 1979). Because the early writers did not recognize these contingencies, research on span of control continues. The reality in most organizations today is a trend toward eliminating management positions and operating under wider spans of control.

Division of Labor

Division of labor is the extent to which jobs are broken down into a number of steps with the responsibility for each step being assigned to specific individuals. Instead of being responsible for an entire activity, employees specialize in doing part of an activity. For example, in unionized television stations, videotape editors are solely responsible for editing videotape. They perform this same standardized task over and over again.

Division of labor is an efficient way of utilizing employees' specific skills. In media organizations, some tasks require highly developed skills. Others can be performed by untrained individuals. However, if all employees were engaged in each step of producing a newscast, all would have to hold skills necessary for performing both the most demanding and the least demanding jobs. This would be an inefficient method of utilizing workers' skills.

Other efficiencies are also achieved through division of labor. Performance skills increase through repetition of a task. Efficiency is also exhibited in reducing time spent in completing tasks as employees become more expert. Training workers to perform specific and repetitive tasks is also less costly. Finally, division of labor increases efficiency and productivity by encouraging specialized creativity. Examples of division of labor of management positions within a television news organization include the *assignment manager* who is in charge of what news is covered each day. He or she creates a storyboard outlining which reporters and photographers will cover which news story. The newsroom *producers* stack the newscast. They are responsible for putting the newscast together, deciding the order of stories, timing the show, and making sure the show flows. They also write stories and edit videotape for the newscast.

Similar positions exist according to division of labor within newspaper organizations. The *city editor* is in charge of all reporters and coordinates all hard-news coverage. The *news editor* is in charge of the copy desk and is the chief person in charge of story selection and placement, copy editing and page design. The *sports editor* is in charge of producing the daily sports section. The television newsroom also has a similar *sports director*.

The belief that organizations should be designed with a high degree of division of labor has been a widely accepted principle. However, this principle can be carried too far. The disadvantages are that too much division of labor causes boredom, fatigue, and stress, which may lead to inefficiency. In addition, with the computerization of media organizations, employees are expected to be able to handle many more aspects of production. For example, many copy editing positions have been eliminated at newspapers, with reporters and editors being responsible for proofing their own copy. Likewise, at many smaller and medium-sized television stations, new employees are expected to be a "one-man-band" with shooting, editing, and reporting capabilities. Although division of labor can be a valuable goal in planning performance in organizations, it is rarely strictly adhered to in most situations.

Departmentation

Division of labor creates a need for coordination of specialists. *Departmentation* describes how specialists are placed together in departments under the direction of a manager. The creation of departments is usually based on the work functions being performed, the target audience, or the geographic territory.

Function. Functional departmentation occurs when organization units are defined by the nature of the work. For example, newspapers are organized into departments of news–editorial, advertising, circulation, production, and business activities. These departments, as well as departments of other media organizations, are engaged in distinct functions of preparing information, reproducing information, distributing information, promoting the product to readers and advertisers, and financing operations of the firm.

Media conglomerates such as Gannett which owns newspapers as well as television stations, can be organized according to function as well as geography. The following job descriptions describe some of the functions of typical management positions in different departments at broadcast and print media organizations. Each of these managers has the responsibilities of hiring and firing personnel within a department.

Broadcast Organizations

1. The Chief Executive Officer (CEO): The chief executive officer is responsible for overall performance of the corporation. Primary responsibilities are for the media's relations with their perspective communities and audiences. The CEO must also coordinate the efforts of all units and oversee the allocation of resources to each.
2. General Manager: The general manager is responsible for the overall management and operation of an individual station. He or she is concerned with matters such as income, expense, budgeting, forecasting, and long- and short-term planning. General managers hire the managers of other departments within the station and oversee the activities of each department.
3. Chief Engineer: The chief engineer is responsible for keeping the station signal on the air. This includes performing special tests required by Federal Communications Commission (FCC) regulation. This person is responsible for maintenance of technical equipment and for ordering new equipment.

4. Sales Manager: The sales manager is responsible for all sales activities of the station. He or she assigns account executives to particular areas or accounts and supervises their activities. He or she sets the rate for the sale of advertising time. He or she must be knowledgeable of market data, retail statistics, audience research, and all other marketing and advertising concerns.

5. Program Director: The program director is responsible for all local, network, and syndicated programming that is broadcast by the station. The program director selects and schedules all programming. The program director also must be knowledgeable of FCC regulations to ensure programming complies. This would be a position concerned with coordination and preparing information.

6. News Director: The news director dictates the style of the newscast and is responsible for all news operations. The news director supervises everyone in the newsroom including anchors, reporters, sports and weather announcers, producers, and assignment editors. He or she also has administrative duties such as budgeting and conducting staff meetings.

Print Organizations

1. Publisher: The publisher is the on-site chief executive officer. This person is in charge of overall newspaper operations, as well as appointing or hiring key department managers.

2. Managing Editor: This person is in charge of compiling the editorial functions of the newspaper into a quality product. This person schedules daily editorial meetings where story ideas are discussed and work assignments are made.

3. Advertising Director: The advertising manager is in charge of selling and creating classified, display, and insert advertising. This person is also responsible for setting advertising rates.

4. Business Manager: The business manager is responsible for handling administrative and general business operations. These may include payroll and personnel matters, accounting procedures, and billing.

5. Circulation Manager: The circulation manager is responsible for selling and delivering newspapers to readers. These duties include marketing and promoting the product, distributing the paper in a timely manner, and collecting subscription fees.

6. Production Manager: The production manager is responsible for procedures that take place once the newspaper content has left the editorial and advertising departments. These duties may include printing, platemaking, and the addition of color and words to newsprint.

The primary advantage of organizing departments according to these functions is that it allows for specialization. It also provides for efficient use of equipment and resources. The disadvantages may be that members of a functional group may develop more loyalty for the group's goals than the organization's goals. Furthermore, in today's computerized media organizations, many functions have been combined. Employees need to be adaptable and be able to assume various functions. Also, all departments must understand the mission of the organization and support and strive for mutually accepted goals. Conflict will arise when different departments strive for different goals.

Target Audience. Audience departmentation is based on division by the type of customers served. One example would be a newspaper organization that has one department to handle home deliveries and another to handle industrial customers. This type of departmentation has the same advantages and disadvantages as product departmentation. For example, if the home deliveries group becomes too competitive with the industrial customers group, cooperation between the two departments will diminish and the organization's overall performance could decrease.

Geographic Territory. Geographic departmentation occurs in organizations that maintain physically scattered and independent operations or offices. Departmentation by territories permits the use of local workers and/or salespeople. For example, media conglomerates such as Gannett own television stations and newspapers across the country. In addition, their large-market newspapers have branch offices to serve suburban editions of their newspapers. Such departmentation creates customer goodwill and an awareness of local issues. It also provides a high level of service.

Different geographic territories become easier to track as media utilize more online services. New versions of media content are being created daily as newspapers, magazines, radio, and television stations go online with their products. Most job openings in these fields require computer-minded people who can provide quality content different from the print or broadcast version. Internet users want a quick product that is updated as often as possible.

Because the new technology cuts across all media, corporations will depend on employees who are able to adapt to continuous changes. Print journalists will have to be broadcast journalists who will have to be online journalists. This scenario has already taken place at a Tribune-owned venture, Chicagoland TV or CLTV, where print reporters are housed with news staffers of the 24-hour cable channel. Both groups provide each other with content. In addition, the newspaper, *The Chicago Tribune*, and the cable product are available online. This type of creativity and openness to new technology will be necessary for all corporations to compete in the future. Distinctions between different departments and even different media will continue to blur as more services are offered online.

HUMANISTIC APPROACH

With rapid change taking place in the structure of media organizations, the need for good human relations increases. The humanistic approach is based on the assumption that work is accomplished through people. It emphasizes cooperation, participation, satisfaction, and interpersonal skills. One word that has been increasingly used to describe the optimal balance of the organizational mix is *synergy*. Synergy is the coordination of company parts so that the whole is worth more than the sum of its parts acting alone (Turow, 1992). A company may have a formal structure intact, but without a willing, satisfied, and competent work force, goals will not be achieved.

The Hawthorne Effect

Mayo (1945) was one of the first to document the importance of human interaction and morale for productivity. He studied individual characteristics such as fatigue to determine the optimum length and spacing of rest periods for maximum levels of productivity. The Chicago Hawthorne plant of the Western Electric Company was the site of the research.

Management at the Hawthorne plant was aware that severe dissatisfaction existed among workers. Mayo and colleagues began to experiment with changing physical conditions to determine which condition would increase productivity. They worked with variables such as lighting, noise, incentive pay, and heating. They found little support for the expected relationship between improved working conditions and improved productivity. Mayo (1945, p. 69) summarized these surprising results:

> The conditions of scientific experiment had apparently been fulfilled—experimental room, control room; changes introduced one at a time; all other conditions held steady. And the results were perplexing.... Lighting improved in the experimental room, production went up; but it rose also in the control room. The opposite of this: lighting diminished from 10 to 3 foot-candles in the experimental room and the production again went up; simultaneously in the control room, with illumination constant, production also rose.

Mayo observed that work output increased no matter how the physical variables were changed. As a result, he realized it was the attention the researchers were paying to the workers that resulted in increased productivity. The workers were so pleased to be singled out for special attention that they tried to do the best they could for the researchers and the company. This effect became known as the Hawthorne effect. As a result of the Hawthorne studies, productivity could no longer be viewed as solely dependent on formal organizational structure.

Cooperative System

Barnard's (1938) ideas also contributed to human relations approaches. Barnard was not a researcher but an executive of a telephone company. He stressed that organizations are basically cooperative systems that integrate the contributions of their individual participants. Barnard defined an organization as an entity where cooperation is conscious, deliberate, and purposeful. Barnard believed that goals were imposed from the top down, whereas their attainment depended on the willingness to comply from the bottom up. However, Barnard did not believe that authority always came down from above, noting situations where leaders claim authority but fail to win compliance. Rather, he believed that authority depended on subordinates' approval.

Barnard (1938) was one of the first theorists to signify the importance of human motivation as crucial to productivity. Material rewards or economic motives were sometimes viewed as weak incentives that must be supported by other types of social and psychological motivations. The most critical ingredient to successful organizations was the formation of a collective purpose. Overall, Barnard (1938) believed that when formal organizations came into operation, they created and required informal organizations. Informal structures facilitated communication and maintained cohesiveness.

Theory X and Theory Y

McGregor (1960) developed two attitude profiles about the basic nature of people. These attitudes were termed Theory X and Theory Y. A Theory X manager believes the average person dislikes work and will avoid responsible labor whenever possible. These managers must respond to this attitude with controls such as punishments if employees fail to produce. Theory X managers also assume that employees prefer to be directed in order to avoid responsibility. Theory X managers were based on the scientific approach to management theory.

Theory Y managers, on the other hand, believe that employees find work as enjoyable as play. They are self-motivated and self-directed. Because employees are committed to organizational goals, they do not need the threat of punishment to be productive. Theory Y workers seek responsibility and are creative in solving organizational problems. Although the beliefs of Theory X and Theory Y managers are quite opposite, McGregor assumes these to be a range of behaviors. Managers can draw on both sets of ideas depending on the situation.

Theory Z

Theory Z (Ouchi, 1981) makes assumptions about the culture of organizations, whereas Theory X and Y made assumptions about individuals. Theory Z also contrasts U.S. organizations (Type A) with Japanese organizations (Type J). Type A organizations are characterized by short-term employment, specialized career paths, rapid promotion, formal control, and individual responsibility. They value individuality over group membership. Social needs are provided by institutions such as churches, neighborhoods, and schools rather than the formal work group.

Type J organizations, in contrast, are characterized by lifetime employment, slow advancement, informal control, consensus decision making, and generalized career paths. Loyalty to groups is of primary concern and more important than individual achievement. Japanese companies reduce incentives to leave the organization and do not rapidly advance employees.

The Theory Z organization attempts to blend the best of both worlds by retaining individual achievement and advancement but also by providing a continuing sense of organizational community. Theory Z is important because it draws attention to the human relations approach to management. It also sets the stage for team-building, which is the basis of many decision-making structures in media organizations today.

Team-building

In today's media organizations, group productivity is often more important than individual task accomplishment. Therefore, managers are needed who can promote teamwork for problem solving and work improvement. According to Blanchard, Carew, and Parisi-Carew (1990), managers who build high performing teams within the structure of their media organizations must understand stages of group development.

When task groups initially meet, they are in Stage 1, the orientation stage. During this period, team members usually have high expectations and are eager about working. However, they are more dependent on authority and need to establish their place in the group. As team members become more familiar with each other and begin working on the tasks at hand, they move into Stage 2, the dissatisfaction stage. Here they begin experiencing a discrepancy between hopes and reality. Some members react negatively toward authority and become frustrated with tasks and plans. In this stage, members experience a discrepancy between early hopes and later realities.

During Stage 3, the resolution stage, the team experiences more satisfaction in working together. Members start to share responsibility and control. They also develop trust and respect.

The final stage that most teams experience is Stage 4, the production stage. Here, team members show high confidence in accomplishing tasks, as well as feel positive about task successes. It is at this level the performance is highest.

Managers who work with teams realize that they must adapt their leadership behaviors according to the stages of group development. In the orientation stage, a more authoritative or directing leader is needed. During the dissatisfaction stage, a coaching leader who is concerned with relationships and tasks is needed to help the group work through conflict. As the team moves toward the resolution stage, the leader can exhibit less directive behavior and become more supporting or relationship-oriented. Finally, in the production stage, the leader functions best as a delegator or just as one of the team members.

Each of these approaches to informal structure is only as useful as the situation in which it is employed. Only when managers consider all situational variables that affect corporate efficiency and productivity can any single structure be successfully used. As a result, contingency theories have been developed that incorporate both scientific and humanistic approaches to management study.

THE CONTINGENCY APPROACH

Different combinations of situational elements require different organizational structures and management behaviors. According to Path–Goal Theory, three important interdependent factors that organizations must consider are forces involving the manager; the subordinates; and the situations (Tannenbaum and Schmidt, 1973). Forces acting on the manager include his or her value system and personal leadership styles such as task-oriented or relationship-oriented. Relationship-oriented behavior is the extent to which the behavior of the manager promotes friendship, mutual trust and respect, and good human relations between the manager and group. Task-oriented behavior is the extent to which the behavior of managers tends toward organizing and defining the relationships between himself and the group, in defining interactions among group members, establishing ways of getting the job done, scheduling, criticizing, and so forth (Fleishman, 1956).

Forces that act on the subordinates include ability, experience, and need for independence. People who perceive that they are lacking in ability may prefer directive managers to help them understand path-goal relationships (House and Dessler (1974). However, subordinates who perceive their abilities as high may resent directive managers. Personal characteristics also include education, experience, and age. Hersey and Blanchard (1972) argued that effective management behavior varies in conjunction with the personal characteristics of subordinates. As employees' maturity level, age, and experience increase, management behavior should be characterized by a decreasing emphasis on task behaviors and an increasing emphasis on relationship behaviors.

Forces that act on the situation include type of organization, time pressure, demands from upper levels of management, and demands from government, unions, or society. These so-called environmental characteristics are usually outside the subordinate's control. If tasks are straightforward, attempts to direct by the leader will be redundant and seen by subordinates as unnecessary. The higher the degree of formality, the less directive management behavior will be accepted by subordinates. Furthermore, when the work group provides the individual with social support and satisfaction, relationship-oriented management behavior is less critical. However, research indicates that relationship-oriented management behavior has the strongest positive impact on satisfaction and productivity for those subordinates who work on stressful or frustrating tasks (Schriesheim & Schriesheim, 1980).

Fig. 4.2 shows the Powers and Lacy (1992) model of television newsroom management that modifies the situational path-goal framework.

The model divides factors affecting job satisfaction into four groups: individual factors, market factors, organizational factors, and leadership. According to the model, these four types of factors influence journalists' perceptions of how successful their organizations are at attaining goals

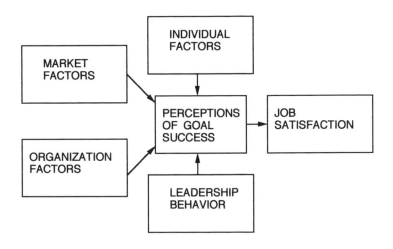

FIG. 4.2. Model of job satisfaction for local television news departments.

such as profit, good human relations, and quality news. If journalists believe their organizations are successful at attaining these goals, their level of job satisfaction increases.

A negative relationship between market size and perceptions of good human relations suggested that local television journalists in large newsrooms perceived news managers to be more task-oriented than those in newsrooms located in smaller markets. A negative relationship was also found between the organizational factor of group ownership and profit success. Local television journalists at group-owned stations perceived no more success at making a profit than did those at independently owned stations.

The most important result of the study for predicting job satisfaction among local television journalists was the relationship behavior of the news directors. Employees were more satisfied with relationship-oriented managers than with management that was task-oriented. Also, job satisfaction related to participation. This implies that news directors should include journalists in the decision-making process if they want satisfied employees who will stay.

Including Women and Minorities
in the Decision-Making Process

When employees feel like they are part of the group and know that what they suggest will be heard and probably implemented, productivity and loyalty increases and stress is reduced. However, knowing how to include employees in the structure and decision-making process becomes increasingly complex as the work force becomes more diverse.

More women and minorities are employed by media organizations today than ever before, although many still reach the glass ceiling when it comes to upper management positions. Nevertheless, the popularity of contingency approaches and Japanese management theories has lead to what advocates say is a "feminine" model of sharing information and encouraging participation in organizations. Rosener (1990) found that men were more likely than women to describe themselves as task-oriented. They view job performance as exchanging rewards for services rendered or punishment for inadequate performance. The men were also more likely to use formal authority and power that comes from their organizations.

Women, on the other hand, described themselves as being relationship-oriented. They were able to get subordinates to transform their own self-interest into the interest of the group through concern for a broader goal. They credited their power to personal characteristics such as charisma, interpersonal skills, hard work, or personal contacts rather than to organizational stature. Women were found to make their interactions with subordinates positive for everyone involved. Women also encouraged participation, shared power and information, enhanced other people's self-worth, and excited people about their work.

Not all men or all women lead in a particular manner, and leadership styles are not mutually exclusive. Women are capable of managing organizations by adhering to the traditional, task-oriented model; some men are relationship-oriented. The larger issue concerns the need for organizations to be willing to question whether traditional command-and-control management is the only way to ensure results. As the work force continues to demand participation and the economic environment increasingly requires rapid change, relationship-oriented behavior may emerge as the management style of choice for many organizations.

Inclusion of minorities in media organizations continues to challenge most media organizations. Because the minority population in the United States is rapidly increasing, the need for skilled minority employees to represent the population has greatly increased as well. Forward-looking media managers must cast a wider net for skilled minority applicants and, more importantly, produce a more hospitably diverse workplace, just to compete for the most talented workers.

One way managers can do this is by valuing diversity in the workplace. Managers can diminish prejudices by acknowledging the problem, addressing negative behavior, and obtaining feedback. According to Brown (1990), successful companies have open and frequent internal communications because minorities translate silence as lack of concern. However, many staffers are uncomfortable in pointing out things that offend them because they fear being perceived as "the minority person" who has no other interests or expertise. Minorities, women, as well as all people from varying cultures need to be comfortable in discussing concerns about the work environment. Valuing diversity in the workplace means recognizing the worth and dignity of others and treating people with respect.

Recognizing Contingencies in Media Organizations

The structure of media organizations affects many aspects of productivity and performance and is contingent on a mix of scientific and humanistic principles. For example, the size of a newspaper may affect how employees express themselves in their writing. Newspapers that were part of a large chain such as Gannett were more likely to advocate activist positions in their editorials and be more critical of mainstream institutions because they perceive themselves to be in powerful positions (Akhavan-Majid & Boudreau, 1995; Demers, 1996). Other examples of structure's influence on conduct are findings that indicate managers of chain newspapers emphasize profits at the expense of quality when compared to independently owned newspapers (Coulson, 1994).

Howard (1973) found that large corporations encouraged the flow of communication and that extensive communication existed; however, much of it was written in the form of reports, memos, and newsletters. Annual evaluation of management performance was required, as were weekly and monthly reviews of station departments.

The structure of the newspaper also affects human relations within the organization. Johnstone (1976) found that in newspaper organizations, face-to-face communication declines as organizations increase in size. He also found that communication in large news organizations flows primarily down the organizational ladder.

Phillips (1976) found that the management behavior of higher level executives set the tone for communication at lower levels of the organization.

For example, a news director who initially had a hands-on approach or participative management style felt obliged to exhibit a more authoritarian behavior when that was what was coming from corporate headquarters. Consultants are sometimes needed to change the overall management environment if a company wants to foster more participation within the entire organization.

Fowler and Shipman (1982) found that newspaper managers evaluated employees on a regular basis and interpersonal communication was the preferred and most often used means of communication. They also found that the perceived atmosphere of the newsroom was related to the amount of participation in which reporters were involved on matters of importance to reporters. The atmosphere was better when reporters participated in decision making.

Likewise, Adams and Fish (1987) surveyed television news directors, general managers, and sales managers and found that participative, or democratic, leadership behavior related to higher levels of job satisfaction. Additional research also has indicated that work dissatisfaction exists when management makes most decisions. An increase in centralization and bureaucratization fosters job dissatisfaction because of diminished autonomy (Joseph, 1983; Polansky & Hughes, 1986).

These studies indicate media personnel are likely to be satisfied when they have more autonomy and are involved in the decision making process. Job satisfaction also increases with additional feedback from supervisors and with opportunities for advancement. In Argyris' (1974) study of the organizational structure of a major newspaper, one reporter commented, "Reporters are an irrational bunch. And the ego is high. You need to hear you're doing well" (p. 49).

STRUCTURAL ANALYSIS

To find out whether or not departments or media organizations as a whole are doing well, effective managers make time for strategic planning. Strategic planning covers a relatively long period of time. It affects many parts of the organization, and it includes the formulation of objectives and the selection of the means by which the objectives are to be obtained. Tactical planning, on the other hand, involves short-range planning such as production schedules and day-to-day procedures. Porter (1980) suggests that managers should periodically analyze the structure of their organizations by conducting a structural analysis. The framework provides a company with a way to understand its own position in the environment. In addition, Porter suggests conducting a competitor analysis to develop a profile of the nature and success of the likely strategy each competitor might take and the environmental shifts that might occur.

There are four diagnostic components to a structural analysis that can also be used for a competitor analysis. These include looking at assumptions of the firm (or the background of the firm and industry), current strategies (how the business is currently competing), capabilities of the firm (both strengths and weaknesses), future goals, and making recommendations. In this process, managers are basically trying to obtain as much information on the formal and informal structure of the organization as possible to identify potential problems, the effect of new technology, the cutback or addition of staff, the opening or closing of divisions, or whatever else is relevant.

Compiling the data for a sophisticated structural or competitor analysis requires much work. There are many sources for field data or published data, much of which is available on the Internet. Top management can stimulate the completion of such analysis by making someone responsible for the effort and by requiring sophisticated profiles as part of the planning process.

SUMMARY

The structure of media organizations is influenced by a wide variety of variables. Scientific approaches to structuring media organizations are concerned with how the parts of an organization fit together in terms of unity of command, span of control, division of labor, and departmentation. Humanistic approaches to structuring media organizations are concerned with the human relations aspect and the assumption that work is accomplished through people. Media managers must consider both aspects as they build their future organizations.

The ability to combine an effective scientific and humanistic structure will rest on managers' ability and willingness to adapt to changing environments. Executives in huge media conglomerates must realize that people who come from different companies with different approaches have no experience working together and thinking about projects that can help other parts of the firm. However, according to Turow (1992), when managers take a synergistic approach utilizing ideas from employees from different areas of the firm, cross-media activities take on a whole new light. Concentration of ownership has changed the structure of most organizations and requires managers to use its holdings synergistically. Utilizing the contingency approach, managers analyze the relevant variables and then choose the appropriate structure. Because these variables are constantly changing, managers must periodically reanalyze and evaluate the efficiency and effectiveness of structure.

CASE 4.1

The Case of Learning about the Bottom from the Top

Easternhouse Broadcasting Corporation owns 12 television stations, 12 AM radio stations, and 12 FM radio stations in the eastern United States. The corporation is divided into two geographic divisions; the Midwest Division has five television stations, six FM stations, and seven AM stations and is headquartered in Chicago. The remaining stations are in the Atlantic Division, with headquarters in Philadelphia. Each division has a president and two division vice presidents, one for television and one for radio. Answering to the regional vice presidents in charge of radio and television are the individual station general managers. Easternhouse also has a corporate headquarters in Washington, DC, with corporate heads for both radio and television. The Midwest Division president is Harvey Milton.

When Milton arrived at work on Monday, he recieved a message to call the Wilson Gaddy, CEO of Easternhouse Broadcasting Corp. The message was urgent, so Harvey called right away.

"Willie, this is Harvey. What's going on," Milton said when Gaddy picked up the telephone.

"What in God's name is happening at WGHT in Cleveland?" Gaddy asked in an accusing tone.

Milton was taken aback by the tone and the question. "What do you mean?" he asked defensively.

"I was at an Eastern Foundation Trustees meeting in Columbus last Friday and all I heard about was the problem with Melinda Raven. What's this all about?"

Milton considered bluffing his way through the conversation, but he knew Gaddy would realize the truth. He replied meekly, "Willie, I don't really know what is going on, but if you give me a couple of hours, I'll get back to you and fill you in."

"I'll go with that Harve. But make it this afternoon. I've got meetings the rest of the morning," Gaddy said as he hung up.

BACKGROUND

WGHT has been in a tight race with WETA for the lead in the early evening local newscast ratings race for 2 years. WGHT was able to take the top spot by 1 rating point during the last two rating periods. Much of this success has been a result of the anchor duo of Jim Haversham and Melinda Raven. After

2 years as a team, they have an excellent rapport. The market surveys show a steady growth in viewer loyalty to the team.

Sandra Godby has been general manger of WGHT for 4 years and has done well in moving it toward being the top station in the Cleveland market. She worked her way up through the advertising department at the station and has a good sense for what viewers want. As has been Milton's custom, he has not dealt directly with Godby; rather, he has followed the chain of command and had Larry Jamison, regional division vice president for television, deal with her. On a couple of occasions, Jamison had mentioned a tendency on Godby's part to be slow in filing reports and providing information about the station.

After Gaddy hung up the phone, Milton called Jamison and asked him if he had heard anything about Melinda Raven. Jamison said he had not, but then he had not talked with Godby or visited Cleveland in about 3 weeks. Milton mentioned his call from Gaddy to Jamison and then hung up.

He immediately called Godby to find out what was going on.

"Sandra, Harve here. I'm a little distressed about some rumors concerning Melinda Raven. What can you tell me about them?"

Following a 30-second pause, Godby began: "Well, you used the right word; they are only rumors. I think it may be a negotiation ploy."

"Why don't you tell me about it," Milton prompted.

"The newspaper ran a story about 10 days ago saying sources inside the station had reported that Melinda was unhappy with her role at the station," Godby explained. The story said she felt she was playing second fiddle to Jim, and she didn't like it. I asked Melinda about the story, and she said she wasn't sure where the story came from. Then she added that she did feel that Jim was condescending to her sometimes.

"Two days later, Cleveland Metro Magazine ran a short blurb in its 'What's Hot in Cleveland' column saying Melinda wants to move to WETA. Again, I asked what gives, and she said I paid too much attention to gossip.

"I'm not sure what is going on," Godby said, "but her contract is up in 6 months, and I have a meeting scheduled with her in 4 weeks. It seems the two might be related."

"Why haven't Larry or I heard anything about this before now?" Milton asked.

"Well, like you said, they're rumors," Godby replied. "I didn't want to bother Larry or you with something that may have no substance. If a problem had developed, I would have faxed Larry a memo, as I have in the past."

ASSIGNMENT

1. What should Milton do at this point concerning Godby?

2. What should Milton do at this point concerning Gaddy?

3. Is there a communication problem in the Midwest Region of Easternhouse Broadcasting? If there is, what causes are behind the problem?

4. What can Milton and others in the Midwest Division do in the future to avoid such surprises?

CASE 4.2

The Case of the New Editor

The *Bloomington Mercury-News* rapidly was becoming one of the best suburban dailies in the Midwest when its editor, Jim Westley, took a job as a business writer for the *Detroit News*. The news staff of eight reporters and two assistant editors at the *Mercury-News* had been together for about 18 months. During that time, the staff had developed a spirit of teamwork that had made them friends and improved the newspaper. The *Mercury-News* had been named the best daily newspaper under 25,000 circulation a month earlier by the Michigan Press Association (MPA).

The circulation of the paper had gone from 14,000 to 17,000 during Westley's 2-year tenure as editor. The advertising linage also had increased 35%. Publisher Janet Gaylord attributed much of the financial improvement to the work of the editorial staff. At the MPA awards banquet, she mentioned that Westley not only brought skills as an editor, but his ability to work with people had resulted in the longest period of staff stability in the paper's 25-year history.

The *Mercury-News* staff was saddened by Westley's leaving, but they knew it was a big break for him. They felt they would continue to remain a close-knit staff. The natural curiosity of the staff about their new editor was answered when Gaylord announced Steve Smith, a former assistant city editor for the *Dallas Morning News*, would be the new editor.

Smith seemed to be a nice guy. He had worked in newspapers for about 6 years—the last 3 in Dallas. He had a degree in history from the University of Michigan. He explained to one staff member that he took the new job to get back to his native state.

Relations between Smith and the existing staff went well for a week. On the Thursday afternoon of the second week, reporter Leslie Bridges came into the newsroom and pounded her desk. When asked what was bothering her, she said, "Our new leader butchered my story to the point that it is unintelligible. I'll be surprised if we don't get sued by someone."

The story involved a lawsuit filed against the local school board by a parents' group over teaching handicapped children. The group contended the board was violating federal law by not providing adequate facilities for their children. The board argued in turn that it did not have the facilities to teach some of the more severely handicapped students. Bridges had written a 30-column-inch review of the case to run the day the court hearing was scheduled to start. Almost half of the story had not made the newspaper.

When Bridges asked Smith about it, he mentioned almost casually that he had miscounted the inches in laying out the story. He said the *Mercury-News* five-column format had thrown him off. Smith told her to rework the story and he would run it on Sunday.

Relations did not improve the next week. During the staff's informal weekly lunch gathering, Dave Simmons, who works general assignment, told the other staff members about what had happened the day before. He had been following a controversy involving 60 homeowners in Bloomington and the builder of their homes. The homeowners said they had been sold houses that were not complete and that had many serious structural problems. The builder said the houses were fine when the deals were closed. Simmons had wanted to attend the homeowners' demonstration, which would be in front of the builder's offices. Smith, however, said no one was really interested in that sort of thing and assigned Simmons to cover the Chamber of Commerce luncheon, where the Chamber was about to reveal its new promotion campaign for a better Bloomington. Simmons had suggested another reporter be assigned, but Smith said rather sharply that he wanted Simmons to do it.

The next 4 weeks saw similar conflicts arise between the new editor and other members of the staff. The weekly luncheons, which had been attended by the old editor but were not attended by Smith, had become gripe sessions. Each staff member tried to outdo the others with a horror story about Smith.

Susan Moore, one of the assistant editors, told the group about the day Smith was writing one of his weekly columns. "He turned to me and asked, 'How do you spell Negaunee?' I said I didn't know and told him to look on the map. He just shrugged, said 'Never mind,' and kept typing. He ended up misspelling Negaunee in the paper."

Five days after the luncheon, the publisher called Moore and the other assistant editor into her office and showed them an unsigned letter complaining about Smith. It said he had undermined staff morale, had shown sloppy work habits, and had shown poor news judgment. The letter went on to say several of the staff had decided to find other jobs.

ASSIGNMENT

1. What are the basic issues in this problem?
2. What should Gaylord do now? Explain.
3. What could Gaylord have done to avoid this situation?
4. What would you do if you were a staff member? Explain.

5. If confronted with the feelings of the staff, what could Smith do to solve the problem? Why would your suggestions work?

CASE 4.3

The Case of Helping Reporters at the *Brighton Light*

Brighton Light publishes 6 days a week, Monday through Friday and on Sunday. It serves a four-county area in the southeast that has an economy based on industry and agriculture. Its circulation, which has declined about 10% during the past 5 years, is 15,506 in a market with 40,000 households. The four counties also are served by two weekly newspapers, both of which are free distribution papers. The *Light* has varied in quality over its 70-year history, going through periods when it was not very good and periods when it won state press association competitions for best small daily newspaper. The 10 years that Sam Davidson has edited the paper have produced good, but not outstanding journalism. Some individual reporters and photographers have won awards during that period.

The newsroom organizational chart for the Light given in Fig. 4.3 shows Davidson oversees three desk editors, who supervise a total of 16 full-time reporters. Two photographers work directly with Davidson.

One morning, Publisher Darlene Hampton asks Davidson to come into her office.

"Sam, I'm concerned about the quality of writing and editing coming from some of our staff," Hampton said to Davidson. "Sandra Hipsome, the English teacher at the high school said she counted 20 grammar, punctuation, and spelling errors on the front page last Sunday. She said she didn't want her students to read the paper because they would learn bad habits. I'm embarrassed. What's going on here?"

"I agree with her, to a degree, although last Sunday was a big exception," Davidson replied. "Two editors were out, one was on vacation and the other caught chicken pox from her kid. But we do have a problem, and it comes from several sources. As you know, we've got a really young staff of writers; five of them have been out of school for less than 1 year, and another three have been with us for less than 2 years. It also seems like the youngsters we've been hiring aren't as good at the mechanics as they use to be, but I don't know why."

"The other editors and I would like to work with them, but we don't really have the time to edit well, much less sit down for a session on writing. We've been averaging about 17 pages of news per day the last few months and that's way above what we use to have. We're just having a devil of a time keeping up," Davidson concluded.

"I understand," Hampton said, "but we have to do something about this. I want you to take some time during the next week and write some recommendations for improving the writing and editing at the newspaper. We can spend some money, but your request for funds needs to be reasonable or I can't get it past the owners. Tell me in detail what you think we can do to improve. We'll get back together this time next week."

ASSIGNMENT

1. Write a report for Hampton detailing ways that the writing and editing can be improved at a reasonable cost.
2. Provide three options/ideas for improvement and explain how and why these would improve the writing and editing.

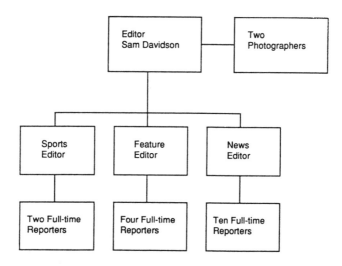

FIG. 4.3. Newsroom organizaional chart of the *Brighton Light*.

CASE 4.4

The Case of How Much Work in the News Bureau

Megan Kenyon had just started her fourth week in the News Bureau at Megastate University (MU). This was her first job after finishing her journalism degree at MU. She had done well in school, with a B+ average and a newspaper internship at a metropolitan daily. So far, she felt the job had gone well. John Silverstein, the head of the News Bureau, had dropped her a note saying he liked the story she wrote about the new telescope acquired by the astronomy department. The note had complimented her on her ability to make the technical aspects of a large telescope easy to understand.

Megan had been trying to produce about four stories a day, with one of them being a longer personality feature. Her "beat" covered some of the less prestigious departments at MU, but as one of her journalism instructors had told her, "Everything and everyone has a story, it is up to the journalists to find it and make it interesting."

As lunchtime approached, Megan started thinking about her three colleagues who had asked her out to eat. They seemed so much older, all in their 40s, that she was a little nervous. But her concern passed quickly as they got to the restaurant and settled into eat. Bob Hammer was the oldest of the group at age 49. He had been at the News Bureau for 5 years, after working 12 years at the local daily newspaper as a staff writer. Joan Collars had been at the News Bureau longest of all the staff, having started right out of college 23 years ago. The final member of the lunch group was Beverly Thomas, who had been a staff writer for the News Bureau for 8 years.

Conversation was cordial as the four ate their lunch. As they sat drinking coffee after finishing lunch, Joan started talking about Megan's work.

"We have been amazed at your work, Megan. Your copy is clean and your story ideas are fresh," Joan said. "We're delighted to have you on staff, but we're curious about how you like being part of our little group."

"The job is just great," Megan said. "The work is interesting, and I've got all sorts of ideas I want to work on."

"We're glad to see your youthful enthusiasm, dear," Beverly said, joining the conversation, "but we are a bit concerned about your work pace. Four stories a day is an awful lot of work. I would hate to see you burn out from too much work. Maybe you should try to pace yourself."

"Oh, I enjoy writing," Megan said, as a feeling of uneasiness crept over her. "I don't think I'll burn out."

"That's how everyone feels at first," Joan said. "But you've been here less than 1 month. After several years, it's a little different. You get a better understanding of what management wants."

"I think what Joan's trying to say is that you don't quite know the lay of the land yet, Megan," Bob added. "The seven of us who have been here a while know the setup pretty well, and we have to be careful with the way we work. MU is one giant bureaucracy you know. Once you set up work patterns, they will continue to expect you to work at that level."

"Bob's right, dear," Beverly said. "We're concerned that you not put yourself in a bad situation in the future. We hope that you hang around for a while, so we're just trying to help out."

"Generally, we aim at 10 to 12 stories a week, including one nice personality piece," Bob said. "Take it from an old newspaper man, the news media won't use even that many stories. We'd be wasting paper by writing too many press releases."

Megan was taken back by all of this. She managed to say she understood and thanked the three for their concern and interest. She left the lunch with a sense of uneasiness, of being on trial. That evening all she could do was think about the conversation at lunch. She wasn't really sure what was going on, or what it all meant to her future. About 9 pm, she decided it would help to talk with someone, so she called her old school roommate, who was working on a newspaper in another city. As her friend said hello, Megan blurted out, "I think I've got some problems here and I need your advice."

ASSIGNMENT

1. Given what has happened, what do you think is going on?
2. What can Megan do to find out what all of this means?
3. If you were Megan, would you change your work habits? If so, in what way?
4. What could be the repercussions of changing work habits?
5. How will the relationship with her co-workers affect her relationship with her boss?

CASE 4.5

The Case of Paper Glut at the *Herald-Telegraph*

Henry Peterson, publisher of the *Herald-Telegraph*, had figured the monthly department heads' meeting would be a quick one. No major problems had come across his desk during the past few weeks. The meeting started at 3:30 pm and he had a 5 pm tee time for golf. He never reached the golf course.

These meetings had been held every Monday of the month for the past 3 years at the 200,000 circulation newspaper. As usual, the first 45 minutes had been somewhat dull. Marie Laraby, the editor, discussed the need for replacing two assistant editors who recently quit. Lynn Madison, the circulation manager, told the other heads about the district manager who had left town with a week's worth of receipts. Robert Atkins, production manager, told the others about the recent problems in color registration.

Larry Lynch, the advertising department manager, was last as usual. Peterson asked what he had to report.

"There is one thing," Lynch said haltingly. "I was concerned about the story that ran in yesterday's paper about how to bargain with auto dealers. It created quite a stir among the local dealers. I'm afraid we might be facing an ad boycott."

Peterson leaned forward in his chair and asked, "What do you mean?"

"Well, right now, the three largest car advertisers have said they don't plan to run their ads next Sunday. Together that amounts to about five full pages. That's a serious loss of money," Lynch said.

"What's their beef?" Peterson asked. "Was there something wrong with the story? I glanced through it Sunday and thought it was straightforward."

"The problem is that they felt it undermined their bargaining positions and that some of the points would be applicable to dealerships back East but not out here," Lynch explained. "They were especially angry that it ran on the same day that the annual auto tab ran."

"Marie, what do you think about this?" Peterson asked.

"A tempest in a teapot," the editor replied. "It was an accurate and useful story. In fact, we got about a dozen calls today from readers thanking us."

"I'm afraid I don't quite consider losing $10,000 a tempest in a teapot," Lynch shot back. "It could get worse."

"Who wrote the story?" Peterson asked. "I don't recall."

"It was a wire story," Laraby said. "We ran it inside in the business section. It was well written and had pertinent information. If the car dealers can't handle the truth, I say too bad."

"Running the story is one thing, but running it on the day they spent a combined $20,000 on an advertising section is another," Lynch said. "Why couldn't you have held the story? It wasn't all that timely."

"I can understand your being upset," Laraby said, "but I don't dummy the business section. Besides, why didn't you tell me about the tab?"

"I did tell you, or at least I sent you a memo. Besides I send out a list of advertising sections and the dates they will run at the beginning of every year. Then I sent a reminder in my weekly memo," Lynch said. "Don't you read your memos?"

"To be honest, I don't read all of the memos that come across my desk," Laraby said. "Listen, we're working short-handed now. Losing two assistant editors this month leaves us understaffed by three assistant editors and one desk editor. I even worked slot last week. I don't have time to read the mountain of memos you and David send. If you want me to know something, tell me to my face, or give me a call."

"You're not the only person short-handed," Lynch replied. "We're missing a sales rep, and I don't have time to call you and repeat messages I have already sent to you. We send memos so you will have some tangible message you can refer to."

"But those memos get lost in all the paper that comes from the various departments and the corporate headquarters, not to mention all the press releases I get," Laraby said. "Besides, I can't ask a memo any questions. If you'd talk to me, I think we'd have a better understanding of what was going on around here."

"You know, I have to side with Marie," Atkins broke in. "It does seem like some people in our organization hold stock in paper mills. What happened to the paperless society our computer systems were suppose to create?"

Peterson, who had been listening to the argument between Lynch and Laraby, interrupted. "We've got a problem here, and it's not just with the auto dealers. We've got to do something about it."

ASSIGNMENT

1. What problem is Peterson talking about?
2. What might be creating the problem?
3. How can the problem be solved?
4. Who will play the main role in solving the problem?

5

TECHNOLOGY AND THE FUTURE

Ask most people to define technology and you will hear descriptions of machines, computers and equipment of various kinds. But technology can be invisible—as simple as a way of doing things, or a structural component of a task. That is because technology generally is a tool, a means to an end. It is the job of managers to determine how well that tool serves its purpose and what effect it has on the very people who use it.

In a media company, this is especially true. Knowing the technology's limitations eases the burden of operating a communications firm. A newspaper photo editor, for example, by understanding the limitations of photo equipment, can determine what situations call for which cameras and which photographers. Similarly, technology determines internal structure—as in the case of the television station manager, who knows that producing the 6 pm news means the work must be divided into journalistic and videographic components, each with its own department and internal working composition. Consequently, technology also determines employee behavior and production efficiency. For instance, as computers become increasingly adept at complex media planning, computerized media brokers may replace media planners in advertising firms, freeing brokers to assume other responsibilities.

Finally, as the pace of technological advances quickens, it is especially important for media managers to understand technology's strategic ramifications. Many media firms—particularly as they produce time-sensitive material—must adequately grasp the market significance of rapidly developing technologies (such as the Internet and its WWW) and learn how and whether to adapt. The decision could mean the difference between new, growing revenue streams and a stagnant, noncompetitive future, particularly as media firms—fattened by mergers and acquisitions—grow more organizationally complex and thus more conservative and slower in their decision making. For example, for years the broadcast industry generally regarded the videocassette recorder (VCR) as a fad without much potential for widespread adoption (Napoli, 1997). But as technologically driven

115

change becomes the norm, media managers must learn to overcome organizational culture and routinized work patterns and biases to deal adequately with change.

A media manager's job is to turn the technology to the company's advantage. To do so, the manager must analyze the organizational role and impact of technology. This chapter examines how a company uses or "adopts" technology, and how technology impacts media organizations—internally and externally. But first a manager must assess an approach to the technology.

APPROACH

How a manager views technology affects the company's performance. A newspaper editor, for example, sets the tone for how well copy editors use pagination terminals. If the editor constantly complains about the computer's shortcomings, staff trust in technology is undermined. If, on the other hand, the editor consistently praises the machine's capabilities and helps staffers understand and master its capabilities and intricacies, then the editor enhances the staff's ability to edit and design pages effectively—in short, the editor enhances productivity.

Of course, the terminal may have something to say about what approach the editor takes. If the machine is simple to operate and consistently performs its intended task, then the editor will see it as one of several tools to aid editing. But if the machine is "cranky"—its performance is inconsistent at best—or if it is hard to master and operate or so prohibitively expensive there are not enough such machines to go around, then the editor's attitude toward it will be antagonistic or, at the least, wary and cautious. Then there is the question of management's expectations regarding the technology. If the editor expects the computer to do simple editing and little more and if that is indeed what the computer is designed to do, then the editor's reaction most likely will be positive. But if the editor expects much more complex and sophisticated design effects that are not within the computer's capabilities, a different, more negative reaction will occur (Sylvie, 1995).

As a result, there are three schools of thought as to how a company should approach technology before the adoption process. These areas are the structural approach, the technological task approach, and the sociotechnical approach—and each essentially relates to how management can *control* technology.

Structural Approach

The structural approach focuses on the management of change and the change in management via the impact on formal devices, such as rules and organizational hierarchy. In other words, this approach sees technology as a planned, controlled instrument of management, which makes conscious decisions concerning the implications of the technology. In this case, structure means considering technology as a tool for managing people (Leavitt, 1965).

A structuralist manager believes that employee behavior does not change by teaching employees new skills, but rather by changing the organization's structure. This manager sees behavioral and attitudinal change as best brought about by devices such as rules, role prescriptions, and reward structures, of which technology is a part. For example, when the newspaper photo editor adopts the latest in photo processing software, he or she primarily does so because the new technology should not change the basic structure of the work needing to be done—photo image development, in this case. In fact, several case studies have confirmed that senior management uses new technology to attain strategic and operating objectives, indicating there are choices of work organization not determined by the technology alone (Buchanan, 1985).

In reality, of course, management does not always have such choices. Although computers have moved into many aspects of organizational life, it does not follow that supervisors and lower level managers have been prepared fully to cope. Sometimes management's computer preparation—its degree of training and level of advanced planning—often lags seriously behind installation of the technology or is narrowly conceived or even nonexistent (Burack & Sorensen, 1976). This is particularly true in media organizations where so much of the work centers around daily deadlines, leaving precious little time for any planning, including planning for new technology. Add in the quickening pace of technological change and it is unsurprising that managers leave the day-to-day technological operations to subordinates.

As a result, it is difficult for media managers to be calculating and control-oriented in regard to structure. Management often relies heavily on employees' skills, talents, and judgment at all phases of production. For example, no longer does the broadcast reporter have to bring video footage back to the newsroom for editing; now videodisk field recorders allow images to be stored directly to a disk and thus editing becomes portable and within the realm of control of the subordinate. Sometimes it might be impractical to view the technology and not see the employee who is going to be using it, which is why many media managers attempt to use the next approach.

Technological Task Approach

This approach complements the structural school, albeit with slightly different focus. Somewhat "functional" in its orientation, this school emphasizes that technology has a certain, observable, direct impact on the employee and on the organization. The technological task manager sees technology as the variable that the manager controls and that determines a response in the organization. In this approach, the manager chooses a technology with the hope that it will enhance the processes and routine tasks of work—that is, increase productivity.

Such a "substitution" strategy can be seen, again, in the case of the photo editor's decision to adopt the latest development software. Here, the editor may wish to give photographers latitude on certain matters so they have the flexibility to shoot effective news pictures, rather than abiding by quality limits that may rule out some pictures. Similarly, the use of digitized graphic systems helps television newscasts upgrade how they package their product. From a device that plays and edits sports highlights as it records live events, to a system that allows "virtual" production of "sets" or locales, technology provides faster and more accurate delivery of images and data—all within the framework of the editing process.

But when a manager substitutes one task for another, more refined one, the potential for problems or trade-offs arises. Going back to the pagination example, the newspaper's editor had hoped to substitute the journalists' (i.e., copy editors') expertise in design and editing for that of the nonjournalists (i.e., blue-collar composing room personnel). The editor' wish was granted, but he also stirred resentment in copy editors, who felt they were no longer doing journalistic work, but composing room work as well (Sylvie, 1995).This has often lead many managers to consider the last approach.

Sociotechnical Approach

This approach lies somewhere between the first two. Here, the manager stresses the needs and actions of those who will use the technology, in addition to examining the technology's attributes and characteristics. Sociotechnical managers see person and machine mutually interacting to the benefit or detriment of the organization. They view technology as dynamic and changing in purpose and use according to its perceived utility (Argyris, 1962).

At first glance, the sociotechnical manager seems to be the norm for today. It is not uncommon to find managers sensitive to employee needs and growth—managers who recognize that formal organizational values sometime infringe on an employee's personal values or skills. As a result, these managers realize that psychological and social planning play an important part in new technology introduction. They evaluate technology not simply according to objectives, but also according to the process of change the technology introduces and its impact on employees' motivations, skills, and organizational competence (Blackler & Brown, 1985). For example, as the cable industry switches to a more compressed (digitized) method of transmitting signals, it will require revisiting home subscribers to install new equipment. That means training and retraining employees in the new hardware system—for everything from installation of cable modems to service to sales—and also maintaining or increasing current levels of service to subscribers.

These three approaches illustrate that management has to have a basic orientation in dealing with technology. They emphasize the element of control, although some research shows managers also view technology in terms of cost and market (Noon, 1994). Regardless, no action occurs in a vacuum and neither does a company's adoption of a new technology. Managers should have a basic objective in mind when deciding to adopt a technology because that objective will in large part determine how well the dynamic process known as adoption—and its opposite, rejection—occurs (Sylvie and Danielson, 1989). This means learning to anticipate and predict somewhat the impact of technology on management and, ultimately, its impact on behavior—of employees and in the market. To do so, we must first reexamine the process of technology adoption and place it in the proper context.

INTERNAL IMPACTS

Technology can have several types of impact: desirable, undesirable, direct, indirect, anticipated, or unanticipated (Rogers, 1986; see Fig. 5.1). But for simplicity's sake and from a managerial standpoint, let us consolidate these consequences into internal and external categories. On the internal side, managers should be concerned with the adoption process and how that process affects the task of managing.

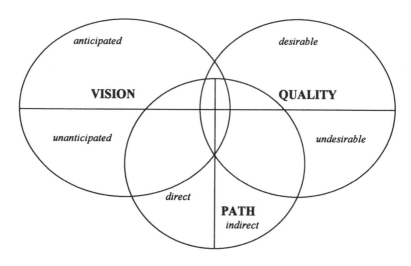

FIG. 5.1.   Types of internal impact.

Adoption Process

When an organization decides to adopt a technology, there are some definite steps (Rogers, 1983) that precede and follow the decision.

Agenda Setting.   This occurs when management identifies problems that may signify a need for a technology. In this step, the manager surveys the industry, related publications, and technological experts for potential solutions. In the media business, technologies seem to often set their own agenda. For example, in the 1990s interest in the Internet has burgeoned to the point where many media companies—particularly newspapers—feel pressured to create web sites to keep pace with the interest and demand for information. More often than not, however, media managers respond to particular needs in the work process as identified by employees.

A media organization's management chooses to introduce or adopt a technology for various reasons. The company believes it can use new technology to obtain some strategic, operating, or control objective and management determines many choices of work and of work organization. Simply put, a worldwide cable news organization, such as Cable News Network (CNN), uses various means of satellite news gathering to give it a long-range toehold in the international television news market. CNN probably could not do as well without this technology. CNN then organizes its staff and work procedures, plans its budgets and markets its programs to take advantage of the technology. More often than not, this decision is an economics-based one, but that is just the beginning.

Matching. In this stage, the manager matches the problem or objective with a technology and then plans and designs a solution.

Let's say *Sandwich Style*, a new magazine, has distribution problems, particularly to newsstands with heavy foot traffic (the magazine heavily depends on single sales for its 3,000-copy circulation). The magazine has spent 2 months courting a variety of distributors trying to stir interest in its product—a guide to "tweeners," middle-aged baby boomer parents who also are the main caretakers for their aging parents. Attempts to sell independent bookstores and retail outlets proved futile; only a small local distributor that handles a handful of magazines agreed to distribute the publication.

The publisher knows new titles such as her's need tremendous support at the newsstand. If sales remain slow, greater control of the problem will have to be taken. Large distributors want to carry only those magazines that sell big, and small magazines, like *Sandwich Style*, are pushed off the shelves. This is a major problem, one that can cause cash flow problems as well as threaten potential advertising sales. The publisher calls an industry acquaintance, a publisher in another city. Both have attended several seminars together. The friend advises, "Try small-scale directs—distribution companies that focus on smaller publications; they tend to offer higher discounts and more personal service." So now our publisher has an idea to consider. It probably will not take long to realize this is the near-perfect match for the problem. But that's a mental match. Now the decision must be made, which brings us to the next step.

Redefining/Restructuring. In this phase, our publisher will want to modify or "reinvent" the friend's idea to fit the magazine's particular situation. The publisher should question whether the organization of the publication's work process is suitable for a small-scale distributor campaign.

In this step, the technology is introduced to organization members, who interact in various ways with the technology. As mentioned earlier, consequences of this interaction can be viewed three ways: (a) direct (changes that occur in immediate response) or indirect (changes resulting from immediate responses); (b) desirable (helps the user or system function more effectively) or undesirable (dysfunctional; does not help the user); and (c)

anticipated (changes recognized and intended by management) or unanticipated (changes neither recognized nor intended).

In one instance, a radio station introduced digital audio software and digital control devices by having them stationed side-by-side to the incumbent
analog equipment. As problems were solved and staff members discovered
what the new equipment could do, the demand increased for the new, easier
tasks and products of the digital equipment. Such a "human guinea pig experience" often works.

In the *Sandwich Style* example, at first glance, the small-scale direct idea
sounds ideal. So the publisher buys contracts with one such distributor. Two
more months pass and *Sandwich Style* is beginning to get the exposure it
needs; circulation is up to 5,000. The problem is that the distributor only
pays 45 % of the cover price for every copy sold, as opposed to 50 % that
other distributors pay; and the payment cycle is slow—210 days after the
off-sale date. That means a lag in revenue, which may mean—at
worst—publishing delays and shutdowns or—at best—smaller commis-
sions for account executives. In addition, the distributor doesn't spend
enough time and energy promoting *Sandwich Style*. In this case we see indirect, undesirable, and probably unanticipated consequences.

A similar outcome occured when newspaper copy editors were introduced to pagination. They were told the computerized process would mean
they would be in total control of the page layout process. There would be no
more worrying about accommodating the production staff's idiosyncrasies
and ignorance of good journalistic format, no more laying out pages by
hand, no more using rulers and pencils. But they later discovered that using
pagination also meant shorter deadlines in some cases, computer de-
lays/glitches, and reorganizing the work day because there were not enough
computers for the staff.

In addition, such employee–hardware interactions can be mental or
physical, pleasant or unpleasant, work or play, and so on. All reactions are
expected in a wide range of areas. Employees voluntarily or involuntarily
respond positively or negatively. Regardless of the attitudes involved, a response or interaction occurs.

A media firm is likely to experience this response fairly quickly because
of the changing nature of the product and the sequential and routinized nature of the work. Although journalists, for example, publish or broadcast
new information daily, they gather that information in a highly structured,
predictable way. Any editor or news director who implements a technology
that interrupts that method will get immediate feedback—determined in

part by the job and task characteristics and values of the user of the technology and in part by the technology's attributes. This interaction is likely to be fed back to management in terms of costs and benefits. This assessment is repeated as the task needs change.

Meanwhile, the magazine publisher decides to make some changes. Receptionists, secretaries, writers, and editors are asked to assemble a list of organizations and their members who might be drawn to *Sandwich Style's* content. A second mortgage is taken out to finance free distribution to human resources departments at 100 large corporations. The publisher also links with several national professional trade associations with members typically in the publication's target age group. This connection gains access to their membership databases and the publisher mails complimentary single copies to all members. Thus, the publisher "reinvents" the typical distribution technology (of simply providing copies in bookstores) to some degree, spending upward of 20% of the total budget on circulation. But the process still is unfinished.

Clarifying.   Another three months pass, and *Sandwich Style's* circulation is up to 7,000—good but not great considering the second mortgage! The publisher checks with the staff to see if the distribution plan has been followed. The check reveals it has. The fault lies with the fact that the returns on complimentary copies has not been high enough to justify the expense. The publisher talks individually with each circulation staffer, stressing the value of making follow-up calls and emphasizing the telephone's role in the process. "Follow up," is the bottom line. The innovation—in this case the method of distribution—has lost its newness and is embedded (via company work routines) in the department's established routines.

As we see, how adopters perceive technology is a very important consideration. This adopter perception can be categorized in terms of *relative advantage* (the degree to which a technology is perceived as being better than the idea it replaces), *compatibility* (the degree to which a technology is perceived as consistent with existing values, past experiences and needs of potential adopters), *complexibility* (the degree to which a technology is perceived as relatively difficult to understand and use), *trialability* (the degree to which the technology may be experimented with on a limited basis before adoption is confirmed), and *observability* (the degree to which nonadopters can see a technology's impact). Each perception or "attribute," then, can lead to good or bad consequences, depending on the organization (Rogers, 1983). Then comes the final step.

Routinizing.   In this phase, the technology is firmly in place and is part of work. Back at *Sandwich Style*, new circulation staffers now automatically receive a telephone "circulation building" manual when they are hired. They also receive rewards for circulation-building ideas—particularly for "affinity programs" that place the publication's name in pertinent markets. For instance, one employee came up with the idea of sending subscription fliers to 10,000 churches nationwide (hoping that conscientious members would take the fliers and buy subscriptions). So in this approach, our publisher has chosen a technology that controls work routines and dictates a certain, somewhat predictable outcome.

In sum, the resulting interaction between employees and technology influences management's perceptions of the technology's usefulness and adaptability. The organization gains experience that will lead it to update its ideas on employee use of the new technology. This, in turn, will lead the organization to modify the desired level of use of the technology. This "learning mechanism" self-adjusts at less than infinitely fast speed. Organizational capabilities, development risks, and other factors shape management's perceptions, which appear as corporate cost–benefit ratios or "project profitability." (Stoneman, 1983; Strassmann, 1976).

Suppose *Sandwich Style's* publisher wants to upgrade the distribution system further by developing a web site. Although many magazines use the Web to promote the printed product, *Sandwich Style* wants to foster communication with "tweeners" across the country and eventually develop spin-off publications. But it means having web-savvy employees —people who can design, service, and maintain the site. The publisher discovers such people are in high demand and may culturally clash with "old style" circulation staff. So selected members of the current staff are trained in the hope they in turn will train their colleagues.

Management's perceptions cause it to redefine its objectives and adjust or restructure the role of the technology to the organization. Once the perceptions form, management uses various methods to reinforce or readjust its technological priorities. Relationships between technology and job content or between technology and organization structure may be mediated by management assumptions, deductions, and objectives. Such mediation may be drastic or gradual, depending on the circumstances (Child, 1972). *Sandwich Style* then may want to gradually use the web site, or place a limit on pages to be created or, eventually, to set standards as to what is considered web-worthy.

Such routinization also may lead to clarification of the technology's organizational meaning to employees and users. Clarification, as indicated earlier, means that as the technology becomes integrated into the day-to-day operations of the organization, its meaning gradually becomes clear to employees. The technology loses its newness and becomes embedded in company operations. *Sandwich Style's* web site, then, becomes part of the furniture instead of some new toy; it no longer represents a change in work. Now it is an accepted way of doing business and, as a result, part of the organization's interactional structure.

Most often devices such as rules, new job descriptions, or rewards of some kind can bring about these changes. For example, one newspaper newsroom switched its structure to topic-team reporting in response to analyses that showed some topics—such as science, health, and medicine—were getting inadequate coverage. The problem was solved; health and science received a much greater share of news space. But there also were policy changes in coverage and display: in essence, a different set of news values also were adopted (Russial, 1997).

Such management adjustment is typical and fairly constant because managing is—by nature—adjustment. Typical managerial functions often include planning, staffing, organizing, controlling, and motivating. Introducing technology requires the use of one or all of these functions at some time in the adoption process. The key is when to perform which function. The next section addresses such managerial impacts.

Technology's Impact on Management

Managers must not evaluate in a vacuum but, rather, look at the operating environment as well. That working environment often indirectly shapes the technology via management perceptions about such issues as competition, market share, and legal regulations, as well as the organization's internal environment. To begin with, these impacts can be described in one word: change. But what kind of change? It differs with the situation and occurs in several areas.

Technology Changes the Nature of Work for the Manager.   The manager of a typical media operation that includes editorial, advertising, distribution and production areas deals with change as a matter of routine. Technology, however, brings about a different change because its role is as basic to media as routine itself. Technology is a tool that affects the very basis of routine.

For example, as magazines change to more automated workplaces (i.e., computers, faxes, and modems), those freelance writers who have not yet adopted and used the technology,—especially the more expensive tools that facilitate communication with editors and the submission of manuscripts—will be affected. Editors will have to weigh the value of the writer's contribution against the ease of producing the story. And as smaller magazines—thanks to portable computers—continue to have more writers located at remote sites, magazine editors will find their staffs becoming more decentralized (Endres & Schierhorn, 1995). This, in effect, changes the way the writer does his or her job. Instead of mailing in a story or waiting to return to the office to write it, the writer now can file the story electronically. That writer's editor no longer has to worry about finding someone to take dictation or extending the copy deadline until the writer comes into the office to write the story. The editor now awaits the story as it comes from a computer terminal—in-house or not. This saves the editor time, which in turn allows him or her to do more with that time. Thus the work methods are changed—probably for the better.

Or consider when a public relations practitioner in a small agency uses teleconferencing—instead of traveling to out-of-town training sessions. This also changes the manager's work climate because there is no longer a reduced staff on what were previously travel days. The manager now is able to do more things instead of filling in for the missing practitioner. The teleconferencing capability will cause the manager to think twice when a practitioner asks to be sent to a training seminar outside the agency's market area. No longer will "no" be an automatic response in that situation because teleconferencing allows the practitioner to pick and choose which training sessions to attend, regardless of their location.

Or suppose a weekly newspaper publisher starts a web site as a means of diversifying the company's interests. This means the publisher will have to change the focus somewhat to include the business of running a site—a technology probably foreign to the publisher, with its own rules of operation, a possibly different set of egos to deal with, different types of content to produce, and different types of audiences to please.

Finally, consider the case of how local TV station news directors will have to reconsider their roles as news providers with the coming of digital television. The new services the technology will allow—specifically, multiple news programs with adjoining data feeds—open up new possibilities for newscasts covering different topics simultaneously. The implications also carry to advertising if each local station decides to transmit more than one channel—and thus complicate the programming choices for consumers.

Technology Affects the Manager's Level of Control. Ironically, many companies adopt technologies to gain greater control over operations—control over the budget, employee behavior, the market, or distribution of the product, among others. Managers often see the technology as a tool that will steer the process more toward short-term objectives or long-term goals. Certainly, technology does help those things to happen.

But it does not always work that way. Remember, technology has desirable or undesirable consequences. Just as computers give the magazine editor more time and thus more control over deadlines and copy standards, it also means the editor becomes overreliant on writers who possess the technology and thus loses some control over the ability to work with possibly more creative writers who may not possess a computer or fax or modem. If the magazine cherishes such creativity, the move to computer standardization and mandated access to the computer may discourage some particularly technophobic writers.

When the public relations agency described earlier added the teleconferencing capability, the employees had routine access to regular training. As employees acquire more experience and better skills, an agency manager no longer has sole knowledge. Again, the practitioner gains through the control of news skills; but the manager "loses" because control of those skill areas is relinquished to the practitioner. The loss comes in the fact that he or she now must place increasing trust in the staff—an occurrence that may be particularly painful for some control-minded executives.

Finally, in the case of the weekly newspaper publisher's new web site, the publisher may retain ultimate authority but unless he has some web experience he must relinquish day-to-day operating authority of the site and must give it to someone schooled in the ways of web operation and maintenance—the staff web page editor or an outside agency contracted to do the job. Surely, that person will have to report to the publisher, but that person also may be gaining more control because the publisher will view him or her as the "web expert" and will be less likely to challenge his or her judgment than would another, more web-savvy owner.

Technology Enhances Planning. This means technology allows managers to become more flexible in setting goals and objectives because it often saves time through increased productivity and efficiency. Also because of the rapid changes in technology, managers have to do advance planning and data-gathering if they are to plan for successful implementation of an innovation.

For example, a medium-sized upstate New York paper considered adopting a voice-mail (audiotex) technology to enhance its personal ads section. Editors and staff looked at personals all over the country—how other papers handled them, the reaction they received, and the success they achieved over the course of 1 year. Problems—public and operating staff reaction, image of the ads themselves, revenue potential, operational adjustments—were anticipated and discussed (Merskin, 1996). Technology also fosters postadoption planning. For instance, an editor on a large metro daily newspaper notices steadily increasing uses for online technology. The editor decides to add 24-hour production of news via instantaneous (real-time) transmission of certain types of news—for example, business and sports—to online users. The editor sees this as an extension of the current print product, old wine in new bottles, and hires more reporters and tells them to just put their stories online. But the editor forgot one thing. Real-time journalism does not work the same as newspaper reporting. Whereas real-time news has the same structure of newspaper news, the continuous release of news makes for shorter, quicker stories with fewer sources and overreliance on regular, routine sources (Aronson, Sylvie, & Todd, 1996). Once the editor realizes this, it is time to rethink the strategy and do some goalsetting about what kind of product should be provided to her customers. Before continuing with the new product, research and testing should be completed.

An emerging technology—by virtue of being a new, unknown, untested, unobserved entity—creates unforeseen problems that require adjustment in planning. Why? Because managers are human, they see a glittering mass of hardware that they often believe will deliver an equally glittering mass of profits (or, at least, savings). Such near-sightedness (and there are degrees of this kind, too) can be avoided somewhat through proper, deliberate, and well-developed planning as well as through testing and observing the technology before it is adopted. Not even the best manager can predict what will happen once the technology is put in place, although there is a positive side. In addition, evidence suggests that new technologies help public relations managers become better strategic planners. A survey (Anderson & Reagan, 1992) showed that by doing more accounting and budgeting work, public affairs policy planning, issues management, media monitoring, and market and demographic data research, public relations managers were able to increase their productivity. At another newspaper newsroom, management adopted new personal computers to perform reporting and writing tasks. The computers allowed the editors to maintain electronic story files whereas previous files consisted of actual newspaper clippings and datebook-type notations. The computer also helped editors maintain a local sources file—easily retrievable—and facilitated story budgeting. Another editor maintained a list of reporters' regular assignments ("beats") and referred to that file whenever doubt existed about which reporter was to cover a certain topic. Still another editor maintained a writing stylebook for reporters' reference (Sylvie & Danielson, 1989).

Technology Generally Forces Managers to Adjust Functionally. This means staffing, organizing, and motivating other managerial functions—also experience the same types of changes discussed earlier. Nowhere is this more evident than in the case of the web, where the onset of publications has shown managers that they must rethink their managerial behavior if they are to make their web sites viable.

In general, a manager staffs by determining human resource needs: recruiting, selecting, and training employees. The Web enforces this function in that it compels the manager to recruit, select, and train employees capable of effectively using the Web. The ease with which this is done depends on the technology and on the company's personnel. Newspapers, for example, have found that web staffing depends on the site's mission and the newspaper's current web expertise. And web staffing levels vary from one-person operations to entire, fully staffed departments to staffs completely composed of freelancers to having the site maintained and operated by an independent web contractor. The growth in web audiences has made some broadcasters turn to full-time management of station Internet offerings through webmasters and webmistresses who manage the flow of information.

Conventional logic has been seemingly cast aside. Consider one editor whose small-town daily started a web page. Print edition staff levels were down. When he could not find any competent local web writers, the editor turned to online recruiting for staffers who would interview subjects by phone and communicate with the newspaper managers by Internet. Their stories were handled the same way as feature-oriented, trend-type pieces. The reporters have to explain their relationship with the newspaper to their sources and an editor assigning a story may notify local sources that an online "reporter" may call.

But some organizational problems developed. Primarily, no one coordinated the story assignments and there was difficulty knowing which online writers were working which stories. So the newspaper created an online editor position to confer with the reporters, make assignments, and promote their copy in daily news budget meetings. Motivational glitches included low online reporter morale regarding source access. "People do not call me back, because it is long distance," one reporter said. "They can't understand how somebody thousands of miles away could be writing a story for the (local) paper."

Why the adjustments? Again, it is because of management's initial view of the technology. Many managers see the Web—and, probably, most technologies—basically from the perspective of, "What can it do *for* us?" rather than, "What can it do *to* us?" The company's goals, objectives, and plans often may predate the purchase of the equipment and usually are based on economic considerations that include costs, labor savings, production efficiency, and continued company profits. An effective media manager adjusts in timely fashion.

So far, we have discussed internal effects. Technology also interacts with external environments. Let us examine how one such external factor—markets—are affected.

EXTERNAL IMPACT

Technology's Impact on Markets

Remember, technology usually is viewed as a tool, a means toward some end. In the area of media markets, managers view technology basically as a means to change the market, hopefully for the better. But that change can take various forms.

Technology Can Expand or Diminish Competition.   In many cases, the technology effectively allows entry into a market that most would have thought closed. It also is possible for a technology to be so expensive that the price drives some companies out of business.

The former began to occur in the late 1990s as the smaller, less competitive wireless cable-TV industry began to use digital compression to more equally compete with their wired counterparts. Briefly put, digital compression allows cable operators to "jam" more channels into less space (by decreasing the bits-per-signal requirement while maintaining quality) for the same price as conventional wired cable TV. The possibility was enhanced by the fact that many cable operators were slow to equip their markets—already prone to signal outages—for the digital signal. Add the interest in the market already exhibited by regional telephone companies and the cable market seemed poised for drastic change.

Similarly, the Internet brought a change to the idea of markets and market definition for electronic newspapers. No longer does a newspaper in, say, San Francisco have the safe, relative monopoly of its print edition when it starts an online version. The electronic edition allows, for example, Taiwanese newspapers to compete with the San Francisco newspaper for the large Chinese and Chinese-American audience—in the advertising as well as in the information markets (Chyi & Sylvie, 1998).

It is easy to see how a technology can diminish competition in some markets by comparing two television stations competing for viewers in the same, basic market. If the leading station decides to enhance its product (and market share) by putting several million dollars into capital improvements—a new and renovated studio, new cameras, new sound equipment, a satellite news-gathering mobile van, to name a few—the result is a clearer, crisper picture with better video footage, more colorful background graphics and better facilities for producing higher quality local commercials. The bottom line means more viewers, which in turn means more advertisers, higher advertising rates, and more prestige for the station. With those cards stacked against it, the competing station—unless it, too, has a large reserve fund or a good line of credit with local banks—may never recover.

This may sound unlikely, but the same thing happened in the late 1980s involving a new newspaper's subscription collection methods. *The St. Louis Sun*—an upstart, tabloid competitor to the incumbent *St. Louis Post-Dispatch*—attempted to generate subscribers via a pay-in-advance billing method and reliance on newstand or single-copy sales techniques. Up to that point, St. Louisans were accustomed to paying for the newspaper after delivery. But The Sun's single-copy sales fell short of expectations and 7 months after its birth the paper failed (Mueller, 1997).

Technology Can Blur Market Boundaries.   The Internet—with its ability to carry written, spoken, and pictorial messages—defies definition. The question arises: When you locate the CNN site on the Web and view a story, are you watching television or "surfing the Web"? If you locate your favorite radio station's web address, are you listening to radio, surfing the Web, or both? Advertisers must be wary as to which market their messages are being transmitted. As media technologies converge, as in the case of the Internet, companies enter markets with much greater ease and thus their products provide adequate substitutes for each other. This encourages market blurring, just as the development of radio and film increased competition for entertainment. A similar situation arose with the rise of cable and low-power television stations, which crowded the market and delivered the same product as broadcast stations (Powers, 1990). Only by differentiating their products can these media create more distinct markets.

Technology Creates New Markets.   Often the first media company to harness a technology has a new market to itself—at least initially. This often occurs when the company has found itself in the situation just described —one in which the market is "fuzzy" (Lacy, 1993). For example, no one knew there was a market for videotext until the technology was mass-produced and introduced to the public and redeveloped into "the Internet." Now many media firms have crawled onto the Web.

For example, Fine Print Distributors started by distributing solely political magazines and other small, regional titles in the southwest. But in the early 1990s, the company bought new computers and converted to a new software program that handles order entry and accounting to help it better track and interpret financial information as well as to comprehensively monitor newsstand distribution. As a result, it now serves chain and independent bookstores, newstands, specialty stores, music stores, and health-food stores in the United States and abroad while launching a subsidiary that sells titles to other distributors and handles billing collections and marketing for publishers. Fine Print has also established itself as a major competitor in alternative magazine distribution.

Technology Provides Revenue Alternatives for Media Companies.

As companies try to weather economic or cyclical downturns, one such hedge often comes via diversification. This idea is not new, of course, but new technologies make the decision somewhat easier and more attractive. This chapter has spent much time discussing the Internet because it holds so many possibilities and carries with it the potential for much impact. For example, it is not uncommon for newspapers to form alliances, use advertising sponsors and/or subscriptions to generate revenue from their web sites (Puritz, 1996). But although many media are creating a web presence, there is some doubt about its potential to raise revenue, especially as an electronic newspaper (Cameron, Hollander, Nowak, & Shamp, 1997). In fact, history is littered with financial technological failures, such as beta video recorders, and many videotext experiments. Still, potentially lucrative ventures still exist. With the future development of digital television—which features pictures of higher resolution and clarity than current analog signals—comes the possibility of simultaneous transmission of data, for example, news, sports, and financial statistics and software. That means that as stations, networks, and program studios switch to the new standard, the sale of high-definition televisions (HDTV) is expected to flourish. The higher production standard also will allow TV news crews to package their programs in such a way as to permit several broadcasts or delivery formats—all of which means increased profits.

Other media companies have used the technology of "branding"—extending their presence as well as their bottom line. In the mid-1990s, for instance, Black Entertainment Television (BET) enhanced its mission of becoming "the preeminent provider of Black entertainment, information, and images" by taking profits from its beginnings as a cable station and parlaying them into four cable channels, an online service, a magazine, a monthly newspaper insert and a chain of theme restaurants. In essence, BET managed itself into strategic partnerships that allowed it to defray capital and technological expenditures and gain expertise in new arenas.

In short, the limit on revenue potential of new technologies is primarily dependent on the innovation of the manager. Witness the craftiness of the person who bought video footage from British firms who run surveillance cameras—for example, fire insurance companies, security firms, and various government agencies—edited and compiled excerpts of authentic, graphic scenes of unknowing couples and created one of the most popular videotapes in Britain. The producer's entrepreneurial spirit is just as strong as that of creators of New Century Network, an online network of dozens of newspaper web sites that offers national advertisers local penetration on those sites. The message is that technology enhances profit.

Technology Redefines or Changes Consumer Use and Behavior.

New technology changes consumption habits. When television was introduced, for example, consumers changed their media behavior—from reading news to watching it (Fullerton, 1988). The Web, for instance, has allowed the consumer to interact with the information—retrieving and sending messages or interacting with the site host. Previously, the consumer was simply a passive listener/viewer/reader of information. Now consumers do not have to wait until noon, 5 or 10 pm, to get a sense of the current weather or short-term forecast; they need only find the local weather map on the Web or, failing that, tune into cable TV's Weather Channel. In fact, cable and satellite technology provide more viewing choices and thus, viewers are becoming more selective in what they watch. The result is evident in the types of channels available: HBO, Cinemax and Showtime (feature films); ESPN (sports); VH-1, TNN, and MTV (music); Lifetime (women's issues);

Disney and Nickelodeon (children's programming); and Pay-TV (special events), to name a few.

Media firms are particularly interested in the phenomenon of technologically encouraged feedback. A Chicago TV station, for example, placed an unmanned camera in a kiosk at a nearby shopping mall, allowing consumers to comment about anything the station produces. Viewers can see themselves during newscasts or on the station's web site. Virtually all newspaper web sites provide either reporters' or editors' e-mail addresses; some provide online "chat" forums where readers discuss news and issues (Gubman & Greer, 1997). Such devices seem to be working; a survey found Internet access and use increased over time among the same group of respondents; and—contrary to experience with other technology where per capita use declines as diffusion of the technology increases—people who used the Internet earlier in the study tended to increase their use over time (Lindstrom, 1997).

As Technology Affects Consumer Behavior, It Also Indirectly Affects Advertising and Promotion Strategies, Method, and Content.   The example most of us are familiar with concerns, again, the VCR. Because the viewer is able to speed (fast-forward) past commercials in programs the viewer has recorded, those commercials in effect lose their audience. This has caused some advertisers to alter their message: shorter, more creative commercials that appear and attract the viewer's attention before the viewer can decide to fast forward, for example. But if the new technologies force advertisers' hands, they also allow advertisers to be more selective about their audiences. Advertisers constantly are looking for ways to target specific messages to specific audiences. Many technologies make this easier. For instance, "push" technology sends web content to users' computers, rather than users having to type in web addresses on their computers to reach the desired site—even to the point of giving the user what she wants, when she wants it.

Advertising on the Web, on the other hand, has proved problematic. There is some question as to whether web ads are recognizable and memorable as print medium ads (Sundar, Narayan, Obregon, & Uppal, 1997). In addition, measuring web audiences—a key to attracting advertisers—has lacked standardization, making accuracy of the audience estimates questionable. The push mechanisms also have been interpreted by some as an invasion of the user's privacy.

On the positive side, because of the inherent targeting efficiencies of the online format, producers of city guide sites—which feature news and entertainment options but may not be affiliated with a local news organization—and other specialized sites have attempted to carve classified advertising niches, for example, in car buying and selling, real estate listings, or employment services. And all the guide sites are competing for local advertising; for example, Microsoft has created Sidewalk—an entertainment-oriented venture that has recruited established cultural writers with an eye toward attracting local and regional advertising. Others, such as the regional Bell operating companies, also have or are planning to have similar vehicles in an attempt to draw part of the local advertising market. A key driving force is national advertisers, who are becoming more intent on reaching geographically targeted audiences via technology filters that compensate for the lack of focused content to buy (Chyi & Sylvie, 1998).

Technology Often Develops Faster Than Attempts to Control It.

As mentioned at the beginning of this chapter, the pace of technological change often exceeds managers' capacities to deal with it. For example, the processing power of a computer has multiplied nearly 700 % since 1970; the number of video channels per home has increased nearly 20-fold; and computer memory is 160 times its 1970 capacity. And as technologies converge, managers will have to devise new and multifaceted strategies to keep their companies on track to meet the challenge. Cox Enterprises, one of the top 15 largest media companies in the United States, is a good example. Founded nearly 100 years ago with the purchase of an Ohio newspaper, the company has grown into several newspapers, radio and TV stations, cable operations and an auto auction firm. Its strategy has been to move quickly into new forms of media. Cox started the first radio station in Ohio, the first TV station in the south, was an early entrant into cable TV, and has done experimental testing of phone service via cable and interactive broadband technology. But Cox also has focused on high growth markets and holds important monopoly market positions. As a result, Cox is well poised to take advantage of new technologies. But Cox—like other media firms—still must be wary of certain tools (e.g., it no longer is in the film and TV production business).

A more efficient marketplace often needs technological standards—either set by the government or the industry. This especially applies in a rapidly changing technological environment and was most recently the case in the development of HDTV and measurement of Internet audience strength and use. For the manager, this means balancing the entrepreneurial spirit with caution; to do any less would be foolish.

SUMMARY

To summarize, technology has internal and external impacts. Managers have to understand that technology demands adjustment and managers must be sensitive as to how and when to manage. As mentioned earlier, a media manager's job is to turn the technology to the company's advantage.

This chapter has examined managerial approaches to technology, the process of how a company uses or "adopts" technology, and how technology may affect media organizations and their markets.

Each of the three basic approachess—tructural, technological task, and sociotechnical—is rooted in a slightly different managerial orientation and each has its advantages and disadvantages. Most modern-day managers use some form of the sociotechnical approach. A media company adopts a technology for its own particular reasons. Then it introduces the technology to employees, who interact in various ways with the technology—depending on the employee and the nature of the task involved. Then management's perceptions and employee reactions prompt a period of adjustment, which ultimately leads to adoption or rejection of the technology.

As a result, the technology affects managerial functions, including planning, organizing, staffing, motivating, and controlling operations (see Fig. 5.2).

In all, technology causes a media manager to manage in an atmosphere of constant change and adjustment. How and when a manager acts has great impact on the company's future.

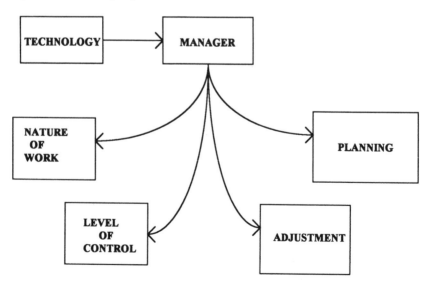

FIG. 5.2.   How technology affects media managers.

CASE 5.1

Real-Time Realignment

As executive editor, Joe Chevalier runs the newsroom of newly created Financial Express (FE) News. It is one of the 13 news agencies that comprise the real-time media industry with financial news wires that use high-speed computer and telecommunication networks to transmit news instantaneously 24 hours a day to worldwide corporate subscribers who need the information to conduct business transactions and industry analysis. Joe was a former editor at a big-city daily newspaper for 5 years before joining FE News.

Subscribers access FE content via a computer screen that lists "headlines." A screen may contain up to18 headlines, which provide the item number, the abbreviated source, the time of release and a textual summary of the subject. FE releases stories in several "takes" (about 45 lines of 1.5 screens) to limit story lengths so information can be released as quickly as possible in as readable a form as possible. Most stories are limited to two pages and many news items contain financial data without text. But often a story is developed in additional takes. FE disseminates about 1,000 news items every 3.5 hours. Stories usually contain fewer words, sentences and paragraphs than comparable items in a print newspaper.

FE staffers—many of them newspaper refugees like Joe—still have to write simply, but practical considerations impose some broadcast-like limitations. Stories usually include fewer sources than comparable newspaper stories. In addition, because of deadline constraints, sources often are less readily available and—because the reporters do not have time and, by virtue of their job, develop some expertise about their subjects—it is not always clear from reading FE stories as to who the source(s) is (are). Reporters regularly use unidentified sources.

All this worries Joe, because he has a gnawing feeling that FE stories are less than objective. At times he feels as if he is working in a fast food restaurant—"cooking" nuggets of information and doing so quickly and without much attention to quality. "This medium imposes on journalism," Joe confides to an assistant. "It demands relevance, speed, and accuracy because of the time element. The readers want it right and fast; they're not interested in style, they're interested in the number. We're writing as it happens and you can see the financial markets react." In addition, Joe's under continuing pressure to upgrade the news to make it more competitive with the other real-time services. FE's corporate parent—a megamedia conglomerate—projects that the industry (where competition can be measured in frac-tions of a second as well as in dollars) will undergo a shake-out in the next 2 years, with probably half of the field surviving.

Joe's trying to decide what to do: On the one hand, he wants to improve the journalistic quality (surely stock traders want quality, too, he reasons); on the other hand, he wants to make FE more competitive. But he fears that enhanced competitiveness means being faster, which he equates with low journalistic quality. He's given up hopes of ever winning a Pulitzer Prize, but he feels journalism should have standards.

ASSIGNMENT

1. In what stage of the adoption process is FE? Based on your interpretation of Joe's feelings, at which stage does Joe want to return? Which approach to adoption does Joe seem to embody?
2. What management changes is Joe experiencing or likely to experience? What functional adjustments will Joe have to make?
3. Research the real-time trade press and develop a list of alternatives for Joe to consider. What new revenue streams might be created in the process?
4. What can Joe do to improve the journalistic quality of FE News and simultaneously make the news more marketable and thus more competitive?

CASE 5.2

The Case of The Technology of Choice

You are the news director of KPUN, a small market network-affiliated television station. Your three rivals—KONE, KFUN and KTUN—have 25, 22, and 29 % of the overall viewership, leaving you with 24 %.

For years, KPUN has been known as the hard-hitting, news-oriented station, with occasional top-notch investigative pieces, popular anchors, and a good sports staff. Your viewers tend to be slightly more educated than average. KONE, your nearest competitor, airs more tabloid-like pieces, emotional tear-jerker stories and sensational "gotcha" journalism. KFUN and KTUN, meanwhile, take middle-of-the-road approaches in news, but feature outstanding weather coverage; KTUN's edge seems to be its highly popular anchors who do a lot of community promotional work while emphasizing national and international news on the air.

KFUN opts for balance in news—local, national, and international—but makes up for it by heavily promoting its total package. No stations have a web presence.

Your station general manager (GM) has just informed you that the upcoming new year will show your budget up 8 % from this year, and you expect it to increase again the following year. About two thirds of any increase you get will be used to upgrade equipment and facilities. With the extra money, however, comes a mandate: The GM wants you to make an upward move in the ratings, at least to second but—given the closeness of the competition—she would like you to shoot for first place. You tell her that an 8 % budget increase is not much to go on, but she says it is comparable to what the other newsrooms in town are getting and that while revenues have grown, costs have kept pace; so there is no hope of hiring additional staff. You will have to use who you have, but more efficiently so as to produce something distinctive that will put you at or near the top.

So you choose to shop for a new newsroom system. You are not sure which way to go, but after reading industry publications and giving the situation much thought, here are your choices so far:

1. *A wire service production system*: A drag-and-drop interface that most likely will be adopted by major U.S. TV organizations by mid-year. It uses a "briefing button" to retrieve information. The reporter types in or highlights a word and instantly accesses a catalog of related material, including wire stories, pictures, sound clips, and maps. It also can retrieve thumbnail video images

and features links to playback and machine control for robotic cameras, still stores, prompters, character generators, and captioning systems. Training on installations has been surprisingly simple, vendors say. The system can be integrated with the wire service's total NewsFocus product. The yearly fee of NewsFocus is based on market size, which is about $9,000 for KPUN.

2. *A multi-task, stand-alone system:* A product that touts itself as a "lens to transmitter" technology, though still not highly adopted by other stations. The system is designed to handle text composition, audio and video browsing, and web publishing. As news feeds come in, the system stores them in low resolution on a server and in full resolution on tape. The user can then browse the low-res video and compose an edit decision list that can then be used in a tape-to-tape suite. With workstation, server software, and browse server, price can vary from $25,000 to $100,000, depending on what the customer wants to accomplish.

3. *A powerful upgrade of a system KPUN already has*: This system uses a database to track scripts, e-mail, wires, and archival data; allows direct access to Internet file exchange and is the next generation of a popular system used nationwide. It will not edit video, but allows the user to view video stored on the video server and adjust the start and end points for playback, which comes in handy for quick cuts. This system can be interfaced with almost any other system. The core software costs about $150 per workstation seat for the servers, and $400 per seat for the database software; the software itself costs about $4,000. The seat prices are expected to fall after the first 10 or 15 clients.

4. *An upgrade of a journalist workstation product:* This product has an additional web publisher application and a backup server; it is made by a company with a good reputation and which offers an integrated system, of which this product is a part. The server allows reporters to perform cuts-only editing and features an undermonitor display that shows the story slug and the piece's running time. The vendor sells the system as a package with its local area network browser, which converts finished video clips to low-resolution files and makes them available to any nonediting station (including producers and news directors) on the network. A four-channel model costs about $100,000 and the workstations run $20,000 apiece.

ASSIGNMENT

1. Choose one of the four options and make a convincing case for it to the GM. Why would the option you choose be a better alternative than the other options?

2. Which technology would most help KPUN vault into the local ratings lead? Which would be least likely to help? Why?

3. Develop a projected budget of all the options and the possible spin-off costs they may prompt. Do a costs–benefits analysis chart and present the findings to the class, which will act as your GM.

4. Should a small TV station enter the web marketplace? Should competition drive or direct that entry? What are the adoption ramifications of creating a web page for a TV station? How would it change a news director's job?

CASE 5.3

At Your Service

It is 2 days until "A" Day—the day your company, ZinesRus, adopts a new technology: a computer-to-plate (CTP) system. In the 20 years it has been doing business as a magazine service bureau (a company that specializes in providing prepress services), ZinesRus has been a leader in the state in the post-typesetting era. With the advent of phototypesetting and offset printing, the firm was an early adopter that learned to placate and calm harried artists and printers faster and cheaper than anyone else. But in 2 days, that may not be true any more.

ZinesRus is in mid-evolution. The company's pioneering founder, Rene, is nearing retirement. He is getting too old to deal with the staff's constant anxiety and complaining on a daily basis. So he has entrusted this next step in the evolution to you, Kerr. You are the operations manager with a journalism degree who has opted to work in production. You love to work with images, but people ... well, that is another story. You find that you are dealing with nonspecialists—staff with little or no formal training in the art and craft of printing but who, through the miracle of computers, can now produce images only professionals could have created 5 years ago.

But you must head toward CTP because if you do not, your clients—several regional alternative magazines—surely will and, thus, no longer need your services. Platemaking previously was a manual process subject to human faults and mishaps, but now computers make it efficient, accurate, and fast. Multiple page programming facilitates large press runs and maintains high quality (i.e., minimal defects). And as the cost of computers and software continues to decline, it brings with it an increased chance that magazines will decide to purchase their own CTP systems and—with it—greater production control. You do not want to see that happen; the future of ZinesRus depends on it.

The problem is the staff. New technology requires bright, flexible people who like to stay on the edge. It may mean education and retraining of some employees, who then can train their colleagues. ZinesRus' staff has shown signs of resistance to training and the subsequent specialization it fosters. They are mostly in their 40s, many of them have been with the company since its inception. They were brought kicking and screaming into the computer era and—despite their protestations—most feel comfortable with computers. But at the coffeepot you often hear talk about "the good old days of hot type." Most staffers are Macintosh disciples, but 40 % now use PCs.

However, most problems come from—and persist with—work files from the one fifth of ZinesRus clients who use PCs.

There are some particular intra staff dynamics that you must master.

- There's Bob, the leader of the conservative faction, which wants to cling onto current technology and resist any new system. "There is nothing wrong with what we've got now," Bob tells anyone who will listen, including you. He fears CTP will force him to factor in more system time for what were once routine output jobs. "The founders (Bob has been with the company since its inception) envisioned this company doing things the old-fashioned way: elbow grease and personal attention to the publisher. We do that and no CTP is going to replace that." Bob vows he will retire first before he works with CTP; he's 63 and has risen to the rank of systems supervisor.

- There's Chad, a twenty-something page designer who is all for CTP, but has no following—unlike Bob, Chad's saving grace is that he is unafraid of any change, regardless of the terms or rules of the CTP acquisition. His work is spotless, although he often complains about outdated technology. "I feel as if I am working with a federation of dunces," he says about the current system. "It is time for a change, Kerr." Chad is well-liked by the staff, but Bob calls him "a flake."

- Then there's Mo, a combative, emotional printer whose perfectionist tendencies have lead to several run-ins with Bob. He would do anything to see Bob quit. The only other thing he cares more about is production and doing his job well. He feels CTP will enhance the company's reproductive capabilities but that, however, designers such as Chad have too much power already. He reasons that CTP will leave him at the mercy of Chad and "his kind" and he worries that CTP may be set up for fixed plate sizes (which poses a problem if ZinesRus wants to expand its clientele). Mo's usually a sullen fellow, but nothing peps him up more than a chance to do battle with Bob.

- Finally, there is D'ann, the voice of reason and the unofficial staff counselor (as well as the most impartial person on staff). D'ann thinks your apprehension is much ado about nothing. But she can be cold and unfeeling at times, when she goes, as she calls it, "on automatic" during an office crisis. D'ann has no trouble with learning any new system and often is her own worst enemy because she is almost too logical. The staff, however, likes her because she is the only woman on staff and they feel protective of what they perceive as her innocence about things—including new technology. You like her pragmatism most of all.

With the new CTP system, you hope to improve the company's proofing and plating in a digital work flow environment. Film output to digital imagesetters constitutes a large part of the bureau's work. But as digital proofs and presses develop, that output probably will decline. Other service bureau owners you have talked to say they are using or considering buying the system, with an eye toward digital presses in the future. As far as you are concerned, you want to be ahead of your clients, who are gaining more and more expertise in putting files together well and more efficiently. Adopting CTP will help the company, because it has four large accounts (and their plate sizes are all the same). But CTP would be inefficient if new clients had varying plate sizes. One resolution could revolve around the Internet—which would create a new area of business (Internet services, multimedia, and related services) for ZinesRus.

ASSIGNMENT

1. Do a costs–benefit analysis of Kerr's options and report your findings to Rene.
2. Let us say Kerr wants to adopt CTP for the firm. What adoption strategies should be pursued? What should Kerr do as to the staff's dominant personalities? Should they be manipulated in some fashion and, if so, how?
3. Explore CTP and compare it with other current prepress technologies. What are the relative costs? Adoption concerns? Training curves? How does the size of an organization figure into adoption of such technologies?
4. What are current concerns—costs, adoption, software development, to name a few—of the magazine industry in general regarding prepress devices such as CTP? How many magazines are bypassing service bureaus and adopting their own pre-press advances?

CASE 5.4

Problems in PR

The Office of Public Relations (OPR) at State University has a problem that faces colleges across the country: how to integrate constantly advancing technology and electronic communication into its news and information service responsibilities. OPR first considered a web site nearly 2 years ago, but a lack of training and skills—plus the lack of a computer systems administrator—technologically crippled the agency. The systems analyst left to go back to college and did not leave detailed instructions as to the maintenance of essential technical equipment. Originally three staffers were responsible for the site but the other two were not consulted once construction started and no one was assigned the site after the analyst's departure.

The office is the university's PR arm. The staff includes one full-time writer, a temporary full-time writer, a publications editor, an assistant director for editorial, an assistant director for minority relations, a proofreader/research associate, an office director, an administrative associate who monitors office supplies and assists with projects and an administrative assistant in charge of news distribution—but no computer person.

Failure to maintain the site hurt its reputation and impeded its ability to disseminate dependable news. A number of computer problems have arisen, including server backup and network problems where the system had to be taken down. Usually, an office member found a quick-but-temporary solution. In the last 2 years, the office has spent about $100,000 for new computers, printers, software, and wiring. But only $2,000 is budgeted for technical support this year, and the analyst line item has been permanently deleted from the office's budget.

The office has established an ad hoc computer team, comprised of administrative associate Chuck Henry, Assistant Director Ellen Daly, and Information Specialist Alexis Keeshen. Henry is responsible for fax distribution of news releases and his office deals with technical problems. Daly is new and is not familiar with technical issues. The office director, Emily Cashore, feels that an administrative presence on the team is essential. No other administrator has extensive computer skills.

Keeshen writes press releases about social sciences and law and tends to "quick fix" technical things without proper supervision. She is one of the few staffers willing to deal with computer problems and sees no need for a permanent computer person. She says that because most problems are minor, those with technical skills and interests should be involved. "Anyone with a liberal arts emphasis does not need to know the technical side of computers," she says.

The office's original homepage did not include a revised mission statement for the office, although one has been in the development stage since the office changed its name 3 years ago (its audiences include the university president, the faculty and staff, their families, and the news media). The page contains no information about campus traditions, maps, or even a link to them. In fact, the staff does not have a realistic and informed clue as to what people would like to see on the page—just some ideas they have gathered from various people on the campus. The office still uses the traditional press release method to distribute information—usually via fax or postal mail. You—a faculty member of the university's management department—have been asked to serve as a consultant to help solve the problem.

ASSIGNMENT

1. What kind of strategic planning should the office do in regard to this problem?

2. What should be done about the agency's online presence? Should it continue or be terminated? Why or why not?

3. Should the ad hoc team be restructured? Should the team be responsible for the site's construction and content? Who should be responsible for updating and maintaining the site?

4. How can the agency make the best use of its current resources in solving this problem? What should be redone to rebuild staff confidence in the site and in its online capabilities? How important is the agency's mission to the web site development?

6

MEDIA REGULATION
AND SELF-REGULATION

Media managers must be aware that the law changes constantly. This chapter discusses how laws affecting media firms have changed and instances when legal advice should be sought. The goal of this chapter is to outline practices and principles that all media managers must apply in order to avoid legal problems. Some online as well as traditional resources for media managers are identified.

This chapter is not intended to be a comprehensive discussion of all areas of law that might affect media firms. It does, however, highlight areas of contemporary interest, and focus on the prevention and response to legal actions. Readers interested in more detail should review the appropriate legal resources referred to throughout the chapter (e.g., the most recent editions of *The Associated Press Stylebook and Libel Manual*, Goldstein, 1996, and *Mass Communication Law: Cases and Comment*, Gillmor, Barron, & Simon, 1998.

PREVENTING LEGAL PROBLEMS

There are general principles and procedures managers at all kinds of media organizations can institute to minimize legal problems. First-time managers must learn and understand the goals of the organization to direct, coordinate and involve the people they supervise. Then, organizational goals must be communicated and implemented by establishing timetables, which can be tied to performance evaluations. Performance evaluations allow managers to quantify performance to promote or fire employees fairly, avoiding wrongful-termination lawsuits.

Performance Assessment and Termination

One of the first things a new manager must do is to ask employees whether they know how their performance is measured. If the performance evaluation process is not spelled out, ask employees for their ideas about performance assessment and how to improve it. Then managers should work with supervisors to develop an equitable and understandable employee performance review process. Employees should be given a personnel manual including job descriptions and duties, organizational employment policies, performance assessment documents and procedures, the company's progressive discipline process, human resources information, and other related materials.

It is especially important to be specific about standards, deadlines, and other appropriate performance measures. All employees should be notified ahead of time when evaluations occur and how to prepare for them. Managers and employees should discuss written goals, performance measurements, and deadlines of evaluations. Rewards for exceptional performance should be clear. New managers can develop ideas for appropriate performance evaluation forms and criteria by obtaining copies of such forms from their own supervisors, or talking to a former teacher or managers at other media organizations (Martens, 1997).

For example, a reporter's performance evaluation might include ratings of:

1. story accuracy;
2. ability to meet deadlines;
3. news gathering skills;
4. ability to suggest and develop story ideas;
5. ability to develop sources;
6. level of awareness and knowledge of the reporter's assigned beat and community;
7. breadth of coverage, including coverage of minorities and minority viewpoints;
8. writing skills, including story organization, importance, style, and word selection;
9. ability to communicate and work with the public, supervisors and other staff members;
10. ability to respond to constructive criticism or feedback

Occasionally, performance reviews will be unsatisfactory. So managers must be familiar with appropriate procedures for disciplining, and if necessary, firing employees. Again, employee handbooks including job descriptions, performance evaluation documents, procedures, and the company's progressive discipline system must be developed and distributed. If termination policies are spelled out in handbooks, and progressive discipline policies and procedures are followed and documented, the company should be protected from wrongful termination suits.

The first time job performance does not meet minimum standards the employee should be notified in writing. The document should explain why performance was unsatisfactory, suggest how to improve, and outline the consequences of failing to improve. For nonprobationary workers, the disciplinary time period for improvement may vary from 30 days for a poor performer's work, to 60 days for an underachieving sales person, or up to 90 days for a tardiness or absenteeism problem.

The employee must be given an opportunity to respond verbally and in writing. The same type of document is used for any employee making a similar infraction to ensure consistency of discipline. If one employee received a reprimand or discipline for a particular infraction, all employees making the same infraction should receive the same discipline.

Falcone (1997) suggested using a step system of due process to discipline employees. The purpose of progressive discipline is to rehabilitate, so employees and employers need a system fair to all. Here are the steps to follow:

Step 1. Clearly state the problem in writing and explain how and why the employee's conduct or performance damaged the company.

Step 2. State a clear and unambiguous warning that failure to improve will result in discipline, up to and including termination.

Step 3. Through progressive written disciplinary actions, demonstrate that the employee's performance did not improve despite repeated written and verbal warnings.

Step 4. Demonstrate that any worker would expect to be fired under similar circumstances because discipline was meted out in a fair and consistent way.

Thus, a wrongful termination lawsuit may be avoided by demonstrating in writing that consistent, predictable steps were taken within the organization to rehabilitate an employee. When an employee is disciplined, discuss the unsatisfactory performance in private and provide a written warning. Place a warning copy in the employee's personnel file and give one to a union representative, if appropriate. Only other employees who need to know about the warning, like an immediate supervisor, should be informed and directed to keep it confidential. That way, the employee's privacy is protected and the company does not risk defamation charges.

Falcone (1997) provided examples of how to write up progressive disciplinary actions, in this case for excessive tardiness.

On April 2, 1998, you had your third instance of tardiness during the previous 2-month period when you arrived 45 minutes late to work. This written warning is to notify you that continued tardiness could result in disciplinary action, and ultimately, termination of your job. You are now being placed in a 90-day disciplinary period during which you must arrive at work on time, or further disciplinary actions, possibly resulting in termination, will occur. This 90-day disciplinary period begins today, April 3, 1998. If you are tardy two more times, you will be given a final written warning before termination.

On May 2, you had your fifth instance of tardiness overall, and your second instance of tardiness since your 90-day tardiness disciplinary period went into effect on April 3, 1998. You arrived 20 minutes late to work. You were given a written warning for your third incident. This notice is to be considered your final written warning for tardiness. If you are late for work again, you will be dismissed.

On May 23, 1998, you had your sixth instance of tardiness in a 3-month period when you arrived 30 minutes late to work. You were given a written warning for your third incident and a final written warning for your fifth incident. It is clear that you have not taken your former warnings seriously. We are waiving our right to dismiss you. If you have one additional incidence of unexcused tardiness in the next 90 days, you will be dismissed from work. If you successfully complete the 90-day disciplinary period, your tardiness and attendance record will continue to be monitored closely. Any further violations will be dealt with seriously and could be grounds for dismissal.

Although it is difficult to fire someone without due process, on-the-spot firings are appropriate for employees who break the law, engage in illegal conduct, endanger other employees, or are insubordinate, negligent, intoxicated, or use illegal substances on company property. If there is any doubt, a manager can suspend an employee until an investigation of the conduct is completed. This allows time to speak to an attorney versed in labor law. Previous disciplinary actions may also be examined to ensure disciplinary actions are fair.

Whether or not a firm uses a termination review process, all managers can ask themselves the following questions to ensure that a termination is fair (Baxter, 1983b). What is the employee's overall record? Are there any mitigating factors that might explain or excuse the employee's misconduct or unsatisfactory performance? Are any statutory problems involved (e.g., regarding race, age, gender, etc.)? Were any job security representations made to the employee? If yes, is the termination consistent with those representations? Are there any public policy concerns? Has the employee received progressive discipline? Is the termination justified? Does it fit the offense?

Employers also need to be conscious of how they fire employees and consider ways to minimize the employee's frustration, anger, and embarrassment. Employees should be told privately and as candidly as possible why they are being fired. The supervisor should do so firmly, yet compassionately, without being apologetic. An apologetic demeanor suggests guilty feelings exist and implies wrongdoing to the fired employee. Employers should limit the amount of information provided to prospective employers calling for reference checks on fired employees. Only the fact and dates of employment and the positions held should be provided. Avoid providing negative information, as the former employee may sue if such information is publicized (Baxter, 1983a, 1983b).

Contracts and Agreements

Managers should establish written procedures for dealing with all sorts of potential legal problems, not just progressive discipline and termination. Instruct employees to document their dealings with interviewees, news sources, business contacts, advertisers, and freelance writers, photographers, and artists. That way, a written record exists if any problems arise later.

Managers and their legal counsel should review important transactions to identify which potential pitfalls should be explained in clauses. Then, clauses spelling out details of possible concern can be included in all contracts. For example, agreements with freelancers should be in writing and signed by both parties. Fees and expenses should be included, as well as what the work's appropriate subject matter is and what its finished form should be (Rauch, 1991).

Due to recent court cases, newspaper managers should ensure that contracts for carriers include appropriate language. For example, if publishers do not wish to provide benefits to carriers, contracts must include language specifically stating that no benefits are provided. Contracts should also state that the plan administrator has the discretion to decide who is entitled to benefits. Contracts might also include an express waiver of benefits (Truitt, 1997a). All types of media firms should spell out all benefits, expectations, agreements, and rights in all contracts.

Documentation of communications with persons outside of the organization is recommended too. Media organizations should establish procedures for dealing with complaints. Irate advertisers, public or private persons who are the subject of stories, readers, listeners, and/or viewers contact such companies regularly.

Employees should be trained to treat all complaints seriously. Employees should be as polite and conciliatory as possible, even if they believe the complaint is baseless because courteous treatment often defuses a situation. Train employees to tell a telephone complainant that they are writing down the facts for internal investigation and then do so, without admitting anything, interrupting, or passing blame. All employees should bring complaints to the appropriate supervisor's attention immediately, to ensure complaints are dealt with consistently. This also prevents a defensive employee from complicating the situation. The supervisor should determine whether the complaint has merit and then send a letter to the complainant, that day, that confirms the call, provides an explanation, proposes a solution, or provides a deadline by which the complainant will be contacted. The same general procedure can be used for written complaints.

Different rules apply in the event of a serious complaint, when a lawsuit is threatened, and when the complainant is an attorney. Instruct employees not to admit anything and immediately refer the matter to top management, along with all available documentation. Top management must then contact an attorney before responding and allow the attorney to handle the problem, when necessary. In any event, employees must feel comfortable about reporting complaints to supervisors, especially complaints caused by employee error or misconduct. If a retraction or letter of apology is needed, an attorney must review it before dissemination. A retraction could repeat the offense and be viewed as an admission of wrongdoing (Rauch, 1991).

Finally, media organizations should publicize their policies internally and have training sessions regarding appropriate procedures and behavior. Never assume that employees have the judgment and experience to deal with legal and ethical dilemmas; even experienced employees can make mistakes. The best way to prevent legal and ethical problems is to anticipate and prepare for them. The media provide information to the public; such organizations must never forget the legal and ethical responsibilities that accompany this role.

GENERAL AREAS OF LEGAL CONCERN

Discrimination

Despite the recent revisiting of affirmative action, discrimination actions continue in corporate America. Actions involving Texaco, Avis Rent-A-Car, Circuit City, and Morgan Stanley have made headlines. Media organizations that cover such cases would appear hypocritical if they engaged in discrimination themselves.

Title VII of the amended Civil Rights Act of 1964 proscribes employment discrimination (or treating an employee unfairly or unfavorably) on the basis of race, religion, gender, or national origin. Prohibited actions include refusing to hire employees based on race or gender, providing unequal conditions of employment, and providing unequal pay for the same job (Lacy & Simon, 1992).

Future media managers must expect to deal with equity issues in an era of legal uncertainty. The results of a poll conducted by the Asian American Journalists Association (AAJA) reveals that 53 percent of Asian-American journalists say equal opportunities for advancement within their organizations do not exist (Terry, 1997a).

Managers can review the American Arbitration Association (AAA; a not-for-profit arbitration group) publication called Resolving Employment Disputes: A Practical Guide, which offers advice on how to design an employee dispute resolution plan for employee handbooks and personnel manuals. A dispute resolution plan could be used to settle sexual harassment and discrimination claims based on age, gender, religion, race, or disability (or wrongful termination, as discussed earlier). The AAA's home page (http://www.adr.org) includes several guides for resolving disputes.

Another discrimination issue media managers may face is whether to extend benefits to employees' same-sex partners. Domestic partners of gay male or lesbian employees must be adequately defined to qualify for benefits. For example, *The Miami Herald's* policy defines same-sex domestic partners as those of the same gender who "share a mutually exclusive, enduring relationship which is intended to be permanent and live in the same residence" (M. Fitzgerald, 1997, pp. 15–16). The National Lesbian and Gay Journalists Association (http://www/NLgja.org) surveyed firms that offer such benefits and developed a booklet entitled "Domestic Partner Benefits: A Trend Towards Fairness." The booklet encourages firms to offer such benefits and provides strategies for establishing them ("Report On Benefits," 1997).

Employee Health and Safety

Employment health and safety are other important management concerns that change often. One recent concern has been establishing and implementing drug-testing policies fairly, primarily because a lack of adequate preemployment screening for drug use and other factors could open up a media firm to liability charges. Firms must avoid hiring employees who may harm or endanger others on the job.

The New York Times Regional Newspaper Group has a drug-and-alcohol free workplace program demonstrating how such policies might be set up. Prospective employees are required to take a urinalysis drug test. Pending completion of the test, applicants accepted for a job must sign forms stating they understand the policy and allow the company to perform the urinalysis and a blood test. The blood test consent is filed and used only when medical treatment is needed for a work-related accident possibly involving the use of drugs or alcohol. Employees hired before the drug policy's implementation sign consent forms allowing the company to test them if job-related accidents occur (Terry, 1997b).

To avoid lawsuits, tests are completed at a federally certified lab that meets stringent guidelines. Chain-of-custody forms identifying the specimen and donor by number are completed to ensure the testing procedure's confidentiality and integrity. The chain-of-custody form, as well as the blood and urinalysis consent forms, are kept on file until a job-related accident occurs or a worker's compensation claim is filed. Employees who refuse to complete forms are notified that refusal is grounds for termination (Terry, 1997b).

Employers can take steps to minimize the likelihood of drug-testing suits. If an applicant tests positive, conduct another, more sophisticated test as a check and give the applicant a chance to explain the result. Sometimes a medical statement can clear up a potential misunderstanding over a positive test. Employees who test positive should be referred to only licensed treatment centers and sign releases so information may be shared with appropriate parties like insurance companies (Berger, 1990).

Managers should require employees to sign a reentry agreement, covering a specific period such as 2 years, after completing treatment. Other suggested provisions include requiring the employee to: abstain from mood-altering drugs or alcohol; agree to random drug testing; agree to continue in follow-up treatment for a specified time; agree to submit a record of all such meetings attended for the employer to verify; and agree that the aftercare treatment is the employee's and/or insurance company's expense (Berger, 1990).

Managers face a much larger variety of health and safety concerns on the job than discussed here. For example, managers must consider how to deal with employee concerns about tobacco or smoke-free work environments, AIDS, and other health problems. The importance of keeping up with regulations (such as the Americans with Disabilities Act) in the trade press and consulting with the appropriate legal expert for advice cannot be overemphasized.

Business Recovery, Disaster, or Crisis Plans

Business recovery, disaster, or crisis plans are developed to ensure employees know how to respond in case of a technical problem, natural disaster, sabotage, crime, or an environmental incident. Although loss of market share, possible harm to public image or credibility, and excessive down-time are concerns, legal and regulatory compliance issues are a primary reason for developing a business recovery plan. Although a disaster plan may not be followed exactly in a real-life situation, it focuses employees' efforts because all know what goals are and what each should do (Gyles, 1997).

A sudden crisis disrupts company operations without warning and is likely to generate news coverage, which may adversely affect employees, offices, revenues, business assets, or the company's reputation. Examples of sudden crises include accidents resulting in significant property damage to company facilities, a natural disaster that disrupts operations or endangers employees, unexpected job actions or labor disruptions, and workplace violence (Irvine, 1997).

A smoldering crisis is a serious business problem that is generally unknown without or within the company that could generate negative publicity when revealed and could result in fines, penalties, legal awards, or other unbudgeted expenses over a certain amount (e.g., $250,000). Examples of smoldering crises include customer allegations of improper conduct, action by a disgruntled employee like serious threats or whistle-blowing, or disclosure of serious internal company problems to employees, investors, or customers (Irvine, 1997).

A crisis plan should clearly identify the types of situations in which the plans are in effect. Media outlets in areas where natural disasters like hurricanes, tornadoes, or floods often hit are especially advised to develop such plans. Emergency management and operations groups should be identified so employees know who is expected to try to come to work and when. Disaster preparedness guides should be developed explaining to employees production or broadcast details such as a list of emergency organizations and agencies, the number of editions to run, whether to print color or black-and-white, and departmental checklists ("Bad Weather," 1997).

The *St. Petersburg Times*, located in a hurricane-prone area, developed a color-coding system identifying certain employee groups who should report to work in an emergency. For example, red and blue teams of production, circulation, and news employees must report to work if the paper expects to produce emergency editions. Yellow and green teams include other employees who report after the storm passes to relieve red and blue team members. Members of each team receive a card identifying their color codes and telephone numbers to call in the event of a disaster situation ("Bad Weather," 1997).

Gyles (1997) suggested an outline for developing a disaster plan including:

- identifying sudden and smoldering crises that are likely to or may occur;
- evaluating critical individuals and departments and identifying those essential for maintaining operations in a crisis situation;
- determining in-house expertise;
- determining critical in-house software and equipment;
- deciding whether and when to use outside consultants (e.g., to aid with a smoldering crisis);
- determining the availability of or purchasing appropriate backup software and/or equipment;
- and establishing a contingency budget and example schedule for the major types of crises.

By planning ahead, media outlets can minimize the occurrence of employee injury and provide coverage to warn local residents of impending danger ("Bad Weather," 1997).

Telecommunications Act of 1996

An example of the changing nature of media regulation is the passage of the Telecommunications Act of 1996. The Act radically changed the broadcast, cable and telephony industries. The major provisions of the Act include: (a) eliminating the 12-station cap on station ownership and raising the TV station ownership coverage limit to 35 % of U.S.homes; (b) eliminating the national radio ownership limits by establishing numerical limits based on market size (the larger the market, the more stations one company may own within it); (c) extending radio and TV license terms to 8 years and streamlining the license renewal process; (d) deregulating cable rates; (e) barring telephone companies from buying cable systems, or vice versa, except in certain limited conditions; (f) repealing the statutory ban against telephone companies providing video programming in their own service areas, with certain requirements; (g) preempting state and local regulations barring cable operators and others from providing local telephone services; and (h) increasing fines for broadcast or cable obscenity from $10,000 to $100,000 (Stern, 1996; Tip, 1996).

Yet by 1997, The Communications Decency Act of 1996, a provision of the Telecommunications Act, was struck down in a Supreme Court ruling. The Act imposed criminal penalties for transmitting indecent or patently offensive material over computer networks to minors. The Society of Professional Journalists opposed it, stating:

> The original law could have made it illegal for reporters to cover stories such as female mutilation in Africa, war atrocities in Bosnia, human rights violations in China and other developments that some might view as offensive. Even medical and science stories could have been subject to the law, depending on interpretation of the law's language (Childs, 1997, p. 3).

In striking down the Act, the Supreme Court accepted a lower court's finding that the Internet's availability and the difficulty of determining its audience's age made it like books or newspapers that deserve the First Amendment's highest level of protection. The court rejected the government's assertion that Internet regulation was justified by its interest in protecting children, which does not justify an unnecessarily broad suppression of adult speech (Mauro, 1997).

Antitrust

Antitrust is another major legal area of interest to media managers. The Supreme Court affirmed in *Associated Press v. United States* (1945) that antitrust laws apply to the media. The Newspaper Preservation Act (NPA) of 1970 gives certain daily newspapers a limited exemption from antitrust laws. Two newspapers within a market may form a joint operating agreement (JOA) when one is in probable danger of financial failure. Under a JOA, the newspapers' advertising, circulation, production, and administrative departments are merged, whereas their editorial departments are kept separate. Proposed JOAs must be approved by the US Attorney General, although administrative hearings often are held before a decision is made. Readers interested in additional information on antitrust, the NPA, and JOAs might read Gillmor, Barron, & Simon (1998) and Lacy and Simon (1992).

A recent antitrust case underscores how rules regarding the practices of media firms can change overnight. In a November 1997 case with implications for newspapers, the US Supreme Court overturned its rule barring manufacturers from fixing the maximum price at which independent dealers and distributors can sell goods to consumers. Newspaper publishers may now establish a maximum price at which independent distributors sell newspapers to the public without automatically violating federal antitrust laws ("Supreme Court," 1997).

In future antitrust maximum pricing cases, plaintiffs will have to prove that the maximum pricing has an anticompetitive effect. Maximum resale pricing should be evaluated using the rule of reason under which a fact finder decides whether the questioned practice imposes an unreasonable competitive restraint. Various factors are taken into account including the relevant business' condition before and after the restraint was imposed, as well as the nature, history, and effect of the restraint. Publishers should seek an antitrust attorney's advice before making any pricing decisions or changes based on this case ("Supreme Court," 1997).

Libel Issues

Libel is an ongoing concern with media managers. For example, a libel award against *The Wall Street Journal* was originally $227 million, but was reduced to $22.7 million in compensatory damages in May 1997 ("For the Record," 1997; Stein, 1997a). And Richard Jewell, identified as a bombing suspect in the 1996 Centennial Olympic Park bombing in Atlanta, reached a $500,000 settlement with NBC over comments an anchorman made on the air after the bombing. He also settled with *Time* with no payment (*Time*, 1997) and CNN for an undisclosed amount. Jewel has libel suits pending against the *Atlanta Journal and Constitution, New York Post* and Disney's WABC-AM ("N.Y. Post," 1997; *Time*, 1997). Obviously, media managers must ensure that safeguards are in place to minimize the chances of a libel action, and cover situations and individuals fairly given these high stakes.

Carter, Dee, Gaynes, and Zuckman (1994) said that the "essential elements common to both libel and slander actions are 1) the making by the defendant of a defamatory statement; 2) the publication to at least one other than the plaintiff of that statement; and 3) the identification in some way of the plaintiff as the person defamed" (p. 46). The *AP Stylebook* (Goldstein, 1996) defines libel as injury to reputation. Libelous words, pictures, or cartoons are those that expose a person to public shame, ridicule, disgust, hatred, or create an ill opinion of a person.

The only complete and unconditional defense to a civil action for libel is that the facts stated are provably true. A second defense is privilege, either absolute or qualified. For a more detailed explanation of libel, its defenses, and who constitute public figures, consult Gillmor, Barron, and Simon 1998, or the most recent *AP Stylebook* (Goldstein, 1996) or *AP Broadcast News Handbook.*

The major causes of libel suits are "carelessness, misunderstanding of the law of libel, limitations of the defense of privilege (including the First Amendment privilege) and the extent to which developments may be reported in arrests" (Goldstein, 1996). Surprisingly, many libel suits result from fact errors in minor stories, court and police news, birth notices, and engagements (Goldstein, 1996).

At least one newsroom editor or manager must be knowledgeable about state and federal libel developments. Advise reporters and editors when they research and write stories that the plaintiff in a libel case, "has the right to try to prove the press was reckless or even knew that what it was publishing was a lie" (Goldstein, 1996, p. 288). Instruct employees to keep careful notes and memos, obtain more than one source for potentially libelous accusations, obtain supporting documents for controversial statements, and obtain the appropriate court documents (such as complaints, cease-and-desist orders, and judgments) when allegations are made. These materials are to be kept in files demonstrating the care taken to ensure stories are accurate. Potentially libelous stories should be reviewed by a legal expert before publication (Gillmor, Barron, & Simon, 1998; Rauch, 1991).

Any postpublication contact with a person claiming to be libeled should be handled carefully, as the response is an important factor in a decision to sue. Judges and potential jurors in a libel-related survey described journalists as irresponsible, lacking decency/courtesy/ethics, invaders of privacy, and arrogant (Dillon, 1997). Journalists should consider how the average person will react when weighing the use of hidden cameras or other potentially controversial news gathering techniques. And editors might consider whether other techniques could be used that would not open a media outlet to libel (Stein, 1997a).

The ABC/Food Lion Case, where a *Prime Time Live* story reporting that Food Lion sold spoiled meat products and encouraged employees to work unpaid overtime, was a suit based on secretive news gathering techniques, not libel as sometimes reported. Although Food Lion's actual damages were assessed at $1,402, the jury awarded the company $5.5 million, which was later reduced to $315,000. The large punitive jury award may have occurred because ABC employees appeared arrogant (Andron, 1997b). Some journalists reported the case as a libel suit, based on releases from Food Lion's lawyers. One juror who favored a high punitive award said, "The people who wrote the articles I have read did not understand the case" (Andron, 1997a, p. 16). The ABC/Food Lion case underscores how important it is for managers, editors, and journalists to conduct themselves with the utmost professionalism.

However, media managers must avoid self-censorship that does not serve the public. Lawyers may evaluate how much a lawsuit would cost rather than whether it could succeed. Small papers, and presumably other small media organizations, have become especially careful about what they publish for fear of surviving a costly libel battle (Garneau, 1991a, 1991b). Although prudence and care always make good sense, a manager must always consider whether the potential suit is meant to intimidate and whether the public interest would be served by publication or broadcast (America, 1991).

Privacy

The right of privacy encompasses "the right to be let alone" or to live one's private life free from publicity (Keeton, 1984). Privacy entitles an individual to prevent the use of, or interference with, personal and intimate aspects of life. Such invasions presumably have a negative effect on a person's psychological well being (Gillmor, Barron, & Simon, 1998).

Journalists may read more about privacy in the most recent *AP Broadcast News Handbook* and *AP Stylebook and Libel Manual* (Goldstein, 1996), which states that once an individual is voluntarily or involuntarily involved in a news event, the right to privacy is forfeited. A journalist should be protected when writing about an individual involved in a matter of legitimate public interest, even if it is not a bona fide spot news event. But publication of a story or picture that "dredges up the sordid details of a person's past and has no current newsworthiness" may not be protected (Goldstein, 1996, p. 290).

The increasing use of computerized records and Internet access appears likely to intensify the conflict between open access to records and individual privacy. Ten years ago, in developing a story to explain why three children were run over by school bus drivers, a *Providence Journal* reporter compared the roster of school bus drivers with Rhode Island state driver's license and criminal records. The results revealed that some had bad driving records and drug convictions, which led to stronger requirements for bus driver background checks. Today, because of the federal Driver's Privacy Protection Act of 1994, drivers in Rhode Island can choose to close their records to the public and news media. The same story could not be done as effectively now (Sullivan & Goldberg, 1997).

The Driver's Privacy Protection Act "closes personal information records including names, addresses, telephone numbers, Social Security numbers, photographs, driver identification numbers and medical or disability information" (Schumacher, 1997, p. 23). Media groups have two options to mitigate the Act: (a) states can pass opt-out laws allowing consumers the option of keeping personal information confidential, making some but not all records open, or (b) media exemptions established by law or administrative rule allowing journalists continued access to personal information. Managers need to discover whether either option has been pursued in their states, and if not, which action is appropriate to take. Thus far, opt-out laws have been the prevalent choice because national press groups have traditionally opposed special treatment for the news media (Schumacher, 1997).

Firms are also feeling the public backlash regarding privacy. America Online (AOL) had to cancel a plan to sell subscriber phone numbers for telemarketing. Lexis-Nexis changed its Internet-based people finder P-TRAK due to vehement public objection to the display of Social Security numbers. Privacy advocates also cite concerns with aggressive marketers annoying consumers, identity theft, and stalkers and radicals gaining access to information through new technologies (Sullivan & Goldberg, 1997).

Poll results document the level of public concern over privacy. According to a Pew Research Center For The People & The Press poll conducted in February 1997, 64% of U.S. adults believe TV news programs invade personal privacy unnecessarily, whereas 57% believe newspapers do the same. In a 1996 Louis Harris/Center for Media and Public Affairs poll, 80% of respondents said the news media often invade people's privacy (Sullivan & Goldberg, 1997).

Protecting privacy takes on special concerns for marketers or others targeting children on the Internet. The Council of Better Business Bureau's Children's Advertising Review Unit (CARU) developed self-regulatory guidelines for marketers to children (which are available at http://www.bbb.org). Online advertisers should make reasonable efforts to ensure that the person paying for the child's online transaction controls it, either by written consent or the ability to cancel an order. Advertisers should have children ask their parents for permission to answer questions, discourage them from using their full names on the Net, and tell them to get their parent's permission before giving out their e-mail addresses to anyone (N. Fitzgerald, 1997). A publication or broadcast station can apply these same principles when adding a children's section to its home page.

As with libel, some journalists believe that the press has not explained its legitimate need for access sufficiently. Journalists must help the public understand why access to government is an issue the public should be concerned with, not just journalists.

Free Press/Fair Trial Issues

Managers and journalists must begin to carefully consider how to publicize the importance of free press/fair trial issues and cover high-profile trials professionally to avoid damaging the image of the profession further. Public and judicial perceptions of the media after the highly-publicized O. J. Simpson and Timothy McVeigh trials suggest,

> "... the news media will be better off saving its litigation energies for technical strikes where the law already is essentially on its side or choosing very carefully when to push the law in unresolved areas, such as access to documents. Today's climate does not seem likely to produce any broad new rights for the coverage of criminal trials." (Brown, 1997, p. 13).

Because of the perceived success of the Timothy McVeigh/ Oklahoma City Bombing trial (e.g., no major delays or disasters), journalists can expect that other judges will copy presiding Judge Richard Matsch's tactics. Matsch took numerous measures to ensure the jurors's privacy and protect the defendant's rights. He " ... issued gag orders limiting press contact for lawyers in the case, denied McVeigh's request to give on-camera interviews, withheld personal information about jurors, and even ordered the construction of a wall in his courtroom between the jury box and the gallery" (Brown, 1997, p. 12). The case may establish a perception in the judicial community that, "secrecy and security should trump openness and access" in high-profile cases (Brown, 1997, p. 13).

Access to Government Information

Media organizations may obtain government information using The Freedom of Information Act, which established a process for requesting information from federal agencies. The Act allows citizens to request any records from the federal executive branch, but does not cover Congress, the federal courts, or state or local governments. Records include documents, papers, letters, reports, films, photographs, audio recordings, and computer tapes (Goldstein, 1996). Managers and employees should be familiar with state laws concerning access. (See Regulatory and and Self-Regulatory Online Resources for Managers for online resources regarding access.)

Copyright

Media managers can expect to deal with copyright protection, which extends to almost anything authored, created, performed, or produced in a tangible or permanent way (Gillmor, Barron, & Simon, 1998). Electronic publishing is a new area of copyright concern. A federal judge recently ruled that newspapers and electronic publishers did not improperly exploit the work of freelance writers by publishing electronic versions of their articles on the Internet. Yet managers must be sure to specify which media are covered in all copyright contracts. Some publications offer additional pay for using articles online (Truitt, 1997b).

Unless a newspaper or firm has a written agreement to the contrary, freelancers retain the copyrights to their works. For example, if a freelance article or photograph about tomatoes is printed without a written agreement by a newspaper and then displayed on its web site or the Nexis database, the use is allowed.

> But if the Webmaster were "to feature, separate from the archive, a special tomato button linking browsers to electronic resources on tomatoes, one of which happened to be the freelancer's article," the use would not be protected. So, managers should obtain written agreements from all freelancers which give the company all rights to their work (Stein, 1997b, p. 24).

Media firms that use or set up web sites for themselves or clients must consider several copyright and publishing liability issues. Unless protected by fair use, uploading and downloading copyrighted works without authorization is an infringement of the copyright holder's rights. Under fair use, portions of copyrighted materials may be copied, but only if it does not undercut the copyright holder's ability to profit. Establish copyright ownership by having all web design firms or employees who worked on the site sign contracts ensuring a complete and perpetual assignment of copyright ownership to the firm. Under the work-for-hire doctrine, web or other materials developed by an employee within the scope of employment belongs to the employer. Typically, a transfer or assignment of rights to the firm lasts for the duration of the copyright (e.g., the creator's lifetime plus 50 years; English, 1997).

Before including preexisting material on a web site, determine what rights the authors may have been granted. For example, if an advertising agency's nonprofit client wanted to post past issues of a newsletter on the web, the agency must determine who wrote the articles. If articles were always written by employees, the nonprofit organization should own the copyright. However, if volunteers wrote articles, because the volunteer gave the right to publish originally does not mean that such a right grants permission to put that same article online (English, 1997).

Before uploading preexisting material, the original written contract should be reviewed to see what the parties intended at the time. Vague contract language that does not clearly delineate future uses will not be considered a grant of rights. Contract language that clearly states that the work can be published in, "technologies now known or hereinafter invented" covers all future uses (English, 1997, p. 94).

Online copyright infringement liability is determined without regard for the intent of the infringer. Anyone who infringes the rights of the copyright holder without authorization is liable, although, "innocent" infringements allow a reduction in damages. A distinction is usually made between a "publisher" and "distributor" when determining liability, unless the distributor knew that the distributed material was illegal or libelous. Thus, management should evaluate a firm's level of involvement in reviewing, editing and passing along website material to determine its liability for online publications on its site (English, 1997).

Deception in Advertising

Advertising managers, publishers, broadcast sales managers, and general managers may need to clear or review an ad to determine whether it is deceptive or appropriate to broadcast or print. Sections 5 and 12 of the Federal Trade Commission Act of 1914 give the Federal Trade Commission (FTC) the power to regulate deceptive advertising and other unfair acts or practices. If an advertiser is injured by a competitor's misleading ad, it may sue under Section 43(1) of The Lanham Act, which provides protection for trademarks. Deception under the Lanham Act is defined as any false or misleading description or representation of fact (Gillmor, Barron, & Simon, 1998; Preston, 1994, 1996).

The current FTC deception definition is composed of three elements: (a) There must be a representation, omission or practice that is likely to mislead the consumer; (b) the representation, omission or practice is examined from the perspective of a consumer acting reasonably in the circumstances, to the consumer's detriment; and (c) the representation, omission or practice must be a material one (Policy Statement on Deception, 1983). Richards (1990) noted that "regulable deceptiveness results only if purchase behavior of a substantial number of people is likely to be affected" (p. 24).

Practices found deceptive include false verbal or written statements, misleading price claims, selling dangerous or defective products without adequate disclosures, not delivering promised services, and failing to meet warranty obligations. Although all claims made in an ad are technically true, if the general impression of the ad is false, it still may be deceptive. That is because the FTC considers whether the entire ad is likely to mislead consumers acting reasonably; it is not necessary for the ad actually to deceive. Nor is it necessary to prove that the advertiser intended the deception (Policy Statement on Deception, 1983; Preston, 1994).

The FTC stated that certain practices are not likely to deceive reasonable consumers, such as misrepresentations regarding inexpensive products that are evaluated easily and purchased frequently by consumers. Such advertisers are less likely to deceive consumers intentionally because they depend on repeat sales for survival. And as long as consumers understand the sources and limitations of such ads, the FTC usually does not pursue cases based on correctly stated and honestly held opinions about a product, or puffery, which is obvious exaggerations about the product or its qualities (e.g., the best or greatest; Policy Statement on Deception, 1983; Preston, 1996–see this source for more information on puffery).

SELF-REGULATION OF AND BY MEDIA COMPANIES

Many media outlets, advertisers, and advertising agencies screen ads before airing or publication to ensure that they are not deceptive nor offensive. Media managers should take clearance and other legal and ethical concerns seriously for both moral and professional reasons. An industry that provides information to society bears a special responsibility to assure its accuracy and fairness. A responsible manager turns the gaze of honest, critical scrutiny to one's own organization or medium because employees look to managers for behavioral cues.

Each media profession develops codes and standards of behavior to help guide ethical behavior. Many questionable practices are not technically illegal; they are simply "wrong" by generally accepted moral standards. (See the next section for Internet resources including online access to certain self-regulatory codes.). Codes of conduct and self-regulatory bodies are useful to managers seeking advice on fair and ethical conduct.

However, critics argue that codes are developed to prevent government regulation. Critics assert industry members are not critical enough of their colleagues and often have ethical standards that are different than the public they are supposed to serve. (Recall how public and industry opinions varied regarding libel and free press/fair trial issues.) Critics also complain that ethical violations typically result in a minor "slap on the wrist"; thus, such codes and bodies do not represent a meaningful front against unethical behavior. Finally, critics assert that if self-regulatory codes were truly effective, would the public have such negative opinions about media firms and their practices?

REGULATORY AND SELF-REGULATORY ONLINE RESOURCES FOR MANAGERS

Major federal agencies are located on the web, with most accessible at The Federal Web Locator (at http://www.law.vill.edu/fed-agency/fedwebloc. html). The U.S. House of Representatives Internet Law Library (at http://law.house.gov/1.htm) provides access to U.S. federal and state laws, as well as some international laws and treaties. For example, for a selected listing of laws and articles regarding privacy and information access go to http://law.house.gov/107.htm.

The Society of Professional Journalists home page (http://www.spj.org) contains a variety of helpful information for media managers. Its FOIA Resource Center link (http://www.spj.org/foia/index.htm) helps journalists and nonjournalists in obtaining information from federal and local governments. Articles and other information regarding access to government documents are included in the online FOI Resource Center.

Editor & Publisher's (E&P) home page (http://www.mediainfo.com/ ephome/index/unihtm/home.htm) sometimes includes articles regarding legal or regulatory issues and an E&P Forum to discuss them. The Newspaper Association of America's (NAA) home page (http://www.naa.org) allows you to access *Presstime* and *TechNews* online, as well as review the NAA's diversity and public policy activities. The public policy link includes information on employee relations, government affairs, legal affairs, and postal affairs, as well as links to the White House, Congress, and Federal Government.

The Radio-Television News Director's Association (http://www.rtnda.org) publishes its Code of Ethics online (http://www.rtnda.org/ethics.html). The Code states that the "responsibility of radio and television journalists is to gather and report information of importance and interest to the public accurately, honestly and impartially." The National Association of Broadcasters home page (http://www.nab.org) includes links regarding current issues, government, legal and regulatory affairs, and TV parental guidelines.

Advertising managers seeking advice regarding deceptive advertising or legal ways to advertise have a variety of Internet resources available. FTC's home page (http://www.ftc.gov) provides information about the FTC in general as well as news releases discussing recent advertising deception cases, consumer and business publications providing guidelines on how to advertise various products and services, and guides for using techniques like telemarketing and 900-numbers. For example, FTC information regarding Infomercials may be found at http://www.ftc.gov/bcp/conline/pubs/products/info.htm. The FTC Bureau of Consumer Protection's Division of Advertising Practices lists its law enforcement objectives, alerting advertisers to the types of advertising, products, or techniques on which it focuses, including infomercials (http://www.ftc.gov/bcp/bcpap.htm).

The Consumer Product Safety Commission's (CPSC) home page (http://www.cpsc.gov) provides information about product safety and recalls. The CPSC Kid's Page (http://www.cpsc.gov/kids/kids.html), which includes tips about playing safely and being a better baby-sitter, provides a good example of a public service home page for children. Managers who wish to communicate with children online might review this page and its contents.

The Council of Better Business Bureau's (BBB) home page (http://www.bbb.org) provides information on how to advertise legally and ethically for local and national advertisers and agencies. By surfing the BBB's advertising review programs pages, one can keep up to date with its national advertising self-regulatory bodies, the National Advertising Division (NAD) and the National Advertising Review Board (NARB). The NAD investigates the truthfulness and accuracy of national advertising. The NARB is the appeals board for advertisers or challengers who disagree with NAD decisions. For local advertisers and others, the BBB's advertising guidelines provide a guide for advertisers and agencies to use when questions arise as to whether an ad claim or technique is ethical.

The Children's Advertising Review Unit (CARU) of the BBB reviews advertising directed to children under 12 years of age and publishes its CARU Self-Regulatory Guidelines for Children's Advertising online (http://www.bbb.org/advertising/caruguid.html). These guidelines provide advice on advertising ethically and accurately to children.

The American Advertising Federation's home page (http://www.aaf.org) provides commentary on recent court cases involving commercial speech. The American Association of Advertising Agencies (AAAA; http://www.aaaa.org) offers information about government activities affecting advertising at their Washington-on-demand page at http://www.commercepark.com/AAAA/washington/washington.html. The AAAA has developed a Creative Code, Agency Service Standards, and Standards of Practice to guide advertisers and agencies. The Public Relations Society of America publishes its Code of Professional Standards for the practice of PublicRelations online at http://www.prsa.org/profstd.html.

The Direct Marketing Association (DMA; http://www.the-dma.org) provides ethical guidelines for direct marketers, including DMA's Marketing Online Privacy Principles and Guidance. Essentially the guidelines cover: online notice and opt out, unsolicited marketing, e-mail, and online data collection from or about children. All marketers operating online sites should make their information practices available to consumers in a prominent place, and should allow consumers an opportunity to prohibit the disclosure of any personal information collected by a marketer. When making decisions on whether to communicate with or collect data from children online, marketers should consider the targeted child's age, knowledge, sophistication, and maturity. The permission of parents or guardians must always be obtained before a sale or collection of data.

SUMMARY

Media law and regulation is obviously very complex. The reader is reminded that media law involves much more than what was discussed in this chapter. Prudent media managers should review the sources cited in this chapter as well as other appropriate sources and counsel to keep abreast of the ever-changing laws, ethical standards, and professional and ethical issues affecting media firms.

CASE 6.1

Developing A Performance Evaluation System

Depending on your interests, contact a newspaper, magazine, radio station, television station, cable channel or system, advertising agency, or public relations firm. Ask to review their performance evaluation system, or develop a system for them. Start out by asking for a copy of the company's overall mission, as well as mission statements developed by the individual departments. (You could choose to develop a performance evaluation system for one department or division, if desired.) If available, review the appropriate performance evaluations forms to see if they are consistent with the firm's mission statement(s).

Next, interview a few employees in various positions regarding the performance evaluation system. See if they know what the major evaluation criteria are and when evaluations occur. You might also ask whether and how the evaluation system could be improved.

ASSIGNMENT

After completing the interviews, generate a list of appropriate criteria to measure performance for a minimum of two different positions that are supervised by a particular manager. Write or revise a performance evaluation for these positions. Then, ask the supervisor to review your evaluations and provide feedback. Revise the evaluations based on the supervisor's comments. Include answers to the following questions.

1. Was the performance evaluations system communicated to and understood well by employees? Why or why not?
2. Was the performance evaluation system used by the company changed? Why were these changes made? Or, if you made no changes, explain why.
3. What have you learned from developing or revising a performance evaluation system?
4. How will completing this assignment make you a better manager in the future?

CASE 6.2

The Case of the Poorly Performing Salesperson

Elaine Miller, sales manager at WCTV, was considering how to handle a problem with one of her salespersons, Rick Folsom. Elaine had been promoted to sales manager 3 months ago, after working at WCTV for 2 years. She earned her promotion by exceeding sales goals every month after her first on the job. She developed a research report using secondary data like *MRI* and the *SRDS Lifestyle Market Analyst*, to analyze the market. Her former boss praised the report, gave a copy to all salespersons, and included a summary of it in the rate card. When her former boss left for a new job in a larger market, he had recommended Elaine as his replacement.

Rick had been a salesperson at WCTV for 2 years. For over a year and a half, his sales performance had been average to slightly above average. However, for the past 6 months, he had not met sales quotas. After her second month as sales manager, Elaine talked to Rick about his performance. He attributed his below average performance to the closing of a major advertiser, Anthony's Fashions. This local clothing store closed because several major retailers, including J.C. Penney's and Dillard's, had opened at the local mall.

Elaine listened to Rick's explanation, then suggested ways to obtain new clients for the station. She asked Rick whether he had set personal sales goals, set up a prospect file of new and inactive advertisers as well as existing businesses that were potential clients, kept up with research and data on the market to use in presentations and reports to clients, came up with new ideas or opportunities to advertise for clients, or asked his clients about their needs and goals (Shaver, 1995). Rick said no, he simply telephoned or visited his clients regularly to see if they wanted to run ads.

Elaine also asked Rick why several of his clients had not paid their bills. She explained that it is a salesperson's obligation to check out a client's ability to pay before running a schedule. Rick replied that he was not aware of that fact; no one had ever really trained him to sell. He had sold time for a radio station before, but that was all the sales training he had. Elaine's predecessor had just hired him and, "cut him loose."

She gave Rick a memo after their first meeting a month ago asking him to focus on sales training for the next month. First, he should read Shaver (1995), *Making the sale! How to sell media with marketing.* She gave him a copy, told him to read it, and asked him to contact her if he had any questions after reading the book. After reading the book, he should establish written personal sales goals, begin to develop a prospect file (with two new and two inactive clients) and develop three ideas for new advertising opportunities for existing clients. In the memo, Elaine told Rick that she would not hold him to sales performance standards that month. She wanted him to focus on doing the background work she assigned to help him improve his future sales performance.

At the meeting a month later Elaine found out that Rick had made a half-hearted attempt at training. For example, he had not developed a prospect file, telling her he had no idea how to do it. She asked him why he had not contacted her to set up a meeting to discuss questions he had about the book or completing her assignments, as noted in her memo. He said he had forgotten. When she asked him specific questions about Shaver's (1995) sales book, he was unable to respond, suggesting he had not read it.

Elaine asked him to read the book again, and she scheduled a meeting with Rick to discuss the book. Elaine instructed him to have a written memo ready for the next meeting that identified the assistance or training he needed to accomplish the tasks she had set for him the previous month. "Base your needs assessment memo on the Shaver book, and be prepared to discuss the book fully," she told him. She said she would be sending him a memo about their meeting outlining what she had asked him verbally to do during the next month, as well as the consequences of not completing these tasks. "Rick, if you do not start to make a serious effort in participating in your training, and ultimately improving your sales performance, your job here could be in jeopardy."

Elaine's "gut feeling" was that Rick was either lazy or unqualified for his sales job. She was surprised that an employee would respond so half-heartedly to a written notice of unsatisfactory job performance. She wondered if there was another reason why he was not responding to her attempts to help him. She wanted to give him a fair chance to improve, but she knew she would have to fire him if he did not take his training seriously and improve his performance. She wondered how to be fair to him yet protect the station at the same time. She had never faced this kind of problem before. "Welcome to management," she told herself.

ASSIGNMENT

Review the chapter and answer the following questions.

  1. Were Elaine's actions in working with Rick fair and appropriate thus far? Why or why not?

2. What steps should Elaine take to identify the training Rick may need? Why?

3. How can Elaine determine fairly whether Rick simply lacks adequate sales training or is truly unmotivated, without opening her station to a wrongful termination lawsuit? Explain your answer and provide examples of what Elaine should do.

4. How can Elaine discover whether there is another reason for Rick's apparent unresponsiveness to her efforts to help him improve his performance? Should she take steps to find out? Why or why not?

5. How should Elaine document the steps she takes to train, or if necessary, discipline Rick? Why?

6. With what other resources or persons should Elaine consult regarding Rick? Why?

7. How should Elaine respond to today's meeting with Rick? To answer this question, write a sample memo from Elaine to Rick about today's meeting.

8. Write a sample memo for Elaine, assuming that Rick does not respond satisfactorily to the meeting scheduled 1 month from now.

9. Write a sample memo for Elaine, assuming Rick does respond satisfactorily to the meeting 1 month from now.

10. What other steps or actions would you recommend to Elaine? Why?

CASE 6.3

Developing an Arbitration System

Depending on your interests, contact a newspaper, magazine, radio station, television station, cable channel or system, advertising agency, or public relations firm. Find an organization that does not have a formalized arbitration system for handling disputes between employees and management, such as sexual harassment, discrimination, discipline, productivity, promotion, demotion, and job termination.

Surf the American Arbitration Association's (AAA) home page at http://www.adr.org. The AAA provides assistance for resolving disputes and has developed specialized rules and procedures to ensure that the dispute resolution process is fair to all involved. Review the guides, rules, and explanations of alternative dispute resolution included to help you figure out how to develop an alternative dispute resolution system or process for your chosen firm.

Here's a basic explanation of dispute resolution to help you get started. Alternative dispute resolution techniques include mediation where a skilled facilitator helps disputing parties reach a voluntary settlement. The mediator serves as an advisor who helps the parties explore issues, discovers each party's needs, and suggests ways to resolve a dispute. However, the disputing parties must resolve the dispute themselves. Under arbitration, a dispute is referred to one or more impartial experts for final and binding determination. Disputing parties agree to present their case to a mutually agreed on and disinterested neutral mediator for a legally binding ruling.

According to the AAA, mediators or arbiters should be people committed to impartiality who have at least 8 to 10 years of experience in the field. A fair and judicious temperament is needed; arbiters and mediators must be patient and courteous. Dispute management skills are a must, as well as a strong academic background and respected professional credentials. Good choices are typically business persons or attorneys with expertise in the particular field.

With both methods, the parties involved control the process. Other advantages are that expensive and lengthy lawsuits can be avoided; arbitration is quicker and often much less costly. Unlike court cases, all information is kept private, preventing embarrassing disclosures for the company or employee. More important, maintaining privacy makes it more likely that the parties can continue to work together after the dispute is solved. The person who assists with or decides the case is impartial and an expert in the field.

For example, parties to a newspaper industry dispute might select an independent and impartial journalist, publisher or attorney who specializes in press law to serve as mediator or arbitrator, depending on case specifics. Many trade or professional organizations use the AAA to resolve disputes. Also, in the less formal setting, participants can tell completely their sides of the story. Relevant evidence cannot be excluded by technicalities, as it often is in courtrooms.

After surfing the AAA's home page, identify the appropriate rules, techniques, and clauses that might be included in a dispute resolution handbook for your firm of choice. Then select two managers and two employees in various departments to interview. The idea is to get as many viewpoints as possible on how disputes have been handled in the organization and how the process could be improved.

If you cannot get an organization to participate, interview managers and employees in various firms in your community. For example, your goal could be to develop an arbitration system to be used by the local professional Advertising Club or Society of Professional Journalists chapter.

After you develop your system, submit a copy of your report to a few more professionals in the field of choice. Review their feedback, surf the AAA's home page again, and make your final revisions.

ASSIGNMENT

Your arbitration report should cover all of the following aspects.

1. A description of the industry, types of companies, and personnel covered by the arbitration system.

2. A summary of the major findings of your research (based on the interviews, background research on the industry and firm or organization, background research on the firm or organization's mission, etc.). Discuss in detail any examples of past disputes that were handled satisfactorily and unsatisfactorily and why. Your summary should also explain how and why the arbitration system will work for this industry and/or organization.

3. A description of the rules and procedures to be followed in mediation and arbitration.

4. A detailed description of the qualifications of persons who might serve as mediators and arbiters.

5. If you are developing the system for a company, explain how and when the dispute resolution process will be implemented. If you are developing the system for an organization or club, explain how and when the dispute resolution process will be implemented.

6. Discuss any other aspects of the process that could assist the parties involved in resolving disputes.

7. Discuss whether the firm or organization should seek the services of AAA in implementing the dispute resolution system and handling future disputes. Explain your answer.

CASE 6.4

Evaluating a Home Page for Copyright Problems

Surf the home page of a media firm, media outlet, or professional media organization of interest. Review the articles, artwork, hot links to other sites and other information or material included in the site. Then carefully reread the section of the chapter on copyright.

If possible, interview whoever developed the web site. Ask if the employee or person developed all site materials or obtained materials from other sources or persons. Ask the employee or person whether copyright protection was secured or considered when developing the web site.

ASSIGNMENT

Develop a report identifying the possible sources or types of copyright problems the firm or organization could have, given its existing web site. Discuss all of the following aspects in your report.

1. Does it appear that all articles and visuals were prepared by employees of the firm or organization? If not, what action should be taken by the firm and why?
2. Do any hot links appear to be featured, separate from archival material, and linked to related electronic resources or indexes? If yes, was the article or linkdeveloped by someone who is not or does not appear to be an employee of the organization? If yes, what action should the organization take?
3. Does the organization encourage uploading or downloading of material for which it does not own the copyright? If yes, what action should the organization take and why?
4. Has the person or employee who developed the web site fully surfed other sites to which the organization is linked? How involved was the employee or person in reviewing, editing, and passing along web-site material? Does the organization appear to have any possible copyright liability as a publisher or distributor?
5. Was the person or employee aware of copyright concerns when developing the web site? Did the person appear to knowingly use material for which the organization had no rights? Of what significance is prior knowledge of a lack of rights?
6. Are there any other copyright concerns raised based on your review of the web site and background research on the organization?

CASE 6.5

Self-Regulatory Analysis of a Web Site
Directed to Children

Select a home page on the Internet that is directed or targeted to children. Such pages could include an advertiser's, toy store chain's or media outlet's web site for kids. Review the site fully. Then review the following advice and guidelines for advertising to or preparing web sites for children.

REview the BBB's CARU self-regulatory guidelines and online guidelines for marketers to children. Information or speeches regarding children's advertising online can be found by searching the entire FTC web site, entering keywords like children, advertising, guidelines, and online. Examples of advice include "The ABCs at the FTC: Marketing and Advertising to Children," found at http://www.ftc.gov/speeches/starek/minnfin.htm, and "Staff Report: Chapter 4—Children and Privacy Online" at http://www.ftc.gov/reports/privacy/privacy5.htm. Review the privacy advice and guidelines at DMA's home page at http://www.the-dma.org. Surf the CPSC's Kid's Page at http://www.cpsc.gov/kids/kids.html for an example of a public service home page for children. Also review any other public service, regulatory, self-regulatory, or commercial web pages or guidelines for children noted in the sites just listed.

ASSIGNMENT

After reviewing these sites, review again the commercial home page for children you selected. Evaluate whether it follows the online guidelines for advertising to children. You may combine the principles noted in all of the advisory or self-regulatory guidelines listed or select one set of advisory or self-regulatory guidelines for your analysis. Prepare a report that includes the following topics:

1. Does the company indicate the age group to which the page is targeted? If not, to which age group does the home page seem to be targeted?
2. Did the company or marketers appear to take advantage of the typical targeted child's age, knowledge, sophistication, and maturity unfairly or unethically when developing the web site? Why or why not?
3. Is the company's information or privacy practices notice prominently displayed and easy to find and read for the targeted age group?
4. Is it easy for the targeted age group to tell that they are being asked to disclose personal information (if applicable)? Has an opt-out mechanism to avoid

submitting personal information been provided? Is it easy for the target group to understand and use the opt-out mechanism? In your opinion, is it pressure-free or are children encouraged too strongly or unethically to get a free gift or something else for providing personal information?

5. Is there a mechanism, easily understood by the typical targeted child, for avoiding future e-mail messages from the advertiser or company? Did you receive any unsolicited e-mail after surfing the site? Was there a mechanism appropriate for the target group in the unsolicited e-mail for refusing future e-mails?

6. Whenever purchase or personal information is sought, is there a prominent message that is easily understood by the target group asking them to seek a parent's or guardian's permission before doing so? Also, is there a mechanism for canceling the purchase, after the fact, by the parent or guardian?

7. Were there any other ethical guidelines or practices that the advertiser or company violated or executed well? What were these guidelines or practices? Why did the company execute them well or violate them?

8. Overall, do you think the company followed the self-regulatory guidelines for advertising to children? Why or why not?

9. Generally speaking, do you think self-regulatory guidelines are an effective way to protect the privacy rights of children surfing the web? Why or why not?

CASE 6.6

Developing Self-Regulatory Guidelines
for a Media Firm

Select a media firm in which you would like to work. (This assignment might be easier if you selected a national level firm or organization.) Then surf the appropriate professional web site or sites for that type of firm. For example, future print or broadcast editors, publishers, or managers could surf the Society of Professional Journalists Code or home page (http://www.spj.org) or the Radio-Television News Code of Ethics online at http://www.rtnda.org/ethics.html. Future advertising managers might surf the FTC's home page (http://www.ftc.gov/), or the BBB's home page (http://www.bbb.org), especially the Advertising Review Programs. See if you can find any other self-regulatory codes or guidelines that seem relevant to your firm's operations.

Then, conduct a search of the firm on Lexis/Nexis. For example, if you selected *The New York Times* as your firm, see whether the paper has been embroiled in any ethical issues in the past 5 years. Those issues might be internal (perhaps involving the sexual harassment of employees) or external (perhaps involving a controversial decision to publish, or not to publish a story). If the firm has not had many major controversies, use Lexis/Nexis to see what the major ethical controversies regarding newspapers have been over the past 5 years. Develop a thorough description of a minimum of five ethical issues to use for developing your code.

ASSIGNMENT

Select at least five major provisions from the self-regulatory codes you found on the web that seem to apply or relate to the ethical issues you researched. Then develop a code of ethics for the firm that features the controversial issues or practices the firm may have or could face in the future. Turn in a report that covers the following aspects:

1. Identify the media outlet or firm you have selected and state why you selected it.
2. Identify and describe in detail the minimum five major ethical issues you found in your research about the firm and industry.

3. Identify and describe the code(s) and code provisions or guidelines you used as a basis for the code you developed.

4. Present your code and its provisions or guidelines. Discuss why it is tailored well to the needs of the firm. Discuss how it improves and/or expands on the self-regulatory code or codes you discussed in question 3.

CASE 6.7

Reviewing Freedom of Information Resources

Select a state of interest and review online and other available sources to discover the applicable information access laws, if any. For example, check out the SPJ's FOIA Resource Center link at http://www.spj.org/foia/index.htm, or the U.S. House of Representatives, Internet Law Library's selected listing of laws and articles regarding privacy and information access at http://law.house.gov/107.htm. Contact the appropriate governmental agency or office for more information about access in your area. If your research into state access becomes too difficult, research access at the federal government level.

ASSIGNMENT

Develop a report outlining what laws, if any, are applicable in your state. Also report on general techniques for obtaining documents from the appropriate state government or agency. Or develop a report outlining the Freedom of Information Act's major provisions and techniques for obtaining information from appropriate federal entities. Write your report so it could be used by reporters or others as a guide for how to request appropriate government documents.

CASE 6.8

Monitoring Broadcast Advertising for Children

Many critics of television and advertising have expressed concern about television advertising for children. As a result, the FCC treats children as a special group of viewers with special rules about advertising. These rules limit the number of minutes per hour of advertising and the connection between program and advertising content. The purpose of this assignment is to examine advertising content aimed at children to see if it meets these standards.

ASSIGNMENT

Please complete the following steps:

1. Check to see if the FCC rules governing children's advertising have changed recently.
2. Using the most recent rules, watch 2 hours of a network-affiliated (e.g., ABC, CBS, NBC) Saturday morning children's programming and 2 hours of an independent's (or nonaffiliated station's) weekday afternoon children's programming.
3. Answer the following questions:
   A. Did the two stations follow the FCC standards about advertising time and content?
   B. How did the two stations compare and contrast? Was one better or worse than the other?
   C. Did you notice any types of advertising that were legal but raised ethical concerns? Were any of the advertisements particularly offensive? Did any of the advertising seem to be misleading? Did any of the advertisements seem particularly manipulative?
   D. Did either station air a commercial for a toy or item featured in a children's program during or adjacent to the program? Was it difficult for a child to tell the difference between the commercial and program? Why or why not?
   E. Would you recommend that either station screen or clear its advertising in children's programs differently? Why or why not?

7

PLANNING

If a manager wants to make effective decisions, he or she must plan. If a manager wants to plan adequately, he or she must make effective decisions. In many ways, the decision wheel presented in chapter 1 could be titled easily a planning wheel. Many of the steps are the same. Despite the similarities, planning and decision making do differ, although these differences tend to be more practical than theoretical.

The planning process differs from the decision-making process because planning is so concrete. Although the decision wheel can be applied to most any decision, business planning takes three forms: strategic planning, intermediate planning, and short-run planning (Fink, 1988; Kreitner, 1986). Strategic planning involves allocating resources to achieve the long-term goals of an organization. These plans can cover 1 to 10 years, but they usually are developed for a 3 to 5 year period. Intermediate planning usually covers 6 months to 2 years and provides reinforcement or correction data for the long-term goals. Short-run planning involves plans for a few weeks or at most 1 year. This type of plan is meant to allocate resources on a day-to-day or month-to-month basis. Figure 7.1 shows how the three plans fit together. The strategic plan fulfills the firm's mission and overall general goals. The intermediate plan involves the general way in which the strategic plan will be pursued, and the short-run plan is how the strategic plan will work on a day-to-day basis.

COMMON CHARACTERISTICS OF PLANNING

All three types of planning have commonalities although the time period, responsible parties, and actual steps vary. Companies have general organizational goals which are fairly abstract statements of what a firm hopes to achieve within given areas of performance. These goals are derived from the organization's mission. Smith, Arnold, and Bizzell (1985) defined an organization's mission as its business domain. It often includes statements

184

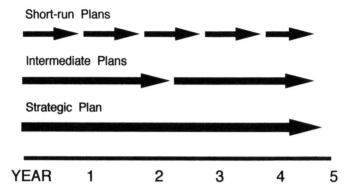

FIG. 7.1. Relationship among strategic, intermediate, and short-run planning.

about the firm's role outside its primary business markets. For example a newspaper's mission might be to provide its readers with a complete and accurate report on the events and issues of concern to its community. The goals associated with this might include: (a) covering all important issues confronting civic organizations, such as the city council, police and fire departments, and school board; (b) covering noncivic issues that relate to individual readers' health and welfare; and (c) covering events and issues that relate to the community's culture and social background. Planning goals help an organization achieve its mission, which should reflect the expertise within an organization. For instance, it would make little sense for a television network news department to pursue a goal of developing an inexpensive but powerful computer because news staff would not ordinarily possess the background or resources to accomplish this.

In order to assess progress, an organization must have operational definitions for measurement. For example, the goal of increasing viewership among long-term residents of the community could be operationalized as increasing ratings by two points during the next 6 months among audience members who have lived in the area of dominant influence (ADI) for more than 10 years. The operational definition must specify in measurable terms the group to be affected (people who have lived in the ADI for more than 10 years), a time period during which the change is expected (next 6 months), and a measurable level of performance that is being sought (two ratings points).

Planning without well-defined goals and assessment procedures is like attending a pot luck dinner where the diner may enjoy the meal, but it will be by chance rather than culinary design. Every plan involves preparation. This characteristic is analogous to the collecting and analyzing of information in the decision wheel presented in chap. 1. The better the preparation, the greater the chances of reaching the goals. A newspaper publisher who embarks on a plan to increase circulation will have little success unless he or she has some idea why people do or do not read the newspaper. Preparation is simply the collection of information about the goals and possible alternatives for achieving those goals. The goals that fit with the mission of the organization and can be operationally achieved are the ones followed by the organization. All planning includes tools for carrying out the plan. The tools are mechanisms for analysis, information collection, and monitoring that assist in developing and executing plans. The analysis tools discussed in chap. 1, financial documents discussed in chap. 10, and the market analysis discussed in chap. 8 are all tools that can be used for planning. Of course, knowing what tools are available for use in planning is not the same as knowing how to apply those tools. The application of tools is learned through experience, practice, and reflection.

Finally, all planning involves a procedure that provides tangible evidence of the process. The steps for achieving the goals and the time frame and resources necessary for carrying out the plan are included in the procedure. The three major business plans are covered in detail in the sections which follow.

STRATEGIC PLANNING

Strategic planning is the long-term process by which an organization pursues its mission and hopes to reach its goals. If a media organization participates in two or more of the three markets—information, advertising, and intellectual—the strategic plan must address explicitly these markets and explain the relationship among them. A television station cannot make plans for the advertising market without including the information market where it will attract viewers. A newspaper cannot plan for the information market without examining the role it will play in the intellectual market.

Smith et al. (1985) used the term strategic management in lieu of strategic planning because the traditional concept of strategic planning did not include control of the plan as it was implemented. They said strategic management includes: (a) analyzing the environment, (b) determining objectives, (c) analyzing strategic alternatives, (d) selecting strategy alternatives; (e) implementing the strategies, and (f) evaluating and controlling performance.

Combining these approaches with the decision wheel in chap. 1 and adding control to planning results in a more refined approach to strategic planning that includes the following steps (as shown in Fig. 7.2):

1. Examine the business environment and past performance.
2. Evaluate available resources.
3. Identify, select, prioritize, and operationalize planning goals.
4. Identify alternative approaches for obtaining goals.
5. Select from the alternative approaches.
6. Implement the plan.
7. Monitor implementation.
8. Evaluate plan's progress and adjust the plan.

As with decision making, the collection and analysis of information is a part of all eight steps in strategic planning. Plans for the future must be grounded in experience and an understanding of current market conditions. The market analysis is the primary method of evaluating the business environment. The internal examination involves how well the firm accomplished its goals in the past and why. Failure to reach goals could have resulted from any number of problems inside the firm, including inappropriate goals, goals set too high, poor analysis of data, inadequate resources, and poor performance.

Evaluate Available Resources

In order to make sure the planning goals can be met, a manager must evaluate at-hand resources. At hand resources include the company's name and reputation, personnel, plant and equipment, and finances. At hand means the resources either are held currently by the firm or can be borrowed easily. Thus, financial resources also include an organization's credit.

Evaluating available resources is important because resources determine whether goals can be achieved, and although resources can be changed from one form to another, the process does not occur as quickly as management would like. If a large metropolitan newspaper needs an experienced award-winning columnist, it will take time to recruit such a writer. The uncertainty of time necessitates good resource planning based on accurate evaluation of which journalists might be good prospects.

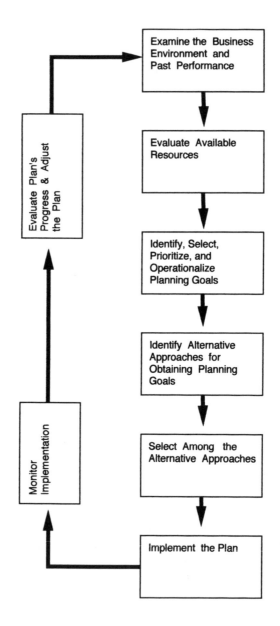

FIG. 7.2. Steps in strategic planning.

188

As the strategic plan develops, evaluations of available resources reveal whether the resources needed to achieve the plan's goals are currently available in the form necessary. When the organization does not have the resources needed by the plan in the appropriate form, the plan must include ways of getting or converting these resources. If the needed resources are not and cannot be made available, then the goals associated with those resources should be reconsidered or not pursued.

No guidelines exist for how many goals a firm needs to identify or select, but all of the selected goals should be obtainable and consistent with the general goals and mission of the firm. Each goal requires resources that are relatively fixed. The more goals a firm pursues, the more competition will exist within the organization for resources. For example, a smaller Ohio newspaper group might select the following goals:

1. Add daily newspapers until the group has papers in markets that make up 20% of the circulation in Ohio (information market goal).
2. Increase significantly the penetration of existing markets (information market goal).
3. Increase revenue from national advertising (advertising market goal).
4. Increase the column inches of display advertising that are run in the paper (advertising market goal).
5. Increase the column inches and percentage of the news hole devoted to letters to the editor and guest columns (intellectual market goal).

The goals listed for the information and advertising markets conceivably could compete for resources. The acquisition of newspapers will cost money, as will efforts to increase penetration. The penetration goal will involve additional spending for the circulation and news departments, as well as money for promoting the changes from the increased spending.

All five goals will consume resources and initially would compete. However, as the plan is placed into effect, the achievement of some of the goals will generate revenue, which then can be applied toward meeting other goals. Timing is important to consider because not all goals have to be reached at the same time. Some can be set for the second or third year of the plan, and some can be made contingent on reaching others.

Identify Alternative Approaches for Obtaining Goals

Almost all long-term goals can be reached with more than one approach, and they often require multiple approaches. For example, a radio station that wants to increase its share of listeners can do so by altering its music format and promoting itself in a number of ways. The aim is to select the most efficient and effective way of reaching or surpassing the goals. The ability to select the "best" approach depends on how exhaustive the analysis procedure is. Often management settles for a less than optimal plan for achieving a goal because not all ideas were identified in the decision-making stage (see chap. 1). Brainstorming is a commonly used technique for generating ideas. It accepts two basic principles of creative thinking techniques: A positive attitude is established, which means criticism is withheld until after ideas are developed; and unusual ideas are encouraged, even if they seem impractical (Whiting, 1955).

Assessing alternatives includes eliminating the ones that are impractical or improbable. Improbability and impracticality can be based on any number of characteristics, including approaches with high risk, high environmental uncertainty, and high resource needs. The list of approaches should be pared to a manageable number of good alternatives for achieving the goals. This usually would range from 3 to 6 methods. Comparison of alternative plans can be as formal or informal as management likes. Formal methods for comparison are discussed in chap. 1 and include cost–benefit analysis, decision trees, and utility theory. From these comparisons efficiency and effectiveness can be determined. Efficiency is measured by the amount of resources needed to reach a given goal, and the most efficient approach is the one that will achieve the goal with the smallest expenditure of resources. Effectiveness is the probability that the approaches will achieve the goals of the plan.

INTERMEDIATE PLANNING

Intermediate planning requires a marketing plan, a financial plan, and a human resources plan. The three must be coordinated with each other as well as with the overall strategic plan.

The main difference between strategic and intermediate planning is the plan itself. A marketing plan must deal with the market mix, which includes product, place, price, and promotion (the four Ps). The marketing mix is applicable to the information, advertising, and intellectual markets. Although they are interrelated, each should have a marketing plan of its own. The product is simply the thing that is sold or given to a consumer in exchange for time or money. In the information and intellectual markets, the product is information and ideas, with their various subdivisions given in chapter 8. In the advertising market, it is the potential attention of consumers to advertising information. The value of the advertising attention depends on the number of viewers, readers, or listeners and the types of people paying the attention.

In most organizations, the product decision is based on the location of older products in their life cycle. Buzzell and Cook (1969) discussed five stages of a product's life cycle:

1. Infancy is when a product enters the market. Sales are low.
2. Growth occurs when the product matures as to who and where it will sell. Sales grow rapidly if the product finds its niche in the marketplace.
3. Approaching maturity is when the established product begins to battle competitors over market share. Sales continue to grow, but at a slower rate than in the growth stage.
4. Maturity occurs when a product finds its place in its segment. Competition continues and sales grow much more slowly than earlier stages.
5. Decline is the final stage when consumers lose interest in the product for whatever reason and sales begin to decline.

With most media products, place is an important part of product. News commodities, such as newspapers and newscasts, are aimed at specific geographic areas. The content reflects this aim. The size, geography, social aspects, cultural characteristic, and political nature of a society affect the places for which news products are designed. Place is also related to price in the United States. Some parts of the country have higher and lower standards of living than others. The same book for example, would face a lower demand due to price in one region than in another.

Place also affects the process and cost of distributing the media product. The cost of delivering a newspaper increases as one moves away from the production site. The cost of distributing a broadcast television program is basically the same within the range of the signal. If the station wants to distribute the program elsewhere satellite transmission would increase costs.

As explained in chapter 8, price will affect demand, but it also determines how much revenue is taken in by the firm. Pricing is a difficult process for many media firms because the joint commodity nature of most media commodities creates extreme uncertainty. Managers are afraid to overprice in one type of market because it will reduce demand in another. Increasing the subscription price for a magazine will reduce circulation, which can affect the price charged to advertisers. Research indicates that newspaper managers often charge less for their advertising and circulation than they could (Picard, 1988).

The traditional way of pricing existing products is to look at inflation, examine competitors' prices, add on additional expenses that have developed, estimate the impact of price on demand, and state the price with a profit goal in mind. The traditional way of pricing new products is to calculate the costs of production and distribution and add a desired profit margin.

The final P in the marketing mix is promotion, which involves persuading people to use the product. Promotion includes advertising, public relations, and promotional activities.

SHORT-RUN PLANNING

Just as the intermediate plans are maps of reaching the goals of the strategic plan, short-run plans are ways of meeting the goals of the intermediate plans. There types of short-run planning are important: budgets, employee planning, and management by objective (MBO).

Budgets are the yearly plan of the organization. They cover the expected sources of money and how to spend that money. The budget must reflect the priorities of the intermediate and strategic plans or the mission of the organization will not be accomplished. Employee planning involves the development of the talents, skills, and aspirations of people within an organization. MBO is where the budget and employee planning intersect. It is an explicit way of setting up objectives, evaluating employees' contribution to those objectives, and allocating resources such as time and money to the successful completion of the objectives.

PLANNING FOR INTERNATIONAL MARKETS

When a media company's long-term strategic plan includes moving into international markets, new issues arise that must be carefully considered within the context of the overall planning process just discussed. The need to plan for international operations is becoming increasingly important for media corporations. Although there have been a handful of multinational media corporations over the years and media products such as films and television programs have been exported to foreign audiences, during the 1980s and 1990s the internationalization of the media industry grew dramatically.

Although the degree to which media and communication companies have internationalized is difficult to measure precisely, the U.S. Department of Commerce (1993) noted that in 1990, 10% of the U.S. work force employed in the motion picture and television production industries was working for the U.S. affiliates of foreign-owned companies. That was twice the rate of employment by foreign-owned companies for the U.S. work force as a whole.

During the same period that foreign companies were investing in the U.S. media industry, U.S. media and communication companies were buying or starting companies overseas. The economics of media production make global operations desirable because once a company has created a media product such as a television program, film, or magazine, it costs almost nothing to distribute it to more people (U.S. Department of Commerce, 1993). Moreover, each additional person who sees the program or magazine spreads the costs of producing that item more widely and thereby increases the media company's profit.

But despite these economics, media companies interested in international expansion face significant barriers. First, most nations—including the United States—have had laws limiting or forbidding foreign ownership of media companies in order to protect domestic media industries from foreign competition and because of concerns that foreign owners might influence content and public opinion in times of war or national crisis. Restrictions on foreign ownership generally have been most stringent for telephone systems, and television and radio stations. Magazine companies and book publishers have tended to be less regulated and, therefore, foreign ownership has been more common in those media sectors.

Many countries not only restrict foreign media ownership but also imports. Europe and Canada, for example, have strict quotas on the importation of U.S.-produced films and television programming (Gershon, 1997). Critics of imported media fear the sheer volume of relatively inexpensive U.S. film and television products will inhibit domestic activity. They also fear the values shown in foreign films and television may undermine national cultures and values—a process known as cultural imperialism.

In the 1980s and early 1990s, however, a number of factors came together to encourage Western countries to open media markets to foreign investment. Improved communication and transportation technologies made it easier for corporations to expand into new markets, and companies in many industries around the world began to globalize their operations.

In order to run expanded operations multinational companies need access to highly developed information transfer systems such as computer networks, sophisticated telephone systems, and databases (U.S. House of

Representatives, 1980, 1981, 1981). That need put pressure on governments to deregulate their domestic telecommunications industries so that consumers and businesses could have access to the latest telecommunications technologies and services—regardless of whether they were provided by domestic or foreign-owned providers. At the same time, there was a general movement to reduce the number of trade barriers between nations in the belief that free international trade would create greater economic efficiencies, help business, and provide consumers with more choices of products for lower prices. These two factors—the need for access to the best communication technology and services and the desire to reduce trade barriers in general—led many developed nations to reevaluate their limitations on media ownership. A number of trade agreements signed during the period, including the European Union agreement among European nations (Gershon, 1997) and the North American Free Trade Agreement (NAFTA) among the United States, Canada, and Mexico, included specific provisions to encourage the opening of media markets to foreign trade and investment.

Whereas changes in the international economy and business environment were pressuring developed countries to make it easier for media companies to operate internationally, changes within the media industry were encouraging media companies to actually take that step.

The growth of the global economy encouraged many media companies to expand by buying media operations in foreign countries. The Canadian company Thomson Newspapers heavily invested in U.S. newspapers during the 1980s as part of its strategic plan for corporate growth, for example. Other companies pursued a similar plan but bought different types of media, becoming multimedia international conglomerates. News Corporation Ltd., Rupert Murdoch's company, started out as an Australian newspaper company but expanded by buying newspapers and television operations in Great Britain and the United States.

The convergence of media technologies also encouraged media companies to expand internationally by eroding the distinctions among the telephone, computer, television, radio, newspaper, magazine, and book industries. Increased competition in many media sectors combined with reduced revenues and profits pressured companies to look for new ways to grow (Turow, 1992). Media companies developed profitable synergies across media products, distributing the same content or concepts through different media. A story idea, for example, could be cross marketed by a multimedia conglomerate through its book publishing and film studios, whereas the soundtrack from the movie could be sold through its record company. Media corporations began realizing these synergies through the acquisition of other, often foreign, companies.

Convergence also encouraged media companies to invest in new lines of business overseas in order to gain experience in those areas. Many of the Regional Bell operating companies, for example, invested in cable systems in Great Britain and other nations to prepare for the day U.S. cable and phone industries were deregulated. Another motivation for overseas investment was media technology manufacturers' desire to gain control of popular content such as films or music to ensure that those entertainment features were distributed in formats compatible with the manufacturers' media technologies (Carveth, 1992; Gershon, 1997; Turow, 1992). Japan's Sony Corp., for example, bought Columbia Pictures to make sure films would be distributed using its home entertainment technologies—a strategy it developed after consumers abandoned Sony's Betamax VCR because not enough movies were available in Beta format. Finally, media companies recognized that investing overseas or setting up joint ventures with foreign partners was a means for getting around the limitations some nations placed on the foreign import of media products. Thus, overseas investment became a way to maintain and increase foreign exports (Carveth, 1992; Gershon, 1997).

As globalization of media continues, it will become increasingly likely that, at some point in their careers, media professionals—whether in broadcasting, publishing, or new technologies—will find themselves working for a company that either has overseas holdings or is itself owned by a foreign company. Thus, ambitious media managers should be prepared to meet the challenges of managing across cultures and across borders.

Examine the Business Environment and Past Performance

As with strategic planning for domestic companies, strategic planning for international media operations begins with examining the business environment and past performances of the country or countries in which a company is considering investing. The questions raised during this process, however, are somewhat different than those a manager faces when looking only at the home market and company. There are a number of factors that influence a decision about where to invest, including the strength of the local economy, the regulatory environment for media, and language and cultural differences that may affect how media are received and what advertising might be sold to support the media product. These factors also affect which media product(s) will be developed.

Media products are generally luxury items. If most residents of a country are living a subsistence existence with little to no disposable income, the market for media products generally is not strong. Advertisers are not interested in reaching markets where consumers have little potential buying power. However, countries with strong economies also generally have highly developed media markets which means stiff advertising competition. Thus, a manager engaged in international strategic planning must balance the analysis of the economic conditions in the country against what is known about the competition for the type of media the company produces.

Sometimes, as in the case of the opening of Eastern Europe, media managers can spot countries that do not necessarily have a strong economy or media industry but show signs of growth in both areas. For example, media corporations from Europe and North America invested heavily in countries after the collapse of the Eastern Bloc in 1989 to the point where the ownership of large segments of Eastern Europe's print media passed into the hands of foreign companies (Hollifield, 1993; Sukosd, 1992).

Other opportunities may arise when developed countries deregulate or privatize a media sector. Until 1984, for example, Germany had only two television networks, which were publicly operated. In 1984, Germany decided to permit commercial broadcasting, which expanded rapidly. Today, although commercial television in Germany is largely controlled by German companies, some foreign media enterprises—including Murdoch's News Corporation Ltd. and the Walt Disney Co. have holdings in German television (Holtz-Bacha, 1996).

Media managers also need to evaluate carefully national regulatory environments. Media companies can face requirements that foreign media be owned partially by domestic partners, or media content and copyright regulations can be troublesome. Copyright is of particular concern in the international media environment. Some countries have not yet signed international copyright agreements, whereas others do not enforce international copyright laws. If a media company were to enter such a market, it might have difficulty protecting its publications or programs from illegal copying or pirating. Such pirating already is widespread in the recording and software industries. If a country has not signed international copyright agreements, then the products a media corporation produces or distributes within that country may be particularly vulnerable.

These economic and regulatory decisions greatly impact the question of what media products a media company should attempt to produce and/or sell overseas. If, for example, the economy of a market is relatively weak and the potential audience does not have a great deal of disposable income, the media manager might want to focus on developing publications or programs that give audiences information that can be used—such as home repair programs or sewing publications—rather than fashion and gossip publications or programs that may not be seen as "necessities" by financially strapped readers and viewers.

Similarly, content regulations in another country could affect a media manager's choice of what to produce there. Many nations have strict laws regarding what media may publish, and content that is routinely published or broadcast in the United States would be censored elsewhere. Great Britain, for example, has more restrictions than the United States on what media can report about criminal justice proceedings and official secrets, whereas some photographs and advertisements depicting women in U.S. magazines would be deemed pornography in some Middle Eastern countries. Such regulations can make it more difficult for a media company not only to produce content for its overseas operations, but also to sell advertising for its foreign editions or programs.

Other elements that affect product and market choices are educational, cultural and language differences. If, for example, the media company is a publishing company, then the manager must examine literacy rates. Only if a major segment of a country's population can read will there be a thriving market for magazines, books, and newspapers. Similarly, if only a small percentage of the population is computer literate or has access to computers, online media services are not likely to be successful.

Cultural differences also are critical in making international media planning decisions. Media content is, by its very nature, something that mirrors and influences the culture in which it is created and sold. That is why so many countries have been concerned about cultural imperialism from foreign-produced media.

For a media manager, it is important to thoroughly understand the local culture of the country where a company is planning to invest. Cultural differences influence how media content and advertisers are received. For example, humor often is culturally based, playing off subtle situations or plays on words that are familiar to people in one culture but often not to their neighbors over the border. Thus, humorous content does not tend to travel well. Similarly, Carveth (1992) noted that *Dallas* was not well received by television audiences in Japan because the television series was based around family conflicts—which violated Japanese cultural values.

Finally, language must be considered. Media content is language-based, regardless of the form it takes. In order to reach an overseas audience, media content must be available in the local language. For films and video, this often means dubbing or subtitles. Publications must be either translated—which is often difficult and fraught with a high risk of error—or produced locally by native speakers in the overseas market. Advertising campaigns or product names that are successful in one language sometimes do not translate well into others.

For electronic media, the issues are even more complex. English has become the dominant language of the new electronic media. But that, by definition, means that non-English speakers cannot access English-based electronic media content and advertisements. Although there is a great deal of non-English content available and people and companies from around the world have web pages available, language remains an issue in the new media. Moreover, some countries are concerned that the growing importance of new media and its domination by English will undermine their local languages. As a result, some governments, such as the French government, require electronic content and media products offered locally to be in their national language. Thus, media companies and their advertisers who wish to make their content available to French audiences must arrange for it to be translated or dubbed.

Evaluate Available Resources

When evaluating the resources available to support international expansion, several important issues surface. First, the manager must decide what the company's primary goal is for internationalizing its operations. The answer to that question influences the answers to the other key decisions that must be made when evaluating the available resources for investing overseas.

The issues the manager faces include how the company should enter the foreign market—by taking its products into the new market or by acquiring existing media companies in that market. The manager also must decide how the new venture will be financed and how much financial risk the company wants to incur. Those issues raise questions of whether the investment should be managed through a wholly owned subsidiary, a partnership, a strategic alliance, licensing, or through some other ownership structure. The manager will then have to decide how the new venture will be organized and managed and how the human resources necessary for success will be found.

The first issue to be considered is, of course, the company's primary goal for overseas operations. The answer to that question usually influences how a foreign investment is structured and managed. Bartlett and Ghoshal (1989, 1990) identified four primary models used by companies to manage cross-border operations and the goals that drive those models.

One model is called *International*. This defines companies that are primarily interested in using overseas operations to distribute their domestic products in foreign markets. As a result, the overseas operation is seen as secondary to the company's main purpose. Control of the foreign office stays with company headquarters, as does almost all of the knowledge needed to produce the product. Information flows one-way from company headquarters to the subsidiary and the overseas operation is expected to return little to the parent company besides profits (Bartlett & Ghoshal, 1989, 1990). Television companies that establish overseas joint ventures in order to get around import quotas on their domestically produced programming would be an example of the international model.

A second model is the *multinational* company, which places more emphasis on its foreign operations. The multinational corporation uses its foreign subsidiaries to develop products for different markets and modifies its strategies and management practices to maximize its efficiency in each of the countries in which it has operations. The emphasis is on producing products that are specifically tailored to local markets. In multinational companies, managers often are hired locally and operate with a fair amount of independence from company headquarters in making daily decisions. A multinational company might be seen as a series of semi-independent but affiliated national companies with similar but distinct product lines (Bartlett & Ghoshal, 1989, 1990). This strategy maximizes the relevance of the company's products to its local audience, but lessens the company's ability to capture economies of scale. Canada's Thomson Newspapers, which owns many U.S. small and medium circulation newspapers, would be an example of this model. Each of its newspapers is produced for a very local audience. Only some of the copy from any given newspaper can be shared with Thomson's other U.S. papers, and even less would be of interest to Thomson's Canadian newspapers.

Global companies—of which Japanese industries provide the best example—think of the entire world as their market and produce products that are designed to be sold universally. Global companies maximize their production efficiencies, and they assume that consumers want basically the same things, no matter where they live. In global companies, most management planning and decision making is made in worldwide headquarters although production may be scattered around the globe (Bartlett & Ghoshal, 1989,

1990). Magazine publishers often take this approach to publishing. Magazines are frequently reproduced by a single company in multiple countries with only minor adjustments to content and translation. Germany's Aenne Burda publishing company, for example, distributes its fashion and sewing magazine Burda Moden in many different European countries (Media Perspektiven, 1994). The U.S. film and television industries also have taken traditionally a global approach to film production. In recent decades, the large budgets required to make films have made it necessary for Hollywood producers to take foreign film markets into account because overseas audiences can make the difference in profit margins. For this reason, foreign audiences have something more than a secondary market for Hollywood studios and films have been produced with global popularity in mind. However, Carveth (1992) and Turow (1992) suggest this may be changing. European audiences are increasingly interested in film with European content, which may eventually move the film industry to adopt the last of the four models of operation—the transnational model.

The *transnational* corporation, which is the model of international management that began emerging in the mid-1980s and 1990s, tries to merge the best of these other approaches while becoming more responsive to consumers' increasing demands that products be somewhat localized. In the transnational corporation, the company is neither centralized in the home market or global headquarters, nor decentralized in all of its outlying operations. Instead, different subsidiaries are assigned different specialties and given the resources and responsibilities to produce them. This approach is designed to make the company both flexible and responsive in meeting local needs, while still being able to combine the efforts of its different overseas operations to gain efficiencies in production and economies of scale.

Corporate managers share planning data with overseas subsidiaries, but those operations also are constantly scanning their local environments for new product ideas, new markets and new efficiencies that they can share with corporate operations around the globe (Bartlett & Ghoshal, 1989, 1990) This two-way learning process is one of the key distinguishing elements of the transnational model. The truly transnational manager recognizes that one of the main benefits of operating in markets around the world is the ability to learn from the people in those markets, gaining new ideas for better products and better ways of doing business.

Germany's Bertelsmann corporation, one of the world's largest multimedia companies, fits the transnational model in many ways. The company operates multiple units with responsibility for different media businesses in countries throughout the world. The corporation uses a decentralized model of management, giving its division managers a great deal of responsibility and authority to develop new products and specialties, while maintaining control through the principle of "leadership from the center" (Bertelsmann, 1998).

The recording industry also could fit in the transnational model. Burnett (1992) noted that although a handful of multinational media companies control the worldwide recording industry—up to 80% of the market in some countries—research has shown that at the same time consolidation in the industry increased, so did the number of new artists and diversity of music available to consumers. Burnett argues that this phenomenon is due to the multinationals' strategy of affiliating with small semi-independent recording labels worldwide, which then search their local music scenes for new talent. Thus the small labels are constantly bringing new music and new artists to the market locally and regionally, which the multinationals then distribute widely if they believe the sound may have appeal.

Once a media company has decided what it wants to accomplish through international expansion, it must decide how it will enter its chosen foreign market. There are two basic approaches. The first is to start its own overseas operations. The second is to acquire an existing media company in that country. If a company's primary goal is to be an international company—that is, to use its overseas operations as a secondary market for its existing products—then it probably would not enter a foreign market by buying another company and its product line. However, multinational, global, or transnational operations might be accomplished through either start-ups or acquisitions. Acquisitions allow the buyer to enter the new market with an already established product, thus reducing the risk of the investment. Much of the globalization of the media industry that took place during the 1980s and 1990s was accomplished through mergers and acquisitions.

A third element of overseas operations that must be planned is the new venture's ownership structure. As with domestic operations, a company's ownership structure directly affects its available sources of capital.

The simplest approach to ownership is to set up the overseas operation as a wholly owned subsidiary—that is a company that the parent company owns and operates entirely on its own. This certainly makes some aspects of operating overseas easier. It simplifies decision making and leaves little room for misunderstandings among co-owners from different countries.

Canada's Thomson Newspapers Corp., for example, operates its U.S. newspapers as subsidiaries.

However, running a wholly owned subsidiary also means that the parent company cannot learn about the new market from a local co-owner or another company that already has expertise in that market. It means that the company must shoulder all of the financial burden of the foreign investment—which can be considerable as operating a foreign subsidiary means additional costs in terms of travel, shipping, and communication between the subsidiary and headquarters. As a result, it usually takes several years for a foreign investment to become profitable.

Another option is to set up a joint venture or strategic alliance with one or more partners. In this arrangement, partners share the risks and costs of the foreign investment and the decision making for it. When the investment becomes profitable, success also is shared. Many countries require that foreign-owned media companies operating within their borders have at least one local partner. In other instances, strategic alliances with local producers are a means for foreign media companies to gain access to restricted media markets. Having a local partner for a cross-border investment can be particularly valuable because the partner can provide contacts with government, industry, and clients, advise on the development of culturally appropriate and attractive content, and help the new venture avoid the mistakes that are inevitable when doing business in a new environment. But even when the partner in a strategic alliance is not a local company, there are significant advantages to the joint venture arrangement. Particularly in technology-intensive media specialties, strategic alliances can help companies share knowledge, tap new innovations, and share the costs of technology development.

Joint ventures have pitfalls, however. Disagreements can arise over strategies for the partnership and authority over decision making. When the partners come from different countries, there can be culturally based misunderstandings. There also is the risk that a company will use an alliance to gain proprietary knowledge of the dominant partner's product line, later dissolving the joint venture and using that knowledge to compete against its former partner. Finally, if one partner is financially weaker than the other, problems can arise if the new subsidiary does not perform as expected and it becomes necessary to subsidize the venture for longer than planned.

Nevertheless, joint ventures have been a common way for media companies to structure their international investments. Examples of such media alliances include investments by Venezuela's Venevision company and Mexico's Grupo Televisa in the U.S. Spanish language television network Univision, with which they also have a programming partnership (Tobenkin, 1997). Another example, is Turner Broadcasting's alliance with a Japanese company to distribute its Cartoon Network in Japan.

A third approach to overseas investment is licensing. In this arrangement, a media company sells to another company the rights to produce one of its specific media products in a foreign market. The company that buys the rights assumes all the risks of making a successful entry into the new market. Usually, the parent company supplies the concept, graphics, and design elements for the product, and the company that buys the license is responsible for translation, production, and distribution. Television programs such as *Wheel of Fortune* and *America's Funniest Home Videos* have been licensed to European media companies. Magazines also are sometimes licensed to publishers in overseas markets.

For the media company that sells the license, this arrangement allows it to widen the distribution of its publication or programming with minimal risk and financial investment. The licensee, in turn, gains the rights to a proven and successful media product, which makes it easier to find an audience and advertisers.

The downside of licensing is that license fees greatly reduce the direct gain the company that created the original publication or programming receives from having its product in a new overseas market. Additionally, the licensor loses control over the production of its publication or program, making it difficult to ensure that its own high standards of quality are maintained. Finally, if the licensee fails in the new market, it can make it difficult for the company that created the media concept to reenter that market with that publication or program with a different licensee or under some other arrangement.

A final, crucial area of planning for the media company evaluating the resources available for an overseas investment is in the area of human resources. Unlike more routine product manufacturing where an initial good idea is mass produced in a routinized manufacturing process, each individual media product—magazine edition, television program, web page, advertisement—is unique and requires the creativity, insight, and specific effort of one or more people to bring into existence. Personnel management across borders is complex. When a media company enters an overseas market, it must conform to local personnel laws. In Germany, for example, most companies are required by law to have a "Betriebsrat," or worker's council, that has significant authority over the company's decisions to hire, promote, and terminate employees, as well as to rearrange work schedules, reassign individuals, and set other work rules and conditions. One German newspaper, for example, tried without success for almost 1 year to rearrange the work schedules of three of its print shop employees to cover vacancies left by retirements. However, management's proposed rescheduling of the remaining employees would have disrupted a car pool shared by two of them, and the newspaper's workers council refused to permit the change. As a consequence, one shift in the print shop was over-staffed, whereas the later shift was severely short-handed. Such a situation would be almost unimaginable to U.S. media managers.

More importantly for media companies, however, is the issue of employee training. Local employees must have adequate management, creative and production skills to meet corporate goals as well as comparable values in terms of the quality and production.

Once a company has evaluated the business environment and performance of a potential overseas market and the resources available for its expansion, the planning process becomes more similar to strategic planning for domestic operations. The company needs to further refine and operationalize its planning goals, identify and select alternative approaches to meeting those goals, and then implement, monitor, evaluate, and adjust the plan. Each of those steps, however, will be carried out in the context of the company's original goals for internationalization, its analysis of the business environment of its target country, the decisions it made about how its foreign operations will be structured, and the effects those structures will have on available resources.

When the company enters the intermediate planning process for its overseas operations, however, managers face additional issues that are specific to transborder media management.

Intermediate Planning for International Operations

During the intermediate planning process for a cross-border media investment, particular attention must be paid to the product aspect of the marketing plan. As already noted, the economy, regulatory environment and culture will affect a media company's choice of what publications, programs, or other media services to distribute. But even after a media company has decided to distribute a particular product, cultural factors must be carefully analyzed. Often differences are so subtle they may be difficult for a nonnative manager to recognize. But in the culturally based world of media, those differences can signal success or failure for the new foreign venture.

If, for example, a magazine or television program features recipes or cooking tips, the producers of that publication or program must make sure the recipes have been adapted for local tastes and the ingredients required to make the food are available. Home repair and other how-to publications or programs must take into account local needs and available products and tools. A program or magazine that teaches people how to build decks and patios, for example, would be useless in a country where the majority of the population live in apartments in cities—as is the case in many European nations. Advertisements must be screened to ensure that they do not offend local mores or insult readers and viewers. One German publisher, for example, received complaints from female readers in Russia about advertisements for Western cosmetics and fashions after the collapse of the Soviet Union in 1991. Readers told the publisher that the upscale products it advertised were unavailable to most Russian women at that time, and that they would be unable to afford the products even if they were available. Readers said the advertisements were depressing and a subtle form of Western elitism.

Even the colors used in publication layout and design, company logos, or program set designs must be carefully reevaluated with the foreign market in mind as color is very culturally significant and can signal different things in different countries. White, for example, is the color of mourning in the Middle East.

Place also is an issue in overseas markets. The transportation and communication infrastructures of many countries are less developed than they are in the United States. The media manager considering a cross-border investment must examine the infrastructure of the target country to see how easy it will be to distribute its products outside of urban areas and whether the costs of widespread distribution will be acceptable.

The promotion process also may change when a company moves overseas. Promotional slogans and even the name of a publication or program may not translate well into other languages. Promotional strategies common in the U.S. such as event sponsorship, live broadcasts, and other techniques for increasing audiences may not be possible or acceptable. Similarly, in many countries, it is difficult if not impossible to collect ratings and readership data, which makes it very hard to do target marketing.

Before entering an overseas market, the media manager must carefully research the promotional strategies that are possible within that country and develop an appropriate marketing plan within that framework.

As with domestic operations, the human resources plan concerns the acquisition and development of people needed to manage the operation and produce the media content. For the global media company the question is where it will find that personnel. One possibility is to send existing managers or key personnel to oversee the new cross-border operation. This ensures that staff are familiar with the goals of the company. Such managers, however, do not know the new market or have contacts in the new environment. For U.S. media companies, it also can be difficult to find Americans who are prepared to go overseas to work. The percentage of Americans who speak a second language and have lived or traveled extensively in other countries is lower than might be found in some other regions of the world.

Another option is to hire people locally for the new foreign office or to leave existing management and personnel in place. The advantages and disadvantages of this strategy are the opposite of those of the first approach. The foreign managers and employees would have local contacts, but they would need training and time to assimilate corporate expectations. In addition, a large measure of corporate control would be forfeited with this arrangement.

Among transnational companies, there is a third approach to personnel management. This approach is to seek the best personnel wherever they are found. Under this approach, a New Zealand executive might manage a U.S. office for a German parent company, or a Japanese national might run a subsidiary in India for a British corporation. Companies using this approach make long-term commitments to these multifaceted, international managers and groom them carefully for top leadership positions where their international outlook, expertise, and experience can be used to guide the transnational organization. For ambitious future managers, this means increased competition for top jobs as companies look throughout the world for the most talented, capable, and adaptable individuals.

When planning market entry into a new overseas operation, most financial planning will be done during the initial strategic planning process. Details of how the new venture will be capitalized during its first few years will be worked out as the venture is set up and the ownership structure is established.

The initial financial plan may need to be reconsidered if unexpected difficulties are encountered. Overseas operations, in general, are expensive to run because of higher travel and communication costs. New start-up media ventures usually require several years before they become profitable under the best of circumstances and, when investing in a foreign market, it can take even longer. Economic downturns are harder for the parent company to anticipate and are likely to throw off initial financial plans if they occur. Hiring a local staff may create greater than expected training costs because the entire staff will need to learn new ways of working even if the parent company buys an existing media company. A media operation may need new equipment and legal expenses may soar as the parent company negotiates with an unfamiliar legal and regulatory environment. Cultural differences between the parent company and the new target audience increase the likelihood that aspects of the media content produced will not be accepted and will need adjustment. Any or all of these factors may affect intermediate financial projections and require emergency funding to support the new venture.

Finally, during the intermediate planning process, managers must establish a benchmark against which to measure their new venture's financial success. Some media companies will consider a new venture successful if, during the intermediate planning period, it is able to generate enough revenue to cover its own operating expenses. Others will not consider the venture profitable until it also is covering the parent company's additional overhead—travel, communication, training, management oversight—for the overseas operation. Some managers will not consider a new venture to be profitable until after it has repaid all of the parent company's initial investment and start-up expenses in addition to covering its own operating costs and management overhead.

Probably the most difficult situation for a media manager occurs if the new venture fails to meet the financial benchmarks the parent company established during the intermediate planning process. At that point, the manager must decide whether the long-term potential benefits of global investment justify maintaining a media operation that is not profitable. The manager also will need to rethink the way the overseas investment has been structured, the way it is being managed, and the publications or programs it is producing. Sometimes a struggling media venture can be rescued by changing partners, managers, the product mix, or by launching an established publication or program with changes. In some cases, however, the only viable decision is to abandon a particular market and focus the company's efforts on other products or other countries.

SUMMARY

Planning is the essence of good management. The process is much like that of decision making, and its success depends on the adequate collection and analysis of information. The processes of planning should involve people from all levels of the organization. Planning takes three basic forms: strategic, intermediate, and short-run. Strategic is long-range planning planning, usually involving 3–5 years. Intermediate planning usually involves periods of 6 months to 2 years. Short-run planning can involve a period of 1 week to 1 year. The marketing plan, human resources plan, and financial plan make up the intermediate plan. The most common form of short-run plan is the yearly budget.

Investing overseas often entails more risk than if a media company were to expand its business in its own home market. However, in today's global economy, overseas investments are becoming more common and more important to the long-term well being of media corporations. International operations give media companies access to larger audiences and more advertisers. They allow them to tap new technologies, new ideas, and new artists or producers from countries beyond their home market. Having subsidiaries in more than one country can help balance a company's finances as a downturn in the economy of one country may be partially offset by an upsurge or stability in the economy of another. Finally, the multinational media corporation often has resources and economies of scale that can give it a competitive advantage as it goes head to head in some media sectors against other strictly domestic media operations.

For these reasons, the pace of globalization in the media industry is increasing rapidly. This means that media managers of the future will have greater need for foreign language skills, multicultural knowledge, and a global outlook. It also means that the media executives of the 21st century will be expected to understand the complex issues that arise when managing media ventures in different countries, have the skills to anticipate those challenges, and the knowledge and ability to plan strategically for success in the global media economy.

CASE 7.1

Adding a New Product

The *Daily Sentinel* newspaper is a profitable stable business with no direct competitive threats (from other media) to its future. Although there are local and state-wide radio and television stations servicing the area, there are no other newspapers. There is a free circulation paper that takes some classified advertising revenue from the *Sentinel* market, but the publisher, Mal McAuley, does not consider the losses significant. The owner's son, Harry, who joined the newspaper after graduating from college, has been trying to interest his father in developing a web site. Mal thinks the idea has potential but sees no reason to rush into development of a web page. He asks Harry to put together a solid strategic plan for consideration. He says the plan must show how the web page would be supportive of the newspaper's mission, which is to provide useful and entertaining information for all the readers in Cheyenne County who are primarily ranchers, small business owners, and government workers. "I want to know in specific terms how this web page is going to help my readers and who is going to pay for it," Mal tells his son. Harry has 1 month to develop the plan and make a presentation to his father, the news editor, the advertising director, and the circulation manager.

Harry sets up a meeting with the advertising department and learns some of the salespeople are worried a web site might impact current customers' commitments to the traditional newspaper. They say they would not like to see customers drop newspaper ads for web advertising. They also want to know if new staff will be hired to handle the accounts because they do not feel current staff can handle accounts for both media. The younger members of the staff are the most enthusiastic and mention the possibility of adding new or different customers to the web site because they have been asked by potential advertisers when or if the newspaper will have a web site. They mention that some ranchers use the Internet regularly to do research for their businesses, and the medical staff members at the local hospital use web pages and the Internet to keep current in their field. Harry suspects that the government employees also use the Internet and web pages to communicate with their central offices, which in some cases are located in Washington, DC. There is disagreement among staff members as to whether there is a local advertising market for a web site.

The news editor tells Harry she is worried that some of her staff will be asked to provide news for the web site. She does not think she has enough current reporters to write "fresh" copy for both the web site and the *Sentinel*.

"And what's the point of just repeating the news online?" she asks Harry. She also challenges Harry to explain why readers would want to have a newspaper web site. "It's a toy for people with too much time on their hands, and I don't think any readers out there care to read local news on a web site," she bluntly tells Harry.

The circulation department tells Harry they do not care what he does because the idea does not seem to have anything to do with delivery of newspapers. Harry suggests that an online newspaper might affect circulation figures, but the manager argues that nothing will replace the newspaper and how it is currently delivered (by truck and local subcontractors).

After his discussions, Harry realizes that the staff members in the three departments do not know much about web newspapers. In fact, he learns that although all the staff use e-mail at work, none use it at home and only five of the younger staff members (in their 20s) know much about this emerging technology. No one is familiar with web pages except a photographer who has a software program he has downloaded from the company computer to produce his private home page.

ASSIGNMENT

What has Harry learned in preliminary interviews with his father and the three departments that would help him answer the following questions?

1. Would a web page fulfill the newspaper's mission? Why or why not?
2. What are the positive and negative factors in the internal (newspaper) and external business environments that Harry needs to consider as he draws up a strategic plan?
3. What resources does Harry have available for the project and what resources would be required?
4. What factors influence how soon a web page could be developed?
5. What data will Harry need before he can present a plan to Mal and the other managers?

CASE 7.2

The Transnational Tightrope: A Case Study in Magazine Management Across Borders

European Magazines Inc. (EMI) publishes a group of magazines that cover the consumer electronics market. EMI publications report on, test, and review new products and developments in consumer electronics. Many of the magazines offer readers classified advertising where new and used consumer electronics items can be bought and sold. The company also publishes catalogs of consumer electronics products and an annual book offers a year-in-review perspective of the industry as well as a forecast of the coming year.EMI is based in Germany, a Western European country with a generally strong economy. The market for consumer electronics in Germany is among the strongest in Europe, so there is solid demand for information about consumer electronics products. EMI has established itself as the leader in that publishing niche in its home country.

Over the past 20 years, EMI also has branched out to sell editions of its magazines in neighboring Western European countries. There is considerable competition in those markets, however, because Western European countries, in general, have strong publishing industries. In each neighboring market EMI entered, there was already a strong domestic magazine covering consumer electronics. So, although EMI's international operations have been successful, they provide a relatively small percentage of the company's total revenues. EMI's bread and butter is still its home country market.

And for a growth-oriented company, that is not entirely good news.

In Germany, the magazine industry is fully mature. Although, the industry's total circulation, revenues, and number of advertising pages have been climbing in the last decade, so has the number of magazine titles being published and, therefore, the competition for readers' attention. More importantly, the magazine industry's real share of the national advertising market has been slipping during the 1990s as television and emerging media syphon off advertising dollars.

In short, EMI cannot expect to enjoy strong or rapid growth in its publishing niche in either Germany or other Western European markets in the foreseeable future.

For EMI's growth-oriented management, that means that the company will have to look outside its Western European region for new opportunities. Because most countries that have economies strong enough to generate a large market for consumer electronics products also already have established magazines serving readers in that niche, the best opportunities for EMI to expand are likely to be in countries with emerging economies, that is, countries where a significant percentage of the people are starting to have some extra income that they can afford to spend on items that are not strictly necessary for survival.

From a management standpoint, investing in a country with an emerging economy entails significant risk. Such countries may require foreign investors to have local partners in order to do business, but local capital to fund initial investments and start-up expenses is often in short supply. Meanwhile, the requirement that investors work with local partners means that company management must be prepared to deal with language, cultural and financial differences even in its internal decision-making processes as it manages the new enterprise.

Perhaps most importantly, if the economy of the new country does not develop as expected, there may be no market for the product the investor produces. In the case of EMI, for example, if it moved into a new country and the economy there did not grow enough for people to have the money to buy consumer electronics, there would be no market for its magazines.

For media companies, the risk can be even greater than for other types of businesses because media products are, by definition, language and culture-based products. For example, a lightbulb can be shipped to another country as long as the electrical currents and light sockets are the same in the new market as in the old and some minor adjustments are made to packaging. However, a magazine publisher has to be sure that every element in the publication's content is appropriate for the new market. Success hinges on getting all of the details right in every single published edition.

Articles must be relevant and of interest to readers in the new market. Items that are advertised or described in stories must be available in that country. Generally, it is most cost efficient for the start-up publication to draw some of its content from material that already has been produced for the company's flagship home market editions. But if the publisher shares content between publications, management must be certain that every shared article has been translated correctly in language, culture, and meaning and that nothing in the content is offensive to readers in the new market. Publication layout and design must appeal to readers in the new country, and the publisher must be sensitive to the fact that colors, symbols, and photographs mean different things in different countries.

Finally, literacy rates are often lower in emerging countries than in industrialized nations, and for a publishing company to succeed, there has to be a critical mass of individuals able and willing to read.

NEW MARKET OPENS

Recognizing the limitations of their own home market, the top executives of EMI decided to expand into foreign markets, particularly into countries with emerging economies and not-yet-mature media markets. Corporate management soon identified a country—Newland—in which it was interested. Newland had the strongest and most consumer-oriented economy in its region, although by Western European standards the living conditions of the population were bleak. Nevertheless, a recent decision by Newland's government to liberalize the economy and open the country to Western investment had drawn a flood of North American and European companies into the market and set off a mini economic boom. As part of its decision to liberalize its economy, the Newland government announced that it would allow limited foreign ownership of the print media, as long as at least 50% of each publishing company continued to be held by a Newland company or individual.

That announcement set off a publishing land rush and Western media companies dashed across the Newland border to grab a piece of the market. Among Newland's advantages as a publishing market were its emerging economy and the resulting strong demand for news and information that would be useful to both business managers and consumers as they came to grips with their new environment.

There also was an almost insatiable interest among the Newlander public in Western products, fashions, and ways of doing things, which boded well for Western publications. Also an advantage was the fact that the country enjoyed comparatively high literacy rates for a nation in its economic situation.

Finally, Newland had a reasonably sophisticated transportation infrastructure in its major cities, making it possible for Western publishers to consider the possibility of printing publications in their home countries and shipping the finished product into Newland.

On the downside, Newland's primary language was unique to the country, which has a relatively small population. Thus, there would be little ability to capture economies of scale in production for Newland, and there would be virtually no opportunities to export editions produced for

Newland beyond that country's borders as was possible for EMI's German and English language publications.

Newland also was different culturally and politically from Germany and other Western nations, and despite the Newland public's interest in things Western, there remained a strong undercurrent of resentment in the population against the incoming Western investors, their ways of doing things and their apparent affluence in comparison to Newland citizens.

The cultural differences between Newland and the West extended to the business culture. Within Newland companies, everything from accounting methods to relationships between employers and employees operated very differently from what would be normal in a Western European or North American company. In Newland, when people took a job, they expected it to be for a lifetime. Pay was low, but employees rarely quit and they generally did not need to worry about being fired or laid off. On the job, productivity expectations were minimal and workers felt little pressure to be efficient.

With the sudden influx of Western investors, the expectations of both managers and employees in Newland changed in some ways but not others. Employees expected that their unwritten lifetime employment contracts would continue, as would their managers' previous standards of productivity. But at the same time, the employees wanted their pay to increase dramatically and their working conditions to improve.

Newland business managers, on the other hand, wanted the chance to become part owners in Western-funded business ventures, and they wanted those ventures to make them rich *quickly.* But with capital in Newland scarce, local managers had little money of their own to invest in new business opportunities.

In the publishing industry, it was no different. Newland publishers' were not familiar with Western business methods. Nor did they have experience doing business in a competitive publishing market because before the government opened the economy, there had been few magazines available in Newland and most received government subsidies. As a result, Newland publishers tended to have unrealistic ideas about how much money they were going to make from their publishing ventures and how much time it was going to take those ventures to start making money—instead of losing it.

Although EMI's management was fully aware of these challenges, company leaders decided that Newland still was an attractive market. Therefore, the company announced that it would begin publishing in the Newland market.

ESTABLISHING THE NEW VENTURE

As required by Newland law, EMI's initial entrance into the Newland market was structured as a joint venture with a local Newland company.

EMI met its partner through a third party, who contacted EMI on behalf of the Newland partner before the Newland government had announced its decision to liberalize its economy. That partner, a Newlander publishing entrepreneur, anticipated his government's decision and decided to find a Western partner with deep pockets. In return, he offered EMI his knowledge of Newland and its readers, his contacts in Newlander government and industry, and the two small electronics magazines he had recently launched that complemented EMI's stable of publications.

Under the agreement worked out, each partner held 50% of the new joint venture. The partnership agreed that it would begin by publishing three different monthly consumer electronics magazines and two annual publications. The monthly magazines included EMI's flagship publication, *Electronic Gadgets Today* and the two small Newland magazines that the local partner published. The annuals included EMI's special yearly electronics industry soft-cover book and its annual catalog.

The fledgling joint venture was named EMI Overseas Ltd. or EOL for short.

EMI's first priority was to establish the monthly magazines in the Newland market and stave off competition from similar publications that might be launched by other Western European publishers. The expectation was that once EOL's monthly magazines established a loyal Newland readership, there would be strong demand for the company's special—and more expensive—annual publications.

But that expectation was only a hunch. Indeed, almost all of EMI's decisions about the Newland market were based on guesses. Because of the suddenness with which Newland's market had been opened by its government and because of the rapid influx of other publishers into the market—each one trying to establish its dominance in a particular market niche—there was no time to do the kind of careful research that would have been done before launching a new publication in a Western European market. Instead, EMI and other Western European publishers simply leapt into Newland without looking. They had only the most rudimentary information about Newland market conditions, readers' habits and desires, and cultural norms. On this occasion, speed of action took precedence over caution and information.

It was a high risk strategy.

Moreover, there was a lot more to setting up a new transnational operation than just deciding what to publish. There was a whole series of critical decisions to be made about how the new Newland magazines should be published, with each decision being important to the ultimate success or failure of the new venture.

Content Issues. A major issue to be resolved by management involved the source and orientation of the content for the Newland publications. A number of options were available. One possibility was to have the magazines produced locally with articles focusing on Newland. A number of Western publishers entered the Newland market using this model of content production.

A second option—again, one widely used by Western publishers breaking into the Newland market—was to use the copy and art that were being produced for a publication's current home market edition and have it professionally translated into the Newland language.

A third choice was a cross between the other two approaches: depend on the local staff to produce some or most of the content for the Newland edition, but also offer them all of the content and art from the company's home market publication so that they could use any material they believed appropriate for Newland readers.

A publishing company using this model also gave the local magazine staff the right to rewrite and refocus the articles borrowed from the parent publication so that the angle of the story would be more appropriate for local subscribers. For example, the German edition of an EMI magazine might focus on the upgrades for a new product promised by the manufacturer in coming months, whereas the Newland version of the story might focus on approaches to maintaining and repairing that same product.

After much consideration, EMI and its joint venture partner decided to use the third content model. It was expected that some content—such as product test results—would be translated directly from the German editions of EMI's publications because the Newland EOL partnership would not have independent product testing facilities. Most of the copy—roughly two thirds of each Newland edition's content—would be produced locally and would be unique to EOL's publications. The other one third would be either test results translated directly or articles published in EMI's German magazines but reworked for the Newland market.

Who Runs the Show? The next crucial questions were how would EOL's Newland publications be produced, where would they be produced, and by whom would they be produced? Again, there was a number of possible options.

Some Western investors published their Newland editions in their home countries and simply shipped the finished product to Newland for distribution to readers. In such cases, the Newland staff or translators usually worked in the company's international headquarters turning out the publication for their distant readership.

Other Western publishing companies set up operations in Newland but staffed them largely with their own personnel. The Newland partners functioned only as advisors and sometimes only as window dressing. Using an almost entirely Western staff ensured that the new publications operated the same way as all of the parent company's other publications, maximizing production and management efficiency and minimizing cross-cultural misunderstandings on staff.

A third organizational structure adopted by some Western investors transplanted Western managers to run the local operation, but hired local workers for nonmanagement positions. This increased the publication's sensitivity to cultural conditions as well as to readers, while ensuring that the business end operated according to Western standards and processes.

Finally, a fourth approach was to completely staff the local venture with Newlanders. This maximized a magazine's relevance to Newland readers and created goodwill among readers and the government by demonstrating that the Western owner was willing to create jobs and share power and prosperity.

After much consideration, EMI agreed to adopt the last structure for its nascent Newland venture. EMI management and its local Newland partners hired Newlanders for both the management and staff positions in EOL. However, EMI insisted that the person hired to head the EOL subsidiary be brought to Germany for extensive training at company headquarters in Western business, accounting methods, and publication production processes. EMI's management also reserved the right to maintain control of major decisions, such as launching a new magazine or any other issue that would have major financial impact on the company. Those decisions would be made in Germany.

Other Decisions.   There were other key issues facing EMI's management in the prelaunch days of its Newland subsidiary. Western publications used higher quality paper, higher resolution photographs and printing processes, and much more color than most Newland magazines before the government opened the market. For this reason, many Western investors arranged to have their publications shipped to Western Europe to be printed, with the finished product being shipped back to Newland for distribution. EMI was fortunate, however. Newland boasted two printing facilities capable of producing high quality four-color glossy publications, and EOL was able to secure a printing contact with one of them.

Another question concerned advertising. Should the EOL subsidiary focus its efforts on securing advertising primarily from in-country sources or from Western advertisers? If the company went after Western advertisers, should the company screen the advertisements submitted for local culture-appropriate content and for product availability?

Although from a financial standpoint, the desirable strategy obviously would be to sell as much advertising as possible and publish it regardless of content, Western publishers had found in the past that such a strategy can backfire in a less developed country. In some instances, local readers had resented the role Western-owned publications played in helping foreign businesses move into the market and compete with local companies through advertising.

In other cases, readers had objected that they could not afford the products that were advertised and accused the Western-owned magazines of using the ads to flaunt Western wealth to them.

In such cases, the result of an open advertising strategy had been to create reader resentment and a loss of subscribers.

The final significant management issue facing EMI and its EOL subsidiary was how the publication would be distributed. In the first months after the goverment opened the market to foreign publishers in Newland, publishers had little choice about distribution. Although the government had opened its publishing market, it had not yet deregulated its magazine distribution system. The government required that all magazines be distributed through the Newland Post—even those that went to newsstands for sale off the rack. Readers and kiosk operators who wanted a publication did not contact the magazine. They contacted the Post. Magazine publishers never knew who their subscribers were or how many copies were sold through subscription and how many were sold on newsstands.

As the distribution system was set up, the Post told publishers how many copies of their publications it wanted. The publisher was paid 90% of the magazine's cover price up front, with the Post keeping the remaining 10% as a sales commission. The Post took responsibility for distributing and selling the magazines and, if some did not sell, the Post absorbed the loss.

The distribution system had worked very well for Newland before the government opened the publishing market to outsiders. In the old days, there had been shortages of paper in the country and, as a result, publishers could not produce enough magazines and newspapers to meet demand. Thus, almost every edition of every publication sold out. That had meant the Post had faced little financial risk in paying publishers for the magazines immediately. At the same time, having the contract for all magazine distribution gave the Post a critical and consistent source of revenue that helped the government provide its citizens with affordable mail service. Loss of revenue from magazine sales would have been a major financial blow to the nation's postal system.

A Good Beginning

The first year of EMI's new venture in Newland went far better than expected. The influx of Western businesses had set off an economic boom in the country and—perhaps even more importantly—the conviction in Newlanders that unlimited economic prosperity was here to stay. Consequently, the conditions for reader interest in nonessential consumer electronics products were ideal. Moreover, the country's long isolation from the West had created interest in information and contact with Western ways of doing things, and so there was strong demand for Western-based publications that carried Western advertising and discussed Western products.

Finally, because EMI and its Newland partner had been discussing a partnership before the Newland government had even opened the market to Westerners, they had been able to set up operations very quickly. Consequently, they were publishing their Western-quality magazines months before most other Western publishers had been able to break into the market.

Not surprisingly, then, the circulation for the three monthly consumer electronics products magazines zoomed during the first year. Circulation for the Newland edition of EMI's flagship magazine, *Electronic Gadgets Today*, topped 75,000 at one point during the first year, an impressive level for a start-up publication in a less-developed country with a population of only 10 million.

EOL's success with advertisers was equally great. Western electronics manufacturers and retailers were no less eager to grab a piece of the Newland market than were publishers, and magazines and newspapers were the most cost-effective way for those companies to advertise their wares to potential Newland buyers. With little competition from other electronics magazines, much of the advertising found its way into EOL publications.

Through the first year, about 30% of the revenue for *Electronic Gadgets Today* came from advertising, whereas the other two monthly magazines were booking about 20% of their revenue from advertising. By comparison, most U.S. consumer magazines depend on advertising for around 54% of revenue, whereas subscription and newsstand sales provide the other 46%.

At the end of the first year, EOL also produced Newland editions of EMI's two annual publications. Those were particularly slick publications, carried lots of advertising and were sold at a premium cover price. They were marketed to Newlanders as Christmas gifts and as status symbols. They were, for example, marketed to Newland companies and executives as something to leave on their waiting room tables for clients to see and read. The newly affluent among Newland citizens also bought copies to display in their homes.

Newland circulation for the Electronics Industry annual book was 50,000 during the first year, and for the catalog, 90,000. Both were immediately profitable.

Although EMI executives were ecstatic about their Newland venture's first year results, that did not mean the company was producing large profits. In fact, only under the most generous calculations could it be claimed that the operations were even breaking even.

With a circulation of 75,000 and 30% advertising revenue, *Electronic Gadgets Today* was bringing in enough cash to cover its direct production costs, including editorial, advertising and printing. The other two magazines were not quite as successful but were still managing to cover most of the direct production expenses for each edition. However, none of the three publications was covering administrative costs, particularly not the higher expenses incurred by EMI's German operations as a result of travel, training of Newland personnel, and other expenses associated with running a transnational subsidiary.

One of those additional expenses included hiring someone fluent in the Newlander language to work in EMI's German headquarters. EMI had realized after its EOL subsidiary published its first magazine that there was no one at corporate headquarters who could read the publications and double check them for quality, accuracy, and possible legal problems.

Some publishers with transnational operations did not worry about having in-house readers for their overseas publications, trusting their foreign employees to produce quality magazines without headquarter's oversight. But EMI felt strongly that the company's reputation had been built on the quality and expertise of its publications. Consequently, EMI executives wanted to make sure the editors and reporters in their Newland subsidiary knew what they were doing when it came to publishing a magazine and knew what they were talking about when it came to writing about consumer electronics products. EMI hired a Newlander who had been living in Germany for some time and had electronics expertise to monitor the new publications.

Their concern was not unwarranted. During the early months of the EOL venture, the local Newland staff proved unable to get their publications out the door on deadline. Instead, they produced the magazines in stages as they were accustomed to doing. This meant that it took 2 to 3 months to get each edition to the printer. Given the fast change in the consumer electronics market, that meant most of the magazines were outdated long before they reached readers.

An honest assessment of the EOL subsidiary's financial standing at the end of its first year would also have had to acknowledge that the operation was not anywhere close to being able to repay its German parent company for its start-up investments or any of the interest being incurred on those loans. Under Western accounting methods, all of those expenses also would need to be covered by revenue from the publications before the overseas subsidiary would be considered profitable.

Still, EMI's executives had few complaints about their Newland venture. They understood that it normally takes several years—and sometimes much longer—before a start-up publication achieves true profitability. They also knew going in that because of the higher administrative costs of managing a transnational subsidiary, it would take even longer for their Newland venture to become profitable than it would have if the company had been domestic.

Finally, EMI's management team was fully aware that advertising and circulation figures for new publications are usually highly unstable for the first few years after start-up as reader and advertiser interest ebbs and flows. Stability and consistent growth comes only when a publication succeeds in building a solid base of loyal subscribers who attract loyal advertisers. For most publications, that happens slowly. So, the fact that the EOL publications were generating enough revenue to cover most of their direct production costs was more than EMI executives had expected.

Thus, at the end of their first year of operations in Newland, EMI executives were quite content.

The Venture Hits Hard Times

If EMI's executives were happy with the results of the first year, their Newlander partner was not. Far from it, in fact.

The Newlander entrepreneur had expected the magazine company to produce a handsome return on his investment in 1 year. Instead, his German colleagues were telling him that the magazines were losing money when all expenses were calculated. The total costs of producing the publications—including interest, overhead, and administrative expenses—were more than what the publications were bringing in from advertising and circulation.

The EMI executives also pointed out that, as an owner of the company, the Newlander partner was expected to continue to provide some of the cash that would have to be pumped into the EOL subsidiary on an ongoing basis until the company became truly profitable—2 or 3 years down the road. And even if his German partners considered his Newland-market expertise as part of his contribution to their joint venture's efforts, as a 50% owner, he should expect to contribute something close to 50% of the money needed to cover continuing financial short falls.

For the Newlander partner, that was simply an impossibility. He did not have the capital and, in capital-starved Newland, neither did anyone else.

In the meantime, there were other stresses on the partnership. Because Western and Newland business practices were so different, there were frequent misunderstandings between the partners. A common business term meant one thing to the Germans and something else entirely to a Newlander.

Because of the Newland law requiring all companies incorporated in the country to have at least 50% Newland ownership, EMI was left with two choices: fold its Newland operations and go home or cover 100% of the venture's losses although its additional investment would not result in a greater share of ownership.

There was never much doubt what the company would do. EMI executives had a long-term view of the opportunities in Newland. The company would stay.

EMI's Newland partner had a short-term outlook, however, and for him, as the company moved into its second year, the situation became decidedly worse.

The first thing that happened was that Newland's economic boom—which had been fueled more by optimism than cash—collapsed. Suddenly, Newlanders realized that the overnight prosperity they had anticipated had not materialized, which meant that many of them had been spending money they did not have and were not likely to recover anytime soon.

At the same time, competition in the Newland publishing market was stiffening. Although EOL's publications had been the first in their niche on Newland newsstands, by the beginning of the second year there were plenty of imitators. Some were copycat magazines that had been started by local entrepreneurs. Most were Western joint ventures run by publishers like EMI that had similar magazines back home and had deep pockets to fund their move into the Newland market.

The combination of increased competition and economic downturn hit the EOL venture hard. Suddenly fewer people had the money to be interested in consumer electronic products, and those people—and the advertisers that wanted to reach them—had a lot more publications from which to choose.

Circulation for EOL's publications plummeted. For *Electronic Gadgets Today*, the venture's mainstay, circulation crashed from a high of 75,000 to 22,000. EOL's other two monthly publications and both annuals suffered similar circulation losses. At the same time, advertising revenues plunged from 30% of revenues for *Electronic Gadgets Today* to 20%, and averaged across all three publications, advertising was generating only 15% of the venture's revenue. EOL's group of publications was no longer bringing in enough money to cover its immediate production expenses.

To make matters worse, in the midst of these setbacks, the Newland Post announced that it was changing the way it distributed magazines. The Post's policy of paying for publications up front and absorbing the risk of selling them was only feasible if it could be sure of selling almost every copy it had. During the days before Western investment, there had been only a few publications available in the country, so selling all copies of all publications had been a sure thing. But with the flood of new publications on the market from around the world, selling every copy was now an impossibility. The Post had no choice but to change the way it did business with publishers.

Under the new system, publishers were still required to distribute through the Post. The Post also determined how many copies of each publication it would distribute. Now, however, it did not pay for the publications when it received them. Instead, the Post waited four weeks and then paid the publisher 50% of the net revenue from sales up to that point—having already taken out its sales commission—and waited another 3 or 4 months to pay for the rest.

In other words, the Post would order 50,000 copies of a magazine and sell 30,000 during the first month. After 4 weeks, it would pay the publisher for 15,000 copies—or half of the total it had sold. The remainder of the revenue for the other 15,000 that had been sold was paid a month or more later when the Post felt it had a final accounting of sales for that edition.

In the meantime, the publisher already would have had to pay all the bills for producing 50,000 magazines, although it had received only a fraction of the revenue from their sales. Moreover, eventually the 20,000 unsold magazines would be returned to the publisher. Those magazines, of course, generated no revenue.

This created serious cash flow problems for all publishers in the Newland market. Moreover, the system shifted all of the financial risk onto the publishers, with only limited means for controlling those risks. Magazine publishers had to rely on the ability of the Post to forecast how many copies of each edition would be sold and, therefore, how many should be printed. If the Post overestimated, the publisher had to absorb the loss.

Worse yet, the Post's new system meant that there was a significant lag time between when an edition was printed and when the Post calculated how many copies of that edition had been sold. In the meantime, the publisher would have printed several more editions without any chance to adjust print runs—and therefore production costs—to account for declines in circulation or, for that matter, to take advantage of increased reader interest.

As the problems created by the Post's distribution system increased, several Western publishing companies met to discuss ways to maneuver around the Newland law that magazines had to be distributed through the Post. The group contacted a magazine distribution company in a country near Newland. The distributor agreed to try to get copies of the Newland Post's subscription and distribution list for each of the publications in the publishers' group. The idea was that the cross-border distributor would use the list to start sending the publishers' magazines directly to Newland readers and newsstands from outside of the country. That would reduce the risk and cash flow problems of the Western publishers involved in the plan, as well as give them control over their own lists of subscribers.

The plan, if the Western publishers were successful, would circumvent their host country's regulations, but the publishers in the group felt it was unlikely that the Newland government would be able to enforce any real penalties against them. Nevertheless, when the group of Western publishers approached EMI's executives about joining them in the plan, EMI declined to participate.

Restructuring, Relaunching, Renewal

By the end of EMI's second year in the Newland market, things were looking grim for the EOL partnership. EMI's Newland partner was shocked by the failure of the venture to produce profits, irritated by the ongoing cultural and professional misunderstandings with EMI, and disheartened by the sharp downturn in the joint venture's fortunes as the country entered a recession. As the second year wound to a close, EMI's Newland partner announced that he was "resigning from the hardships of the market."

EMI was without a partner.

EMI was not alone in facing this crisis. Western investors around the country were experiencing similar problems as their capital-short Newland partners faced the recession with empty pockets. Under pressure from the business community, the Newland government repealed the law that required 50% ownership by a Newlander citizen in order for a publisher to do business in the country.

EMI was now free to go into the future using the corporate structure of its choice for its Newland operations.

The choices, of course, were several. EMI could restructure EOL as a wholly owned subsidiary. It could look for a different partner—another Newland investor or a Western partner —or it could decide to cut its risks by shutting down EOL and licensing its publications to another publisher.

In the face of the recent hardships of the Newland market, Western publishers were doing all three things. Some of them were leaving the market altogether. With the first wild "gold rush" into Newland over, the fallout among publishers was beginning. Only the best, hardiest, and most determined were going to be able to stay.

Even as EMI's management team were considering these options, the phone rang. On the other end was the chairperson and CEO of another German publishing company that had entered the Newland market the previous year with a magazine that focused on crafts and hobbies. This new publisher, Hobby Magazines Inc., had also encountered problems with its Newland partner. The chairperson of Hobby Magazines suggested that his company and EMI form a new joint venture for their Newland operations.

EMI's management team was intrigued by the possibility. For one thing, although crafts and hobbies had little to do with consumer electronics, at least Hobby Magazines was producing the same type of publication EMI was, that is, a special interest magazine that provided readers with news they could use. As far as EMI was concerned, that made Hobby Magazines a better fit for a partnership than a movie star or fashion magazine publisher.

Nevertheless, examination of Hobby Magazines' record in Newland was a bit discouraging. The company had been a late entrant into the market and had already reorganized its Newland subsidiary twice. Circulation of its hobby magazine had never been strong in Newland and had declined with the recession, just as EMI's publications had. The pool of potential advertisers for the hobby publication was smaller than for EMI's consumer electronics magazines and the companies producing hobby supplies had much smaller advertising budgets.

Still, the hobby magazine was a proven performer in Germany and in other Western European countries where Hobby Magazines Inc. had operations. If EMI managers took a long-term view, they had reason to believe that it might be equally successful in Newland 5 or 10 years down the road when the economy stabilized and the citizenry started having more disposable income and leisure time.

Moreover, Hobby Magazines Inc., although a German incorporated and managed company, was actually owned by a major Canadian magazine publishing company. Thus, if EMI partnered with Hobby Magazines, EMI's executives would have the advantage of working with a management team that shared their language, culture, and business outlook, while being backed by the very deep pockets of a truly multinational publishing corporation.

After several months of negotiations, the two companies agreed to go forward together in a joint venture. The newly created partnership was not 50–50, however. With EMI bringing in five publications and Hobby Magazines bringing in only one, the joint venture was structured with EMI holding 94% of the company and Hobby Magazines only 6%.

One of the first orders of business for the new partnership was to relaunch one of EOL's consumer electronics magazines. The magazine, one of those originally started by the Newland partner, had never overcome its production problems. The publication's focus had wandered from issue to issue and content was usually outdated by the time it reached readers. During the recession, both readers and advertisers had abandoned it, and circulation had fallen below 10,000 with advertising producing less than 10% of revenues.

After careful consideration, EMI decided not to kill the publication but, instead, to relaunch it. They pulled the publication off the market for several months and hired a market research company to survey remaining readers about why they read it. The survey results identified a central area of the magazine's coverage that had attracted readers. That became the new focus of the publication.

Once plans for the new focus were completed and the publication was redesigned to have a new look, EMI hired a public relations firm to advertise the relaunch of the made-over magazine. Initial response to the relaunch was quite positive, with circulation climbing above 15,000 for the first 2 months of the new publication and advertising producing about 17% of the magazine's revenue.

With the market beginning to shake out and the number of magazines published in Newland falling, EMI's management team recognized that it was time for their Newland subsidiary to change the way it did business. Up until then, the venture had been operating as a start-up company, a phase in the life cycle of organizations during which quick decisions and risk taking are important. But as the other would-be publishers in the Newland market departed, EMI's management realized that they needed to focus on a long-term strategy for slow, stable growth. EMI temporarily shelved plans to buy, launch, and absorb additional publications in Newland. Instead, it started an ongoing program of market research to help its existing magazines be more successful. The company also began bringing on new employees, doubling its staff in just 1 year. Finally, a marketing firm was hired to develop a consistent advertising and marketing plan for each of the publications.

EMI also came up with a plan to minimize the problems caused by the Newland Post's distribution system. The company placed an advertisement in each edition of each of its publications offering readers a small gift for sending in their names, addresses, and comments to the editors. This not only provided EMI with reader feedback, it also allowed the company to start developing a list of its readers and subscribers.

With a basic subscriber list in hand, EMI was able to start developing programs to improve reader retention—a key issue in publishing.

Almost immediately, these changes began paying dividends. By the end of the third year of operation, circulation for the subsidiary's flagship *Electronic Gadgets Today* had climbed more than 45% from its low at the crash, topping 32,000. Circulation for the other two consumer electronics products monthly magazines was more than 25,000 and one of the annuals sold more than 60,000 copies during the third year of operations.

Advertising revenue also was climbing. By the end of the third year, *Electronic Gadgets Today* had averaged a 33% advertising-to-editorial-pages ratio for the 12 months and had, in one memorable issue, broken the 50–50 mark. For the company as a whole, about 20% of the Newland subsidiary's revenues were coming from advertising and the percentage was slowly climbing. Although the company was still slightly in the red for all of its operations for the year, it had finished the year showing strong and steady growth on all fronts.

EMI's executives projected that, all things remaining equal, they could expect the Newland subsidiary to be booking 40% of all its revenues from advertising by the end of the next year—their fourth in the market. They expected to achieve profitability—true profitability—the year after.

Five years to profitability had been about what they had expected going into the Newland market and, despite a few surprises along the way, the company was pretty much on track. For EMI's management team, that meant only one thing: It was time to begin looking for a new market in another country with an emerging economy. It was time to expand their transnational operations again.

ASSIGNMENT

Answer the following questions based on information in the chapter and in the previous case.

1. Which of the models of cross-border investment do you think the German company was using with its Newland project—international, multinational, global, or transnational? Which aspects of their plan make you think it is that model? Which aspects of their plan do not fit that model?

2. Why would a publisher consider printing a magazine in its home country and then shipping the finished product overseas? What would be some of the disadvantages of doing that?

3. What would be advantages and disadvantages to each of the models of content production that different Western publishers were using to launch magazines in the Newland market?

4. What would be the disadvantages of each of the different organizational structures considered by EMI and its partners as a way of producing the Newland magazines?

5. Do you think that EMI or the managers of its subsidiary should have involved themselves in screening Western advertising before putting it in their Newland magazines? If so, what criteria should they have used for accepting or rejecting an ad?

6. Under the initial system whereby the Post paid for magazines up front and absorbed all losses, there were still some disadvantages for publishers. What would some of those disadvantages have been? Do you think the advanatages of the system outweighed the disadvantages of it from the publisher's point of view?

7. Do you agree with EMI's decision to hire someone at its German headquarters to read and monitor the Newland magazines for quality? Would it have been better for EMI to have done as many other publishers did—that is just

trust their Newland employees to publish a high quality magazine without headquarters' oversight?

8. Would you have stayed in a market that required you to pay 100% of the operating costs of a business venture while only receiving a 50% share of the ownership? Why or why not?

9. What do you think about the Western publishers' attempt to make an end-run around the Post? Was that ethical? Should EMI have joined them?

10. Given EMI's situation after its Newland partner quit, what would have been the advantages of each of the choices it could have made for restructuring it Newland publishing operations? What would have been the disadvantages of each choice?

8

MARKET ANALYSIS

At its simplest, a *market* is where goods and services are bought and sold. This selling process requires demand by consumers and supply by businesses. Market analysis is an effort to understand the interaction of supply and demand in the market. This interaction starts with the media company and involves consumers, competitors, government regulation, and the general nature of the economy. The actions of firms, government agencies, or consumers affect the entire market. Market analysis allows managers to understand the market so changes can be anticipated and actions can be taken.

Every market is defined geographically by the area in which a company sells its product or service. For example, a newspaper's market is defined by the area in which copies of the newspaper can be obtained by home delivery or newsstand and newsrack sales. A television station's market is determined by the ability of viewers to receive the signal.

Media organizations are unusual because they participate in more than one type of market with the same commodity. An automobile dealership sells cars to people and is, therefore, in the automobile market. However, a magazine company can sell copies of magazines to readers and space in the magazines to advertisers. The multimarket nature of many media firms creates a complexity that makes media management an especially difficult challenge.

In order for media managers to meet the challenge, they must be able to analyze demand and supply in the various markets. The complexity of the market process, the difficulty of generating accurate data, and the nature of the decision process make many managerial decisions risky. However, market analysis reduces this risk by yielding information and analysis that fits into the hub of the decision-making wheel explained in chap. 1. Because information and analysis are central to decisions, market analysis is central to any major changes in the nature or price of media commodities.

This chapter provides an overview of the nature of media markets, the economic environment in the markets, and how factors that affect firms in these markets can be analyzed.

230

STEPS IN MARKET ANALYSIS

Market analysis has five steps: (a) Identifying the type of market, (b) understanding the general goals of a manager's organization, (c) specifying the nature of demand for a firm's commodity, (d) identifying the market structure, and (e) examining the economic environment.

Types of Markets

Media firms function in one or more of three types of markets (Lacy & Simon, 1993): *advertising*, *information*, and *intellectual*. The information market is where readers, viewers, and listeners seek a variety of information. In exchange for this information, they pay money or make their attention available for advertisers. The advertising market is where advertisers buy space or time from media organizations to present their products and services to the viewers, readers, and listeners. The intellectual market is where individuals and social groups seek ideas and information that will help the groups pursue their goals within the society. This market is the equivalent to the marketplace of ideas developed by John Milton and amplified by John Stuart Mill.

These three markets are connected for some media because media commodities can be joint products, which means two or more markets are served with a single production process. For example, a newspaper firm prints newspaper copies with information that can be sold to readers and advertising space that can be sold to advertisers. The connection is even stronger because readers use advertising as information.

All three types of markets are important for news media. The information and advertising markets generate revenue for business survival, but it is the intellectual market that gives news media their special place in society. Yet this market is the most difficult to examine because there is no direct exchange of money for a product. This difficulty does not mean the market can be ignored. It is the supply and demand interaction in the intellectual market that the First Amendment was designed to protect. The Hutchins Commission warned in 1947 that if media organizations ignore their responsibilities in this market, the special protection offered by the First Amendment could be revoked by society (Commission on Freedom of the Press, 1947). In a more direct relationship, the regulation of broadcast television by the federal government traditionally carries with it an obligation to serve this market.

The issue of a media company's responsibility to society emerged during the 1990s as an important element of the debate about government's influence on media content. The creation of a ratings system for television programs, efforts to censor on-line content through the 1996 Telecommunications Act, and anger over media coverage of Princess Diana and her death all represent the public's concern about news media's emphasis on scandal and sensational events. Managers of media companies, especially news organizations, must consider their impact on society and their contribution to the intellectual market in market analysis and planning.

One last problem in dealing with these three markets is their interrelationship. People use what they learn in the information market for decision making in the intellectual market, and they buy newspapers for advertising as well as news. Because people use content in ways not intended, it is difficult to predict the demand behavior of readers, listeners, and viewers.

Despite the complexity of identifying and separating business behavior in markets, it is necessary to do so. Managers need to be aware that decisions affecting one market have an impact on the other markets. Lack of awareness about the interrelation can increase government intervention into their affairs.

Goals

A *goal* is the purpose of some behavior. Before this term is applied specifically to media management, it is worthwhile to step back from the individual goals and examine the origins of organizational goals. Goals flow from the basic purposes of an organization. For example, some organizations are commercial and seek a profit, whereas others are noncommercial and nonprofit. The following section starts with general purposes and then defines goals for media organizations.

General purposes refer to the reasons that media organizations exist. A company may want to make a profit or change society, but whatever it seeks to do, its goals will reflect the financing that media organizations receive. Altschull (1984) listed four patterns of financing media: *official, commercial, interest,* and *informal.* The official pattern involves government control of media content through rules, regulations, and decrees. The purpose is to promote the goals of the government entity controlling information. The commercial pattern presents content that reflects the view of advertisers and their "commercial allies, who are found among owners and publishers" (Altschull, 1984, p. 254). The purpose is to make profit for the owners. The interest pattern generates content that reflects the goals of the special interest group that produces the content. The purpose is to promote the aims and ideology of the interest group. The informal pattern produces content that reflects the goals of the relatives and acquaintances who provide money to produce the content (Shoemaker, 1987). The purpose of the media organizations becomes the achievement of the goals of the individuals and groups who finance these organizations.

Although U.S. media markets involve a commercial pattern of financing, the official pattern is also important. In the U.S. hybrid system, the commercial pattern is affected by government regulation. The extent of regulation and its impact varies with changes in political power. Government also influences commercial media by serving as a source of news.

General purposes are useful in understanding a communication system, but particular goals of individual media organizations show a great deal of variability. Goals are the planned results of decisions by the organization's managers. The variation of goals among commercial enterprises has not always been considered an important factor in market analysis. The assumption of traditional economic theory is that companies attempt to maximize profit. In reality, firms often pursue goals other than profit maximization.

Just as the "rational" person assumption of traditional decision theory (see chap. 1) has come under criticism as unrealistic, so the assumed goal of profit maximizing has been attacked (Greer, 1980). As a result of the debate concerning business goals, several theories emerged during the 1960s that start with alternative goal assumptions. Williamson (1964) said managers maximize their own utility because the separation of management from ownership means strict profit maximizing need not be observed. Managers spend some profits to enhance their utility through staff, expense accounts, office suites, executive services, and other perks. The staff helps to reduce insecurity and expand power, whereas the perks enhance status and prestige. Cyert and March (1963) rejected the assumptions of profit maximizing because people within an organization pursue many goals and because managers tend to seek satisfactory profits rather than maximum profits. They also said firms do not have perfect knowledge, a traditional assumption for rational decision making and profit maximizing.

In place of maximization, Cyert and March (1963) postulated a coalition theory of behavior based on three areas of behavior inside the firm—goals, expectations, and choice. These areas of behavior involve interaction among people in an organization to determine how that firm will behave in the marketplace.

Behavioral theories have received research support, which indicates that organizational behavior is complex and that goals vary with time from organization to organization. The important point is that the goals of an organization must be understood at the time a market analysis is undertaken. A television news department facing intense competition from another station might reduce profit by spending more on the newscasts in an effort to increase its audience. Management sees this as a necessity because the dominant newscast charges the highest prices for advertising time. A daily newspaper without direct competition might try to gain the largest profit margin it can by firing newsroom staff. In both cases the goals are neither right nor wrong; they are simply the goals that have been adopted.

The process by which goals are established and changed fall within the realm of earlier chapters, but market analysis begins with the goals of all firms in the market. Managers must clearly understand their firm's goals in order to pursue them. Managers also need to understand as best they can the goals of competitors in order to react to their behavior.

Nature of Demand

Demand in a market is measured by the number of people, households, or firms wishing to buy a product or service. For example, if the number of minutes of advertising sold by a radio station is greater this year than last, demand is said to have increased. The economic theory of perfect competition states that demand is related to four factors: the price of a commodity, the price of the commodity's substitutes and complements, the income of consumers, and the taste of the consumers (Stigler, 1952). *Price of a commodity* means the amount of money it cost to get one unit of that commodity. The *price of substitutes* is the unit price of another commodity that might be used in lieu of your company's commodity. For example, *Time* and *Newsweek* are considered by many readers to be acceptable substitutes, so the price of one can affect the demand for the other. *The price of complements* is the price paid for a commodity that is used with the one your company produces. For example, dip is a complement for chips. For some people, a television set and a VCR are complements. *Consumer taste* is a catchall term for the wants and needs that individual buyers have for various commodities. The impact of consumer taste on demand is related to the quality, or perceived quality, of media commodities.

Price. Price is related negatively to demand for most products and services. As the price of a product goes up, the demand for that product will go down, and vice versa. The degree to which demand changes when prices change is called *elasticity of demand*. If a 1% increase in price results in a decrease in demand that is greater than 1%, demand is elastic. If a 1% increase in price results in a decrease in demand less than 1%, demand is inelastic. If a 1% decrease in price results in a 1% drop in demand, the result is unit elasticity.

Price elasticity is a measure of how sensitive demand is to price changes. *Inelastic demand* means demand is not very sensitive, whereas elastic demand means it is. With inelastic demand, an increase in price often can result in an increase in revenue because the decline in demand can be offset by the increase in revenue. For example, a city magazine entitled *Downtown* has a circulation of 100,000 per month. With a price of $1 per copy, *Downtown* has a monthly circulation revenue of $100,000. If this magazine has inelastic demand, an increase in price to $1.25 may cause circulation to drop to 90,000, but the company actually will increase its monthly revenue to $112,500. The loss from the drop in circulation was less than the gain from the increase in price.

The price increase may seem like a good idea, but the fact that advertisers buy space based on the number of readers means a reduction in circulation could cause advertising revenues to drop. If a 10% drop in circulation for *Downtown* caused a 10% decline in advertising, the circulation revenue increase would not make up the decrease in ad revenue. The connection between the advertising and circulation markets means the elasticity in both markets must be considered when changing price in one.

Companies with elastic demand must be careful with price increases because demand may drop so much that the revenue increase generated from a price increase will not offset the loss from declining customers. Continuing the previous example, *Downtown* might have an elastic demand. In such a situation, the price increase to $1.25 could cause in a drop in circulation to 75,000. The monthly profit would then be only $93,750. Combine this decline with the loss in advertising revenue from losing 25,000 readers and the price cut would be disastrous. Elasticity usually is related to the number of acceptable substitutes. The greater the number, the greater the elasticity.

Price of Substitutes and Complements. The price of substitutes is important also in determining demand. The ability to substitute one service or good for another allows consumers to shop for a better buy. Whether an acceptable substitute will be used depends on its price relative to the commodity being considered. As the price of a substitute decreases, the demand for the original commodity will decrease because buyers will get a better deal buying the substitute.

The relationship between the price of a commodity and its substitute is called the *cross-elasticity of demand*. If a 1% decrease in the price of a substitute causes a 1% drop in the demand for a commodity, the cross-elasticity of demand is unitary. If a 1% decrease in the price of a substitute causes a drop greater than 1% in the demand of a commodity, the cross-elasticity of demand is elastic. If a 1% drop in the price of a substitute results in a drop in demand for a commodity less than 1% the cross-elasticity of demand is inelastic. In effect, the cross-elasticity of demand is a measure of how well one commodity substitutes for another. The more elastic the demand, the greater the substitutability.

For example, if a competitor for the city magazine *Downtown*, which sells 100,000 copies per month, increases its price to $1.25, the cross elasticity will be elastic if Downtown gains more than 25,000 readers. The cross-elasticity will be inelastic if the gain in readers is less than 25,000. The important managerial consideration is not whether the demand is strictly elastic or inelastic but the degree of elasticity. An inelastic relationship between magazines still can benefit the firm that holds its price when a competitor has a price increase.

Demand for a commodity is related negatively to the price of complements. As the price of complements increases, the demand for the commodity decreases because it is more expensive to use the two in conjunction. For example, if the price of coffee increases, the demand for sugar decreases because less coffee is being consumed. It is difficult to establish a relationship among media complements based on price. However, one could say that public relations releases are complements for news content. As the amount of news content declines, the demand for press releases will decline, all else being equal.

Income. As a person's income increases, the overall demand for products and services will increase because he or she has more money to spend. The proportion of income spent on a given commodity, such as information, does not necessarily remain constant for all incomes. The percentage of a person's income spent on a type of good or service depends on that person's needs and the price of the various products. A person who makes $30,000 may spend 20% a year on food. The same person making $50,000 might spend 12% if he or she ate the same type of food after the increase in income, or he or she might spend 21% if this person decides to eat only at the most expensive restaurants.

People vary in their demands for information. People who make a living by selling or using information, such as stockbrokers or writers, tend to spend a higher percentage of income on information because it becomes an investment for future income growth. However, most people will spend a smaller percentage of their higher income on information because much of their media use is for entertainment. As income increases, these people are more likely to substitute travel or live entertainment for information as entertainment.

Overall, an increase in income will result in increased expenditures on media, but the increase may not necessarily be proportionate to the income gain. This is where individual taste comes into play.

Consumer Taste. Consumer taste is an umbrella term for the reasons people want and need goods and services. Unlike the role of price and income in demand, little theory exists to explain how changes in consumer taste affect demand because of the difficulty in measuring taste. At best, it can be said that as taste changes, demand changes.

When examining markets for media organizations, it is worthwhile to understand how people use information. The following list shows a classification system for information use (Lacy & Simon, 1993), based on research about the uses and gratification of media content (Severin & Tankard, 1992) and dependency theory. Type of use includes *surveillance, decision making, diversion, self-understanding,* and *social-cultural interaction.*

A *Surveillance*—People use information to check the environment to see what issues and events might interest them. This monitoring can identify new information about old issues and events of interest, or it can identify new areas of interest.

B *Decision Making*—This is the purposeful use of information to decide on a course of action or to form an opinion or belief. Information that a person encounters usually is judged to be relevant or not relevant to the decisions. This use involves seeking specific information about a particular decision.

C *Diversion*—Information used for entertainment, amusement or distraction that may include, but is not limited to, material that is enjoyable, such as movies, television shows, books, and feature articles. This type of information provides utility to a user. The benefits flow from the acquiring and understanding of the information and not from its application to another process. The entertainment need not be pleasant. For example, a well-written feature on a person or an account of a crime might fit in this category. This use has emotional effects on the user.

D *Social-Cultural Interaction*—Communication is a central part of group membership. Social and cultural groups share information in a process that allows members to identify common ground on which they can establish interaction. The exchange may be about serious issues, such as the goals and processes of the group, or about less serious matters, such as shared interest in sports. Such group communication will take many forms. All such communication that helps either to bond members or to separate members from groups fits under this heading.

E *Self-understanding*—People use information to evaluate and determine their beliefs, values, and philosophy about life and themselves. Information helps people to reflect on these issues, which in turn affects how people interaction in social groups.

Surveillance means people use information to keep up with what is happening around them. Decision making involves the use of information for selecting among various options. Diversion is the use of information for entertainment, distraction, and enjoyment. Self-understanding involves using information to gain a better insight into one's psychological state. Social-cultural interaction is the process of using information to establish and promote group membership and survival.

Consumer taste is important in understanding the markets for media commodities because price is not as important as content in determining demand. In other words, demand for media content is less elastic with respect to price than with respect to content (Lacy, 1989). Consider the growing use of the WWW. Most web sites remain free to visitors, but that does not guarantee a high number of hits. The *USA Today* site is among the 10 most visited sites on the Web because of its range and depth of information.

The use of information is related to the content provided by a media organization. Information used for decision making tends to be very concrete, whereas information used for diversion need not be detailed and may even be inaccurate. A book that provides better self-understanding will be more difficult to write than a light television program aimed to divert people momentarily.

Market Structure

Market structure is the way the market is organized. This structure comes from the collective behavior of all firms and in turn affects the individual behavior of all firms. The market structure faced by a media company begins with the geographic limitations of the market. After the geographic limits are defined, structure depends on the nature of the media commodity, the number of competitors, and the barriers to entry in the market. The nature of demand is related to market structure because it affects the nature of the media commodity.

Geographic Limits.   Geographic limits establish who will have access to a commodity by determining the area in which buyers and sellers interact. Several factors come into play in determining geographic boundaries of markets, but they fall into the areas of costs and revenues. If serving a geographic area costs more than the revenue generates, most businesses will not serve that area. The costs include production, distribution, and selling costs. *Production costs* are the expenses a company has from creating its product or service. *Distribution costs* are the expenses from delivering a product or service to the consumer. *Selling costs* are the costs of getting people to buy the product or service, which include promotion, advertising, and commission expenses.

Revenue is classified as circulation and advertising revenue. *Advertising revenue* comes from transactions in the advertising market, such as selling time or space to advertisers or selling classified ads to local readers. *Circulation revenue* comes from transactions in the information market, such as selling magazines or newspapers to readers or cable service to viewers.

The relationship between costs and revenues determines the geographic market, but this relationship varies from company to company and from medium to medium. A newspaper, for example, will circulate primarily in areas where it attracts advertising. Thus, the farther away a person lives from the businesses that advertise in a newspaper, the less likely that person is to be in the newspaper's geographic market. But this observation varies with the newspaper. Some large daily newspapers circulate in areas distant from their primary advertisers because they feel it is part of their responsibility to the intellectual market to provide news across a wide geographic area. Some newspaper groups have been criticized for not fulfilling this public service obligation when they cut back distribution in high cost areas (Blankenburg, 1982).

Television faces a different type of geographic limit. The range of broadcast signals traditionally has determined a television station's geographic market. The signal fades as one moves away from the transmission point. The development of technology has reduced the impact of this limitation. Stations, such as WTBS in Atlanta, have the ability to distribute programming around the county by satellite and cable. The dependence on advertising revenue tends to limit the geographic market, but production and distribution technology also help to determine the geographic market.

Nature of Commodity.   Once the geographic limits of a market are defined, the commodity must be examined. A *commodity* is the physical good or the service provided by a company. The term commodity is used because media content has the physical aspect associated with a product, while at the same time it provides a service. The analysis of media commodities starts with the uses of information mentioned earlier. In addition to types of use, the content of media can fall into several categories based on four dimensions (Lacy & Simon, 1993): geographic emphasis, nature of information, information format, and topic of information. These four dimensions and their subdivisions are presented in Table 8.1.

Geographic emphasis concerns the geographic location addressed in the content. The emphasis may involve events at the local, state, regional, national, or international levels. It may also be nonspecific with regard to geography. The definitions of geographic emphasis given in Table 8.1 are ones that have been used in media research, but specific definitions may vary from firm to firm.

The second dimension addresses the nature of content, which has three main subdivisions. The content can be advertising, which is information placed in designated space or time bought by an organization in an effort to influence attitudes and behavior. This involves advertisements designed to make people aware of a product or service, to give price information, to give information about quality, or to create a positive image of a product or service.

The second subdivision is *news*, which is content prepared by a media organization's news staff and placed in space not bought by an advertiser. This news generally falls into three categories: hard news, which emphasizes conflict and violence; analysis, which is an effort to give context about an event, trend, or issue; and opinion, which is someone's or some organization's position about an event, issue, or trend.

The third subdivision of nature of information is *feature material*, which is used broadly to represent all content not fitting into news and advertising. Feature material includes what journalists traditionally call feature stories, but it also includes film, books, and nonnews television and web programming, such as sports, comedy, drama, music, and a variety of other content.

The third dimension is content format, which can be written, visual, or audio. Written information is conveyed with words on paper or a screen. Visual information is presented with film, video, still photographs, and graphics. Audio information is received by a person's ears. The three can be combined in various forms, and various media have different degrees of these three formats. For example, most printed matter is written and visual; radio uses audio; and television uses visual, audio, and sometimes written formats. Media convergence concerns the delivery of all these formats through a single technology—the computer. The Web has not created a new information format, but it allows people to combine existing formats and use them interactively.

The fourth dimension is topic area, which deals with particular topics covered in the information content. The eight subcategories presented in Table 8.1 are used often, but they are not the only possible categories. These categories have been used because they have meaning to media users and the media people who create content.

These four dimensions allow a manager to develop a profile of media content. This profile is important because the nature of a commodity determines whether it will meet the demand of the readers, listeners, and viewers in a market. For example, a segment of people in a city may be interested in getting hard news about local government, schools, and sports because they play a role in the social-cultural interaction in the community. A media commodity that does not contain a high degree of information in these areas may not meet the demand of this segment.

Number of Competitors.   Firms compete when their products or services can be substituted for each other. The greater the cross-elasticity of demand, the greater the competition. As the number of competitors increases, the probability increases that a buyer can and will substitute commodities for one another.

Economic theory can be categorized on the basis of the number of sellers in a market and the nature of the commodity. Perfect competition theory assumes many sellers and homogeneous products that are perfect substitutes. Monopolistic competition assumes many sellers and heterogeneous products that are differentiated into submarkets by location, advertising, and the nature of the product. Oligopoly theory assumes few sellers and either heterogeneous or homogeneous products. Monopoly theory assumes one seller and one product serving a market (Litman, 1988).

Identifying the number of competitors in media markets is not always easy because the commodities produced by various forms of media are not good substitutes in all markets. For example, television news and newspapers are different in many ways. They are not good substitutes for many people, but others find them to be acceptable substitutes. An additional complicating factor is that television stations do not charge users for content, whereas newspapers do. This makes a measure of cross-elasticity of demand between newspapers and local TV newscasts difficult or impossible to determine.

TABLE 8.1

Classifications of Media Content

I. Geographic Emphasis

    A. *Local*—Information about the county, city, or neighborhood in which a reader lives.

    B. *State*—Information about events and issues affecting the state in which a reader lives.

    C. *Regional*—Information about the region of the country in which a reader lives (e.g., the Great Lakes region).

    D. *National*—Information about the U.S. government and other events affecting the country or a part of the country outside the region.

    E. *International*—Information about countries outside of the United States.

    F. *Nonspecific*—Information that has no geographic connection, such as personal advice.

II. Nature of Content

    A. *Advertising*—Information put in the newspaper by a group or individuals in order to influence the reader to take some action or to make the reader aware of an issue, event, product, or service.

        1. *Awareness Advertising*—Information that attempts to bring an event, issue, product, or service to the reader's attention.

        2. *Price Advertising*—Information about the price of a product or service.

        3. *Quality Advertising*—Information about the quality or reliability of a product or service.

        4. *Identity Advertising*—Information that is designed to create a positive image of a product or service in the minds of the readers.

    B. *News*—Information that is prepared by the newspaper's staff or by another news-gathering organization. The news organization does not receive pay for printing this information.

        1. *Hard News*—Information that deals with disaster and physical or ideological conflict. The emphasis is on a specific event or series of events.

        2. *Analysis*—Information that is meant to improve understanding of an event.

        3. *Opinion*—Information about someone's or some organization's position concerning events, trend, or issue by providing context.

    C. *Feature Content*—Material that does not fit into news and advertising. This includes feature articles in print material, books, films, video, and much of the content on the Internet.

III. Content Format

    A. *Written*—Information conveyed with text.

    B. *Visual*—Information conveyed primarily with visual images and symbols other than words and letters.

    C. *Audio*—Information that people receive through their ears.

IV. Topic Area

    A. *Government*—Information concerning an official governing body.

    B. *Business*—Information concerning groups and individuals involved in commerce or trade.

    C. *Sports*—Information about athletic efforts and athletes.

    D. *Science*—Information concerning the natural

    E. *Schools*—Information about systems of education and members of those systems.

    F. *Crime*—Information about people or groups who violate laws and about people and groups who enforce the laws.

    G. *Leisure Activities*—Information about things people do for entertainment and those who provide entertainment.

    H. *Sociocultural Activities*—Information about actions that affect the society and culture in which the readers live. This includes information about marriages, deaths, and activities of noncommercial organizations.

Portions of this table are from Lacy and Simon (1992, pp. 32–33). Copyright by Ablex Publishing. Reprinted by permission.

As a practical tool, however, managers can classify other media commodities as excellent, good, adequate, poor substitutes for their commodities. Two daily newspapers headquartered in the same city usually are excellent substitutes in the information and advertising markets. A daily produced in the next county that covers a wide area may be a good substitute for the local daily in the information market, but only an adequate substitute in the advertising market, and a poor substitute in the local intellectual market. A local television newscast might be an adequate substitute for a local newspaper in the information market but a poor substitute for supermarket advertising. On the Web, the CNN and *USA Today* sites are excellent substitutes despite one being produced by a newspaper company and the other by a television company.

Despite the difficulties, identification of competitors is crucial to decision making in the market. In addition to identifying competitors, their behavior must be monitored across time because the nature of a commodity can change.

Barriers to Entry. The last factor in market structure involves the barriers confronting a company that wants to start a firm in a market. Types of barriers to entry vary from industry to industry and even from market to market. Three important barriers to media organizations are high fixed costs, regulation, and the market power of existing firms. The term high fixed costs means the firm faces a great deal of expense just to operate. These fixed costs do not vary no matter how many pages a magazine or newspaper has or how many minutes a broadcast program contains. Fixed costs cover expenses, such as buildings and equipment, that are necessary to produce just one copy of a newspaper or one minute of broadcasting. The high fixed costs of running a daily newspaper come from the expense of having printing presses, computer systems, and a large staff to collect news. Television news has high fixed costs, but they are not as high as those at daily newspapers. Magazines have low fixed costs because they can hire printers and freelancers for writing.

In addition to fixed costs, media organizations also have variable costs, which are those that increase with each additional unit. For example, adding another page to a newspaper increases variable cost because that extra page or copy uses more ink and paper.

Table 8.2 shows how fixed and variable costs change as production increases for a newspaper. The cost of owning a printing press is $1,000 per day, whereas the cost of ink and paper is $0.25 per copy. Producing one copy, the average fixed cost is $1,000. But the average fixed cost drops to $1 with a circulation of 1,000 and to $0.05 with a circulation of 20,000. This rapidly declining average fixed cost contrasts greatly with the stable average variable cost of $0.25. The rapid decline in average fixed cost contributes to the rapid decline in average total cost, which equals fixed plus variable costs divided by number of units produced.

High fixed costs are related to the cycle of the publication or broadcast. Daily media firms have higher costs than do weekly or monthly ones, because daily media must own more equipment to reduce the uncertainty of having someone else produce their commodity. These high fixed costs generate economies of scale, which means the more units that are produced, the lower the average cost per unit. This is shown in Table 8.2 by the declining average fixed cost. Thus, each additional reader or viewer adds nothing to fixed cost. Additional expense comes only through the variable cost.

High fixed costs act as a barrier to entry because they require a large investment of money to start a business. Because start-up money usually is borrowed, paying interest increases operating costs, which means the price of a commodity will be higher and demand will be reduced. In addition, established firms with high fixed costs enjoy the economies of scale to a greater extent than will new firms. Established firms sell more units, which lowers their average cost. Older firms usually have a higher profit per unit or lower unit price because their costs per unit will be lower. Either way, a new firm entering an industry with high fixed costs is at a disadvantage.

Technology development is connected to fixed costs. Efficient technology, such as high speed offset presses, can add to economies of scale. At the same time, less expensive technology, such as personal computers, can lower barriers to entry by providing low cost quality products. During the 20th century, technology has increased barriers to daily newspaper markets.

TABLE 8.2
Costs of Producing a Newspaper

Circulation	Fixed Cost Per Day	Average Fixed Cost Per Copy	Cost of Paper & Ink Per Copy	Total Cost	Total Cost Per Copy
1	$1,000	$1,000.00	$.25	$1,000.25	$1,000.25
500	$1,000	$ 2.00	$.25	$1,125.00	$ 2.25
1,000	$1,000	$ 1.00	$.25	$1,250.00	$ 1.25
5,000	$1,000	$ .20	$.25	$2,250.00	$ .45
10,000	$1,000	$ .10	$.25	$3,500.00	$ .35
20,000	$1,000	$ .05	$.25	$6,000.00	$ .30

However, technology has lowered entry cost for weekly newspaper markets during the past decade. The growth of online publications has lowered barriers because computers and server time are cheaper than printing presses.

Regulation can be a strong barrier because the government can exclude companies through a licensing procedure. Historically, the broadcast industry was regulated to control the public airwaves and to reduce chaos in markets from overlapping radio bands. Many argue that broadcast companies are licensed to operate and in return they owe service to the public in the intellectual market. The ability to enforce this public service aspect has been curtailed by deregulation, but the assumption of television service remains an important public policy issue. The 1996 Telecommunications Act aimed to reduce regulation and increase competition. However, 2 years after its passage, competition in the cable and telephone industries remained underdeveloped.

Regulation also plays a role in determining the number of competitors. Antitrust law was developed to counteract efforts by large organizations to use their market power to exclude unfairly other firms and keep new firms from entering a market. The assumption underlying antitrust law is that people are best served by many sellers, which keeps price down and improves efficiency. The main antitrust laws and the issues they address were presented in chapter 6. The impact of these laws on market structure is to limit behavior that might reduce the number of firms in a market.

Regulation is a response to the illegal accumulation and application of market power, which is the third main barrier to entry. Market power lets a firm influence the factors that affect demand. The more market power a firm has, the more influence it has over price and quality decisions. A company with a great deal of market power that wants to maximize profit will increase prices to increase revenue and lower quality to cut costs.

Whether market power, or its use, is illegal depends on how that power was accumulated and how it is used. Market power that is used to further increase power by fixing prices or excluding competition can be challenged under antitrust laws.

As the number of firms in a market increases, consumers have more potential substitutes. The availability of substitutes moves power from companies to consumers. This consumer power keeps prices down and improves quality, but it also reduces profits. From a manager's viewpoint, competition limits power and increases uncertainty. But in the long run, competition can be beneficial to a firm because it forces it to react to consumer demand. These reactions will reduce the chance of the company producing inferior commodities that lower demand across time.

Economic Environment

The first four steps in market analysis have concerned the actual markets in which the media firms operate. The final one is called the economic environment, and it concerns general business conditions. As with all businesses, media companies take raw materials and people's skills and turn them into information they can sell. These inputs include products, such as paper, and skills such as the writing and reporting ability of journalists. The production processes use capital equipment, such as television cameras and printing presses, and require financing.

The process and acquisition of inputs and financing are influenced by general economic conditions within and outside the particular market. This section deals with three of these conditions: availability and price of inputs, availability and cost of financing and investment, and general economic conditions in the market.

Availability and Prices of Inputs.   People in the computer industry use the acronym GIGO to explain poor performance. It stands for "garbage in, garbage out." This applies to media organizations as well. If inferior journalists, salespeople, and managers are used, the commodity produced will not be of high enough quality to retain readers, viewers, and listeners. The same can be said of raw materials.

The flip side of high quality inputs is price. Just as media firms serve markets as sellers, they also enter markets as buyers. The quality of the inputs is a matter of availability and price of intermediate goods and services, which are goods and services used to produce other goods and services. The most important input for media firms is labor, which refers here to all people who contribute to the production process. The price media organizations will pay for raw material and labor depends on supply and demand. As the price paid for labor (wages) increases, the number and quality of people available will increase. As the price paid decreases, the number and quality of people available will decline. Many news organizations underpay journalists, which has resulted in many good journalists leaving the field (Weaver & Wilhoit, 1996).

Availability and Cost of Financing and Investing.   As with all business, managing media firms involves financing the operations. This requires that long-term costs be paid for as well as the expenses of day-to-day operations. Firms have three basic ways of financing: using *revenue, borrowing,* and *expanding ownership*. Revenue financing involves firms paying for goods and services from the revenue they generate in day-to-day operations. *Borrowing* results in firms paying for the use of money from financial institutions or investors. *Expanding ownership* requires selling part, or all, of the control of an organization either to a person, firm, or the public through the issuance of stock in the company.

Most business expenses, which accrue from day-to-day operations, are paid with revenue. Borrowing money to pay for operating expenses is a sign that a company may be in trouble. If this behavior extends over a long period, the company most likely will fail.

Borrowing and expanding ownership are used more for long-term financing. For example, a company that produces several magazines may want to move to a larger office. This will be financed most likely through borrowing. On the other hand, a newspaper group that wants to expand and buy more newspapers can either borrow the money or sell stock in the company. The advantage of the former is that the current owners retain control. The advantage of the latter is that the newspaper group does not have to pay interest on that money at a prescribed rate. Stockholders, however, will be paid dividends, but management has more flexibility with this form of financing.

An important aspect of financing is long-term investment. Investment can take the form of better technology, such as improved printing facilities, but equally important is investment in human capital. Human capital includes the skills, knowledge, and talent of the people who work in an organization. This human capital is generated through education and training.

The long-term success of a media firm is related to its investment, which is related in turn to the availability and costs of financing that investment. If interest rates are high, the expense of borrowing can be a long-term burden. An example is the Ingersoll newspaper group, which financed expansion in the 1980s with money borrowed at high interest rates. As a result, the company had to sell all of its U.S. newspapers because they could not pay off the debt with revenues.

Expanding ownership also can have high costs. Public trading of stock requires that the management be aware of the price of the company's stock. The price is related primarily to profit performance, although other factors can come into play. This means managers at public corporations often must cut costs during economic downturns to keep profits up. This cost cutting can have a long-term impact by lowering the quality of the commodity and services, which result in declining demand.

General Economic Conditions. How well the economy is performing is summarized by general economic conditions and is reflected in the employment rate, inflation rate, and the cost of borrowing money (interest rates). Media organizations, like most businesses, perform better when the economy is prospering. However, economic conditions are cyclical, with expansions being followed by recessions. When consumer disposable income and business advertising budgets decline, profits and quality of media commodities tend to fall.

If revenues decline because of deteriorating economic conditions, management can react by cutting expenses, cutting profit margins, or both. *Profit margin* refers to the percentage of revenue that goes to the company as profit. It is determined by dividing the profit, which is what is left over after expenses are subtracted from revenue, by the total revenue. If a company is not willing to lower its margin during economic hard times, it must cut expenses. This means firing people and, perhaps, accepting inferior raw material. However, if it will lower its margin, the company may be able to get through the bad economic conditions with little drop in quality. The long-term impact of quality reduction is difficult to measure, but it does occur.

Whether a company can reduce profit margins is often dependent on the type of ownership. As discussed earlier, publicly owned companies tend to be less likely to lower profit margins. However, private ownership is no guarantee of how managers will react to poor economic conditions. The reaction of a given firm to economic conditions is a function of the organizational goals and the nature of the mangers and owners.

One special area of concern during difficult economic times is the intellectual market. The tendency to cut costs at news organizations often results in canceling expensive investigative projects. Sometimes news organizations will be less aggressive in covering businesses because they fear the advertising loss. This tendency is unfortunate because readers, viewers, and listeners need and expect the ideas and information news organizations can provide.

In many ways, poor economic conditions may offer long-term growth opportunities for media organizations. A newspaper, magazine, or television news organization that can provide useful information during uncertain times may be able to capture a larger market share. This strategy, of course, requires a firm to improve its commodity when economic conditions suggest cutting costs. Such a strategy is risky but should be considered. At the very least, media managers must be aware of the long-run implications of cutting their contributions to the intellectual market.

Overall, the economic conditions work as constraints on decisions and actions by a media firm. During good times, they offer opportunity for expansion and growth. During bad times, the economic conditions test the flexibility of a company to contract without reducing its commitment to its readers, viewers, and listeners.

ANALYZING THE MARKETS

Managers need to analyze their markets for two reasons. First, market analysis is needed for specific projects, such as changing the nature of the commodity or starting a new media company. Second, periodic analysis is useful to monitor the firm's market position. The first type of market analysis is part of strategic planning and was discussed in chapter 7. This section discusses how a manager might conduct a periodic analysis of markets.

The analysis includes the examination of market structure, organizational goals, the nature of demand, and the economic environment. The information and advertising markets are addressed together. The analysis of the intellectual market is discussed separately.

Information and Advertising Markets

Market Structure. The first step is to understand the market structure. This involves asking six questions:

1. *What is our firm's geographic market?* The answer to this question is relatively simple. It is determined by management decisions as to where material will be available. Although the answer is simple, the question is important. The geographic market affects the answers to the other questions.

2. *What is the nature of our firm's commodity?* This question addresses the content of the media commodity and is related to the breakdown of information content in Table 8.1.

3. *Who are our competitors and how do their commodities compare and contrast with ours?* This question concerns the cross-elasticity of demand and should be approached from a consumer's viewpoint. No media commodity can be everything to everyone. People sometimes will substitute one media commodity for another even when the two do not appear to be good substitutes. Market analysis must determine which commodities are potential substitutes and to what extent this substitution might take effect.

   Although content is most important in considering substitutability, price also plays a role. If a media commodity becomes too expensive, people will use another commodity that is less expensive, even if it was previously less expensive.

4. *How difficult is it for new firms to enter our market?* This question deals with barriers to entry. If it is difficult for a new firm to start in a market, your company has more discretionary power. This question addresses whether fixed costs are high and whether there is extensive regulation in the industry. One way of answering this question is to examine how many new firms have started and survived in your market and similar markets during the past 10 years. The higher the start-up and survival rate, the easier it is to enter.

5. *What barriers contribute to this difficulty?* This question is an extension of the previous question and deals with the future of these barriers. Cost barriers to entry are a function of technology. Web sites use relatively inexpensive equipment and do not require large staffs to generate content and to distribute it. Daily newspapers are the opposite. Radio stations cost less to start than television stations because radio requires less expensive technology. Being aware of technology trends and uses will help answer this question.

6. *Will the structure of our market change in the immediate future?* The answer to this question comes from the answers to the other six. Are new commodities coming out that can be substitutes for yours? Will government policy change? Will technology lower the barriers to entry? The more volatile the market structure, the more uncertainty a manager faces. The less concentrated the market structure, the less control a manager has in implementing decisions.

The Organization's Goals.   The second step is to examine the firm's goals. In strategic planning this means goals for specific actions. In a general market analysis, the manager must ask three questions:

1. *What are our firm's specific short-term and long-term financial and quality goals?* Almost all commercial organizations have stated financial goals, although many organizations have no explicitly stated quality goals. However, explicit goals are crucial because people find it difficult to work as a team to achieve vague or unspecified goals.

Financial goals involve profit goals and revenue goals. Once revenue goals and profit goals are determined, the roles of expenses can be determined. All goals should be obtainable.

Quality goals are related to financial goals. First, quality is related to expenses. All else being equal, a media firm that spends more will have higher quality. Of course, all else is never equal. The individuals who work within an organization also affect quality. But, in general, the greater the expenditure, the more likely quality will increase. Second, the quality of the media commodity is related to revenue through price and demand. Higher quality results in higher price, but it also can result in greater demand.

2. *How well are we achieving these goals?* The answer to this question rests on the ability to measure performance. Financial performance is relatively easy to measure. Quality performance is more difficult. Managers usually measure quality with their sense of what makes quality, content analyses, and surveys of readers, viewers, and listeners.

If goals are not being met, the reason is important. Such failure can be because the goals are set too high, the firm simply is not performing well, the market is too competitive, economic conditions are creating problems, the prices are too high, or some combination of these factors.

3. *Should we consider changing, adding, or dropping any of the firm's goals during the immediate future?* The answer to this question comes from the entire market analysis. Other factors contribute greatly to this decision. For example, as new media developed, some newspaper companies diversified by buying television and radio stations. The acquisition of new forms of media resulted in redefining the organization's goals. As market structure changes, competition can decrease or increase. Either one can affect specific performance goals for a given period.

The Nature of Demand. In this step, the manager should ask these questions:

1. *Has demand for our firm's commodity changed?* Change in demand is relatively easy to determine. It involves comparing demand in one time period with demand in another. In newspaper and magazine markets, demand is measured by circulation and penetration. In the television and radio markets, demand is measured by ratings and share of audience. In book, movie, and recording markets, demand means the number of units or tickets sold.

2. *If demand has changed, was it because of changes in price, price of substitutes and complements, consumer income, consumer taste, or quality of product?* The answer to this question is difficult to determine because more than one cause often underlies changes in demand. The answer to this question comes from the evaluation of competitors in the section about market structure. Variations in pricing are easiest to address because price is easy to measure. Changes in consumer taste and substitutability are more difficult because they involve content, which is not easy to quantify. However, these two factors often tend to be the most important in determining changes in demand.

The best approach is to analyze the nature of your commodity and the nature of possible substitutes across time to see if the patterns of commodity change mirror the trends in demand. Did demand for your commodity change when a competitor changed its content or price? Care must be taken, however, because many factors come into play.

3. *Are there any indications that demand will change in the immediate future?* This question is even more difficult than the first two because it requires prediction of future trends. It may be that trends of increasing or decreasing demand will continue or level off. This question becomes crucial because it is the basis for most long-term planning.

Economic Environment.   Analyzing the economic environment is also important. This area of analysis deals primarily with the amount of resources that will be available to a firm and to the users of its commodity. Three questions should be answered here:

1. *Will unemployment in your market increase or decrease in the near future?* This question concerns demand for information and is related closely to question 1 in the nature of demand section. If unemployment increases, people in the market will have less money to spend and demand for some media products will drop. Demand for others may grow. For example, broadcast television viewing might increase if people have less money for other forms of entertainment. Any effort to estimate future demand must take employment trends into consideration.

2. *Will business activity in your market increase or decrease in the near future?* This question deals primarily with demand in the advertising market. If unemployment increases, business activities in many areas will decrease. Not all business activities are affected equally, however. Decline in purchasing power affects the purchase of larger items, such as houses and cars, more than the demand for food. But even food demand can be affected because people will buy cheaper types of food as income drops.

   If business activity decreases in a market, advertising will decline for many businesses, although not necessarily all. Advertising is looked on as less important for many businesses than providing a good product or good service.

3. *What will happen to the interest rate in the near future?* This question addresses the long-term operations of a media organization. Plans to expand the number of media outlets or improve equipment usually are related to the ability to borrow money. The higher the interest rate, the more such an expansion will cost in the long run. If the interest goes up, more future revenue must go toward paying off the debt.

Intellectual Market

The purpose of the analysis is to determine whether the social contract implicit in the First Amendment is being met by news organizations. As mentioned, this market is served by information acquired through the information market and advertising. However, some news organizations, especially newspapers, have sections that are designed specifically to address public policy issues. These are the editorial and op-ed pages.

The analysis of the intellectual market involves four questions. These questions are not exhaustive, but they will help managers explore how well their companies are serving this market.

1. *How much of the content carried in our news commodity deals with the context surrounding issues and events?* Traditionally, news media have concentrated on events, often of a fast-breaking nature. The needs of a complex society extend beyond this type of coverage. Just as important is why and how events unfold and issues develop in society. This is the context that is needed for individuals to have informed opinions about policy issues.

2. *How balanced is content concerning controversial issues?* News organizations usually assume a responsibility to present several sides to a controversy. This approach lies behind the development of op-ed pages, which carry opinions that contrast with those expressed in the newspaper's editorials.
   In most markets, adequate performance in the intellectual market requires diversity of opinion in the editorial and op-ed pages. This is determined by examining content related to important issues across time.

3. *How well are events and issues covered across time?* One criticism of news organizations is that they tend to be erratic in coverage. A great deal of time and space will be spent on topics that grab attention, but these topics fade from attention after a few weeks. This tendency results in sensational stories dominating news, whereas more complex and subtle stories are neglected. Serving the intellectual market requires a news organization to be aware of the long time frame associated with some important issues and trends.

4. *Do our goals include serving the intellectual market?* If a news organization does not address this market explicitly in its statement of goals, it probably is not serving the intellectual market well. Goals are the basis for decisions. If no goals exist concerning this market, few decisions will address issues associated with meeting demand. News media managers may be aware of these types of goals, but it is easy to neglect them in the everyday operation of a news organization.

SUMMARY

The analysis of a market is part science and part art. Quantitative research is crucial to analyzing markets, but measurement problems limit the accuracy of some research. Managers need to be able to identify the limits of particular research and be able to fill in holes in that research with their own judgment and experience.

Market analysis plays two important roles. First, it allows for better day-to-day decisions. You make better decisions about where to go when you know where you are. Second, market analysis is the central part of long-term strategic planning. Going back to the decision wheel presented in chapter 1, market analysis is part of that wheel's hub. This analysis provides information basic to decisions within the organization.

The analysis of the information and advertising markets addresses four areas: market structure, organizational goals, nature of demand, and the economic environment. The analysis of the intellectual market deals with the way news media organizations fulfill their responsibility to members of the society in which they operate.

CASE 8.1

The Case of Examining a Local Television News Market

You are the news director at WWWB, which has 165,000 households in its area of dominant influence (ADI). Of these households, 95% have television, 50% have multiple television sets, 72% are cable subscribers, and 80% have VCRs. The metro area, which is part of the ADI, has 110,000 households with the same percentages for multiple TV sets, cable penetration, and VCR penetration.

Your station is an ABC affiliate. WBBB is the NBC affiliate and WPPR is the CBS affiliate. The market has one independent station, WXZX. The cable system carries a Public Broadcast Station, two commercial stations from a large metro area 100 miles away (WERE), three super stations, forty specialized channels, three premium channels, six public access channels, and five pay-per-view channels.

All of the network affiliates and the distant metro stations have local newscasts at 6 pm. The winter ratings period just ended. The average weekly ratings and shares for the 6 pm time slot for the previous four ratings periods were:

		Shares		
	Spring	Summer	Autumn	Winter
WWWB	18	20	22	26
WBBB	38	38	36	34
WPPR	10	10	10	9
WXZX	6	6	7	5
WERE	2	2	2	2
All Other channels	26	24	23	24

˙Winter was the most recent ratings period

		Ratings		
	Spring	Summer	Autumn	Winter
WWWB	9	10	13	15
WBBB	19	18	21	20
WPPR	5	5	6	5
WXZX	3	3	4	3
WERE	1	1	1	1
All Other channels	13	12	13	14

Each of the newscasts lasts 22 min. The geographic breakdown of numbers of stories for news and sports for the three local evening newscasts for the four periods were:

The following tables breakdown the stories by the type of presentation for the four periods:

WWWB				
	Spring	*Summer*	Autumn	*Winter*
ADI	10	11	12	13
State	3	2	2	2
National	3	3	3	2
International	3	2	1	1

WBBB				
	Spring	*Summer*	*Autumn*	*Winter*
ADI	11	10	10	10
State	2	4	4	3
National	3	3	3	4
International	3	2	3	3

WPPR				
	Spring	*Summer*	*Autumn*	*Winter*
ADI	8	7	7	8
State	3	3	4	3
National	5	5	4	4
International	3	4	4	4

WWWB				
	Spring	*Summer*	*Autumn*	*Winter*
Anchor read with no video	9	8	7	6
Anchor read with video	6	6	5	6
Reporter package with video and reporter taped before newscast	4	5	6	6

	Spring	Summer	Autumn	Winter
WBBB				
Anchor read no video	9	10	9	10
Anchor read with video	5	5	6	5
Reporter package	5	4	5	5
WPPR				
Anchor read with no video	10	11	10	11
Anchor read with video	6	4	6	5
Reporter package	3	4	3	3

ASSIGNMENT

Using only the data given in the previous tables, answer the following questions as best you can.

1. What is the nature of WWWB's product?
2. How has that product changed across the four periods?
3. How does your product compare to those of your competitors?
4. Has the demand for your newscast increased or decreased during the four periods? By how much? By what percentage?
5. What reason for the change in demand is suggested by these data?
6. If you wanted to continue the trend, what would you suggest for the content of the newscast? Why?

CASE 8.2

Evaluating Content on the WWW

The WWW is a conglomeration for sites from a variety of people and organizations. The content on such sites varies as greatly as the nature of the people who created the sites. If an organization wants to create a commercial site, it should systematically analyze the content of existing sites to identify competitors.

This case requires that you use the content categories provided in the chapter to analyze content on the Web. The first step is for the class to select three sites. One site should be an online newspaper. The second should be an entertainment-oriented site, such as one set up by a movie studio or television network. The third should be a site created by a company that sells products and/or services to consumers, such as an automobile company or catalogue site.

Using Tables 8.1 and 8.2 complete the following assignments.

ASSIGNMENT

1. Go to each of the three sites and randomly select ten pages to examine. Using the five classifications of information use from page 218, determine which uses best fit the content on the pages. Can the information be used for surveillance, decision making, diversion, social-cultural interaction, or self-understanding? (More than one use can apply to a given page.) Why did you classify the content as you did?

2. Using the same pages selected for assignment 1, classify these pages according to categories in Table 8.1. What is the geographic content of these pages? What is the nature of the content? What content formats are used? What topic areas are covered?

3. On the basis of the classifications in assignments 1 and 2, what segments of the Web audience are the sites aimed at? Do you think the sites are designed for specific types of gender, age groups, lifestyles, or income groups? If so, why do you believe so?

CASE 8.3

The Case of Analyzing a Suburban Newspaper Market

Molly McLane has always liked a challenge, but the new one she is facing is unlike anything she has ever faced. Her latest assignment from Howard-Slipps Newspaper Corp. is to take six weekly newspapers in the suburbs around Detroit and make them into a viable group that can compete in a media-rich environment.

Howard-Slipps is a well-established group of about 30 daily newspapers and six television stations. This project will be their first expansion into the weekly newspaper industry. Howard-Slipps just acquired six independent weeklies in six Detroit suburbs, all within Oakland County. The cities in which the weeklies are located are: Pontiac, Southfield, Troy, Novi, West Bloomfield, and Birmingham. The Detroit metropolitan area includes three counties: Oakland, which is north and northwest of Detroit; McComb, which is north of Detroit; and Wayne, which includes Detroit and other suburbs.

Molly has worked for Howard-Slipps for 7 years. For 6 years she was publisher of a medium-size daily in Ohio. About 1 year ago, she was appointed head of the Nondaily Division of Howard-Slipps. She came to Howard-Slipps from a job as publisher of a group of 14 weeklies in Ohio. Her assignment as head of the Nondaily Division is to develop a long-term strategy for acquiring midwest weekly newspapers, primarily in metropolitan areas. As part of this plan, Howard-Slipps has decided to buy existing independent newspapers or small groups rather than start new newspapers. The cost of starting new newspapers and building goodwill is seen as being higher than buying existing newspapers and reshaping them into competitive groups in the information and the advertising markets.

The Detroit area has been selected as the test market for three reasons:

1. Some advertisers in the Detroit metropolitan area still hold bad feelings toward the metro dailies, *The Detroit News* and the *Detroit Free Press*, about the big increase in advertising prices following the creation of a joint operating agreement between the two newspapers in 1989. There is also some residual anger among readers about a strike that started in 1995 and continued for almost two-years.
2. The main competition for the newspapers in the area is a group of 11 twice-weekly newspapers called the Times & Sentinel (T & S) Newspapers. Molly thinks these newspapers are not doing an adequate job serving the readers.
3. The six independent newspapers were available at good prices.

The exact strategy for the Detroit suburban market is now being formu-
lated. Molly has put together a task force to examine the markets and come
up with a plan. You have been hired as a consultant to analyze the market
based on the following data.

MARKET DATA

The 11 T & S newspapers are published on Wednesdays and Sundays. Six of
these newspapers are located in the cities where Howard-Slipps has bought
newspapers. In all six cases, the T & S newspapers have a circulation lead
over the Howard-Slipps papers. Two of the other T & S newspapers are located in McComb County and the other three in western suburbs of Wayne
County, where the corporate headquarters are located.

The T & S papers are the only other newspapers with editorial offices in
the six cities in which Howard-Slipps has newspapers. The two Detroit dailies have Oakland County bureaus that serve these cities. The cities also are
served by a total market coverage shopper that covers all of Oakland
County. The T & S newspaper sell at the newsstand for $0.50 a copy ($1 a
week) or for $0.75 a week for home delivery.

The six T & S newspapers average about 36 pages per edition, of which
17 pages are new. The following are average percentages of the news- editorial pages in T & S newspapers filled with the various types of news about
the hometown suburb:

Hometown government	6.5%
Hometown law enforcement	1.8%
Hometown sports	6.0%
Hometown business	1.0%
Hometown societal news	14.4%
Editorials about the hometown	3.3%
Total hometown copy	33.0%

Of the remaining 67% of the news hole, 35% is about other suburbs in
Oakland County, which is taken from the other T & S newspapers, 10% is
about the county in general, 10% is about other happenings in the Detroit
three-county area, and 12% involved information about events outside the
Detroit metropolitan area or information that has no geographic emphasis,

such as syndicated material. Of this 67% 3.5 percentage points are nonhometown editorials and opinion pieces.

The variations in percentages among cities is only slight. The T & S newspapers draw from each other extensively. The T & S newspapers have three news-editorial offices. One is at the printing facility in Pontiac. It contains the news staffs for Pontiac and West Bloomfield papers. The office at Southfield houses the staffs for Southfield and Novi, and the office in Troy contains the news-editorial staff for Troy and Birmingham.

The number of households in each city and the circulation of the T & S newspaper in that city are:

City	Households	T & S Circulation
Pontiac	30,769	15,922
Southfield	27,963	13,175
Troy	26,075	14,645
Novi	11,428	5,999
West Bloomfield	51,111	23,599
Birmingham	9,258	5,396
Total	156,604	78,736

The circulation of the other six T & S newspapers equals 32,921 for a total of 111,657 circulation for the entire group.

The penetration of the morning *Detroit Free Press* in Oakland County is 29%, whereas the circulation of *The Detroit News*, which is the afternoon newspaper, is 20%.

The six suburbs fall into two types. Pontiac, West Bloomfield, and Troy include a relatively large amount of business and/or industry. Each has a distinct downtown shopping area. Southfield, Birmingham, and Novi are primarily commuter cities with the residents working in other parts of the metro area. The shopping areas for these three cities are located primarily in malls within the city limits.

All six cities have fairly high average incomes and education levels. With a few exceptions, most of the neighborhoods would be classified as middle-to-upper middle income. The exceptions include some very wealthy and lower-middle income neighborhoods.

Portions of the T & S newspapers also are available on the WW through one central location. On the T & S Web site, readers will find the top three stories of the week from each of the 11 newspapers, links to various other news pages, and all the classified advertising from the 11 papers. The site receives about 15,000 hits a day.

ASSIGNMENT

Using the aforementioned data and the concepts in this chapter answer the following questions.

1. How would you describe the geographic market for the T & S newspapers you will compete against?
2. How should Howard-Slipps set up its geographic markets? Will each paper have a separate market, or will the papers be seen as serving a larger market together?
3. What should be the nature of the Howard-Slipps newspaper commodities in the Detroit Market? Why?
4. How will this commodity compare with those of the T & S group?
5. How well is the T & S group serving the intellectual market?
6. How should Howard-Slipps react to the T & S Web site?
7. How can the Howard-Slipps newspapers serve the readers better than the T & S newspapers?

CASE 8.4

The Case of Starting a City Magazine

You have been hired as a consultant for a corporation that produces magazines—Caine's Publications. This corporation currently has business magazines in 10 large cities across the United States. It also publishes several other special interest magazines. Management plans to enter the field of city magazines. However, the company wants to begin in one city before expanding into others. For reasons involving cost savings, Caine's will start a city magazine in one of the following three markets: Denver, Pittsburgh, or the Tampa–St. Petersburg area. Caine's eventual market selection will be based on detailed market research, but they only plan to research two markets because of the expense involved in conducting the research. You have been hired to analyze these three metropolitan markets and to select two for further research.

Plans call for the monthly magazine to be a general-circulation magazine primarily carrying articles about cultural, social, and entertainment activities in the metropolitan area. However, it also will carry some in-depth articles about local government and business. The magazine will be aimed at the entire metropolitan area and not just the central city.

The audience will be primarily middle to upper-income households. These are the people with discretionary income to spend on social and cultural activities. The advertising market will be those companies that attract these types of people.

The competitive environments for these markets are as follows

Denver has two separately owned and operated general circulation daily newspapers, and there are four other dailies in the five-county metro area. The suburbs have an extensive newspaper market, with about 24 weeklies, most of which are group-owned. The Denver market has thirteen television stations and 33 radio stations.

Both Tampa and St. Petersburg have a daily general circulation newspaper. The four-county metro area has one other daily, and about 12 weekly newspapers can be found in the smaller cities and towns in this area. The metropolitan area also has 15 television stations and 35 radio stations.

Pittsburgh has one daily newspaper. However, the Kent Newspaper Company recently purchased 5 of the 10 other dailies located in the five-county Pittsburgh metropolitan area. Kent managers have announced they will organize to compete more intensely with the Pittsburgh paper in the suburbs. There also are about 18 weekly newspapers in the metropolitan area. The Pittsburgh area has nine television stations and 28 radio stations.

Each of these markets also has one monthly magazine. In Denver, the magazine is called *Denver Today*. It has been in existence for about 4 years and is owned by a family that has no other media interests in the area, although the company owns 10 small daily newspapers throughout the Mountain region of the country. The magazine contains cultural and entertainment information with an emphasis on feature articles about people in these areas. Additional material includes articles about the Denver art scene, the local symphony orchestra, local theater productions, and movies. It is a slick monthly that averages 44 pages. It carries about 12 pages of advertising. It is rumored to be have lost about $250,000 last year. Paid circulation was 25,000 last year. *Denver Today* set up a web site 1 year ago with its top six stories of the month, links to other sites, advertising from the printed version, and updated schedules of entertainment and cultural events. The sit has about 10,000 hits, and 2,000 visitors per week.

The Tampa area monthly is called *Florida West* and is in its second year of existence. It is a news-oriented magazine with long stories about business, government, and other organizations in the Tampa Bay area. It tends to have aggressive reporting, especially about business. It averages about 40 pages a month, of which 30% is advertising. It carries some entertainment and cultural information, but these tend to be short reviews and reports that account for about 10% of the news space. The first-year losses were well over $1 million, but this included the start-up cost. The magazine has been praised by media critics in the local newspapers and has a circulation of about 30,000. The magazine is owned by a company with similar successful magazines in Los Angeles and Phoenix. The company also has several national specialty magazines. From the beginning, *Florida West* has had a web site that is available free to subscribers. It also has advertising and weekly schedules of entertainment, art, and cultural events in the metropolitan area. It receives about 20,000 hits and 2,500 visitors a week.

Pittsburgh has a magazine entitled *Pittsburgh*. It is only in its sixth month of operation and is owned by a company that also owns a local network affiliated television station. The magazine emphasizes entertainment and contains a great deal of graphics and color. It averages about 32 pages a month and always has a long piece about a local figure connected to the entertainment world. The remaining articles tend to be short, much like the articles in *USA Today*. Its paid circulation is about 15,000. It has an average of 10 pages of advertising a month, with the majority of ads coming from television, movies, and book companies. No figures are available about profits.

ASSIGNMENT

Despite the presence of an existing magazine, these three cities have cost savings related to production facilities and none of the existing magazines is well established. These markets are the most favorable for starting a city magazine. Your job is to use the aforementioned information and the following tables to suggest which two markets would be best for conducting detailed research in preparation for starting a city magazine. Explain the basis for your recommendation, including a discussion of market demographics and an analysis of the extent and nature of competition in the market. The case involves selecting the appropriate categories of data to use for making the decision and the particular type of data that will help best (total dollars, per capita dollars, or changes in expenditures). Total expenditures and income represent an absolute amount of economic power, whereas expenditures and income per household represents how much discretionary spending and income there is in a market. The higher the income and expenditure per household the more likely the households will have money to spend on media. Changes across time represent trends in expenditures and income. Increasing data show economic growth, whereas decreasing data show a declining economy.

The data are revised to reflect statistics as close to reality as possible.

TABLE 8.3

Retail Sales Data for Tampa–St. Petersburg, Denver, and Pittsburgh Metro Areas

	Tampa–St. Pete	Denver	Pittsburgh
Year 1: Total retail sales	14,910	14,327	13,525
Year 2: Total retail sales	19,681	18,336	15,513
Year 1: General merchandise sales	1,734	1,526	1,982
Year 2: General merchandise sales	2,283	1,944	2,373
Year 1: Food sales	3,302	2,783	2,817
Year 2: Food sales	4,032	3,323	3,503
Year 1: Auto sales	3,765	3,641	3,114
Year 2: Auto sales	4,706	4,566	3,993
Year 1: Gasoline sales	862	811	793
Year 2: Gasoline sales	911	857	840
Year 1: Apparel sales	533	676	673

Year 2: Apparel sales	709	861	750
Year 1: Furniture sales	900	921	652
Year 2: Furniture sales	1,180	1,173	821
Year 1: Eating and drinking	1,557	1,622	1,297
Year 2: Eating and drinking	2,047	2,072	1,541

Note. Figures are in millions of dollars. The data reflect analysis of stastistics from a variety of sources, including *Editor & Publisher Market Guide*, New York: Editor & Publisher Inc., 1988, Author and the U.S. Census.

TABLE 8.4

Income, Household and Farm Product Data for Tampa–St. Petersburg, Denver, and Pittsburgh Metro Areas

	Tampa–St. Pete	*Denver*	*Pittsburgh*
Year 1: Population	2,014,319	1,739,385	2,198,649
Year 2: Population	2,670,100	2,186,670	2,420,300
Change in population Year 1 to Year 2	32.6%	25.7%	10.1%
Year 1: Number of households	837,308	690,096	842,377
Year 2: Number of households	1,112,000	892,520	923,779
Year 1: Estimated disposable personal income	28,033,994 (Thousands)	26,722,404 (Thousands)	31,096,000 (Thousands)
Year 2: Estimated disposable personal income	49,947,700 (Thousands)	47,101,518 (Thousands)	46,227,730 (Thousands)
Year 1: Income per capita	13,917	15,363	14,143
Year 2: Income per capita	18,700	21,540	19,100
Year 1: Income per household	33,481	38,723	36,915
Year 2: Income per household	44,916	52,774	50,042

TABLE 8.5
Retail Sales Data per Household for Tampa–St. Petersburg, Denver, and Pittsburgh
Metro Areas (thousands of dollars)

	Tampa–St. Pete	Denver	Pittsburgh
Year 1: Total retail sales	17.80	20.80	16.10
Year 2: Total retail sales	17.70	20.54	16.79
Year 1: General merchandise sales	2.07	2.21	2.35
Year 2: General merchandise sales	2.05	2.18	2.57
Year 1: Food sales	3.94	4.03	3.34
Year 2: Food sales	3.63	3.72	3.79
Year 1: Auto sales	4.50	5.28	3.70
Year 2: Auto sales	4.23	5.11	4.32
Year 1: Gasoline sales	1.03	1.18	.94
Year 2: Gasoline sales	.82	.96	.91
Year 1: Apparel sales	.64	.98	.80
Year 2: Apparel sales	.64	.97	.81
Year 1: Furniture sales	1.07	1.33	.77
Year 2: Furniture sales	1.06	1.31	.89
Year 1: Eating and drinking	1.86	2.35	1.53

TABLE 8.6
Percentage Change in Retail Sales Per Household for
Tampa–St. Petersburg, Denver, and Pittsburgh Metro Areas

	Tampa–St. Pete	Denver	Pittsburgh
Year 1 to Year 2: Total retail sales	-0.1	-0.2	+4.3
Year 1 to Year 2: General merchandise sales	-0.1	-0.1	+9.4
Year 1 to Year 2: Food sales	-7.9	-7.7	+3.4
Year 1 to Year 2: Auto sales	-6.0	-3.2	+16.8
Year 1 to Year 2: Gasoline sales	-20.3	-18.6	-3.2
Year 1 to Year 2: Apparel sales	0.0	+1.0	+1.3
Year 1 to Year 2: Furniture sales	-1.0	-1.0	+1.3
Year 2: Eating and drinking	-1.1	-1.1	+2.2

TABLE 8.7
Percentage Increase in Retail Sales for Tampa–St. Petersburg, Denver,
and Pittsburgh Metro Areas

	Tampa–St. Pete	Denver	Pittsburgh
Year 1 to year 2: Total retail sales	32%	28%	15%
Year 1 to Year 2: General merchandise sales	32%	27%	20%
Year 1 to Year 2: Food sales	22%	19%	24%
Year 1 to year 2: Auto sales	20%	25%	28%
Year 1 to Year 2: Gasoline sales	6%	6%	6%
Year 1 to Year 2: Apparel sales	33%	27%	10%
Year 1 to Year 2: Furniture sales	31%	27%	26%
Year 1 to Year 2: Eating and drinking	31%	28%	19%

TABLE 8.8
Additional Demographic Data about Tampa–St. Petersburgh, Denver, and Pittsburgh

	Age Distribution Year 2		
	Tampa-St. Pete	Denver	Pittsburgh
Under 5 years	5.2%	7.4%	5.8%
5–17 years	17.1%	20.5%	19.1%
18–24 years	10.6%	14.2%	12.2%
25–44 years	23.4%	34.9%	25.6%
45–64 years	22.2%	14.2%	23.9%
More than 65 years	21.5%	8.8%	13.4%
Median Age	38.6	28.9	33.4

(continued)

	Education Attainment and Unemployment		
	Tampa–St. Pete	*Denver*	*Pittsburgh*
Percentage that finished 12 years or more of school	62.5	80.5	67.3
Percentage that finished 16 years or more of school	12.4	24.6	14.1
Percentage of work force unemployed in Year 2	5.2	4.1	6.1

CASE 8.5

Analyzing Radio Competition

A radio station makes money by attracting a specific segment of the listening audience. The segment is attracted by playing music or having news and talk that will appeal to members of that segment. However, it is not always clear which stations are competing against each other for audience because listeners of the same age can be interested in a variety of programs.

This assignment involves two steps. First, listen to the radio stations in your market that would be most likely to appeal to an audience under 50 years old. Classify the groups on the basis of the age group most likely to be attracted to the programming. Use the following age groups: 18- to 30-year-olds, 30- to 40-year-olds, or 40- to 50-year-olds. Give the reason for your decisions. Feel free to conduct research about these stations if it will help you identify their target audiences. This could include newspaper and magazine articles about the stations and ratings reports. The second step is to assume you are starting a station in your city that will try to attract people in the 30- to 40-year-old age group. How many stations will you have to compete against? What type of programming to you think will work best in attracting listeners to your station? The programming can be similar or not to existing stations, but you should explain why your station will attract listeners better than potential competition.

9
MARKETING AND RESEARCH

With the increasing competitiveness of the media industry, marketing and research activities are central to the job of media management. Marketing activities revolve around decisions about the four P's–*product, pricing, placement* (distribution), and *promotion*. In order to make these decisions, managers need answers to questions about their customers. For media managers, the two types of customers are their readers, viewers, or listeners and their advertisers. A broadcast manager might use research to determine whether viewers like and trust the local news anchor. A newspaper publisher might use research to determine the types of stories readers enjoy. A manager at an advertising or public relations firm might use research to choose the most effective advertising campaign. All media managers need profiles of their customers to market their space or time to advertisers.

This chapter allows the reader to develop a broad perspective on marketing and research. Many marketing decisions, research questions, methods and information gathered are common across media organizations. The basic types of research questions and methods used by media organizations are presented.

THE MARKETING FUNCTION

Marketing is the "process of planning and executing the conception, pricing, promotion, and distribution of ideas, goods, and services to create exchanges that satisfy individual and organizational objectives" ("AMA Board," 1985, p. 1). The underlying *marketing concept* is that the successful company is the one best at determining what consumers want and then meeting those desires more effectively than competitors (Kotler, 1980). The marketing concept has been the accepted philosophy driving marketing strategy for more than 40 years. However, prior to that time, marketers believed that consumers had similar preferences and would purchase anything marketers developed and sold. Consumers are now viewed as diverse and selective in their purchase decisions. In the case of broadcast, cable, and print media organizations, important purchase and related behaviors include viewership, readership, and listening behaviors. In the case of the advertising or public relations firm, the purchase of an advertised product or the development of a positive attitude toward a product or issue are important behaviors. When companies maintain or advertise on a web site to publicize or sell their media and other products, the number of web or ad hits and related purchases are the measured consumer behaviors.

Proper *product positioning* is considered the basis for successfully satisfying consumers and understanding their purchase behavior. Product positioning is accomplished through a coordinated marketing strategy; that is, the four P's are compatibly designed to provide a consistent and desirable picture or image of the product being offered. Few products meet the needs of all consumers, hence a product's position is often *targeted* to a *segment* of the potential audience.

The content and advertising of broadcast, cable, Internet, and print media products can be developed to cater to the tastes of a specifically defined target audience, just as manufacturers create products with characteristics designed to meet the needs of their markets. A well-positioned product typically has one or at most two defining attributes or usage benefits that differentiate the product from competitors in the same category. Advertisers communicate the position of the product (media or otherwise) to create the desired image in the mind of the consumer. Often media products are designed for audiences that advertisers desire to reach. In this case, the advertiser and the media manager target the same audience, and the media manager also targets the advertiser by targeting the advertiser's audience. Alternatively, the media manager may accept the audience attracted by the editorial content of the media vehicle, then find advertisers interested in targeting that audience.

The mushrooming accessibility of cable and the WWW has supported the emergence of new media products that are customized for more narrowly defined audiences than traditional broadcast and print media. The interactive nature of many web sites allows any one individual to become a target for a customized message, with the individual determining the nature of the message. The Microsoft/NBC joint cable and Internet venture, MSNBC, allows an individual to customize a web page experience, as do many other web sites.

The development of the marketing concept and the new product positioning strategies marked the onset of the need for a new organizational function—marketing research. Marketing research provides a way for media managers to discover the needs and wants of their audiences and determine how best to meet them.

THE MARKETING RESEARCH PROCESS

It is important that research is conducted systematically and objectively to ensure the quality of the information obtained. No manager wants to spend tens or hundreds of thousands of dollars gathering information unless that information is an accurate reflection of reality. *Systematic* research is well planned and organized. All the details are outlined in advance of data collection. *Objective* research is void of bias. Research bias appears in many forms, but often it is a result of the researcher's preconceived desires or expectations for the outcome of the research study.

Stages of Marketing Research

The process of marketing research is similar to the research process in other areas of study. There are eight stages to the process.

Research Question Development. This stage is also referred to as setting research objectives. The research question may be about a particular problem, such as: "Why do consumers buy one product rather than another?" or "Which newspaper design do readers prefer?" Some researchers prefer to set objectives rather than state questions. For example, the second question phrased as an objective would be "Determine the newspaper design readers prefer."

Secondary Research Review. A researcher reviews the available information on a topic of interest before conducting his or her own research. Often, enough data are available to save the time and money necessary for a new research study. Secondary research is used very often by media managers and is discussed later in the chapter.

Primary Research Design. The researcher develops a plan or a *design* for the study. The design for the study is driven by the research questions.

Data Collection Procedure. The specific data needed to answer the research question are identified and a plan is created to appropriately collect the data.

Sampling Design. Due to financial and time constraints, researchers study a subset of the population of interest. This smaller group is called a sample, and must be representative of the population of concern. A design for obtaining a representative sample must be outlined.

Data Collection. The data are collected. Often this is the most time consuming and costly part of a research study.

Data Processing and Analysis. Data are typically edited or verified before being analyzed. Verification reviews the data for completeness and bias, then data are coded for analysis and entered into a computer program.

Report Writing. The final stage is the writing of a report that clearly details the study, the results obtained, and how the results answer the research question(s).

TYPES OF RESEARCH AND RESEARCH QUESTIONS

The type of research problem suggests which method to use. Having knowledge of research method options enables managers to decide between competing research proposals submitted by outside suppliers (including evaluating the research design, methods, questionnaires and sampling techniques used) or to design and implement research in-house. Managers also must be able to understand and interpret research findings in order to use the results effectively.

Before designing a research study, three issues can be considered. First, how much is already known about the problem at hand? Second, how much information is needed about each audience member? Third, how important is it that the results of the study are generalizable to other people and situations? The answers to these questions direct the researcher to some types of research and not others. The following is a discussion of the different categories of research available and some considerations for choosing any one of them.

Primary Versus Secondary Research

Primary research is research that is conducted for the specific purpose at hand. Its main advantage therefore, is that it has been designed by the researcher to answer the specific question posed and is likely to provide the needed information. Secondary research has been conducted for purposes other than the researcher's. As such, it may not provide the exact information that is needed. However, secondary research has advantages. When comparing secondary to primary research, secondary research is often cheaper, easier to collect, more quickly accessible, and provides sufficient, if not perfect, information.

Media managers regularly use secondary research information. Most often the secondary research is in the form of syndicated research. Syndicated research data is an integral part of media research. It can be used to answer research questions about the audience (a print vehicle's readership, a broadcast vehicle's listeners, a television program's viewers), the effectiveness of an advertising message (message research), and the placement of advertising by advertisers (advertising activity research). *Syndicated research* is research that is conducted on an ongoing basis by a specialized firm. The research is not contracted to meet the special needs of any one company, but is conducted to serve a group of companies in the industry. Any company can purchase the information. Some of the most common syndicated research data that are used by media organizations are produced by companies including A.C. Nielsen, Arbitron, Simmons Market Research Bureau, Gallup and Robinson, and Starch INRA Hooper (see Fletcher & Bowers, 1991 for a detailed review of syndicated research sources).

Exploratory, Descriptive, and Causal Research

Exploratory research is typically performed when a researcher is approaching a relatively new topic and little information is available to guide the study, hence the term exploratory research. Research questions may not be well defined and there may be many issues of interest that cannot be narrowed down to become the focus of the study. As such, exploratory research can identify key variables, issues, or ideas that help the researcher better understand the general problem and define more specific research questions. A television network might be interested in developing a new type of programming to attract a younger audience but still maintain adult interest. In order to generate concepts for such a program, they might choose to speak to small numbers of parents and children and test ideas in a focus group situation. This would allow for free thinking and the emergence of important ideas that might not have been in the mind of programmers. This exploratory research situation would identify directions for the development of the new programming, and a more well-defined set of research questions to be studied.

Descriptive research, as its name implies, is research that describes a group of people or a situation in detail, across a set of characteristics defined in the research questions. Descriptive research is very common in media organizations. A local newspaper interested in updating its nonnews features, such as the comics section, might analyze which comics satisfy reader interest and which can be safely dropped without losing readers. They might also want to identify popular replacement comics. The newspaper could conduct a survey of its readers to identify how many of them read each of the strips and if there were any others that might be preferred. Descriptive research is useful for identifying segmenting characteristics of the audience and in estimating the actual sizes of those segments.

Most of the questions that managers ask are inherently causal in nature. Whenever a manager considers strategic options, he or she is really asking "which of these strategies will create or cause the outcome I desire?" Only *causal research* can answer questions that specifically pose a question about a strategy causing an observable effect on an outcome, typically audience behavior. A broadcast television network programming executive considers the placement of a program expecting the decision to affect the size and characteristics of the audience for that program, and the programs appearing before and after it.

Causal research, however, is difficult and expensive. It requires the accumulation of research over time, which allows researchers to examine a variety of causes and to control for competing theories as to why behavior occurs. No one research project can establish causality. Because business decisions often do not allow time for extensive causal research, media managers usually accept the ability to predict behavior reliably as a replacement for understanding causal relationships.

Designs for Data Collection

Once the researcher has defined the problem, reviewed secondary data, and decided that primary data collection is necessary, a design is developed for the study. Exploratory research is typically conducted using *qualitative research* designs. Qualitative research is intended to provide a relatively quick insight into a problem so that further action can be planned. Qualitative research typically uses small convenience samples, rather than large representative samples, and relies on subjective or intuitive data collection and analysis. The results of a qualitative research study should not be used as a definitive information base for risky decision making. Qualitative research techniques include the *focus group* and the *depth interview* techniques.

A focus group consists of 8—12 people who represent the population of concern and is facilitated by a trained moderator. Focus groups provide an open-ended response situation where synergy among the participants enhances the generation of ideas. Discussions typically last between 1-1/2 and 2 hours. Information collected during a focus group is considered to be valuable. However, focus group data cannot be generalized to the greater population with confidence due to the small number of people in the study and the unique nature of interaction of the focus group.

Depth interviews are often unstructured personal interviews that allow the trained interviewer to deeply probe the reported behaviors and feelings of the interviewee for up to 2 hours. The advantage of this type of interview is its ability to generate a great deal of information for any one individual. It also provides unexpected information. However, it is more costly than the focus group and other types of data collection methods. It also suffers from the problem of small sample size and limited generalizability.

Descriptive research is often conducted using *quantitative* methods such as *survey* or *observational* methods. Quantitative methods use larger samples and allow researchers to generalize the results to other people and situations. The survey method is also called a self-report method because it asks people to tell the researcher about their behaviors, attitudes, or opinions and their characteristics relevant to the managerial problem. A survey consists of typically the administration of a questionnaire specially designed to answer the research questions. The questionnaire is administered face to face, through a phone interview, or is sent through the mail for individual self-administration. The results of a survey provide a profile of the group of interest along a set of characteristics identified by the researcher as needed information.

Surveys are often cross-sectional, or performed at one moment in time. Sometimes, a *longitudinal study* is appropriate when data collected at more than one point in time are needed to evaluate the research question. For example, National Purchase Diary, Inc., analyzes market share trends for brands by collecting purchase diaries monthly from respondents.

Observation is a method that does not rely on the self-report of the individual, but observes the behaviors of individuals of interest through various means. The observation can be obtrusive (known to the individual) or unobstrusive (unknown to the individual). Some of the more widely used types of observational data collection methods include scanner data, Nielsen or Arbitron ratings of program viewership, and the tracking of Internet users' surfing behavior. A.C. Nielsen and Arbitron provide current data on television audience size and composition. Scanner data is often used at point-of-purchase sites such as grocery stores to collect information on purchase behavior. Many grocery chains provide preferred customer cards that are scanned each time a purchase is made. The customer receives a coupon of unknown value as a reward for each instance of purchase when the card is used. Because the customer has registered a self-profile of demographic information with the grocery chain to receive the card, the list of purchases is associated with that individual's demographic profile. Finally, *content analysis* provides a means of objectively investigating media content. Content analysis often is used to examine typography, layout, and makeup in newspapers and magazines. (See Wimmer & Dominick, 1991, for more information about these research methods.)

The ability of descriptive research to describe accurately a large population relies on two elements of research. First, the sample studied must be randomly selected from the larger population the sample represents. Randomness requires that biases connected to income, gender, ethnic background, and other factors be absent in the sample. There is no way to guarantee the absence of biases, but random sampling allows researchers to reduce and estimate the probability that these biases exist. The second element is a large sample size. The larger a random sample, the less likely it is to be biased. Large is a vague term, but most samples should be larger than 400, and a sample of more than 1,000 works well for representing millions of people.

Strictly speaking, causal research can only be performed using *laboratory experiments*. Laboratory experiments are used when control over extraneous conditions is important and feasible. Laboratories are not necessarily sterile white labs, but are controlled situations. Sometimes movie theater situations are created for laboratory experiments testing reactions to ads or new television programming. The same newspaper lifestyle section could be tested in a laboratory situation where one group of individuals reads one version, and a second group reads the second version in a controlled setting without disruptions. This type of experiment is more likely to ensure that differences in reaction to the two lifestyle sections are due to the content of the sections and not some external contaminating factors. However, the disadvantage of the laboratory experiment is that the exposure was unnatural, and exposure to the lifestyle section in the person's home may be different than in the contrived setting, resulting in a different reaction to the section.

Because of laboratory experiments' limitations, experiments also are conducted in natural settings and are called *field experiments*. For example, two versions of a newspaper lifestyle section are tested by delivering one version to residents in one geographic region of a city and a second version in another market region. Reader reactions are monitored in both regions to determine which section was preferred. The advantage of a field experiment is that real-life conditions are present. However, the disadvantage is that real-life conditions lack researcher control and allow a multitude of factors to influence the outcome. Hence, the researcher may never be sure that the difference in reader reactions was solely due to the difference in the lifestyle section of the paper.

These two critical designs involve concerns about internal and external validity. In order to have internal validity, an experimental design must isolate the cause–effect relationship between the managerial factor of concern (the independent variable) and the desired audience behavioral outcome (the dependent variable). When an experiment has internal validity, the probability is high that only the independent variable caused the dependent variable to change. External validity occurs if the experimental results can be generalized to other situations and people, in other words, in real practice. To do this, the sample used in the experiment must be randomly selected from the larger population.

It is impossible to have perfect internal and external validity in the same experiment. Internal validity requires control over all factors extraneous to the independent and dependent variables of concern. Controlled lab situations enhance internal validity, but then decrease external validity by removing the real world extraneous factors. Conversely, external validity requires that extraneous variables not be controlled, as in field experiments. However, once extraneous variables are allowed to fluctuate, internal validity suffers. So the researchers always trade-off.

Basic Versus Applied Research

Basic research is typically used to identify general principles of practice for media managers. In that sense, basic research answers more general research questions than *applied research*. For example, if an advertiser were to ask, "Which type of advertising strategy creates a more positive attitude toward the advertised brand, comparative or single-sided?" this question could be best answered using a basic research approach. At first, this may appear to be a very specific question, but in many ways it is a general question. We would expect the results of a study designed to answer the question to provide information that would be generalizable to all brands, product categories, companies that could be advertised, and even to any medium of advertising such as radio, television, newspaper, magazine, or the Internet. In this sense, the answer to the question has general applications, and the advertising account executive could use this principle for future decisions.

On the other hand, applied research answers a specific question, and the results of the study are not intended to be generalized to other situations. Applied research is typically conducted to obtain information for a specific decision in one unique situation. For example, at the time of the death of Princess Diana, one of the tabloids might have conducted a study to identify the reaction of their readers to the publication of the paparazzi photos showing the princess in the automobile before her death. The uniqueness of this situation (the widespread adoration of the most arguably widely recognized woman in the world, her history of being hunted by the paparazzi) illustrates how the results of this study could not be generalized to other situations. Another more commonplace example would be a study designed to identify the best celebrity endorser for a new budget line of clothing at Sears. The combination of the factors of Sears' image, clothing, and a budget line create a situation that would not likely be duplicated. The results of such studies provide information for the manager to take action, but not information that can be used again.

The biggest advantage of basic research is its development of principles of practice or its generalizability or repeated usability of the results of one study. Its disadvantage is that it requires more resources (money and time) to conduct. The advantages of applied research are that it takes fewer resources than basic research, and it can answer the specific question at hand. Given the time and money constraints on gathering information for decisions, applied research is performed often despite its disadvantage of limited use in other decisional situations.

TYPES OF APPLIED MEDIA RESEARCH

Media companies ask some of the same applied research questions regardless of the nature of the company. The research questions can be categorized based on the nature of their content. The following is a discussion of five basic types of applied media research and how the information gained is used to market the media company.

Audience Research: Secondary Data

Audience research studies questions about the characteristics of present and potential target audiences. A company can perform primary audience research or access the many secondary, syndicated sources of audience data. *Target market research* is a common type of audience research that identifies the characteristics of potential audiences. Two of the basic characteristics studied are *demographic* and *psychographic*. Demographic characteristics include age, education, gender, marital status, occupation, income, and geographic location. Psychographic characteristics describe the individual's lifestyle, activities, interests, and opinions, and are virtually unlimited in nature. Psychographics include reactions to media content, preferences for media vehicles, and perceived images of media companies and spokespersons.

A popular method for categorizing audience members into eight categories based on demographic and psychographic profiles is available from Stanford Research Institute (SRI). SRI's Values and Lifestyles (VALS 2) typology categorizes consumers into three overall categories of self-orientation and presumes they are motivated by principle, status, or action. It further differentiates the self-orientation categories based on the amount of resources (education and income) available to the groups. See Schiffman and Kanuk (1997) or the SRI web site (http://future.sri.com/ovalshome) for more details. The VALS segmentation approach is based on the idea that consumers buy products that provide satisfaction and give meaning to their identities (Graham, 1989), hence consumers in the same segment may view the value of products similarly.

Another commonly used psychographic service is the Yankelovich Clancy Shulman's Monitor. The Monitor surveys respondents' values and attitudes, tracks trends, and uses this information to segment respondents into groups (Wickham, 1988).

One very important psychographic is media habits, or the present media usage of the individual. These characteristics are easy to measure and very useful for clustering individuals into audience segments that share a common set of characteristics. The audience segments become targets for the media product of concern, such as a new magazine, a newspaper column, television programming, or a new ad campaign. Media habits not only describe the segment, but provide information to the advertiser for message placement. Media habits can be obtained during target market research. However, the placement of an advertisement is typically guided by secondary data provided by syndicated research companies. The media planner can select, and the media buyer can purchase, time and space in the vehicles identified as efficiently reaching the target audience. This same secondary data can be used by any media firm to identify its own audiences and audiences of competitors.

Several companies provide syndicated audience data for print and broadcast vehicles. For print vehicles, Simmons Market Research Bureau (SMRB) and Mediamark Research Inc. (MRI) are two major companies used by advertisers. Both companies estimate readership rather than circulation to provide a more accurate estimate of the numbers of adults who actually read the magazines or newspapers. SMRB samples 19,000 households and conducts personal interviews with one adult in each household to estimate the readership of many consumer magazines and newspapers. They estimate readership by identifying adults who report having read a recent issue of the print vehicle. MRI conducts personal interviews with more than 20,000 adults and estimates readership based on the respondents report that they are certain of having read the print vehicle during the previous publication interval.

Both SMRB and MRI provide demographic and various product category usage data breakdowns with the estimates of readership. The information allows advertisers to locate their target market by its media habits. For example, SMRB data from 1989 show that the percentage of *True Story* readers who smoke cigarettes is much higher than expected based on the cigarette smoking rate in the general population, and is much higher than found in the readership of most other consumer magazines and newspapers studied (Simmons Market Research Bureau, 1989). Consequently, this information tells the media manager that ads placed in *True Story* are more likely to reach cigarette smokers than ads placed in other magazines.

Advertisers also use Nielsen and Arbitron for information regarding broadcast television, cable, online, and radio audiences. Nielsen provides audience measurement data for television, cable, and the Internet, and Arbitron reports audience data for radio, cable and online use. These services also offer specialized and customized reports, in either printed or computer-ready form.

Both Arbitron and Nielsen assign stations nationwide to only one viewing region based on whether they are the stations primarily tuned to by viewers in a given metropolitan area. These nonduplicated, mutually exclusive market areas establish by county the area to which viewers tune. Nielsen calls them designated market areas (DMA), whereas Arbitron calls them areas of dominant influence (ADI). Arbitron defines an ADI "as a geographic survey area created and defined by Arbitron based on measurable patterns of television viewing" (Guide, 1987, p. 37). Each county in the continental United States is assigned only to one DMA or ADI. Another commonly used market definition is the total survey area (TSA) or the total market area in which viewing or listening takes place. The metro survey area (MSA), which generally corresponds to the U.S. Government's Office of Management and Budget's standard metropolitan statistical area (SMSA), is a geographic area that includes a city and the area nearest to the station's transmitter (Guide, 1987).

Viewers and listeners are measured in rating and share estimates. For example, a TV rating refers to the estimated percentage of the number of TV households that is tuned to a program at one time. In other words, a *rating* is the number of households watching a TV show divided by all the households with TV sets. A TV share refers to the estimated percentage of households using television (HUT) during a specified time period that is watching a program. A *share* is the percentage of households watching a particular program divided by the total households with TV sets turned on during the time the program is available. Similar formulas are used for radio, but radio ratings examine listeners instead of households because much of radio listening occurs outside the household.

Advertisers and agencies compare the ratings and shares of different programs on different stations and channels to decide which ones to buy. Media managers are especially concerned with the results of these studies because they determine the value of their media space for advertisers. They base advertising prices on ratings and shares. The broadcast measures are taken daily, but are focused on critically four times each year during the "sweeps" periods.

The term *reach* refers to the percentage of the audience that is exposed to a vehicle, ad, or program in a given period. *Frequency* refers to how often that audience is reached. An advertiser may select a particular medium, or combination of media, based on whether the product is sold to the public at large or a specialized segment (such as basketball fans). Historically, one might expect to reach more viewers using television because this medium typically attracts larger audiences. One might achieve higher frequency using radio because spots are cheaper and an advertiser can purchase more of them (Lancaster & Katz, 1989). However, the growth of cable and direct satellite channels has resulted in the fragmentation of television audiences into smaller segments. Increased use of the WWW holds the potential for even more fragmentation of TV audiences, reducing the reach available through television programming.

Listening and viewing habits are measured typically by using diaries (survey), meters (observation), or telephone surveys (Beville, 1988). Diaries are booklets in which viewers and listeners record which stations they watch or listen to and when. Meters automatically record when each set in a home is turned on and off and to which station each is tuned. One of the commonly used telephone survey methods is day-after recall, in which respondents are called to determine their listening and viewing activities from the previous day. The coincidental method also is used commonly. Households are called at random during the time period of interest and respondents are asked what they are watching or listening to at that time (Wimmer & Dominick, 1991).

Managers must keep a few limitations in mind when evaluating audience data. Respondents may not be careful, or honest, when reporting their viewing and listening habits. A meter records only which channel is tuned in and when by the respondent pushing the appropriate button(s)—it does not record whether anyone stayed in the room to watch. In addition, diary reports tend to underestimate the audiences of independent stations; such stations typically earn higher ratings in reports based on meters. The three major national TV networks (ABC, CBS, and NBC) have raised concerns over the reliability of data based on people-meter estimates. Questions about improving the cooperation rate of households in the Nielsen sample, metering more households, and developing ways of dealing with respondents who become tired of pushing buttons to indicate what they are watching have been raised (Walley, 1990).

Obviously, advertisers use different kinds of secondary data for different kinds of advertising problems and questions. There are many companies (listed in Table 9.1) that provide information about consumers and their product and media usage habits to advertisers and advertising agencies (Broadcasting/Cablecasting Yearbook, 1991; Solomon, 1989).

Interestingly, print and broadcast managers also use some of these same sources. Various sources are available to newspaper managers seeking secondary information (see Table 9.2). Managers should consult local organizations like the Chamber of Commerce or other local economic development offices for market information. State agencies concerned with economic development also may provide information. State or regional press associations sometimes compile primary and secondary market information. The creative manager consults these and other sources when developing a market kit (*Broadcasting/Cablecasting Yearbook*, 1991).

TABLE 9.1

Sources of Advertising Research

Source	Service
Sales and Marketing Management's Survey of Buying Power	Provides data for buying power, household income, and retail sales by type of store and merchandise.
Standard Rate and Data Service (SRDS)	Provides data on consumer spendable income, retail sales and the number of households. Also publishes *The Lifestyle Market Analyst,* which breaks down the population geographically, demographically, and psychographically.
Simmons Market Research Bureau (SMRB)	Provides demographic and media usage information for light, medium, and heavy users of more than 500 product categories.
Mediamark Research Inc. (MRI)	Provides demographic and media usage information for light, medium, and heavy users of many product categories.
ScanTrack (Nielsen) and Behavior Scan (IRI)	These two companies provide retail sales data obtained using supermarket scanners.
Broadcast Advertising Reports	Provides data on competitive expenditures in the broadcast medium.
Leading National Advertisers	Provides data for magazine and outdoor advertising expenditures in various media. Publishes Ad $ Summary.
Nielsen Retail Index	Provides data regarding consumer sales and retail prices and relates them to competitors.
National Yellow Pages Monitor	Provides reports on yellow pages advertising.
Outdoor Advertising Association of America	Provides case studies and reports on uses of outdoor advertising.
Traffic Audit Bureau	Audits outdoor circulation.
Point-of-Purchase Advertising Institute	Provides research reports and a newsletter.
Yankelovich Partners	Provides the Monitor study of consumer social values as well as customized research services.
Competitive Media Reporting	Provides data on advertising occurrences, expenditures, creative and broadcast verification for more than 90,000 brands across various media to advertising agencies, advertisers, broadcasters and publishers.
Gallup and Robinson	Provides copy testing, tracking studies, concept testing, media research, research on claims substantiation, spokesperson testing, event sponsorship, custom research and international testing.

Various industry groups provide assistance to the broadcast or cable manager for developing sales kits, as well as market or industry data (Solomon, 1989). A number of companies provide research services for radio, television, and/or cable broadcasters (*Broadcasting/Cablecasting Year-*

TABLE 9.2
Sources of Newspaper Research

Source	Service
Newspaper Association of America (NAA)	Provides data about the attractiveness of newspapers as an advertising medium. Also publishes the annual *Facts About Newspapers* report.
Magazine Publishers of America (MPA)	Provides research on circulation, readership and effectiveness.
Starch Ad Research	Conducts print advertising readership studies.
Editor & Publisher's Market Guide	Provides facts and figures about all U.S. daily newspaper markets, including estimates of number of households, local population estimates, estimates of disposable personal income, kinds of industries, important shopping centers, and the number of banks.
Sales & Marketing Management Survey of Buying Power	Provides information on the population, retail sales, and buying power of U.S. markets.
Standard Rate and Data Service Newspaper Advertising Source	Provides rate and production information for daily, weekly, college and university, and minority newspapers. Includes data about U.S. markets including income and retail sales.
Audit Bureau of Circulations (ABC)	Audits the circulation of newspapers and periodicals.
BPA International	Audits the circulation of business publications and special-interest consumer magazines.
U.S. Bureau of the Census:	Publishes data and indexes providing the demographic, social, and economic characteristics of U.S. markets, as well as annual Census updates in the Statistical Abstracts.
Ad Track	Weekly USA Today & Louis Harris poll to determine the effectiveness of a major ad campaign.

book, 1991). Some of these companies provide information also used by print and advertising managers (see Table 9.3)

Audience Research: Primary Data Collection

A media manager may choose to conduct a primary audience research study to answer questions not answered by syndicated data. A newspaper manager who is aware of changing readership and market conditions can capi-

TABLE 9.3

Sources of Broadcast Research

Source	Service
National Association of Broadcasters (NAB)	Industry organization that works on broadcast issues. Provides research advice and assistance to members.
Television Bureau of Advertising (TVB)	Provides research services and data including trends in television and other media, trends in advertising volume, and ad revenue figures and forecasts. Publishes TVBasics annually, which contains a wide variety of statistics.
Association of Local Television Stations (ALTV)	Provides lobbying and reports for local TV stations affiliated with the Fox, WB, UPN, and PaxNet networks, as well as independent stations.
Advertiser Syndicated Television Association (ASTA)	Provides reports and sponsors workshops to improve understanding of use of syndication.
Cabletelevision Advertising Bureau	Provides reports on cable audiences and advertising and produces *Cable TV Facts*, a compilation of cable information.
Radio Advertising Bureau (RAB)	Provides information, data, and research about radio advertising, ad sales, new business development, consumer behavior, other media, and creative and marketing concepts. Publishes Radio Marketing Guide and Fact Book, Sound Solutions, Format Profile Reports, and the 24-hour online internet marketing resource center called RadioLink.
FMR Associates, Inc.	Provides perceptual and programming studies, weekly call-outs, format opportunity, and vulnerability positioning studies. Also provides testing of TV commercials and programming simulation tests.
Frank N. Magid Associates Inc.	Provides consulting and research services for broadcast and new media. Methods for local, national or international studies include telephone interviewing, personal interviewing, focus groups, mystery shopping, mail surveys, theater testing and online testing. Provides many research services including market baseline studies, brand equity or extension studies, positioning studies, talent or personality surveys, promotion or campaign testing, and slogan testing.
Arbitron	Measures radio audiences and provides software used to analyze and integrate its quantitative measures with qualitative measures and other local market data. The software allows stations and ad agencies to customize survey areas, dayparts, and demographics to support target marketing strategies.
Nielsen Media Research (NMR)	Measures TV audiences through 9 syndicated services used to buy sell, plan and price TV time, as well as make programming and scheduling decisions. Measures daily TV, cable and home video using people meters or diaries.

286

Electronic Media Rating Council	Reviews rating services' methodology to ensure users of credible data. Also has developed Minimum Standards for Electronic Media Rating Research.
MORPACE International, Inc.	Provides television, cable, telecommunications and computer technology research and consulting. Customized studies include: ongoing customer satisfaction research, image and brand-related studies, analysis of service trials, analysis of possible acquisitions, new product development research, analysis of potential pay channel and pay-per-view market penetration, and analysis of petential new revenue.
SRI Consulting	Provides consulting and strategic research for communications, entertainment and information industries.

talize on an opportunity to attract new readers to help offset other declining readership segments. On the other hand, if the manager does not know the demographic composition of a neighborhood that traditionally has provided large numbers of readers is changing, trying to increase circulation may prove to be futile. Thus, the prudent manager conducts or contracts research studies regularly to keep abreast of market changes. The major types of research used by newspaper managers include circulation, readership, and advertising studies.

Circulation Studies. "Newspapers are almost always defined by geography—in their names, their local news and advertising, and their distribution" (Sohn et al., 1986, p. 99). Geography is important to local newspaper managers because it defines the area in which readers are attracted. Circulation studies reveal the newspaper's market share, the market share of competing media, existing circulation patterns, and areas of potential circulation growth (Mauro, 1980). A newspaper manager then can conduct a situation or market analysis to determine which areas to target for increasing circulation.

Readership Studies. Readership studies help a manager to describe the people who live in those target areas. Although descriptive survey demographic studies are the most common type (Willis, 1988), psychographic and media usage questions also may be included in readership studies. Studies that include demographic, psychographic, and media usage questions reveal who reads the newspaper, why, which sections particular reader segments prefer, and the benefits they accrue from reading the paper. Results suggest ways to attract new readers. For example, a large metropolitan newspaper might develop a special lifestyle section to appeal to upper income city residents who are moving to a particular zip code. A small town newspaper might increase soccer coverage in the sports section when research shows that it is becoming an important activity for children and their parents. This type of study also incorporates product positioning research.

Studies incorporating demographics, psychographics, and media usage may be used to measure the characteristics of audiences for competing media. Information about who exclusively reads each local daily, weekly, and shopper, who reads a combination of these publications and why, and how these and other publications are used may reveal untapped readership segments.

Advertising Studies. Some information derived from audience research is used to attract advertisers to the media vehicle. Advertisers are attracted to a medium for its efficient reach or coverage of an audience that is desirable to the advertiser. Advertisers want to reach the greatest numbers of their desired target audience for the least amount of money. A media manager or media representative sells media time to media buyers using a media kit that includes an estimate of media efficiency known as the cost per thousand (CPM) for reaching the desired audience. Characteristics of the desired audience have been identified through audience research. The coverage of the media vehicle can be obtained through secondary data sources. CPMs, which may be used for intramedia or intermedia comparisons, allow comparisons of one medium or vehicle with another to find those that are the most cost efficient. This information is packaged in a *media kit,* which is designed to position the media product as an ideal vehicle for the advertiser.

The basic CPM formulas are as follows (Sissors & Surmanek, 1982):

For Print Vehicles:

$$CPM = \frac{\text{Cost of one page black \& white (or appropriate size and color) x 1000}}{\text{Circulation or number of prospects reached}}$$

For Broadcast Vehicles:

$$CPM = \frac{\text{Cost of one unit of time x 1000}}{\text{Number of homes or prospects reached by a given program or in a specific time period}}$$

Media managers at smaller newspapers, radio stations, or cable channels with small budgets might use published data to develop a media kit. Census data, Sales and Marketing Management's *Survey of Buying Power, Editor& Publishers Market Guide* and Standard Rate and Data Service's various publications on newspapers, magazines, radio stations, and TV stations might be found at the local library and consulted for market information. Local, state, or national trade associations also may provide data about industry trends.

Audience research may become even more important because of the continued segmentation of broadcast audiences. With increasing competition from pay cable, pay-per-view, subscription TV, satellites, and VCRs, managers expect that the competition for broadcast audiences will intensify. This means that the competition for advertising dollars will intensify as well.

Competitive Media Activity

Data on past and present *media activity of advertisers* can be purchased from Competitive Media Reporting. The data can be provided in many forms and list advertiser purchases in competitive vehicles. Advertising agencies are most likely to use this data, however other media managers can identify the buying patterns of a desired advertiser to gain insight into desirable media buys.

Product Positioning Research

Product positioning research identifies the product characteristics that are desired by the audience. It is assumed that the position of any product, including media vehicles, is a function of the audience's perceptions of the product. The perceptions are determined by the uncontrollable individual characteristics of the audience, but also by the controllable product characteristics, product price, distribution, and promotion strategy. Studies of audience perceptions of products are considered product positioning research. Its purpose is to discover a product's unique attribute (or combination of attributes), to reposition a product to better meet the needs of the audience, and to diagnose why audiences are not attracted to a product. It can include other factors such as how a product compares to similar competitive offerings.

Positioning research is often performed using exploratory and descriptive methods, such as a survey of the audience or perhaps focus groups with audience participants. Identifying consumer habits, lifestyles, behaviors, and desires through primary target market research provides information that can be used as a basis for product positioning.

For media organizations, the greatest positioning concern may be the audience's image of the company. In this case, the media company is the product. Examples include a cable company concerned with maintaining its subscribers as well as its franchise. In 1997, Ted Turner prohibited his CNN employees from appearing in films to avoid the reduction of their credibility with viewers. Other broadcast news divisions and newspapers are concerned with their credibility as well. In an effort to revamp their image during the Fall 1997 campaign, ABC implemented an irreverent campaign, designed by TBWA Chiat Day North America, for watching television and ABC programming. Initial focus group pretests of the campaign indicated a negative reaction from the viewing audience, but ABC officials moved forward despite these reports (Robins, 1997). The effectiveness of this campaign will be determined by the bottom line outcomes of viewership and the resulting ad dollars ABC receives for placement of advertising during their programming. A new cable network's name is critical to the successful positioning of the network, because it may be one of the only pieces of information audiences hear about the new network.

Positioning research can identify the audience perceptions along these important characteristics. In fact, a broadcast station has a mandated concern for community views about programming, including how well the station covers local issues and problems. The FCC notes that licensees should try to discover local broadcasting "tastes, needs and desires" (*Ascertainment*, 1976; *En banc*, 1960, p. 2312; *Primer*, 1971). It evaluates licensee performance in this regard by considering how responsive programming is to local needs rather than how a licensee arrives at programming decisions (*Revision*, 1984).

At the media content level, studies of audience reactions to and preferences for broadcast and cable programming, news and magazine articles and format, and the structure and content of web sites are critical to maintaining audience commitment. Media managers then sell their audiences, commitment behaviors (measured through audience research) to advertisers.

Several types of research designs can be used to conduct positioning studies. Call-out phone survey research is used to evaluate the popularity of a radio station's present and future musical offerings. "Hooks," which are representative 10- to 30-second song excerpts, are played over the phone to respondents of a one-shot study or members of an ongoing listener panel. Both types of respondents report whether they like or dislike each hook (Rich & Martin, 1981).

Television managers also are concerned with determining how popular their programs and on-air personalities are. A manager might conduct a mail or telephone survey, focus group, or personal interviews to determine whether his news talent and newscast is favored by the local community. Results may be used to determine local news anchor changes.

Media Content: Formative and Evaluative Research

Evaluative research determines how well the media content conveys what it is intended to convey. Causal research methods such as experiments are often used to conduct this research. This research is extremely common in advertising agencies where advertisements are tested before use (pretest message research) and after use (posttest message research).

Test marketing can be used to evaluate audience tastes for broadcast and cable programming, print editorial content, web site structure and content, as well as advertising. For example, an ad might be shown in one market before it is shown nationally in order to project what its effect on consumer behavior might be. Ads might be shown in two different markets or on a two-way cable system in one city, with subscribers in one part of the city seeing one version of a program or commercial and those living in another area seeing another version. Results of a random telephone survey would reveal which program version earned higher ratings or which commercial spurred more sales.

Formative Media Content Research. Media organizations can test their products before committing full resources to them. Production companies and television networks pretest programming and advertisers pretest their ads.

Concept testing is a method used to test the potential popularity of a program or the potential effectiveness of the key selling concept in an ad before it is viewed by the general public. A concept might be tested by having respondents read a one-page written summary of the program or showing them a mock-up of a commercial made using slides and an audiotape. Respondents may be invited to a theater to view a pilot program. After viewing, they report their feelings about the program to help network executives determine how popular various characters and endings might be (Fletcher, 1981).

One type of formative field experiment is the test market. Advertisements or programming or editorial content can be run in small, controlled markets so their performance is tested in a more natural setting. Advertisers can do a split run in print vehicles, which allows two versions of the media content to run in different geographic areas. This allows a test of comparative performance.

Major advertising agencies conduct formative or pretest message research to help develop new ads and predict how well a new ad will meet the advertising objective before actually placing the ad. The prediction of an ad's performance requires causal research and experimentation. An advertiser might use a laboratory study to measure the audience's attentiveness to an ad or on which areas of an ad the audience might focus. Sometimes, the advertiser checks to see if the brand is placed in a position that the audience will notice. This type of a laboratory study might utilize a pupillometer, which measures pupil dilation, an indication of interest, or an oculometer which tracks eye movements. The advertiser could also ask the audience about its psychological reactions to the ad after exposure. This type of study also allows an advertiser to compare the performance of more than one format for an ad and then choose the one that performs best. Some other typical advertising objectives that are tested experimentally are related to an ad's ability to create brand awareness, change attitudes toward the brand, and create purchase behavior.

Summative Media Content Research.

Summative research can determine whether the appropriate message was conveyed to the target market. This allows the media manager to evaluate if the media content objectives were actually accomplished. This type of study is typically performed in the field during a campaign.

Summative advertising research information can also be purchased as secondary data from one of several research firms. Starch INRA Hooper and Gallup and Robinson are two major firms that provide syndicated data on the performance of ads in broadcast and print media. The disadvantage of the data from these firms is that they are limited in scope and their ability to provide answers to specific questions an advertiser might have about an ad's performance.

Starch scores provide information about how many individuals saw a print ad, how many noted the brand name or logo, and how many read at least one-half of the copy of the ad. Gallup and Robinson can provide television ad information indicating the percentage of viewers recalling the ad one day later, the number of ideas communicated by the ad, the primary idea communicated by the ad, and the audience's report of being favorably persuaded by the ad.

SUMMARY

All media managers must understand research from a broad perspective in order to use it effectively. Advertising, newspaper, network, cable, and on-line technology managers use similar kinds of data and research techniques in different ways and obtain information from the same research sources. Managers also should understand the research data and techniques their counterparts use. Hopefully, managers will use this knowledge to serve their own media organizations, clients, and especially their audiences more effectively.

Before designing a research study, three issues can be considered. First, how much is already known about the problem at hand? Second, how much information is needed about each audience member? Third, how important is it that the results of the study are generalizable to other people and situations? The answers to these questions direct the researcher to some types of research and not others.

Some of the research categories that are important to effective media management are primary, secondary, syndicated, exploratory, descriptive, and causal research. Applied research methods include audience, product positioning, formative, and summative research. Data collection designs available to the researcher include focus groups, in-depth interviews, surveys, and experiments. By collecting information about the consumer, the media manager can make more informed strategic decisions and market the media vehicle to advertisers.

CASE 9.1

The Case of WZZY's Dilemma:
Do We Need A New Format?

Todd Backer was thrilled—he had finally been appointed programming manager at a major market radio station. However, he had a big job on his hands. WZZY had been ranked either 10th or 11th in the Dallas market for years. A succession of program managers had tried to improve WZZY's record, with limited success. Part of the problem was that the top four stations had been successful at maintaining their high rankings for years. Two reasons were that their formats, musical selections, and on-air personalities were popular and their station images were well developed. WKCK and WCTY cornered the market on country. WKCK, otherwise known as Kickin' Country, had been a strong number one for years. WKCK relied on its traditional country format, playing the music of "old" artists like Charley Pride and Loretta Lynn, coupled with traditionalists like Randy Travis. Kickin' Country also had a strong news department, known for live, on-the-spot coverage of breaking news.

WCLS, the second-ranked station using a middle-of-the-road format, attracted the 25- to 45-year-olds and was known as the local sports leader because it carried high school and college football and basketball broadcasts.

WCTY was content with its third place ranking in the market because it used the contemporary country format that appealed to younger, more prosperous, country fans (who were attractive to advertisers because of their buying power). Finally, the fourth-ranked WTOP played contemporary top 40 hits, appealing to the lucrative 18- to 24-year-old market. WTOP was very successful at promoting itself with this segment, sponsoring local music festivals and college events.

Todd's mandate was to improve WZZY's standing—or else. WZZY's format was presently album-oriented rock (AOR), featuring artists like the Rolling Stones, Eric Clapton, and ZZ Top. Todd's "gut feeling" was that this format was a major part of the problem. WRCK, another station in the market that had been ranked sixth for years, also used an AOR format. Todd felt there just was not enough interest to support two AOR stations.

Todd discussed this problem with the general manager and owner, Bob Curtis, and suggested that the station conduct research to determine if his suspicion was correct. He also wanted to discover what other formats the station might adopt. Curtis agreed, but also wanted the research project to suggest which audience segment (or segments) to target. He wanted to be certain that this new format would attract listeners advertisers wanted to reach. Curtis directed Todd to recommend a research project which would accomplish all of these goals.

To help him focus on format, Todd needed to do research on radio formats. *The Broadcasting/Cablecasting Yearbook* (1991) provides a breakdown of the radio programming formats used in the United States and Canada. McCavitt and Pringle (1986) and Head and Stirling (1990) provided descriptions of the major formats, including:

Adult Contemporary/Hit Music—appeals to persons 18- to 34-years old. Emphasizes currently popular songs and artists and uses a broad array of current and classic hits to appeal to a wide range of adults.

Album-Oriented Rock (AOR)—appeals to persons, especially men, 18- to 34-years old, and includes current hits and oldies, with a strong emphasis on artists. Album cuts, and occasionally the entire side of an album or CD, are played. Mixes less popular songs from successful albums with classic rock hits.

Beautiful Music—known as good or easy listening; traditionally background, instrumental versions of slower tempo hit songs and oldies.

Big Band/Nostalgia—appeals to persons age 35 and older, who prefer the music of the 1930s, 1940s, and 1950s (nonrock only).

Black—features Black artists and music. Playlist may include gospel, soul, and other traditional Black recordings.

Contemporary Hit Radio (CHR)/Top-40—appeals primarily to 18- to 24-year olds, but also attracts listeners aged 12- to 34. Playlist consists of top-selling pop and rock singles. Oldies are played occasionally.

Classic Rock/Oldies—appeals mostly to listeners older than 30. Features hits from the 1950s and 1960s.

Classical—plays recorded classical music, as well as live opera, symphony, and chamber music performances. Appeals to people who are well educated and who are in higher socioeconomic categories.

Country—appeals to men and women 25- to 64-years-old in all socioeconomic categories. Specialized versions of this format include traditional and contemporary country/country-rock (music appealing to both country and rock audiences).

Jazz—appeals mostly to persons in high socioeconomic categories. Usually has limited appeal.

Middle-of-the-Road (MOR)—appeals to adults 25- to 45-years old. Includes vocal and instrumental versions of contemporary, nonrock popular music, and standard hits and makes extensive use of on-air announcers. Typically a heavy emphasis on news, sports, weather, traffic, sports events, broadcast talk, and interviews.

News—appeals to people 25- to 54-years old, mostly to better educated men. Consists of local, regional, national, and international news, features, analysis, commentary, and editorials. Programs cycles of 20 or 30 minutes are developed because it is assumed audiences will tune in only for short periods of time.

Urban Contemporary—appeals to Blacks 18- to 49-years old, but also attracts other people. Basically a combination of jazz, disco, and dance-beat rock and roll. Format varies widely by station and market.

Talk—appeals to people 35- to 65-years old. Features interviews and audience call-ins about many different subjects. May also feature psychologists, marriage counselors, and sex therapists who encourage listeners to talk about their personal problems.

ASSIGNMENT

1. How can Todd determine whether the AOR format is the problem? What kind of research project should he recommend?
2. Should Todd recommend more than one study? If so, which research project should be conducted first and why? Which aspect of the problem should be researched second, and so forth.
3. How can Todd determine which audience segments might be good potential listener targets before the research project begins?

CASE 9.2

Analyzing A Media Market

You have just been hired as the head of the media department at Acme Advertising Agency. (Assume Acme is located in the largest major city near you.) You are the top media planner for the agency, as well as department head. Acme is a small agency with only 10 employees in its media department. Acme's clients are mostly local, but the agency has begun to attract a few national clients because of its outstanding creative reputation. Your predecessor worked for the agency for more than 20 years, but left because these national, and some local, clients were complaining that they did not understand why certain media buys were made. They also complained that they did not receive adequate justification for the media buys that were made.

As you sift through your predecessor's desk and files, you note a woeful lack of information about the local media, and essentially none about the national media. Basically, the files contained rate cards and recent copies of syndicated radio and television ratings reports. You call your predecessor, who says that he simply "knew the market by heart" and did not need much documentation for the various media. He tells you that he thought it was a big mistake for the agency to solicit national clients. They were too demanding and were always nitpicking about details. You quickly realize that you do not have the information on hand that you need to do your job.

You report your impressions to your boss, the agency's owner, who agrees with your assessment and directs you to develop the data base you need. "We don't have any big media projects due right now. Unless something comes up, spend the next 2 weeks putting together the information we need to bring our media department into the 21st century. Develop an analysis of the local media market that we can use and suggest what outside sources of data we might buy. As you know, we serve local and national clients in a number of different areas: a major local bank, a national manufacturer of packaged goods, a major national wine producer, a major local grocery chain, a major local automobile dealership, a national catalog selling men's and women's clothing and household goods, a major local department store, and a prominent local restaurant, to name a few. Keep these clients in mind when you develop your analysis, but also consider that we're going to try to attract other major local and national accounts over the next few years. We need to be 'up to snuff' with the big agencies, if possible. But remember: We're a small agency. So prioritize what you need so I can figure out a way to buy the essentials for you now and buy other materials as funds become available."

Develop a market report for your boss that evaluates and compares the major local media outlets. Compare the merits and demerits of the major local print, broadcast, outdoor, and direct mail outlets. Also include any other important local media vehicles that are unique to the major city nearest you. Provide a basic description of each vehicle and its audience, providing information about its most popular features or programs, as well as audience composition data. Avoid the tendency to rely solely on information provided by each vehicle. Also seek out information that describes the demographic and psychographic composition of the market, as well as purchasing habits and the level of local discretionary income. Also find out as much as you can about local media usage habits.

Review the *Gale Directory of Publications & Broadcast Media* and the *Broadcasting/Cablecasting Yearbook* to find out what the major media vehicles are in your city. Examine Census data, Sales & Marketing Management's annual *Survey of Buying Power, Editor & Publisher Market Guide,* and any Standard Rate and Data Service publications for market and consumer information. Also review SRDS's *The Lifestyle Market Analyst,* which breaks down the U.S. population geographically and demographically and includes lifestyle information on the popular interests, hobbies, and activities in each market. Also review other appropriate sources of information about your market, its residents, and their buying patterns. The WWW can provide access to a variety of data. A search engine, such as Yahoo (www.yahoo.com) and Altavista (www.altavista.com) can help find sites with data. Possible starting places include the Arbitron site (www.arbitron.com) and the U.S. Census Bureau site (www.census.gov).

Consider what other syndicated research reports you might need for your agency besides syndicated ratings reports for broadcast. For example, consider whether your agency should purchase the *Simmons* and/or *Mediamark* reports, as well as other local, regional, or national sources of syndicated research. Also consider any other sources of information that might be appropriate for the agency to purchase. Evaluate the merits of these sources and recommend which ones your agency should buy. Prioritize and explain your choices.

ASSIGNMENT

Develop a report for your boss that includes all of these elements:

1. An analysis of the consumers in your market and any major segments that may be good targets for your clients. Provide any tables that support your analysis.

2. An analysis of the various major media vehicles in your market. The strengths and weaknesses of each vehicle should be discussed and cost efficiencies compared.

3. An analysis of the national and/or local sources of syndicated research that should be purchased by the agency. Review the merits and demerits of each and rank each source in order of importance to the agency.

4. An analysis of any other sources you recommend for purchase. Review the advantages and disadvantages of these sources and rank each source in order of importance to the agency.

5. An analysis of how all of this information will be used by the agency. For example, describe how your local market and media analyses can be used now in developing media plans. Discuss how each syndicated research source can be used to develop media plans for current clients. Also discuss how each source might be used for potential clients.

6. Recommendations on the sources of information that must be purchased right away. Present timetable for purchasing other sources of information. Justify your decisions.

CASE 9.3

Measuring Newspaper Quality

Assume you are the director of marketing research for the local or national newspaper of your choice. The publisher of this paper is concerned about a research trend that suggests circulation is beginning to decline. The publisher wants you to develop a study to test editorial, as well as reader, assessments of the quality of your paper. The goal is to identify the paper's strengths and weaknesses in order to find out what actions are needed to stem a circulation decline. She suggests that you consider the criteria found in Leo Bogart's book *Press and Public: Who Reads What, When, Where and Why in American Newspapers* (1989, see pp. 258–265) and George Gladney's Newspaper Excellence: How Editors of Small and Large Papers Judge Quality, *Newspaper Research Journal,* Spring 1990, 58–72.

ASSIGNMENT

Write a preliminary research proposal for the publisher that includes the following:

1. Suggest an appropriate method for conducting research regarding newspaper quality. Describe the type of research, appropriate subjects, sample size, and so forth that you think will assess quality best. Decide whether separate studies are needed to examine editorial and reader perceptions of quality. Describe the appropriate methodology, if you think separate studies are needed.
2. Provide a preliminary list of questions or a questionnaire that demonstrates how you think quality should be measured for each study you propose.
3. Provide a rationale for why you chose the quality measures you did for each study you propose. Explain how the questions or questionnaire items will measure assessments of quality from both an editor's and reader's standpoint.
4. Provide a timetable. Explain when you think the research project(s) should be conducted and why. Discuss how long you think it will take to complete the study or studies and provide information regarding when each stage in development and implementation will take place. Also state when you expect to present the results.
5. If the newspaper has a web site, discuss whether you should include this site in your analysis and how the measures of quality applied to the web site might differ from those applied to the print version.

CASE 9.4

Should the News Anchor Be Fired?

Jane Smithies, news director at KDTV, summoned the station's marketing and research director, Jack Johansen, in for a meeting. It seemed that the ratings for the early and late-evening newscasts were slipping. "Walter Dobson may no longer be the news institution he once was," Jane told Jack. "It's your job to find out. We have to find out why ratings are slipping and take action. Otherwise, we'll quickly slip from number two to number three in this market and we can't afford that."

Jack was well aware how competitive the market was. A loss of just a few ratings points usually meant thousands of dollars of lost advertising revenue. The station had to be very careful in taking any action, whether trying something new or resolving a problem. Any change that resulted in even a minor ratings loss was usually felt in the pocketbook.

"Jack, you've got to find out whether Walter is the problem or whether changes are needed in the format and content of our newscasts." Jane also told Jack that he needed to present a brief summary of the kind of research the station could conduct to solve this problem, or whether it would make better sense to hire an outside company to evaluate the problem and propose solutions.

ASSIGNMENT

Pretend that you are Jack Johansen. Prepare a report that explains whether the station should conduct research itself or hire an outside consultant to evaluate the news programs. Explain the rationale for your decision. Consult your local library for information about broadcast research and broadcast consultants. Also interview a local broadcast manager (or invite one to speak in class). Pretend that KDTV is located in your home market and make suggestions accordingly. Prepare a report that includes the following information:

1. Suggest the type of research that might be conducted. Prepare questions that would assess fairly whether the anchor or the program is the problem. Suggest the best methodology for finding this out. Explain why this methodology is the best one for solving this problem.
2. Evaluate the advantages and disadvantages of conducting research in-house versus hiring an outside consultant. Is it better to have an independent party plan the research and make a judgment in this case? Why or why not?

3. Suggest which local research company, national research company, local consultant, and national consultant might be suited best for solving this problem. Present the advantages and disadvantages of using each.

4. Recommend the best way to address this problem. Explain why the station itself should conduct the research, or who should be hired. Be sure to justify your answer.

CASE 9.5

Dealing With Cable Customer Dissatisfaction

You are the manager of the cable system in your city (or the nearest city). You are concerned about the constant complaints from customers regarding service. You received 20 letters this week alone; you shudder to think how many complaints the receptionist received by phone. You also are concerned because the local city government is beginning to make noise about the poor level of service the cable company provides.

You have decided to conduct a survey of subscribers to identify what the major problems are and how they might be solved. You have never conducted a survey before and you really cannot afford to hire a research firm. You must find a way to design a study that can be conducted by you and your employees.

ASSIGNMENT

Prepare a report describing how you could design and conduct such a survey from scratch, using only company employees and resources. This report should include the following:

1. Identify and describe the appropriate method to use to conduct the survey and how it can be handled in-house. In other words, what kind of a survey can be handled by local cable employees and why?
2. Discuss which sources of free or low-cost information might be consulted for developing your consumer survey. Explain how these sources can be used and why they are appropriate for this situation.
3. Explain how questions for the questionnaire will be developed. In other words, how can you find out what the major problems are before you conduct the survey? How can you decide which questions to include in the survey and why? How can you allow for employee input on which questions should be included? How can you allow for community input on which questions should be included?
4. Provide examples of the types of questions that will measure accurately what your major service problems are.
5. Suggest other questions that should be included, if any, besides questions regarding the problems and their solutions? Describe the other types of questions that might be included and explain why they are or are not needed.
6. Make a decision regarding the kind of survey you should conduct. Explain and support your decision.

CASE 9.6

Researching and Marketing the WWW

The emergence of the WWW as a commercial entity has created a boom in web pages. Despite this boom, the number of commercial locations making a profit remains low, and the types of content people want and will pay for remains a mystery. This assignment has two parts. The first involves designing research to collect data on web use, and the second involves designing a marketing plan to promote a web site.

ASSIGNMENT

Assume you are thinking about starting a web site for an existing media company. It could be a magazine, newspaper, television news operation, or any other form of media. You need to know how many people currently access the web on a regular basis, and what they look for when they do access the Web. Describe the way you would go about finding out this information. This assignment requires that you explain who you would study and how you would study them. In other words, what method would you use to answer your questions? Why? How would you sample the people you study? Why? How would you measure web use? What sort of problems do you think might limit your ability to collect data or create invalidity conclusions about your research?

Assume that you will start a commercial web site for students at your university. You need to examine the four P's of marketing before your start the site. You can do this by answering the following questions:

1. What type of content would you have on your site? Why would this attract students at your university? What might be some problems with this type of content? Would it be expensive to create? Would it offend people enough to affect your commercial success?

2. How would you pay for the web site? Would it involve subscription or advertising revenue? Who would advertise on your site? Explain your decisions.

3. Do enough of the students have access to computers and modems to build an audience? How expensive might a server be?

4. How would you promote the site so people would know it was available? What types of advertising or publicity would you pursue?

10

BUDGETING AND DECISION MAKING

Managers use a variety of types of information in the process of making decisions. This chapter discusses how media managers use accounting information for making decisions, planning the future, and controlling organizational behavior. Most people think of accounting as indecipherable and sometimes meaningless columns of numbers representing debits and credits. Indeed, accounting information often is presented in annual reports and budgets as rows and columns of dollars and cents.

Despite the financial emphasis, accounting provides meaningful, nonfinancial information describing the past, present, and future status of an organization. Without accounting information, managers would lack the necessary information for planning, decision making, and evaluating performance; organizations would have poorly defined goals, if they were to have goals at all; and managerial learning and organizational growth might never occur. Consequently, accounting provides essential information for the day-to-day activities and long-term growth and survival of organizations.

A manager is faced with a wide range of accounting information. The information a manager chooses to use in making a decision depends on several factors, including the manager's level in the organization, the long or short-term nature of the decision, the organization's size and complexity, and the nature of the firm. Regardless of the variety of types and forms of accounting information available to managers, one form of information managers use extensively is the budget. Thus, the focus of this chapter is on how managers develop and use budgets in planning and controlling the functions of a media organization.

TYPES OF ACCOUNTING INFORMATION

Accounting activities are divided into *financial accounting* and *managerial accounting*. Financial accounting provides information about an organization's health to outsiders. Managerial accounting provides information about the day-to-day operation of the company for managers to use in planning and budgeting. Although both are related to managing an organization, this chapter concentrates primarily on managerial accounting.

Financial Accounting Information

Financial accounting refers to the preparation of materials, such as annual reports, for use primarily by individuals external to the organization. Such materials are used by the general public, regulatory agencies, owners, investors, creditors, taxing authorities, and industry associations. For example, a public media company's annual report may reveal the culture and values of that organization. The annual report's cover design, letter to shareholders, and information about planned investments and acquisitions reveal what management considers important to the firm's long-term success.

A balance sheet also reveals a great deal of information about a company. Let us consider how to analyze a balance sheet using an example for a fictitious broadcast group with seven television and two radio stations called Callas Communications (see Table 10.1). The long-term objective of Callas Communications is primarily to acquire more television stations and, if possible, other media and communications-related properties in the future. Another goal is to identify and acquire stations that have the potential for substantial long-term appreciation and profitability. Callas' management looks for personnel who can aggressively manage these stations to maximize profits, allowing the company to purchase more stations. Callas' seven TV stations are network affiliates of ABC, CBS, NBC, or Fox.

This background information is important for evaluating Callas' balance sheet, which reflects the financial status of a corporation by listing its assets and liabilities. It serves as a stop-action photograph of a company on a given date. When a series of balance sheets are examined together, they reveal how the company behaved across time.

The balance sheet is divided into major sections called *assets, liabilities* and *shareholder's equity*. Assets are resources that a company owns or that are owed to a company. Liabilities are amounts of money that are owed by the company in some form to a person or organization. Both assets and liabilities take many forms, but the total assets minus the total liabilities reveals the company's financial health. The difference between assets and liabilities is shareholder's equity, which represents the value of the company that belongs to the owners. The balance sheet gets its name from the

TABLE 10.1

Consolidated Balance Sheets for Callas Communications

| | December 31, | |
	1996	1997
Assets		
Current Assets		
Cash and cash equivalents	$ 76,098	$ 444,602
Accounts receivable, less allowance for doubtful accounts ($505,759 in 1995 and $391.910 in 1996)	20,869,263	21,645,960
Film contract rights	4,650,692	5,021,280
Other current assets	3,083,819	7,827,972
Total current assets	28,679,872	34,939,814
Property and equipment, net	25,705,700	26,849,615
Film contract rights and Other noncurrent assets	2,980,489	3,427,662
Deferred financing fees less accumulated amortization ($2,947,833 in 1995 and $4,049,724 in 1996)	11,879,623	11,345,329
Intangible assets		
Goodwill	60,154,095	60,962,282
Network affiliations	198,353,310	198,353,310
Broadcast licenses	54,317,488	54,317,488
	312,824,890	313,633,080
Depreciation	(20,373,673)	(28,144,992)
Net intangible assets	$292,451,210	$285,488,080
	$361,696,904	$362,050,508
Liabilities and stockholders' equity (deficit)		
Current liabilities:		
Accounts payable	$ 4,228,495	$ 3,213,571
Accrued interest	4,476,488	4,857,102
Other accrued liabilities	2,800,052	3,598,027
Film contract rights payable and other current liabilities	5,556,854	7,662,692
Total current liabilities	17,061,889	19,331,392
Long-term debt	272,719,996	281,248,667
Film contract rights payable	2,935,627	2,706,742
Deferred tax liability and Other noncurrent liabilities	25,495,392	24,881,817

Commitments

Redeemable preferred stock	36,390,000	36,390,000
Stockholders' equity (deficit):		
Common stock	67,173	69,425
Additional capital	37,491,361	36,437,716
Accumulated deficit	(29,272,158)	(36,300,728)
Less: Unearned compensation	(1,192,376)	(2,005,023)
Note receivable from officer		(709,500)
Total stockholders' equity (Deficit)	7,094,000	(2,508,109)
	$361,696,904	$362,050,508

fact that assets always must equal liabilities and shareholder's equity. Several of the terms in the balance sheet shown in Table 10.1 need defining:

Assets. *Current assets* include money or other resources that are converted easily to money. For example, accounts receivable include money owed the company for services or products rendered. Inventories are those objects that can be sold readily for cash.

Investments and other assets are resources that come from investing other resources. Property, plant, and equipment include land, buildings, and equipment owned by the company. Because some media organizations, such as daily newspapers and television stations, require a large fixed investment, this category is often a large portion of assets for these firms. Depreciation represents the value of property, plant, and equipment that has been used up in the operation of the organization. If a newspaper or TV station buys a computer system, a certain percentage of the cost of that system becomes depreciation each year until the value reaches zero. One can look at property, plant, and equipment as investments in future production. As that investment is used for production, it declines in value, which must be represented on the balance sheet.

Goodwill, publication, and *broadcast rights* represent the value of any legal rights a company has to publish or broadcast and the value of how people feel about the company. Goodwill is the value of the company's reputation. A problem with these categories is that they are hard to measure. Quite often, a company will figure its liabilities and owner equity and the difference between these two and its assets will be goodwill. Just as equipment depreciates, goodwill has a limited life. People who watch television stations have viewing preferences that change, have multiple viewing options due to DSS, cable, and VCRs, and have outside TV interests. Goodwill for these people ends. This loss of goodwill is amortized across the line and is placed in the balance sheet to show this loss of this asset.

In reviewing Callas' balance sheet, a large part of the company's assets are listed as intangible assets, especially network affiliations. It appears that Callas may have simply listed the difference between assets and liabilities as intangible assets. Given the aggressive acquisition stance the company takes, one would expect to see a large amount under intangible assets and under liabilities in the next section of the balance sheet.

Anyone considering an investment in Callas would be wise to be cautious. All of Callas' stations are VHF network-affiliated stations. Network affiliations are valuable, as there are a limited number of very high frequency (VHF) channels available in each market. Television station broadcasting on the VHF band have had some competitive advantage over ultra-high frequency (UHF) stations. This advantage is diminishing, however, as viewing options increase. Plus the major networks' share of the viewing audience nationwide has been declining for several years. Such a high reliance on intangible assets may indicate a company in, or potentially in, financial trouble.

Liabilities and Shareholder's Equity. Current liabilities are debts that are due within a relatively short period of time. Besides the typical short-term debts that many companies pay like salaries, a company like Callas has interest payments on the high level of debt the company carries, given its goals of acquiring media properties. Also note the long-term debt or noncurrent liabilities. These are liabilities that extend for 1 year or more. For example, if a company sells bonds, the amount owed the bond holders would be noncurrent liabilities.

The large amount listed under long-term debt also indicates the company's long-term goal of acquiring properties. For example, during the past year Callas acquired a Fox affiliate in a top 10 market for approximately $175 million in cash and the assumption of certain liabilities. The purchase price and liabilities are reflected in the long-term debt column for 1997. Another acquisition the previous year is reflected in the 1996 long-term debt. Obviously, the owners and stockholders believe that these station purchases will pay off over the long term; otherwise they would be unwilling to acquire so much debt.

This debt is reflected in the shareholder's or stockholder's equity section, which shows a deficit. Shareholder's or stockholder's equity represents the resources of the company that belong to the owners in one way or another. For example, if the company had earned a profit, any retained earnings listed would be the amount of profit that remains in the control of the managers of the company.

In the case of Callas Communications, both preferred (voting) and common (nonvoting) stocks are listed under liabilities. Should the company ever liquidate, the holders of preferred stock would be compensated first. Presently the stockholders' equity is a deficit, so anyone considering an investment in Callas must be cautious.

Although a balance sheet is used generally by outsiders to evaluate the financial position of the company, a series of balance sheets also can help managers. They are not so much generators of information for decision making as they are warning signals. By monitoring the balance sheets across time, one can get a sense of whether the company's financial position is improving or deteriorating.

If the ratio of assets to liabilities is increasing, the company is doing well. If the ratio is declining, it could be doing better. In reviewing Callas' balance sheets for 1996 and 1997, it appears that the company could be doing better. Intangible assets increased slightly in 1997 when the stockholders' equity showed a deficit.

Another item to note is the "Note receivable from officer" listing under stockholders' equity. The company made a personal loan to an officer of the company with an annual interest rate of 8%. Other stockholders or potential investors might legitimately question the wisdom of making personal loans to officers from company funds. Such a loan may indicate that questionable accounting practices are used by the company.

MANAGERIAL ACCOUNTING INFORMATION

Managerial accounting emphasizes the accounting information needs of the manager for decision making. Budgets and income statements are developed to aid managers in assessing whether organizational goals are being met. Budgets and income statements are the accounting information formats most frequently used by managers.

Budgets and Income Statements

A *budget* is a statement of the planned use and acquisition of financial resources for meeting specific goals during a particular period of time. Budgets quantify the objectives and specific goals of the manager's department or company. Budgets provide direction for decision making and are an integral part of the planning process. Consequently, budgets are used as detailed and coordinated plans for the future.

Budgets also set performance standards or criteria for evaluation. At the end of the budgeted time period, an income statement is generated. The *income statement* reflects the actual expenditures and revenues for each category listed in the budget for the time period. A comparison of the budget and income statement for the same time period allows the manager to evaluate the unit's performance and provides necessary information for controlling the functions of the department.

Annual budgets are prepared for the business and each of its departments, and each budget is subdivided into 12 monthly periods. The budget for the business is called the profit plan or master budget plan; departmental budgets are known as operating budgets. Long-range budgets also are developed, but typically only at the level of the business as a whole.

Table 10.2 illustrates a master budget plan for radio station KHIT-FM, which was recently purchased by Callas Communications. KHIT is a top-40 hit music station serving a geographic area with a population of about 250,000. The area includes a major state university and several smaller colleges with a combined student population of about 60,000. KHIT's market serves as a regional medical center and has an automotive manufacturing plant and regional recording studio. A major regional discount and grocery retailer maintains its headquarters here, as well as a national insurance and investments company. The area's median income is around $45,000.

The summarized master budget plan displayed in Table 10.2 reflects the budget for the business as a whole. The actual profit plan would include operating budgets from each department. The budget is comprised of expenses, which are the costs associated with running the radio station, and revenues, which are the sources of income for the station. Table 10.2 shows the proposed allocation of financial resources to the various departments in the radio station as expenses, as well as the revenues expected from specific sources for the coming year.

The major source of revenue is generated from the selling of airtime for advertising. The advertising revenue is categorized by geographic source; local advertising accounts for 77.8% of the station's sales revenues, and national/regional advertising accounts for 23.2% of revenues. Total expected revenue is calculated by subtracting the sales representatives' commis-

TABLE 10.2
KHIT-FM Budget

Station Revenue & Expense Items	Dollars
Revenues	
National/regional advertising	210,000
Local advertising	740,000
Total projected sales	950,000
Agency and rep commissions	(95,500)
Other revenue	50,000
Total projected net revenue	904,500
Expenses	
Departmental operating expenses	
Engineering	37,000
Program production	135,000
News	30,000
Sales	184,000
Advertising and promotion	60,000
General administration	300,000
Nonoperating expenses	
Depreciation	52,123
Interest	16,400
Total expenses	814,523
Pretax profit	89,977

sions, which depend on the amount of sales. Miscellaneous additional revenue is added to calculate the projected total revenue for the coming year.

Projected operating expenses are itemized by department and indicate each department's forecasted financial needs. The two types of expenses itemized in the budget are operating and nonoperating expenses. Operating expenses include the day-to-day costs of running the radio station. The operating expenses of a radio station might include the cost of using an outside news service, music license fees, subscribing to an audience ratings service, and the compensation of employees.

Nonoperating expenses include other costs that are not incurred from operating the station, such as the depreciation of equipment and interest to be paid on any outstanding loans. Depreciation is a common nonoperating expense because equipment loses its value and eventually needs to be replaced.

The departmental operating and nonoperating expenses are summed to calculate the projected total expenditures for the coming year. Total expenses are subtracted from total net revenues to calculate the projected business profit before paying taxes. For radio station KHIT, the expected profit for the coming year is $89,977.

Table 10.3 shows this year's budget in comparison to the previous year's income statement for radio station KHIT. A comparison of last year's actual expenses with the projected figures developed by the new owner shows some important differences. For example, more revenue is expected from

TABLE 10.3
Annual Budget for Radio Station KHIT

Station Revenue & Expense Items	Dollars This Year	Dollars Last Year Actual
Revenues		
National/regional advertising	210,000	200,000
Local advertising	740,000	725,000
Total projected sales	950,000	925,000
Agency and rep commissions	(95,500)	(93,500)
Other revenue	50,000	40,000
Total projected net revenue	904,500	871,500
Expenses		
Departmental operating expenses		
Engineering	37,000	34,000
Program production	135,000	130,000
News	30,000	30,000
Sales	184,000	180,000
Advertising and promotion	60,000	55,000
General administration	300,000	298,000
Nonoperating expenses		
Depreciation	52,123	50,123
Interest	16,400	13,400
Total expenses	814,523	790,523
Pretax profit	89,977	80,977

local and national advertising sales and other revenue. A spending increase is planned for program production, engineering, advertising, and promotion. These figures reflect the planning and decision-making activities of several managers at KHIT.

The budget for the coming year was developed by the new sales manager, general manager, and the existing programming director over the course of 3 months of discussions, data gathering, and decision making. Callas Communications brought in two new managers from other stations with track records of increasing revenues. The company purchased the station because management felt a strong additional profit potential was likely, given the large student population and diversified economy in the market.

Presently, the economy is strong in the market, so the new managers want to take advantage of this quickly. The auto manufacturing industry often experienced downturns, so profits must be increased quickly to improve performance before another downturn begins. Also, the new managers want to educate local and national advertisers about why increasing their advertising budgets would help their businesses. The new sales manager had successfully retrained sales personnel before to increase sales and develop new accounts. The revenue projections were based on this manager's previous successes.

The general manager felt another strategy should be developed to increase other revenues over the coming year to satisfy the owners. Several general strategies might be utilized: (a) the staff could work harder to maintain existing revenues; (b) costs could be cut; or (c) other types of revenue could be sought.

The sales manager was already working on the first solution. The second solution of cost cutting would improve the situation in the short run, but the long-run consequences could affect the station's ratings negatively, thereby reducing advertising revenues in the future. Budget amounts were increased slightly for engineering, program production sales, advertising, promotion, and general administration to maintain the station's quality. These increases were judged to be the smallest possible to maintain quality and cover planned projects for the coming year. The news department budget was not increased as management felt the station's 18- to 44-year-old core audience listened because of the station's music selections, not its news coverage. The general manager also noted that she would work with all department heads to trim the budget where possible without sacrificing quality.

The programming head, who had been retained by Callas, proposed an idea to promote the station while generating additional revenue. The station could align with the city, local advertisers, and the regional recording studio to promote a concert on the riverfront every spring. The city had an annual spring festival to celebrate the end of the area's long winters and foster community spirit. The programming manager thought a free concert featuring artists who recorded at the regional studio would be a natural tie-in.

The station might conduct a T-shirt design contest to be entered by students from the local university and colleges for the concert. The winning T-shirt design could be produced and sold by sponsoring advertisers at their businesses, and at the concert itself. KHIT could promote the contest and concert on the air and locally through its cosponsors. In addition, the station could attract business for their advertisers by selling T-shirts in their stores. Any advertising for the T-shirt promotion also would be advertising for their participating clients, the station and the concert.

The extra $5,000 in the advertising and promotion budget for this year reflected the minimum cost of promoting the event. The extra $10,000 in other revenue represented a conservative estimate of the additional revenue to be gained from T-shirt sales. The increases in engineering and program promotion represented the estimated minimum cost to broadcast the concert. Presumably the recording studio could be counted on to share production costs.

The three managers agreed that the concert and T-shirt idea was worth a try. The recording studio also featured artists popular with the station's target market. If the concert was successful, as expected, it would only become more profitable in years to come. And it might lay the groundwork for establishing another concert in the late summer/early fall when college students returned to school.

The budget developed for KHIT's coming year represents the desired future status of the radio station based on the decisions of the management team that prepared the budget, keeping the corporate owner's goals in mind. The budget provides spending guidelines for the department heads and sets performance expectations for the sales staff. In particular, this budget sets a criterion for evaluating the short-range decision to promote the station through the concert and T-shirt promotion. If T-shirt sales generate additional revenues of at least $10,000, and advertising sales are increased as projected, then KHIT might choose to repeat the promotion the next year. If the outlined expectations are not met, then the radio station probably would not choose the same strategy for the coming year.

The example of radio station KHIT illustrates how annual budgets are developed and used for short-range planning and routine decision making. Long-range budgets are used for plans of 5 years or more and cover more nonroutine decisions. Whether a manager makes a fairly routine, short-range decision or a nonroutine, long-range decision is often a function of the manager's level in the organization. The types of budget information a manager needs and uses for decision making are affected by the long- or short-term nature of the decision itself.

The steps in the decision-making process are reviewed in order to explain how managers use budgets. Two important aspects of the process also are discussed: how short-range versus long-range decisions affect the use of information and how the differences in organizational levels affect managerial decision making.

MANAGERIAL DECISION MAKING

Managerial decision making, like most decision making, is a process that consists of six stages, as shown by the decision-making wheel in chap. 1. Collecting and analyzing information plays the central role in the this process, but managers at different organizational levels collect and use information differently.

The case of KHIT illustrates this process. The sales manager identified the possible increases in advertising revenue through discussions with sales personnel and advertisers, and by evaluating local and national economic indicators. The sales manager viewed the opportunity from the perspective of how it would affect the department during the coming year. The general manager, on the other hand, specified the overall organizational goal of increasing profits in comparison to last year. The sales manager informed the general manager of the opportunity to improve sales performance through training and mentoring the sales staff. The general, sales, and program managers reviewed several strategies and selected the concert and T-shirt contest because they appeared to be relatively cost-effective ways to increase profits. But all managers were involved to ensure that the organizational and departmental perspectives were considered.

This example also demonstrates how the budget is used for implementing the solution. The income statement will be used to monitor the solution because it provides information about the performance of the solution. Both can be reviewed to refine the solution in future years. All three managers understand that if profits are not increased in the next year or two, all may lose their jobs.

Long-Range Versus Short-Range Decisions

Short-range decisions are often routine decisions, the type that a manager has some degree of experience in making on a regular basis. Because of the manager's experience with a routine decision, information about alternative strategies, and the results of the those strategies are accumulated. As a result, routine decisions usually involve less risk, and the decision outcomes are more predictable than in nonroutine decisions.

Routine decisions are evaluated within some short period of time, perhaps a few months. So, if short-range decisions have unexpected negative consequences or do not produce the expected results, changes can be made quickly to minimize the impact of the undesired outcomes.

Nonroutine decisions are made infrequently and have long-range effects and consequences. Such consequences are difficult to anticipate. For example, the decision to invest resources in new equipment, such as a new system of computers for a newspaper, has a short-range consequence of increasing costs during the fiscal year of the purchase. However, the long-range consequences may be more difficult to determine and forecast. For example, desired long-range outcomes would be increased writer productivity and efficiency in the production of the paper itself. But an unanticipated, long-range consequence of using video display terminals was repetitive motion injury, which could have been avoided by purchasing ergonomic furniture and materials. So background research is needed to evaluate the likelihood of those outcomes, and to predict the value added to the paper in the long run.

Managers should also evaluate problems to see if an unexpected, and more cost effective, solution may be found. For example, major metropolitan papers like *Newsday* and *The New York Times* have tried to find a cheaper and faster way to make color proofs. Some newspapers have purchased high-end color copies to use for making page proofs and ad proofs. Such copiers cost $50,000 or more, but can print a proof in 3–4 minutes for $0.37, rather than 20–30 minutes at a cost of $7 each.

Presently these copiers are more cost effective for papers generating large numbers of color proofs (Toner, 1997a). But these copiers may come down in cost over time, making such a system cost effective for smaller papers. Newspaper managers can keep up with such innovations by reviewing the "Operations" section of *Presstime* each month. Managers in other media firms can check their trade publications each month for similar cost-saving ideas.

Even more difficult to predict than expected positive long-range outcomes are long-run negative, unexpected results of decisions. An example of present concern is whether the Internet will draw readers away from newspapers. Many newspapers have published online editions to retain readers and prevent erosion of classified advertising. Yet publishing online may discourage some potential subscribers from purchasing a subscription. Newapaper managers must keep abreast of Internet trends to ensure that readers and revenues are not lost to the new medium.

The fact that future outcomes must be predicted makes long-range decision making more difficult than short-range decision making. Long-range decisions often involve some large investment of capital, making the decision even riskier. In a recent survey, 347 respondents reported that the average daily newspaper planned expenditures of $1.8 million in the coming year. Respondents planned $83.4 million in software purchases, up from $46.3 million the year before. Publishers are continuing to replace proprietary systems and first-generation desktop publishing systems with personal computers. The planned expenditures for such computers grew from $104 million in 1996 to $150.5 million in 1998 (Toner, 1997b). And newsprint expenses alone represent about 15 to 20 percent of a newspaper's advertising budget (Rudder, 1997).

Obviously, companies have more to lose if the purchase does not produce the desired outcomes. The decision also is evaluated over a longer period of time. For example, it will take 1 year or more before newspaper management will notice all the effects of purchasing new personal computers and software. Broadcast managers must consider whether, when, and what to buy when making a decision about updating to a high-definition television system.

Long-range decisions most often occur at higher levels in organizations, and shorter range decisions occur at middle and lower levels. Higher level management makes the riskier decisions and takes responsibility for decisions that affect the entire organization. Middle and lower level management make decisions that are more routine, are less risky, and result in consequences that directly influence their departments. The level of decision making and the nature of the decision affect the type of information the manager needs for the decision-making process. Indeed, the type of budget information managers use and evaluate varies based on these same factors.

Levels of Planning, Decision Making, and Information Needs

The nature of planning and decision making varies with the organization level at which each process occurs. At the highest levels of management, decisions are made determining the firm's policies and general guidelines for evaluating the company's performance. This is what the owners of Callas Communications do. The information top management uses is often summarized and future-oriented. For example, information about future market share, economic indicators, and other market performance measures are forecasted and then used by upper level management to predict revenue and profit goals for the coming year.

Middle level management typically deals with using resources efficiently and effectively. At this level, managers need information to develop operating budgets. Often decisions need to be made about investing in new equipment, services, or people. For example, KHIT middle managers may recommend purchase of better remote broadcasting equipment if the planned concert becomes an annual event. A newspaper's managing editor might decide to buy a new advice column about the Internet if readers indicate an interest in this service and information.

Lower level management deals with more structured, routine tasks and uses information from inside the organization. Decision rules are communicated, preferably in verbal and written form. The information used is very detailed and typically unambiguous. At this managerial level, information is not necessarily forecasted for future concerns. For example, KHIT's engineering director must decide which engineer will work overtime at the remote concert broadcast.

DEVELOPING THE MASTER BUDGET PLAN AND DEPARTMENTAL BUDGETS

Developing budgets is one part of the planning process where decisions are made about the available resources for achieving goals. Generating the master budget plan for the entire business can take some time, usually 3 to 6 months, depending on the size, nature, and complexity of the organization. Managers at all levels of the organization participate in the effective development of the master budget plan. At the highest level, a budget committee might consist of the company president, the controller, vice president of sales, and vice president in charge of production. In a media organization, the budget committee includes the top manager, the controller, and all department heads. This committee establishes budget goals for the company that directly affect the budgeting at the departmental level. The budget committee also reviews and approves departmental budgets.

A budget director, who reports directly to the controller, coordinates budgets at the departmental level. The budget director prepares a timetable for the development and approval of the operating budgets and works with managers in the development of each departmental budget. The master budget plan is assembled and submitted to the budget committee and then the board of directors for approval. Finally, the budget director is responsible for preparing and distributing performance reports, based on the previous year's budget, to the budget committee and department managers.

Forecasting

A key element of generating budgets is forecasting. *Forecasting* is an effort to predict future events and trends and anticipate their implications for the company. Granger (1980) listed three types of forecasting: event outcome forecasts, event–timing forecasts, and time series forecasts. With event outcome forecasts, a manager tries to predict the consequences of an event. For example, how will the closing of the regional recording studio in town affect KHIT–FM? With event–timing forecasts, a manager attempts to predict when a specific event will take place. For example, if a growing city has only one network-affiliated television station, that station's management would be interested in knowing when a second network affiliate might enter the market. With time series forecasting, a manager attempts to predict the effects of a series of phenomena on the business. For example, what effects will the listing of employment notices on the Internet have on a newspaper's classified ad linage?

The benefits of accurate forecasting seem obvious, given the central role of information in decision making. As with most valuable things, accurate forecasting is not easy. So many factors can change and the possibility of measurement errors is so great, that accurate long-range forecasting is as much an art as a science.

Despite the limitations, however, budgeting requires some forecasting. Kreitner (1986) listed three types of forecasting: informed judgment, surveys, and trend analysis. Informed judgment involves the forecasting of events and trends by an individual or group, based on a knowledge of the topic being forecast. Informed judgment is used extensively in the creation of most short-term budgets. Surveys are efforts to anticipate the future by asking questions of a sample of people that represent a larger group. The idea is to draw conclusions about the future of the larger group based on comments from a small percentage of that group.

Trend analysis extends historical trends found in data about the past into the future, with some alterations based on assumptions of change. Because everything changes to a degree, all trend analysis must address key factors that shape the event being forecast. For example, if KHIT's advertising staff is extending trends in advertising sales, the staff needs to specify assumptions about changes in overall business sales. The staff might assume, based on predictions by government economists, that retail sales in their market would increase 5% during the next year. Using this figure, the staff could come up with an estimate of retail sales. From this figure, they could estimate their revenue during the next year by applying the percentage of local retail sales that they have received as advertising revenue during the past 5 years.

KHIT's staff might also use the trade press and Internet resources to review economic indicators. For example, *Advertising Age*, *MEDIAWEEK*, *Broadcasting*, *Presstime,* and other trade publications typically carry articles about actual and projected advertising expenditures. Economic information may be found at the Census Bureau's home page (http://www.census.gov/econ/www), the Dow Jones Business Directory (http://businessdirectory.dowjones.com) or The Financial Data Finder (http://www.cob.ohio-state.edu/dept/fin/osudata.htm).

All budgeting requires some forecasting. And it is important to deal explicitly with assumptions about the changing economic environment. Otherwise, a station will underestimate revenues during a booming economy and overestimate revenues during an economic downturn. Two principles tend to hold true: the longer the range a budget covers, the more important forecasting becomes, and the longer the range a budget covers, the harder it is to forecast accurately. This in effect is the forecasting dilemma. The only solution is to invest in several methods of forecasting for the long range and to hire competent forecasters.

Departmental Operating Budgets

Although forecasting plays a role in the annual departmental budget, the need for extensive forecasting is minimized by the data from previous years' income statements and budgets, and from the expertise of the people within the departments. Informed judgment plays a key role, although this should be bolstered by available data in the marketplace.

The department budget is the central document for controlling the finances of an organization, and it plays a direct or indirect role in most decisions. Table 10. 4 shows the newsroom budget for a daily newspaper with a circulation of 100,000. The departmental operating budget is set up on an annual basis, with at least monthly updates on past spending and resources that remain available.

All budgets are broken down into categories of expenses considered to be important in running the business. Which expense categories are important varies from medium to medium and from company to company. At the newspaper represented in Table 10.4, payroll is divided into salaries for full-time employees, overtime paid to full-time employees, and money used to pay part-time employees, called correspondents and freelancers. A larger newspaper might lists photography salaries separately from those of writers and editors. It also might differentiate between regular part-time employees (correspondents) and irregular part-time employees (freelancers). The important consideration is that budget categories and

TABLE 10.4

Operating Budget and Income Statement for the News/Editorial Department of a 100,000 Circulation Daily Newspaper

Item	This Year	Last Year
Payroll		
Salaries	2,000,000	1,980,000
Overtime	39,000	39,000
Correspondents and freelancer	93,000	91,000
Office supplies	40,000	37,000
Research material		
Computer time	120,000	100,000
Books, magazines, papers	1,000	5,000
Travel	50,000	50,000
Photography supplies	40,000	38,000
News services	164,000	160,000
Syndicated material	124,000	120,000
Other news/editorial	75,000	75,000
Total	2,746,000	2,695,000

subcategories reveal how the money is being spent within the department in a way that allows for decision making.

The amount of money allocated to a budget category reflects its relative importance to reaching the goals of a department. For example, management at the newspaper represented in Table 10.4 decided to spend more on an online research database service this year. The cost of this online database is shared with other departments at the newspaper. Resources were cut for books, magazines, and newspapers because some of these materials will now be available through the online database. Expenditures for overtime and travel were also cut to help pay for the database. The correspondents and freelancers expenditure was increased so the paper can hire someone to train employees to use the online database and to hire temporary help when big stories break.

The importance of budget items can change across time to reflect the long-term plans of the organization. The commitment to using the online database is seen in increased payroll and office supply expenditures. The paper's management plans to reward employees who use the database effectively, and additional office supply purchases of paper and an additional printer are in the budget. On the other hand, a plan that would increase profit by controlling costs would reveal payroll reductions or keep them stable as revenues increase.

The operating budget can be thought of as an ideal for the year's spending. But with news media, the ideal rarely happens. This is why managers often end up shifting money from one category to another, and may even get additional resources from the top management of the media organization. If a famous person like Princess Diana or Mother Teresa died, as happened in 1997, news organizations will ignore the operating budget to a degree. Money will have to be shifted and new resources found. A budget is a map, but detours are expected. A quality news operation often will require deviations from the budget to accomplish important company goals

Budgeting Methods

The department heads are usually in charge of generating their department operating budgets. They are most familiar with their department's needs. But they are not as familiar with the business environment as the employees who maintain contact with those outside the organization. The reporters, camera crews, salespeople, and receptionists are the ones who deal with news sources, readers, listeners, viewers, and advertisers. For this reason, the informed judgment of the department heads must reflect the experience of their workers.

Budgeting methods involve two considerations: the flow of information and the assumed starting point of the budget. The flow of information can be either upward, downward, or both. Upward flow means the information goes from employees to the managers. Downward flow is the reverse, and both means a two-way flow occurs.

In the departmental budgeting process, information must flow both ways to generate an effective budget. Managers need information from employees in order to understand what they need to do their jobs effectively. At the same time, workers need to understand the budgetary constraints that face their organization so they do not squander resources.

Although this flow of information will be greatest during the budgeting period, it should continue all year long. The budget is a starting point. Actual expenditures must be compared to the budget throughout the year. Employees need to know how expenditures compare to the the budget process throughout the year. This is especially true of journalists. A journalist who understands the budget and can argue for a big story within its constraints is more likely to have management's support than one who does not understand what a particular story request means to the department's budget.

The second consideration is the assumed starting point of the budget. Typically, it is assumed that last year's operating budget reflects the needs of the department. The previous year's funding levels become the starting point for this year's budget. This approach is similar to trend analysis because it assumes the trend represents what is needed. The shortcoming is that it perpetuates any miscalculations or errors from previous budgets.

An alternative starting point is called *zero-based budgeting*, which assumes that every budget starts at zero and managers must justify all expenditures. It is easier to identify inefficiencies or wastefulness using this method. However, the process is far more time consuming than basing expenditures on last year's operating budget.

An example of how the two might come into play can be found in Table 10.4. Suppose the editor finds in the income statement that only $89,000 was spent last year on correspondents and freelancers, which was $2,000 less than budgeted. The new budget could start with the $91,000 in last year's budget, although that amount is not needed based on last year's performance. An inflation figure of $2,000 can be added. Using this method, the request for $93,000 is probably more than what will be used.

If zero-based budgeting is used, the editor has to justify the $93,000, which would be hard to do based on last year's performance. Most likely, the amount needed for correspondents would be the same as the previous year, plus the $2,000 inflation figure, which would equal $91,000. This assumes no major change in the use of correspondents and that their payment will increase at the inflation rate from the previous year. However, the editor might have to shift money from other places if an online database trainer is hired or temporary help is needed.

Despite the seeming appeal of zero-based budgeting to the overall organization, it is not a commonly used process in media organizations. First, the increased demand on time is a problem for many managers who already have too many responsibilities or who do not enjoy dealing with numbers. This latter problem is especially true in newsrooms where many people consider themselves to be "word" and not "number" people. Second, this approach takes power away from departmental managers. Money is power, and departments can become adversarial rather than cooperative as they compete for budgets. Many of those who have power do not like to risk giving it up, which is what zero-based budgeting can do. In effect, the goals of the individual managers can interfere with what is best for the organization.

Some compromise between the two assumptions is best. Justifying budget items is an important process in identifying areas that no longer need as many resources; this allows the shifting of resources to new areas. As shown in Table 10.4, resources could be shifted from books, magazines and papers to computer time on the online database. However, the time requirements to justify all budget items would overburden many smaller organizations. If the budget director actively identifies areas that are waning in importance within departments, the department heads can deal with these categories without having to justify totally all budget items.

SUMMARY

Accounting practices fall into two categories: financial and managerial. Financial accounting is used primarily by those outside the organization and is typified by the balance sheet. The balance sheet is a picture of the assets and liabilities of an organization at a given point in time. It summarizes the financial well being of that organization.

Managerial accounting is aimed at generating information for decision making. The most important forms of managerial accounting are budgets and income statements. A budget is the plan for how the organization will spend money during a given time period. The income statement is a summary of how money was spent in previous time periods. The master budget plan covers the entire organization, whereas the departmental operating budget deals with the plans for the individual departments within the organization.

Forecasting plays an important role in budgeting. The longer the period covered by a budget, the more important and difficult accurate forecasting becomes.

The information flow for budgeting within an organization should be upward and downward through the organization structure. It is also important in budgeting to consider whether last year's budgeted expenses are the appropriate starting point for creating next year's budget, or whether all managers should start at zero in making up their budgets. Usually, a compromise between the two approaches is best.

CASE 10.1

Analyzing the Performance
of a Media Company or Outlet

Obtain a printed or Lexis/Nexis copy of an annual report for a media company. Review the annual report for information about the company, paying special attention to the balance sheet and any accompanying explanations.

ASSIGNMENT

Write a report analyzing the company's annual report. Discuss whether the company seems to be in good financial health and why. Also discuss whether the company's expenditures and performance over the past year seem prudent. Answer all of the following questions in your report.

1. Does the company seem to be managed well, financially speaking? Why or why not?

2. Did the company appear to operate profitably? Why or why not? (If the company reported a deficit, explain whether it seems to be indicative of a problem, or whether it simply represents something like a one-time major purchase that should contribute to the long-term good of the company.)

3. Do the major expenditures or purchases mentioned in the report seem reasonable, given the company's goals? Why or why not? (Be sure to identify the major expenditures and their amounts when answering this question. Also note if no major expenditures are listed in the report.)

4. Do you see any accounting practices or items in the report that appear questionable or representative of poor accounting practices? If yes, identify these practices or items and explain why you think they are questionable.

5. Would you recommend that someone invest in this company? Why or why not?

6. What other ideas, impressions, or comments do you have after analyzing this company's performance?

CASE 10.2

Forecasting Advertising Sales

Select a local newspaper, local magazine, broadcast station, cable channel advertising market, or advertising market for any other local media outlet. Try to predict whether advertising sales will increase or decrease for that media outlet over the next year. Review Shaver (1995), especially chapter 5, Local Market Research, for ideas on completing this assignment. Shaver (1995) mentioned other data sources besides those listed here.

To get started, contact the local Chamber of Commerce to get information about economic indicators. Review any local business publications or the business section of your local newspaper for information about the market's economy or business openings or closings. Review relevant national trade or industry publications for information about trends in or forecasts of advertising sales.

Also review online sources like the Census Bureau's home page (http://www.census.gov/econ/www), the Dow Jones Business Directory (http://businessdirectory.dowjones.com) or The Financial Data Finder (http://www.cob.ohio-state.edu/dept/fin/osudata.htm). Visit the online home pages for trade or industry publications and conduct online searches for forecasting or advertising sales articles or data. For example, visit *Advertising Age* at http://www.adage.com, or *ADWEEK* at http://www. adweek.com. Access *Presstime* or *TechNews* online at http://www.naa. org/index_nojava.html. Check out *MarketScope* at http://www.naa. org/marketscope/index.html for the latest in daily newspaper advertising and marketing intelligence. Review *Broadcasting & Cable* online at http://www.broadcastingcable.com. Ask your professor for other online sources to check out.

ASSIGNMENT

Write a report indicating whether the sales of advertising should increase or decrease for your media outlet over the next year. Include the following sections in your report.

    1. Discuss the overall economic indicators for your market. For example, are many new businesses opening in the market? Are many businesses closing? What is the market's unemployment level? What are the largest employers in the market? What are the major retail centers and how successful are they?

Are there any major positive or negative economic events expected in your market? If yes, how might they affect advertising sales?

2. Can advertising sales in general be expected to increase or decrease during the coming year? Why?

3. Identify the types of firms, products, or services for which advertising should increase or decrease during the coming year. Explain why these increases or decreases are predicted.

4. Explain whether your media outlet can expect advertising sales to increase over the coming year and why. Provide suggestions for new clients to approach. Provide ideas for other ways to generate additional revenue through advertising sales, based on your research.

CASE 10.3

Forecasting to Purchase a Radio Station

Develop a report forecasting economic conditions in a particular market for each of the next 3 years. The report should include, at minimum, the following types of economic activities: employment, manufacturing, retail sales, local taxes, housing sales, and advertising expenditures. The purpose of the report is to decide whether Callas Communications should purchase a radio station in the market selected. Recall that Callas' long-term objective is primarily to acquire more television stations and, if possible, other media and communications-related properties. Callas seeks to identify and acquire stations that have the potential for substantial long-term appreciation and profitability.

Select a market to study that can be researched through the library or online economic resources. Collect data about each of the areas listed previously, at minimum, from the past 5 years. Interview people who are knowledgable about market economic indicators, including economists, business people, the local government economic development staff, employees from local media advertising departments, government officials, and business reporters.

Review chap. 10 as well as local business publications, or the business section of the local newspaper, for information about economic predictions or indicators. Also review online sources like the the Census Bureau's home page (http://www.census.gov/econ/www).

ASSIGNMENT

Prepare a report of three to five pages that forecasts economic activity in the selected market. The report should discuss the economic indicators just listed for each of the next 3 years. Conclude the report by predicting the strength of the market's economy during the 3-year period and whether the economy will be strong enough to warrant Callas'purchase of a radio station there.

CASE 10.4

Analyzing a Budget

Focus on a student newspaper, radio, or television station. Ask the director for a copy of the media outlet's budget, preferably from the last several years. Review the budget to see the outlet's mission statement or goals and how expenses have changed over time. Then have the director visit the class to discuss the budgeting process, including major purchases made during the budgeting period reviewed.

ASSIGNMENT

Write a report assessing the outlet's budgeting process. Answer all of the following questions in the report. Be prepared to share the report with the media outlet's budget director.

1. Does the outlet use last year's budget as the starting point for the annual budgeting process, zero-based budgeting, or both? Should the outlet change its starting point? Why or why not?

2. Which items or categories in the budget have the largest allocations? Why?

3. Do the categories of expenses in the budget seem complete? Do additional categories need to be added? Why or why not?

4. Does it appear that one or more categories of expenses have changed in importance over time? Why?

5. Which employees are involved in the budget development process at the media outlet? Should other employees be involved? Why or why not?

6. How does information flow during the budgeting process at the outlet: upward, downward, or both? Should the flow of information be changed? Why or why not?

7. Does the media outlet seem to be trying to fulfull organizational goals through its budgeting process and actual budget allocations? Why or why not?

8. Does the media outlet have a good, effective budgeting process? Why or why not?

CASE 10.5

Cutting the Budget at KHIT-FM

The general manager at KHIT-FM just informed the sales and programming managers that the employees of the local automotive company will be going on strike tomorrow. The strike is expected to last several weeks, possibly several months, creating a major problem in the local economy. The general manager wants to retain plans for sponsoring a concert with the regional recording studio, as top management at Callas Communications agree that it represents a strong profit venture. Other ways of maintaining profitability must be found.

Review Tables 10.2 and 10.3, the master budget plan for KHIT-FM. (The nonoperating expenses shown there are fixed and cannot be changed.) Also review the information about KHIT-FM discussed in this chapter. Consider other ways to cut the budget or develop additional sources of revenue, given the impending strike. Try to estimate the amount of advertising revenues that KHIT-FM may lose due to the strike.

ASSIGNMENT

Create a new budget that will meet the profitability requirements of Callas. Make suggestions as to which parts of the budget may be cut and explain why. Write a report which answers all of the following questions.

1. How much advertising revenue may be lost due to the strike? How was the estimate calculated?
2. How should KHIT-FM respond to the possible strike? Which budget categories should be cut (and by how much) or eliminated if the strike lasts for several weeks or months? Why?
3. What additional sources of revenue might the station tap? Explain ideas for generating additional revenue for the station, given the impending strike.
4. Present a new budget for KHIT, using the format shown in Table 10.2.
5. Explain why the new budget will allow the station to meet its profit goal for next year (or increase pretax profits by $9,000, from $80,977 to $89,977).

EXTENDED CASE STUDIES

CASE 1:
The Case of Profits vs. Public Interest:
Clearance at KCMO-TV

Television stations across the country are often faced with *clearance* issues. Clearance is the process station managers use to decide whether to air a potentially controversial advertisement or program. This case, which is based on the types of clearance issues that occur in today's broadcast media, features fictitious characters at a fictitious station facing a fictitious situation. However, the types of clearance problems featured are designed to represent the kinds of problems and issues that media managers face in the real world. (For example, see the sections of this case entitled *Background on the Food and Drug Administration (FDA) and Prescription Drug Advertising* and *Background on Controversial Advertising Clearance*, for an example of the types of clearance problems media managers presently face.)

THE CASE

General Manager Sue Parsons was concerned about the upcoming annual visit from her station's group owner, Jeb McGowan of Capstone Communications. Parsons had recently overruled General Sales Manager Steve Smith's decision to accept advertising for Valtrex, a prescription drug used to treat genital herpes outbreaks in adults with normal immune systems. She also overruled Smith's decision to accept advertising for psychic advisors, as well as liquor advertising from Seagram's during the past Christmas season. Although McGowan's annual visit typically dealt with concerns about profitability and maintaining the quality of local news, she knew clearance

333

would be a big issue in this year's meeting. Complicating matters was the rumor that McGowan would soon sell Capstone to a large, nationally known communications conglomerate, Randolph-Reed Communications.

Several stations in the Capstone group had begun airing television advertisements and infomercials that might be considered controversial in the market (Kansas City). For example, some Capstone sister stations had accepted the Valtrex ads she turned down. Valtrex ads had also run locally on the cable channels Comedy Central, E!, CNN, and MTV. Other Capstone stations had aired infomercials for psychic hotlines. Parsons knew that McGowan would probably ask her to begin accepting at least some of these types of advertising on KCMO. This would be the first time she would have to advocate a position with which she knew McGowan would disagree.

Parsons had already met with KCMO management to communicate her feelings on the matter and discover how her colleagues felt about accepting such ads. Parsons told them that she felt accepting such ads was contrary to serving the public interest. "First, what actual benefit does calling a psychic advisor provide? Does it make our viewers think that we condone or believe in psychics when we choose to air psychic infomercials?

"Second, what does it say about us if we are willing to air ads for a herpes drug and psychics? How does this affect viewer perceptions of the credibility of our newscasts? How does this affect viewer perceptions of our support of socially beneficial causes in the community? I think when we seriously consider all of the potential negatives, accepting these ads just isn't worth it."

Some of her management staff agreed. Program Director John Nelson felt airing such ads would harm KCMO's good reputation in the community. Public Affairs Director Annie Atkins agreed, as did Press/Publicity Director Harry Williams. "Our newscast is rated number one, and we do a lot of community work with the United Way and local family and children's charities," Williams said. Atkins added. "We've had special newscast segments based on ABC's Children First series. I don't want to see us undo all of that goodwill for a few extra bucks from some ads for a herpes medicine or hard liquor."

However, Business Manager Pete Paulson, General Sales Manager Steve Smith and Research Director Janice Rubenstein disagreed. The station needed additional revenue to achieve profitability goals set by the group owner. "We've got to start selling more advertising if we all want to keep our jobs," said Smith. "ABC has improved in national ratings, but we're still way behind NBC's prime time numbers. We all know that makes it harder for us to sell airtime. Plus, *ABC News with Peter Jennings* is no longer the number one newscast. If the numbers for our local newscast go down as a result, we're going to be in big trouble. Where are we going to make up revenue like that?"

Paulson, Smith and Rubenstein also pointed out that other local stations had accepted seemingly controversial ads without any harm to their reputations. They concluded: "McGowan's not likely to fire us; we're doing fairly well, given ABC's national ratings and the success of our local newscast. However, we've got to be realistic. If we go along with McGowan, air controversial ads, and then get a negative reaction, we can say we were going along with his directive. That'll save our skins if things go bad."

Parsons replied, "Will it really save our skins? McGowan may not be able to fault us, but our neighbors might. We live in this community. We'll have to hear about it at Rotary meetings, on the golf course, at the playground, everywhere. I have serious concerns about the direction the broadcast industry is taking, both in relaxing advertising clearance and the tendency toward tabloidlike sensational news. What's going to happen to our credibility in this community if we don't hold the line?"

Paulson reminded his colleagues that another station in Kansas City, KSMT, had aired ads for the contraceptive Depo-Provera. Stations in other cities including Boston, Seattle, Nashville, and Columbus had aired Depo-Provera ads as well. Depo-Provera was the first prescription drug brand to gain FDA permission to mention the brand name and condition the product treats in a television commercial. The ad carried the tagline, "Be sure of your plans. Be sure of your birth control" ("TV Ad," 1997).

The competing station had aired the Depo-Provera spots only after 10:30 pm. The spots were scheduled during late night so only adults would see the ads. Apparently, there had been surprisingly few complaints to the local competing station. Smith pointed out, "If KSMT can get away with airing an ad that directly mentions it's for birth control, why can't we air one in late night mentioning herpes?"

In the meeting of her management team, Parsons agreed that response to the Depo-Provera campaign had been surprisingly limited. However, she reminded them, "Other local stations haven't had to deal with the backlash from the Christian community over *Ellen*." A small but vocal local Christian group had raised objections over the airing of the *Ellen* "coming out" episode, where the main character revealed she was a lesbian. "If we air controversial ads too soon, especially those dealing with contraception or other issues of sexuality, we could be labeled 'indecent' by these folks. Can you imagine what a field day our competitors, both in television and print, could have with that? We all know that Andy Dalgliesh will eat us alive in his column in the *Kansas City Star*."

Parsons pointed out that the local group, CDTV or Christians for Decent Television, headed by a local Baptist minister, the Rev. Johnny Mason, had labeled KCMO the "anti-family" station. "If we start airing controversial ads, we're just playing into the hands of CDTV. Even worse, CDTV is now being advised by the Christian Family Coalition (CFC). CFC sent CDTV a media watch kit, which includes advice on how to monitor TV programs and advertising. This kit includes things like sample letters to send to TV stations, advertisers and local leaders to complain about undesirable programming and advertising. The kit also shows how to write press releases and orchestrate a local media campaign against an offending station or advertiser."

Parsons continued: "Rev. Mason told me that CDTV will monitor *Ellen* and any other program that espouses values he finds un-American and un-Christian. CDTV will tape each program, documenting which local and national advertisers ran ads. CDTV will also transcribe any offensive dialogue or portrayals to use in news releases. If you're concerned about revenue, what kind of an effect would that have on our bottom line? Mason told me, 'We want to be sure that God-fearing Kansas City residents are aware of the filth airing on your station.'"

Paulson said, "Everyone knows that Mason and the CDTV don't represent the average Christian or person in this community. The overwhelming majority of Kansas City residents are normal, decent people who don't condone Mason or his methods. He always makes these big threats, and nobody pays any attention to them. He complained about the Depo-Provera spots, but nobody backed him up or his threatened boycott of late night programming."

Parsons countered, "I agree—there was no real response to the Depo-Provera spots. But that was before Mason got advice from the CFC. We have to expect that Mason's response to any future campaigns or programs he finds offensive will be more sophisticated. Besides, it's one thing to mention birth control. It's another thing to talk about herpes because it is a sexually transmitted disease. Sure, we could air Valtrex ads late at night. But I know Mason will say something like, 'Now KCMO is advocating a medicine for a disease of sinners engaging in premarital sex.' You know the other local stations and newspapers will give him coverage. Do we really want to do something that will knowingly encourage this kind of attention?"

Rubenstein spoke up, "Sure, the other media outlets will give Mason some coverage. But they don't want to encourage him. They all know he could turn around tomorrow and attack them. He thinks the *Star* is a 'swill of liberal stench' for running "Doonesbury." And there are plenty of programs on the other networks about which he could complain. I think it's a shame that we even have to think about what Mason's going to do. Isn't there something called the First Amendment that's intended to prevent the chilling of free speech?"

Finally, Paulson asked Parsons, "Is there any truth to the rumor that McGowan is selling out to Randolph-Reed?" "I don't know," Parsons replied. "That may be why McGowan is coming. We all know that if he sells, it's possible that some of us may lose our jobs. Historically, Randolph-Reed isn't known for coming in and cleaning house. But I think we all know that we'd better be careful here. Randolph-Reed management's position on ad clearance is an unknown. This may not be an issue with them. So if McGowan does sell, we want to be sure we have a good reason for doing something that may change the image of our station."

"What do you suggest?" Smith asked. Parsons replied, "I personally believe the best we can do in this situation is support whatever we truly believe is right to McGowan. Obviously, you all know that I'll argue against accepting these ads. I know that several of you will argue for accepting them. I'd like those of us on each side to meet and come up with a spokesperson to present views to McGowan. That way, whatever happens, we'll all know both sides were presented fairly. We'll all have to live with the consequences, so each side should have the chance to express its views."

In closing the meeting, Parsons thanked her colleagues for their frankness and useful insights. "We haven't had a big philosophical disagreement like this in a long time. We may be facing a lot of big changes around here if we air these ads and if McGowan sells to Randolph-Reed. So let's think about how to disagree and face big changes together, yet continue to be a good team. On that note, let me know by tomorrow at five 5 pm who will present each side of this controversy to McGowan.

"Finally, we need to develop contingency plans on how to deal with the possible responses of community leaders, Rev. Mason and the religious community, and our media competitors if we decide to accept ads or infomercials for hard liquor, Valtrex, and psychic advisors. I'd like each of you to develop a one-page summary of the potential reaction to airing controversial ads and how to deal with it. We all know that McGowan may order us to air them. So we must be prepared to respond quickly. I'd also like each of you to propose procedures for clearing ads, especially controversial ones. We have to ensure that our employees can clear ads effectively. We want to ensure that if a controversial ad airs, it meets all legal requirements and we've considered the ethics and consequences. That way, we'll be better able to deal with any controversies which may arise."

ASSIGNMENT

Read the following background sections and then answer each of the following questions.

1. Did Parsons handle the difference of opinion over clearance properly? Should representatives of each side of the controversy be allowed to present their views to McGowan? Or should Parsons have done so herself? Explain your answers.
2. How concerned should Parsons and her management colleagues be regarding the possible response of Rev. Mason, CDTV, and the CFC? Why?
3. How concerned should Parsons and her management colleagues be regarding the possible response of McGowan? Why?
4. How concerned should Parsons and her management colleagues be regarding the possible change in ownership? How much should that contingency influence their decisions and actions? Why?
5. How concerned should Parsons and her management colleagues be regarding the reactions of other local media outlets? Why?
6. What type of leadership style does Parsons exhibit? Do you think she is an effective leader? Why or why not?
7. How effectively does Parsons communicate with her employees? Do you think she is an effective communicator? Why or why not?
8. Develop a contingency plan for dealing with the potential responses to airing controversial ads. Identify the possible reactions from community leaders, religious leaders and competitors. Explain how KCMO management should respond to those reactions. Explain and justify your recommendations.
9. Develop an advertising clearance policy report for KCMO. Detail the policy areas to include, the policy sources to consult, which types of ads should be banned outright and why (if any), and which employees should be involved in deciding whether to accept controversial ads. Designate one employee who should be responsible for advertising clearance on a day-to-day basis. Also include any other guidelines or information which should be included in the policy report to aid employees in clearing ads. Explain your recommendations.

BACKGROUND ON BROADCAST ORGANIZATIONS

Commercial television stations depend on the sales of national, regional, and local advertising for profits, and also may receive funds from national commercial television networks. They may carry network programming, originate syndicated and paid programming, and compete with other stations for a share of the viewing audience. Network affiliates tend to sell more advertising and earn higher profits than independent stations. Today, stations aligned with Fox, for example, may be more profitable than independents were in the past.

Most stations have established mechanisms for reviewing ads. The sales and traffic departments typically monitor advertising content and preview ads before they air. The sales manager oversees traffic, but a station's general manager usually makes the final decision on whether to accept a controversial advertisement for broadcast (Wicks, 1991a).

Most stations have policies for political advertising, product acceptance (e.g., whether ads for certain products will be accepted for broadcast), copy acceptance, advocacy or issue advertising, product protection (e.g., separating competing ads), and time standards. Larger stations may have policies for mail and direct-selling accounts, bait-and-switch advertising, contests and games, demonstrations, medical products, free offers, and guarantees (*Center for Law & Social Policy*, 1971; Linton, 1987; Rotfeld, Abernathy, & Parsons, 1990; Wicks, 1991a).

National advertisers generally review their own ads to avoid litigation. National advertisements are cleared initially within agency and advertiser organizations, including both the agency's and advertiser's legal departments, in storyboard form. Then, the media reviews an ad in storyboard form. The national television networks and other print and broadcast media have developed advertising codes. After an ad is cleared, it is produced, and final clearance begins. First, the agency grants final clearance, then the advertiser and its law firm, and finally the media. Regulation after broadcast or publishing is mainly the responsibility of the FTC, although there are a number of government agencies that regulate various aspects of advertising. The FTC also publishes guides that make recommendations regarding advertising for certain industries and products.

Stations might consult the National Association of Broadcasters (NAB) and the networks for advice. Larger stations may contact advertisers or visit a store. Stations might review ads by perusing scripts, storyboards, a product sample, or a label or package insert, before and/or after production. Claim substantiation, or authentication of demonstrations or testimonials, could be requested as well.

Station managers may occasionally resolve differences between competing advertisers. Commercials may be challenged by competing advertisers, who must present supporting data. Outside technical expertise may be called in, and ads will be withdrawn only if the complaint is found valid. Viewer complaints also may be investigated, and ads possibly discontinued until complaints are resolved (Miracle & Nevett, 1987; Zanot, 1985).

Stations vary in how their policies are communicated. Stations may codify policies in a manual, have mostly written policies, use mostly memoranda, use the last NAB Code, or convey policies verbally. Staff policies are communicated either through making their existence known, discussing them with staff, or encouraging or requiring the staff to read them. Generally speaking, policies are communicated verbally to employees on a day-to-day basis (Linton, 1987; Rotfeld et al., 1990; Wicks, 1991a; Wicks & Abernethy, 1997). Stations having written policies tend to request substantiation of ad claims and reject ads more often (Rotfeld et al, 1990; Wicks, 1991a).

Wicks & Abernethy (1997) suggest that TV clearance employees who consider their ethical values important are willing to take a stand to promote those values. And that stand apparently results in significantly different clearance outcomes that protect viewer and advertiser interests. TV clearance employees who consider ethical values important tend to work at stations where more types of ads are banned outright. Plus, managers who consider ethical values and avoid negative reactions like viewer complaints when clearing ads reject more ads. Employees who consider earning the highest possible profits for their stations and avoiding negative reactions such as advertisers canceling ad schedules appear more likely to work at stations banning fewer ad types.

BACKGROUND ON THE FOOD AND DRUG ADMINISTRATION (FDA) AND PRESCRIPTION DRUG ADVERTISING

In August 1997, the FDA issued proposed guidelines that clarified the requirements for TV and radio prescription drug advertising. The goal is to make prescription drug ads more understandable to consumers. Broadcast ads for direct-to-consumer promotion of prescription medicines may now identify the drug's name and condition it treats. Such ads must include information about any major risks, as well as instructions for obtaining more detailed information about the advertised drug's uses and risks. The FDA will evaluate the effects of this change for 2 years to determine whether additional requirements are needed ("FDA to Review," 1997).

The Federal Food, Drug, and Cosmetic Act requires ads promoting medical uses of prescription drugs to include a brief summary of all important information about the advertised drug, including side effects, effectiveness, and contraindications. Previously, broadcast ads that only mentioned a drug's name but did not identify the condition that it treats were exempt from the brief summary requirement. Print ads easily met the brief summary requirement because such information is included in ad copy. However, it is difficult if not impossible to include this same information in broadcast ads due to time and space constraints. Before this change, broadcast ads typically mentioned the drug's name but did not make any claims or mention the condition treated. These reminder ads were exempt from the brief summary requirement ("FDA to Review," 1997).

Now, instead of the brief summary, the pharmaceutical advertiser must provide a way to ensure that consumers can easily obtain complete product information. For example, broadcast ads might include: (a) a toll-free telephone number for consumers to access detailed product information by phone, fax, or mail; (b) references to print ads containing a brief summary of the product labeling (e.g., see the Valtrex ad in the June issue of *SPIN*); (c) a WWW home page or Internet address or URL with complete product labeling information; and/or (d) a statement that physicians, pharmacists, and veterinarians (if an animal drug is advertised) may provide more product information. The FDA is also encouraging prescription drug advertisers to provide consumers with easy access to consumer-friendly, nonpromotional information about the advertised product ("FDA to Review," 1997).

A TV campaign for Depo-Provera, a female contraceptive injection product, was the first prescription drug spot that identified the brand name and condition. Depo-Provera was also the first female contraceptive advertised on television. The 2-two-minute spot, a long commercial by today's standards, included at least a full minute devoted to the legally required summary of warnings and side effects ("Drug makers," 1997).

The Depo-Provera spots premiered on local stations in Kansas City, MO, Seattle, WA, Columbus, OH, and Nashville, TN, as well as the USA Network, Sci-Fi Network, and Black Entertainment Television cable channels. The ads were after 10:30 pm on WDAF-TV, the Fox affiliate in Kansas City. "Obviously, we are trying to put it in at a time period when the primary viewing audience is adults," said WDAF General Manager Ed Piette (Gellene, 1997).

In fact, most stations airing the Depo-Provera ads restricted them to dayparts when children are not in the audience. Such ads are also likely to air in programs where the content and audience viewpoints are compatible with a contraceptive. This is because broadcasters historically have been wary of birth control ads. A number of stations rejected the Depo-Provera ads, citing policies banning birth control advertising ("TV Ad," 1997).

Depo-Provera is administered by injection four times a year. Although it costs about the same as oral contraceptives, it is not nearly as widely used as birth control pills. Younger women are more likely to use Depo-Provera. The Depo-Provera commercials target 18- to 44-year-old women. Presently, Depo-Provera accounts for about 7% of the $1 billion domestic birth control market ("TV Ad," 1997).

However, the airing of such ads is likely to upset religious groups that oppose birth control. Some television stations accept public service ads promoting condom use to stem the tide of AIDS. Most stations do not accept ads for condoms or other birth control methods.

Another concern with airing pharmaceutical advertising stems from possible unanticipated side effects and social controversies. For example, women's groups have questioned Depo-Provera's widespread use because research may link it osteoporosis. A women's advocacy group contends that Depo-Provera is prescribed to some minority women against their will. Thus, any station airing Depo-Provera ads, or ads for any other pharmaceutical, may open itself to criticism from interest groups (Kirk, 1997).

The FDA is facing criticism from consumer groups for changing the guidelines for prescription drug advertising. Consumer groups have called for more stringent guidelines on pharmaceutical advertising, arguing that some drug company ads have been misleading. The FDA changed the guidelines after lobbying by the Republican Congress and advertisers (Kirk, 1997).

Consumer groups and prescription drug advertisers are involved because the stakes are high. Drug company advertising on television has grown dramatically over recent years. Competitive Media reports that spending on direct-to-consumer prescription advertising almost doubled from 1995 to 1996 to $596.5 million. Network TV spending increased from $10 million in 1995 to $53 million in 1996 (Kirk, 1997). Spot television advertising (or national and regional advertisers buying ads on local stations directly rather than through the national TV networks) stands to benefit from the FDA's relaxation of requirements. It is estimated that pharmaceutical advertising may bring as much as $1 billion in incremental spot TV advertising business (Brodesser, 1997).

Consumer groups are also concerned because the emphasis is shifting from targeting ads to doctors to targeting pharmaceutical ads to consumers. Consumers cannot always diagnose their own ailments accurately nor can they write prescriptions. Thus, they may pressure their doctors to prescribe unnecessary drugs (Kirk, 1997).

Prescription drug advertising is increasing for several reasons. Probably the major cause is the success of recent campaigns. The success of the baldness drug Rogaine TV ads and nicotine patch advertising for quitting smoking has encouraged the drug companies to advertise. Another reason is the rapid growth of managed-care health insurance. Consumers, who change doctors more often, are more informed about their medical histories. As a result, they become more aware of new medications, which may be less expensive than other treatments. Increased use of the Internet, which provides consumers with access to more information, may be another reason for the growth of drug advertising (Kirk, 1997).

BACKGROUND ON CONTROVERSIAL ADVERTISING CLEARANCE

Ads for controversial products, like condoms and liquor, have caused debate when their advertisers broadcast ads on television. TV broadcasters, especially the ABC, CBS, and NBC networks, have avoided controversial products. The networks cite reasons of taste and public perception, fearing boycotts by religious groups and others who might be offended (Millman, 1996).

The wall that has prevented condom manufacturers from airing their ads on the networks and their affiliated stations has received its first crack. Two network affiliates, Seattle's KING-TV and KCPM-TV in Chico, CA, began airing Ansell's LifeStyles condom ads in late September of 1996. Carol Carrozza, Ansell's marketing director, asked the ABC, NBC, and CBS networks' and 44 local affiliates to air the LifeStyles condom ads. Initially, three affiliates agreed to air them, but KPRC in Houston backed out after further thought. All three stations are NBC affiliates ("Two network," 1996).

Carrozza and other condom firms report that television managers are wary of airing condom ads because some consumers may think it means the station condones illicit sexual behavior. Carrozza said that the stations accepting the LifeStyles ads "have taken a stand with us for education about safer sex." She also said, "Beyond public service announcements, this acceptance of our advertising appears to be the first move any major network affiliates have taken to balance the tidal wave of sexually provocative programs that ignore responsible behavior" ("Two network," 1996, p. 49). The commercial features a computer-animated skeleton giving all the reasons he never used condoms in his lifetime.

The Atlanta-based Durex Consumer Products approved Ansell's action. "We use cable television stations, including MTV and Comedy Central, because we think these channels are hitting our target audience," said Jim Hourigan, Durex's director of sales planning. "There still remain editorial constraints from the networks, and that is why we have not targeted them for our advertising programs" ("Two network," 1996, p. 49).

Another clearance first occurred recently, with a few TV stations accepting ads for hard liquor. A Corpus Christi, TX station, KRIS-TV, was the first to accept a hard liquor ad (Lafayette, 1996). Frank Smith, KRIS's owner said: "There hasn't been much negative reaction here among the regular public–although the newspapers are doing their damnedest to get it" (Pruzan, 1996, p. 8). Until this campaign, distillers obeyed a voluntary code banning hard liquor ads on television.

A representative of the NAB, an industry lobbying organization, said "We oppose any advertising ban on any legally produced product.... We believe that local decision-making, not a federal ban, is the right approach regarding this or any other advertising issue" (Lafayette, 1996, p. 3). Yet a congressman introduced legislation to ban TV and radio ads for hard liquor in response to KRIS-TV's airing of the Seagram's ads.

The spots for Seagram's Crown Royal brand on KRIS-TV ran between 9 pm and 10 pm, the final hour of network prime time and after the 7 pm family hour. Smith added, "I'd run them anywhere they want to run them." Smith believes liquor ads sales would be a plus for TV stations because distillers spend more than $200 million on print advertising annually. "There's a lot of money in that business. We're trying to open the door for the whole television business" (Lafayette, 1996, p. 3).

Smith feels there is nothing unsavory about airing liquor commercials, adding "This is the industry that accepts psychic advertising" (Lafayette, 1996, p. 3). He said he aired ads for a small local liquor store about 8 years earlier and "we got complaints only from prohibitionists." The ads named prices for specific brands of liquor and hundreds of spots ran over a 6-week period.

However, the networks and other stations are unwilling to air liquor ads, particularly at a time when the government is concerned with tobacco advertising. ABC reported that it does not accept distilled spirits advertising on the network or its owned stations. NBC and CBS have similar policies. NBC's President and CEO Bob Wright said he was concerned that an NBC affiliate would air liquor ads but the networks have no control over what their affiliates accept. Smith's reaction was "It's my television station. He does things on NBC that I don't like, but I don't bitch" (Lafayette, 1996, p. 3).

Fox's sales president Jon Nesvig said of clearing liquor ads: "You're going to expose it to kids somewhere. We'll let our friends from cable go first" (Lafayette, 1996, p. 3). Cable networks have also expressed misgivings about airing liquor ads. A Turner Broadcasting (e.g., CNN, TNT) spokesperson said: "If and when liquor ads on broadcast and cable become commonplace, then Turner Broadcasting might look at it at that time to see if we would include that category on our networks" (Lafayette, 1996, p. 3).

Many beer advertisers feel the airing of distilled spirits ads will ultimately affect ads for beer and wine. Liquor advertisers may have started advertising on TV in the hopes of causing a ban on all TV advertising for alcohol. Liquor sales volume dropped about 30 % between 1980 and 1995, with consumers switching to light beers, wine, and bottled waters. Beer and wine advertisers spent about $750 million in broadcast advertising in 1995, whereas liquor advertisers spent about $230 million in print and outdoor ads. So, a ban on all alcohol ads might make it easier for liquor advertisers to regain market share (Millman, 1996).

Anheuser-Busch pulled all beer advertising from MTV to avoid criticism for selling to underage drinkers. The move was intended to avoid criticism in response to the airing of liquor ads on TV. Anheuser-Busch's move was also in response to the FTC's investigation of a Schlitz Malt Liquor commercial that aired on MTV during the program *My So-Called Life*. This program is targeted to teens (Ross, 1996).

Whether accidental or not, placement of beer ads in programs targeted to teens may occur because of run-of-schedule (ROS) media buying. Most ads are aired on a ROS basis, meaning that they are not program-specific and can air anytime during the day. For example, a Budweiser ad ran at 2 p.m. on December 17, 1996, during ESPN2's NBA Inside Stuff, which is designed to appeal to teens (Ross, 1996).

In addition, abandoning the liquor ad code opens the door for alcohol related products that would attract young viewers. George Hacker of the Center for Science in the Public Interest said "These products, like margarita mixes or low-alcohol refreshers with fruity, sweet flavors resemble nonalcoholic beverages and mask the taste of alcohol. Given that the liquor industry has begun to target entry-level consumers in magazines like

Rolling Stone, Details, and *Spin,* transferring that kind of advertising into broadcast means that millions of teenagers will be receptive. It is very difficult to design a message that will appeal to a 21-year-old and not an 18-year-old" (Millman, 1996, p. 1).

Two Baton Rouge stations that accepted liquor ads faced complaints. WVLA-TV (NBC) and WGMB-TV (Fox) in Baton Rouge were among 21 TV stations that ran liquor ads for Seagram's Crown Royal Canadian whiskey ("Liquor ads," 1996). Most stations that aired the ads had no complaints although the President, FCC, and members of Congress were angered by the liquor ads.

Competing stations in Baton Rouge did not accept the liquor ads, or condom ads, citing their inappropriateness. Managers at competing stations also said that hard liquor has more punch than beer and wine, making it easier to abuse. They are concerned a congressional backlash over liquor advertising might lead to a federal ban of all alcohol advertising. WAFB General Manager Ron Winders said, "It's very shortsighted ... It shows the lack of a long-term responsibility as a broadcaster. It's certainly the wrong time to get into a controversy with Congress and the FCC" ("Liquor ads," 1996, p. 9).

Indeed, President Bill Clinton expressed concern that liquor ads could encourage young people to drink. FCC Chairman Reed Hundt said abolishing the liquor ad ban was, "disappointing for parents, and dangerous for our kids." Reed urged self-regulatory action to avoid FCC action and advised broadcasters to reject the ads (Millman, 1996). President Jim Hedlund of the Association of Local Television stations summed up political reaction: "The bully pulpit the president and Reed Hundt are taking would make the vast majority of broadcasters leery about accepting these commercials" (Millman, 1996, p. 1).

Advertisers contend that they should not be harassed for advertising a legal product. "The focus should be less on whether people are advertising than how they're advertising," said Daniel L. Jaffe, executive vice president of the Association of National Advertisers. "Alcoholic beverage products, like some other kinds of products, can be very dangerous when abused. They should be advertised with care and judiciousness. That should be the focus of government attention" (Millman, 1996, p. 1).

Black Entertainment Television CEO Robert Johnson said he would air any liquor ads his cable network was offered. "The issue of restricting these ads is hypocritical, based on outdated myths and morality issues. I think we're getting into dangerous ground when we're substituting morality for fundamental rights" (Millman, 1996, p. 1).

BACKGROUND ON DEREGULATION

During the 1980s, the FCC deregulated commercial radio (*Deregulation*, 1981) and television (*Revision*, 1984). Policies and guidelines on ascertainment, program-length commercials, program logkeeping (program logs were the official daily record of all material aired on a station), and the amount of commercial time to air per hour were relaxed or eliminated. Shortly thereafter, other practices including guidelines regarding deceptive advertising (*Elimination*, 1985) and the Fairness Doctrine were deregulated (*Inquiry*, 1987; *Syracuse Peace Council v. Television Station WTVH*, 1987). Due to the relaxation of the deceptive advertising policy, local broadcasters no longer need to exercise particular care when deciding to accept advertising that is the subject of an unadjudicated FTC complaint, or to review the reliability of every prospective advertiser (*Elimination*, 1985). And the Fairness Doctrine required licensees to present alternate views on controversial issues in certain circumstances.

Local broadcasters now have more individual discretion in deciding how to serve the public interest. However, more discretion may be accompanied by greater uncertainty about whether a station is serving the public interest. Policies are now less specific about how public interest responsibilities are fulfilled. New broadcast managers might review the 1960 policy statement and ascertainment primers for guidance in determining how to meet public interest requirements.

The former NAB TV Code was the most important self-regulatory mechanism for local broadcasters, providing guidelines regarding commercialization, clutter, and clearance. The NAB Code Authority Board also cleared commercials for national and regional advertisers. Ads precleared by the NAB were typically cleared by the networks (although the networks still determined for themselves whether a commercial would be accepted; "Agencies, Networks," 1983). After the Code's demise, the networks assumed primary responsibility for clearance. However, concerns over clearance effectiveness were raised in 1987 when ABC, CBS, and NBC cut back their Standards and Practices divisions as a cost-cutting move (Davis, 1987).

As a result of the events of the past 20 years, individual station management has more commercial decision-making freedom than ever before. At the same time, station responsibility for ascertainment or determining how the local community views station policies was relaxed by the FCC. The FCC no longer concerns itself with ascertainment methodology, but only with how responsive stations are to community needs (*Revision*, 1984). So managers may decide what new policies to implement and how to determine what community views are of them.

Licensee discretion is essentially "penalty-free," as the FCC also eliminated license challenges based on commercial time considerations. Violations of the deceptive advertising policy are now considered only in "character" proceedings, which rarely occur (*Policy Regarding Character*, 1986). The FCC considers ascertainment satisfactory if "programming presented by the licensee satisfies its obligation" (*Revision*, 1984, p. 1101).

The FCC said that competitive market forces would regulate the industry. For example, viewers would not watch and advertisers would not buy time on stations airing too many commercials. It noted a decline in public complaints about advertising as support (Commercialization, 1981; *Revision*, 1984).

BACKGROUND ON ADVERTISING CLEARANCE AND DECEPTIVE ADVERTISING REQUIREMENTS

The FCC noted early on that it expected stations to investigate potential advertisers (*KMPC*, 1939). It originally attempted to regulate advertising content (Public Service, 1946), but later relinquished most of its responsibility in this area to the FTC (*FTC*, 1987; *Liaison*, 1987). However, the FCC noted that licensees did have obligations regarding deceptive advertising (*Elimination*, 1985):

> Broadcasting licensees must assume responsibility for all material which is broadcast through their facilities. This includes all programs and advertising material which they present to the public. With respect to advertising material, the licensee has the additional responsibility to take all reasonable measures to eliminate any false, misleading, or deceptive matter .... This duty is personal to the licensee and may not be delegated (*Report*, 1960, p. 2303)

These clearance measures included taking reasonable steps to assure every prospective advertiser's reliability and reputation, and ability to fulfill promises made to the public (*Licensee*, 1961), especially those of "questionable character" (*KMPC*, 1939, p. 730). Broadcasters also had to exercise particular care when deciding to accept advertising that was the subject of an unadjudicated FTC complaint. The FCC expected more diligence when a station employee prepared ad copy or directly examined ad claims, and acted when a station failed to implement adequate clearance practices (*NAB Legal Guide*, 1984). However, most of these clearance requirements were eliminated in 1985. The FCC simply noted that stations are still responsible for all material that is broadcast on their facilities *(Elimination,* 1985). It is left to stations to decide how to fulfill this responsibility.

Before deregulation, most stations had mechanisms for clearing deceptive advertising; many had standards dealing with traditional areas of concern like political and children's advertising (Linton, 1987; Wicks, 1991a). Larger stations probably have more policies for more specific areas of ad content or sales techniques, such as mail and direct-selling accounts (e.g., buying products by calling an "800" number). Perhaps this is because the FCC formerly expected stations of greater size and resources to make a correspondingly greater effort to screen deceptive advertisements (*Center for Law & Social Policy*, 1971).

Large-market stations, which are often quite profitable, sell more of their commercial time inventory to national or regional spot advertisers (Wirth, 1977). This also may explain why larger organizations have more advertising policies. They must deal with more types of advertisers.

BACKGROUND ON INDEPENDENT RESEARCH ON TV ADVERTISING CLEARANCE PRACTICES AND POLICIES

A professor specializing in advertising clearance research conducted a national survey of the advertising clearance practices and policies of television stations (Wicks, 1991a, 1991b). A 62.6 % response rate (482 of 769 commercial television stations polled nationwide) was achieved. The percentage of respondents by network affiliation status (e.g., ABC, CBS, NBC, Fox, or independent stations) and broadcast band (e.g., UHF, VHF) was similar to actual proportions.

At most stations, the sales manager was responsible for deciding whether or not to accept ads for broadcast on a day-to-day basis. Although the average time sales managers, as a group, spent reviewing ads was 5 hours per week, the most common response was 1 hour per week. About 84 % of responding managers saw an ad they declined to accept air on another market station. Most managers conveyed advertising policy decisions verbally. The national breakdown of employees responsible for reviewing ads is found in Table C.1.

The percentage of stations having certain policies is shown in Table C.2. The average station has 12 advertising policies however most stations do not have formalized advertising policies. Regarding the form most policies were in, only 66 stations reported having policies codified in a manual, 56 had mostly written policies, 113 favored memos, and 139 conveyed policies verbally. Policies were communicated as follows: 87 stations required their employees to read their policies; 34 encouraged them to; 139 communicated policies through staff discussions; and at 94 stations the supervisor told each employee individually about policies. Thus, the average station "stores" and "communicates" its policies verbally. Stations nationwide also consulted certain sources when making decisions about whether to accept a questionable advertisement. The average station used about five sources to make decisions regarding ads (see Table C.3).

The average amount of commercial time aired per hour was 12:15, below the old FCC guideline. Only a minority exceed it (18 of 426 responding, or 4.2 %). Stations also were asked if they accepted infomercials or program-length commercials. Of the 470 stations responding, 77.9 % (or 366) accepted them and 22.1 % (or 104) did not. The average station airs five infomercials per month. The minimum was zero and the maximum was more than 100.

In a survey of infomercial clearance practices, 95 % (or 468 of 491 respondents) accepted infomercials for broadcast (Wicks, 1994). The breakdown of employees primarily responsible for clearing infomercials on a day-to-day basis was: 37.4 % (175 of 468) program managers, 32.7 % (153)

TABLE C.1
Employee Responsible for Clearance Review

Employee	Percent of Stations	Number of Stations
Sales manager	52.1	248
General manager	15.6	74
Program director	7.8	37
Operations manager	5.9	28
Station manager	5.7	27
Traffic manager	3.4	16
Broadcast standards	2.7	13
None	.5	3
Other	6.3	30

Note. N = 476.

TABLE C.2
Station Advertising Policies

Policy Area	Percent Having Policy	Number Having Policy
Political advertising	96.6	460
Product protection (separates competing ads by a certain amount of time)	85.1	405
Contests and games (restrictions on how they are advertised)	84.7	403
Movie trailers (bans or restricts the airing of violent or sexy movie ads)	82.8	394
Mail order/direct selling (restricts the use of direct response ads)	80.0	381
Product acceptance (bans certain types of products outright)	79.0	376
Issue advertising (bans or restricts ads about controversial issues)	78.6	374
Copy acceptance (bans or restricts certain copywriting techniques)	78.4	373
Contraceptive advertising (bans or restricts contraceptive ads)	77.9	371
Children's advertising	69.1	329
Bait and switch (bans advertising one product at a very low price and trying to get the consumer to buy another, more expensive one, at the store)	67.4	321
Time standard (limits the amount of commercial time to be aired per hour)	67.4	321
Interruption standard (limits the number of commercial breaks per hour)	62.8	299
Guarantees (restricts advertising warranties or guarantees)	49.6	236
Free offers (restricts the use of free offers in ads)	48.9	233
Medical products (bans or restricts how medical and/or health products are advertised)	46.4	221
Demonstrations (guidelines on how to demonstrate products in ads)	25.8	123

Note. $N = 476$.

sales managers, 10.5 % (49) general or station managers, and 19.4 % (91) other station employees. The average monthly proportion of infomercials for which substantiation was requested was 9.7 %. The average monthly proportion of background checks of infomercial advertisers was 16.0 %.

TABLE C.3
Station Policy Sources

Policy Source	Percent Usually Consulting	Number Usually Consulting
Station policies	75.6	360
FCC publications	66.0	314
Former NAB television code	61.6	293
NAB	55.5	264
Group owner	42.0	200
FTC publications	39.5	188
Local or state consumer agency	34.0	162
BBB	31.3	149
Network	26.5	126
Network code	19.3	92
Group code	17.9	85
BBB code of advertising	14.3	68
BBB ad review committee	6.9	33
NAD/NARB case reports	6.7	32

Note. N = 476.

The average number of questionable infomercials banned was 2.2 (out of 12 identified in the questionnaire). Most respondents (97.2 %) reported accepting infomercials because they represented a source of additional revenue for their stations.

Of the 23 respondents who did not report accepting infomercials for broadcast, almost 70 % (16 of 23) worked at VHF, network-affiliated stations. The main reasons why infomercials were not accepted were: inconsistent with the station's operating philosophy (17), inconsistent with the station's image in the community (17), and inconsistent with the stations programming norms (16). Of these 23 stations, seven had formal written guidelines banning infomercials (Wicks, 1994).

In a survey of advertising and infomercial clearance practices, with a response rate of 40.6 % (or 364 of 896), respondents reported airing about 10 infomercials per week (Wicks & Abernethy, 1997). The majority accepted infomercials for broadcast (96.4%), whereas only 13 or 3.6 % of respondents reported their stations did not accept infomercials for broadcast.

Stations were asked for what percentage of all standard (e.g., 30-second) and infomercial ad submissions they requested substantiation (e.g., support for claims made in the ad) per month. Substantiation was requested for an average of 8.3 % of monthly standard ad submissions, and 25 % of monthly infomercial submissions. Stations were also asked what percentage of all ad submissions they rejected per month. For standard ads, the average rejection rate was 1.6 %, and the average infomercial rejection rate was 6.3 % of the monthly total of infomercial submissions (Wicks & Abernethy, 1997).

Sales managers were responsible for advertising clearance on a day-to-day basis at most stations (see Table C.4; Wicks & Abernethy, 1997). A number did not reply to this question, which had been asked in previous surveys with no indication that the question was difficult to complete or understand. Thus, the researchers wondered whether some stations were reluctant to admit that they did not assign clearance responsibilities to a particular employee.

The researchers also asked respondents whether they had written advertising clearance policies, verbal policies, or no policies at all. Forty-four stations or 12.1 % indicated that they did not have ad clearance policies. Of those having policies, 158 or 43.4 % only communicated policies verbally, whereas 162 or 44.5 % communicated policies verbally and in writing (Wicks & Abernethy, 1997).

Stations were asked how stringent their advertising clearance standards are during certain dayparts (with 1 = *least stringent* and 7 = *most stringent*). Standards were most stringent on Saturday mornings when children are

TABLE C.4
Employee Responsible for Clearance Review

Employee	Percent of Stations	Number of Stations
Sales manager	24.7	90
General manager	10.7	39
Program director	7.7	28
Operations manager	5.0	18
Station manager	1.0	4
Traffic manager	7.7	28
Broadcast standards	1.9	7
None	12.1	44
Other	5.0	18
Did not answer	24.2	88

Note. N=364

likely to be viewing (average = 6.5), slightly less stringent during early fringe and prime access (e.g., 3–7 or 4–8pm, depending on time zone; average = 5.8); and least stringent during late fringe and late night (e.g., 10pm–5am or 11pm–6am) when few children are likely to be viewing (average = 3.3; Wicks & Abernethy, 1997).

Respondents were asked how readily their stations would accept certain ad types, even if they have yet to be submitted (with 7 = *always accepts* and 1 = *never accepts*). The averages for responses were: AIDS public service announcements (PSA) = 5.5, infomercials = 5.4, condom or safe sex PSA = 4.7, condom ads = 3.8, psychic ads = 3.4, and 900 phone number ads = 2.4.

CASE 2:
The Case of Capital Investment and *The Call & Journal*

The Call & Journal, in its 87th year, is one of the city's leading Black newspapers and as its chief financial officer, you are proud to help run such a forward-looking publication. And as the publisher's right-hand employee, you are poised to bring your newspaper into the 21st century.

You have noticed that many of the daily newspapers in the state already have web pages and you want *The C&J* to be in the forefront of technology among the city's Black papers. But you are not quite sure that the Internet is the same thing as the other innovations—color, pagination, and computers in general—that *The C&J* has adopted. You want to do your homework before you help set *The C&J* on a course it should not take. You sit down to assess the newspaper; here is what you know.

History and Market.   Your paper was founded to help combat racial discrimination. The founder, a member of the local NAACP chapter, received several death threats and once was beaten by the KKK. *The C&J* gained a following for its stand against Jim Crow laws and thereafter made civil rights its number one content priority, with the only major content change coming in the 1970s with the addition of sports and entertainment sections.

In the 1980s, the newspaper changed ownership and began to emphasize positive African-American images while continuing its focus on local civil rights matters. The paper served as a forum for discussion of racial change in the city and the publisher often served on civic boards and agencies, promoting progressive change.

Today, the paper has evolved into probably the city's most respected and read Black newspaper. The seven-person editorial staff has won several state and national journalistic awards with reporting focused on politics, social, school, business, religion, sports, health, and entertainment matters.

Its readers are married and middle class, typically Democratic voters who own their own homes and earn about $37,000 annually. Specifically, 42% are 35- to 54-years-old, 25% are 24- to 34-years-old, and 20% are 55- to 65-years-old. Forty-five percent earn between $30,000–$50,000; 32% earn $20,000–$29,000 and 15% earn $51,000–$99,000. Thirty-three percent graduated from college; 31% have some college education and 25% did not graduate from high school.

The C&J distributes its 22,000 press run via newsstands and neighborhood hawkers at churches and grocery stores. There are a few subscriptions, but newsstand sales—at $0.50 a copy—account for 85% of sales. Some 36% of readers live in the inner city; the rest are strategically targeted through direct mail, churches and other organizations. The competition consists of three other Black weeklies: *The Examiner-Post, The City Weekly,* and *The Beacon,* with circulations of 20,000, 13,500, and 25,000, respectively.

The Examiner-Post considers itself the voice of the city's underprivileged and progressive thinkers. It is a free publication distributed similarly to *The C&J* but without the latter's marketing savvy. It is published by a prominent local clergyman who is a former city-wide office holder and still active in civil rights issues and controversies. Its content consists mainly of the latest injustice or sensational crime in the Black community, with a heavy dose of news about local Black churches and the rest a hodgepodge of syndicated sports, opinion, and entertainment fluff about celebrities and civil rights issues. It is produced using 1970s computerized cold-type machinery; production quality typically varies from decent to sub-par. Its readers tend to be skewed—with nearly two thirds—the city's older, Black middle class vanguard.

The City Weekly is an upstart, 5-year-old publication that targets (about three fifths) the up-and-coming, younger Black professional with an income in the $30,000–$40,000 range. Content tends to focus on how-to-succeed stories, networking, new business opportunities as well as stories about 1980s- and 1990s-era Black celebrities. The publication has a well-designed, almost magazine-like quality, with advertising that tends to reflect the aspirations of success: heavy on new automobiles, technology, and fashion outlets. There is little mention of the civil rights struggle in the publication, which has doubled its size in the last 3 years.

The Beacon is owned by one of the city's elder statesmen who has put it up for sale. He and his family are seeking to get out of the publishing business altogether. *The Beacon's* circulation is down 7,500 from 2 years ago because of several factors: the publisher's failing health, *The C&J's* innovation, *The City Weekly's* niche and the limits on the market to support four similar publications. *The Beacon* has not attempted to change its content mix, preferring to focus on education and crime issues in the Black community and—unlike The C&J—*The Beacon* ignores the economic and cultural upheaval the city continues to experience.

The City.   The metropolitan area of 1.2 million is the largest in its region and the largest in the state. The economy is built on energy, medicine, high technology, and higher education. The city's school system is the seventh largest in the country, with nearly 175,000 students. Ethnically, the city's diverse, with a multicultural population of 25% Hispanic, 24% African American, 7% Asian American and the rest Caucasian. The minority communities are growing whereas the White population continues to decline.

Continuous Improvement.   *The C&J* prides itself on striving to constantly upgrade its product. High-quality software and hardware are no strangers to the staff. It uses digital technology to receive much camera-ready advertising. It is a fully paginated newspaper, with all pages designed and produced via personal computer.

It has conducted reader surveys, which have served to suggest new products. One such result is *C/J Youth*, a 7-year-old tabloid for teenagers, written by high school students, edited by a *C&J* staffer, and distributed at a dozen local high schools. Another is a newsletter distributed to current and potential advertisers; the publication touts *The C&J's* virtues in terms of content, ad reach, and circulation.

The Problem.   Just like any small business, *The C&J* constantly faces financial problems. Traditionally, Black newspapers use technology to complete an obvious, specific, labor-intensive task (e.g., word processing, design, layout and photo-imaging). But the Internet represents a great unknown.

The publisher knows his readers well. But he is unsure as to whether a web page is the best device to extend circulation and provide more services to readers. Neither he nor you have any idea as to how many readers *have access* to the Internet, much less if they *use* it. But you have a nagging sense that if you do not hop on the Internet express, it will pass you by (along with your competitors, especially *The City Weekly*, although none have a web page yet). So the publisher is considering investing in the necessary equipment. He has one bid from an Internet service provider and the estimate is $15,000—including the cost of new computer equipment (computer, monitor, scanner, modem, and phone lines). This will allow web page creation, online editions, access to newsbreaking stories online, and dialogue and interaction between staff and readers. This *does not include* what it would cost to include archives (i.e., previous editions), allow the 15-person staff to receive and send information via e-mail, network the staff computers, and allow the staff to access the Internet—those items were not included in the bid request. The paper would have to secure a loan to finance the purchase. He is not sure whether the paper should seek more bids because that will only delay the inevitable.

He has asked you to figure out what this will all cost him in terms of next year's budget. "Can't we amortize or depreciate some of the cost?" he asked.

You assure him it can be done, but that you'd like to have more bids so you can prepare a worst–and best-case scenario. You also remind him that he can partly recoup the costs of such a major purchase for *The C&J* via tax planning that annually deducts a percentage of the costs from income over the life of the asset. You advise that he can use either straight-line depreciation (in which an equal annual value is placed on the equipment for the life of its usage) or declining value depreciation (in which each year is assigned a different value, with the assumption that the value diminishes over time).

"For how many years?" he shoots back.

"Depends on the IRS code," you say, adding that it is usually 5 years for technical equipment but that you would have to check with the tax accountant to be sure.

"OK," he sighs.

"Let's work up a few budgets, see what the tax situation can be and decide whether we need to go web-light or web-heavy in terms of our costs. If Uncle Sam's going to help us out, we might as well take advantage of him. And check with a couple of banks to see what kind of interest rate they'd give us. You and your assistant get to work and see how we can save money and not compromise our long-term interests."

ASSIGNMENT

1. Check with at least four Internet service providers and get estimates for the new computer equipment *The C&J* will need.

2. Once you have decided which estimate is best, contact two or three local bank loan officers about what it would most likely cost *The C&J* (or a paper similar to it) to take out a loan to buy the equipment. Determine both the interest and life of the loan and compare the costs with the option of a direct cash purchase.

3. Research the probable shelf life of the equipment and prepare a depreciation table (using either straight-line or declining value depreciation) for a 5- or an 8-year period, depending on your findings.

4. Examine current Internal Revenue Schedules and the current code, consult with a local accountant or tax advisor, and determine the current allowable length for depreciation of the equipment. Also, determine for what kind of tax write off *The C&J* (or a similar-sized publication) could qualify and for how many years.

REFERENCES

Adams, J. S. (1963). Toward an understanding of inequity. *Journal of Abnormal and Social Psychology, 67*, 422–436.

Adams, R. C., & Fish, M. J. (1987). TV news directors' perceptions of station management style. *Journalism Quarterly, 64*, 154–162, 276.

Adler, S. J. (1991, October 9). Lawyers advise concerns to provide precise written policy to employees. *The Wall Street Journal*, pp. B1, B5.

Akharana-Majid, R., & Boudreau, T. (1995). Chain ownership, organization size, and editorial role perceptions. *Journalism and Mass Communication Quarterly, 72*, 863–873.

Agencies, networks battle over censor's role. (1983, November). *Adweek*, p. 52.

Aldag, R. J. & Brief, A. P. (1978). *Task design and employee motivation*. Glenview, IL: Scott, Foresman & Co.

Alderfer, C. P. (1972). *Existence, relatedness, and growth*. New York: Free Press.

Allen, M. W., Siebert, J. H., Haas, J. W., & Zimmerman, S. (1988). Broadcasting department impact on employee perceptions and conflict. *Journalism Quarterly, 65*, 668–677.

Altschull, J. H. (1984). *Agents of power*. New York: Longman.

AMA board approves new marketing definition. (1985, March 1). *Marketing News*.

America, A. (1991, May). Anatomy of a libel suit. *Presstime*, pp. 6–10.

Anderson, R., & Reagan, J. (1992). Practitioner roles and uses of news technologies. *Journalism Quarterly, 69*, 156–165.

Andron, S. (1997a). Message to journalists more about trust than law. *Quill, 85(7)*, 15–16.

Andron, S. (1997b). Scratched car saves ABC. *Quill, 85(7)*, 14–15.

Argyris, C. (1974). *Behind the front page*. San Francisco: Jossey-Bass.

Aronson, K., Sylvie, G., & Todd, R. (1996). Real–time journalism: Implications for news writing. *Newspaper Research Journal, 17(3–4)*, 53–67.

Armour, S. (1997, December 6). Team efforts, technology add news reasons to meet. *USA Today*, pp. 1A–2A.

Ascertainment of Community Problems by Commercial Broadcast Applicants, 57 FCC 2d 418 (1976).

Associated Press v. United States. 32 6 U.S. 1 (1945).

Bad weather checklist. (1997, October). *Presstime*, 44.

Barge, J. K. (1994). *Leadership: Communication skills for organizations and groups*. New York: St. Martin's Press.

Barnard, C.I. (1938). *The executive functions*. Cambridge, MA: Harvard University Press.

Bartlett, C. A. & Ghoshal, S. (1989). *Managing across borders: The transnational solution*. Boston, MA: Harvard University Press.

Bartlett, C. A., & Ghoshal, S. (1990). Transnational management. Homewood, IL: Irwin.

Bass, B. M. (1983). *Organizational decision making*. Homewood, IL: Irwin.

Bass, B. M. (1985). *Leadership and performance beyond expectations.* New York: Free Press.

Baxter, R. (1983a, August 29). Avoiding liability in firing employees. The National Law Journal, pp. 20–21.

Baxter, R. (1983b, September 12). Managing the risks in firing employees. *The National Law Journal,* pp. 20–21.

Becker, L., & Kosicki, G. M. (1997). Annual survey of enrollment and degrees awarded. *Journalism & Mass Communication Educator, 52*(3), 63–74.

Bendix, R. (1956). *Work and authority in industry.* New York: Wiley.

Bergen, L. A., & Weaver, D. (1988). Job Satisfaction of daily newspaper journalists and organization size. *Newspaper research Journal, 9*(12), 1–13.

Berger, W. (1990, September). Drug testing: Watchdog or witch–hunt? *Folio,* pp. 100, 102–106.

Bertelsmann, A. G. (1998). *Bertelsmann principle* (online).Available at: http://www.bertelsmann.de/bag/englisch/portrait/unternehmenskonzeption.html

Beville, H. (1988). *Audience ratings: Radio, television, cable* (rev. ed.). Hillsdale, NJ: Lawrence Erlbaum Associates.

Blackler, F., & Brown, C. (1985). Evaluation and the impact of information technologies on people in organizations. *Human Relations, 38*(3), 213–231.

Blanchard, K., Carew, D., & Parisi-Carew, E. (1990). One Minute Manager Builds High-Performing Teams. New York: William Morrow & Co, Inc.

Blankenburg, W. B. (1982). Newspaper ownership and control of circulation to increase profits. *Journalism Quarterly, 59,* 390–398.

Bogart, L. (1989). *Press and public* (2nd ed.). Hillsdale, NJ: Lawrence Erlbaum Associates.

Bramlett–Solomon, S. (1992). Predictors of job satisfaction among black journalists. *Journalism Quarterly, 69,* 703–712.

Bramlett-Solomon, S. (1993). Job appeals and job satisfaction among Hispanic and black journalists. *Mass Commmunication Review, 20*(3–4), 202–212.

Braus, P. (1992). What workers want. *American Demographics, 14*(8), 30–35.

Broadcasting/Cablecasting Yearbook. (1991). Washington, DC: Broadcast Publications.

Brodesser, C. (1997, September 8). Spot TV: Drug ads are a shot in the arm. *ADWEEK,* MO–14.

Brown, B. (1997). Jury still out on McVeigh trial. *Quill, 85*(7), 12–13.

Brown, K. F. (1990, July/August). The new newsroom: Challenges of hiring and keeping minorities will force newspapers to learn to adapt. *ASNE Bulletin,* 9–10.

Buchanan, D. A. (1985). Using the new technology. In T. Forester (Ed.), *The information technology revolution* (pp. 454–465). Cambridge, MA: MIT Press.

Burack, E., & Sorensen, P. F., Jr. (1976). Management preparation for computer automation: Emergent patterns and problems. *Academy of Management Journal, 19*(2), 318–323.

Burnett, R. (1992). The implication of ownership changes on concentration and diversity in the phonogram industry. *Communication Research, 19*(6), 749–769.

Butler, J. M., Broussard, E. J., & Adams, P. (1987). Stress and the public relations practitioner. *Southwestern Mass Communication Journal, 3,* 60–79.

Buzzell, R. D., & Cook, V. (1969). *Product life cycles.* Cambridge, MA: Marketing Science Institute.

Cameron, G. T., Hollander, B. A., Nowak, G. J., & Shamp, S. A. (1997). Assessing the potential of a full–featured electronic newspaper for the young adult market. In C. Warner (Ed.), *Media management review* (pp. 15–28). Mahwah, NJ: Lawrence Erlbaum Associates.

Carter, T., Dee, J., Gaynes, M., & Zuckman, H. (1994). *Mass communication law in a nutshell* (4th ed.). St. Paul, MN: West.

Carveth, R. (1992). The reconstruction of the global media marketplace. *Communication Research, 19*(6), 705–724.

Center for Law and Social Policy, 23 RR 2d 187 (1971).

Child, J. (1972). Organization structure, environment and performance: The role of strategic choice. *Sociology, 6*(1), 318–323.

Childs, K. (1997, July 5). Problems persist despite CDA ruling. *Editor & Publisher*, 3, 35.

Children's Television Report and Policy Statement, 50 FCC 2d 1 (1974).

Chyi, H. I., & Sylvie, G. (1998). Competing with whom? Where? And how? A structural analysis of the electronic newspaper market. *Journal of Media Economics, 11*(2), 1–18.

Collins, B., & Guetzkow, H. (1964). *Social psychology of group processes for decision making.* New York: Wiley.

Commercialization on TV Stations, 49 RR 2d 391 (1981).

The Commission on Freedom of the Press. (1947). *A free and responsible press.* Chicago: University of Chicago Press.

Cook, B. B., Banks, S. R., & Turner, R. J. (1993). The effects of work environment on burnout in the newsroom. *Newspaper Research Journal, 14*(3–4), 123–136.

Coulson, D. C. (1994). Impact of ownership on newspaper quality. *Journalism Quarterly, 71,* 403–410.

Cyert, R. M., & March, J. G. (1963). *A behavioral theory of the firm.* Englewood Cliffs, NJ: Prentice–Hall.

Davis, L. (1987, July/August). Looser, yes, but still the deans of discipline. *Channels*, pp. 33–34.

Davis, R. (1957). *The fundamentals of top management.* New York: Harper and Row.

Demers, D. (1996). Corporate newspaper structure, editorial page vigor, and social change. *Journalism and Mass Communication Quarterly, 73,* 857–877.

Denison, D. R. (1990). *Corporate culture and organizational effectiveness.* New York: Wiley.

Deregulation of Radio, 84 FCC 2d 968 (1981).

Deutsch, M. (1949, February). A theory of cooperation and competition. *Human Relations, 2,* 129–132.

Dillon, J. (1997, September 27). Contradictory impressions of libel. *Editor & Publisher,* 64, 48.

Driver, M. J., Brousseau, K. R., & Hunsaker, P. L. (1993). *The dynamic decision maker.* San Francisco: Jossey–Bass Publishers.

Drucker, P. F. (1983). The effective decision. In E. Collins (Ed.), *Executive success: Making it in management* (pp. 464–475). New York: Wiley.

Drug makers to debut TV ads providing more information. (1997, August 9). *Dallas Morning News*, 4F.

Dyer, W. G. (1995). *Team building: Current issues and new alternatives.* New York: Addison–Wesley.

Elimination of Unnecessary Broadcast Regulation, 50 Fed. Reg. 5583 (1985).

En banc programming inquiry. (1960). 44 FCC 2303.

Endres, F. (1988). Stress in the newsroom at Ohio dailies. *Newspaper Research Journal, 10*(1), 1–14.

Endres, F. (1992). Stress professional classes: Causes, manifestations, coping. *Journalism Educator, 47*(1), 16–30.

Endres, F., & Wearden, S. (1991). Personality and perceptions of professional job stress. *Journalism Educator, 46*(1), 54–65.

Endres, K., & Schierhorn, A. (1995). New technology and the writer/editor relationship: Shifting electronic realities. *Journalism and Mass Communication Quarterly, 72,* 448–457.

English, E. (1997, March/April). Avoiding copyright and other legal pitfalls in setting up your Web site. *Journal of Advertising Research,* 92–95.

Falcone, P. (1997, February). The fundamentals of progressive discipline: Employee discipline. *HR Magazine,* 90.

FDA to review standards for all direct–to–consumer RX drug promotion (1997, August 8). U.S. Department of Health and Human Services News Release. *HHS News.* Available at: http://www.fda.gov/bbs/topics/NEWS/NEW00582.htm.

Fielder, F. (1967). *A theory of leadership effectiveness.* New York: McGraw–Hill.

Fink, C. C. (1988). *Strategic newspaper management.* New York: Random House.

Fink, S. L. (1993). Managing individual behavior: Bringing out the best in people. In A.R. Cohen (Ed.), *The portable MBA in management* (pp. 71–112). New York: Wiley.

Fitzgerald, M. (1997, October 4). Benefits to homosexual partners. *Editor & Publisher,* 15–16.

Fitzgerald, N. (1997, October 13). Online safeguards. *ADWEEK,* 23–24.

Fleishman, E. A. (1956). A leader behavior description for industry. In R. M. Stogdik & A. E. Combs (Eds.), *Leader bahavior: Its description and measurement* (pp. 104–119). Columbus: Ohio State University Bureau of Business Research.

Fletcher, A. D., & Bowers, T. A. (1991). *Fundamentals of advertising research* (4th ed.). California: Wadsworth.

Fletcher, J. (Ed.). (1981). *Handbook of radio and TV broadcasting.* New York: Van Nostrand Reinhold.

For the record. (1997, June). *Presstime,* 35.

Fowler, G., & Shipman, J. (1982). Pennsylvania editors' perceptions of communication in the newsroom. *Journalism Quarterly, 61,* 822–826.

Franklin, J. (1997, December 29). Employment projections, table 4a. *BLS Home Page,* http://stats.bfs.gov/news.release/ecopro.table4.htm.

Fullerton, H. (1988). Technology collides with relative constancy: The pattern of adoption for a new medium. *Journal of Media Economics, 1, 75–84.*

FTC, FCC in liaison agreement on ads. (1987). RR Current Service, 2d, 11, pp. 212–214. (Originally published April 27, 1972.)

FTC v. Raladam Co. 283 U.S. 643 (1931).

Garneau, G. (1991a, April 20). Press freedom in deep trouble. *Editor & Publisher,* pp. 11, 44.

Garneau, G. (1991b, April 20). To err on the side of publishing. *Editor & Publisher,* pp. 9–10.

Gaziano, C., & Coulson, D. C. (1988). Effect of newsroom management styles on journalists: A case study. *Journalism Quarterly, 65,* 869–880.

Gellene, D. (1997, July 9). Drug firms airing ads for female contraceptive. *The Los Angeles Times,* D–3.

Gershon, R. A. (1997). *The transnational media corporation: Global messages and free market competition.* Mahwah, NJ: Lawrence Erlbaum Associates.

Giles, R. H. (1983). *Editors and stress.* New York: Associated Press Managing Editors Association.

Gillmor, D., Barron, J., & Simon, T. (1998). *Mass communication law: Cases and comment* (6th ed.). Belmont, CA: Wadsworth.

Gladney, G. (1990). Newspaper excellence: How editors of small and large papers judge quality. *Newspaper Research Journal,* 58–72..

Goldstein, N. (Ed.). (1996). *The Associated Press stylebook and libel manual.* Reading, MA: Addison–Wesley.

Graham, J. (1989, February 13). New VALS 2 takes psychological route. *Advertising Age,* 60, 24.

Granger, C. W. J. (1980). *Forecasting in business and economics.* New York: Academic.

Greene, C. N. (1972, October). The satisfaction–performance controversy. *Business Horizons,* 32–40.

Greer, D. F. (1980). *Industrial organization and public policy.* New York: Macmillan.

Griffin, R. W., & Moorhead, G. (1986). *Organizational behavior.* Boston: Houghton Mifflin.

Grunig, J., & Hunt, T. (1984). *Managing public relations*. New York: Holt, Rinehart & Winston.

Gubman, J., & Greer, J. (1997, August), *An analysis of online sites produced by U.S. newspapers: Are the critics right?* Paper presented to the Association for Education in Journalism and Mass Communication, Chicago.

Guide to understanding and using radio audience estimates. (1987). *Arbitron radio market report reference guide*. New York: Arbitron Ratings Co.

Gyles, B. (1997, June). Living to tell. *Presstime*, 45–50.

Hamner, W. C., & Organ, D. W. (1978). *Organizational behavior: An applied psychology approach*. Dallas: Business Publications.

Haney, W. V. (1973). *Communication and organizational behavior* (3rd ed.). Homewood, IL: Irwin.

Harrison, E. F. (1987). *The managerial decision–making process* (3rd ed.). Boston: Houghton Mifflin.

Head, S., & Stirling, C. (1990). *Broadcasting in America: A survey of electronic media*. Boston: Houghton Mifflin.

Heller, F. A., & Wilpert, B. (1981). *Competence and power in managerial decision–making*. Chichester, England: Wiley.

Hersey, P., & Blanchard, K. (1972). *Management of organizational behavior: Utilizing human resources* (2nd ed.). Englewood Cliffs, NJ: Prentice–Hall.

Herzberg, F. (1968). One more time: How do you motivate employees? *Harvard Business Review, 46*, 53–62.

Herzberg, F., Mausner, B., & Snyderman, B. (1959). *The motivation to work*. New York: Wiley.

Hofstede, G. (1980). *Culture's consequences: international differences in work–related values*. Beverly Hills, CA: Sage.

Hollifield, C. A. (1993, August). The globalization of Eastern Europe's print media: German investment during the post–revolution era. Paper presented to the Association for Education in Journalism and Mass Communication, Kansas City, MO.

Holtz-Bacha, C. (1996, May). Media concentration in Germany: On the way to new regulations. Paper presented to the International Communication Association, Chicago, IL.

House, J. R., & Dessler, G. (1974). The path-goal theory of leadership: Some post hoc and apriori tests. In J. G. Hunt & L. L. Larson (Eds.), Contingency approaches to leadership (pp. 60–75). Carbondale: Southern Illinois University.

Howard, H. H. (1973). *Multiple ownership in television broadcasting: Historical development and selected case studies*. Unpublished doctoral dissertation, Ohio University, Athens.

Huber, G. P. (1980). *Managerial decision making*. Glenview, IL: Scott Foresman.

Inquiry into Section 73.1910 of the Commission's Rules and Regulations Concerning Alternatives to the General Fairness Doctrine Obligations of Broadcast Licensees: Notice of Inquiry, 2 FCCRcd 1532 (1987); Report of the Commission, 2 FCC Rcd 5272 (1987); Memorandum Opinion and Order. 3 FCC Rcd 2050 (1988).

Irvine, R. (1997). What's a crisis, anyway? *Communication World, 14*(7), 36.

Ivancevich, J. M., Lorenzi, P., Skinner, S. J., & Crosby, P. B. (1994). *Management: Quality and competitiveness*. Burr Ridge, IL: Irwin.

Janis, I. L. (1982). *Groupthink* (2nd ed.). Boston: Houghton Mifflin.

Joffe, B. (1989, July). Law, ethics and public relations writers. *Public Relations Journal*, pp. 38–39.

Johnston, W. (1987). *Work force 2000*. Indianapolis: Hudson Institute.

Johnstone, J. W. C. (1976). Organizational constraints on newswork. *Journalism Quarterly, 53*, 5–13.

Jones, T. (1996, July 18). Big media deals on a roll. *Chicago Tribune*, (3):1.

Joseph, T. (1983). Television reporters' and managers' preferences on decision–making. *Journalism Quarterly, 60,* 476–479.

Jurczak, P. R. (1996, August). *Newsroom Cultures, newspaper acquisitions and the community: A case study of Pittsburgh newspapers.* Paper presented to the Association for Education in Journalism and Mass Communication, Anaheim, CA.

Katz study says Birch, Arbitron paint different portraits of radio listening. (1988, July 11). *Broadcasting,* 71–72.

Keeton, W. (Gen. Ed.). (1984). *Privacy. In Prosser & Keeton on Torts* (5th ed). St. Paul, MN: West.

Kiesler, C. A., & Kiesler, S. B. (1969). *Conformity.* Reading, MA: Addision-Wesley, 849–869.

Kirk, J. (1997, July 8). FDA may relieve TV advertisers. *Chicago Tribune,* D1.

KMPC, The Station of the Stars, Inc., 6 FCC 729 (1939).

Kodrich, K. P., & Beam, R. A. (1997, August). *Job satisfaction among journalists at daily newspapers: Does size of organization make a difference?* Paper presented to the Association for Education in Journalism and Mass Communication, Chicago, IL.

Kolodny, H., & Stjernberg, T. (1993). Self–managing teams: The news organizations of work. In A. R. Cohen (Ed.), *The portable MBA in management (pp. 290–314).* New York: Wiley.

Kotler, P. (1980). *Marketing management: Analysis, planning and control* (4th ed.). Englewood Cliffs, NJ: Prentice–Hall.

Kreitner, R. (1986). *Management* (3rd ed.). Boston: Houghton Mifflin.

Lacy, S. (1989). A model of demand for news: Impact of competition on newspaper content. *Journalism Quarterly, 66,* 40–48, 128.

Lacy, S. (1993). Understanding and serving readers: The problem of fuzzy market structure. *Newspaper Research Journal, 14*(2): 55–67.

Lacy, S., & Simon, T. F. (1992). *The economics and regulation of United States newspapers.* Norwood, NJ: Ablex.

Lafayette, J. (1996, June 17). Texas TV ads for liquor spur call for federal ban. *Electronic Media, 3.*

Lancaster, K., & Katz, H. (1989). *Strategic media planning.* Lincolnwood, IL: NTC Business Books.

Leavitt, H. (1965). Applied organizational change in industry. In J. March (Ed.), *Handbook of organizations* (pp. 1144–1170). Chicago: Rand McNally.

Lewin, K. R., Lippitt, R., & White, R. K. (1939). Patterns of aggressive behavior in experimentally created social climates. *Journal of Social Psychology, 10,* 371–299.

Liaison between FCC and FTC relating to false and misleading radio and TV advertising, RR Current Service 2d. 11, p. 201 (1987). (Originally published February 21, 1957).

Licensee Responsibility with Respect to the Broadcast of False, Misleading or Deceptive Advertising, 74 FCC 2d 623 (1961).

Likert, R. (1961). New patterns of management. New York: McGraw-Hill.

Lindstrom, P. B. (1997). The Internet: Nielsen's longitudinal research on behavioral changes in use of this counterintuitive medium. *Journal of Media Economics, 10*(2), 35–40.

Linton, B. (1987). Self–regulation in broadcasting revisited. *Journalism Quarterly, 64,* 483–490.

Liquor ads on TV stoke local fire. (1996, June 21). *Greater Baton Rouge Business Report, 9.*

Litman, B. (1988). Micoreconomic foundations. In R. G. Picard, J. P. Winter, M. E. McCombs & S. Lacy (Eds.), *Press concentration and monopoly* (pp. 3–34). Norwood, NJ: Ablex.

Locke, E. A. (1968). Toward a theory of task motivation and incentives. *Organizational Behavior and Human Performance, 3,* 157–189.

Martens, D. (1997). The first–time manager's survival guide. *Presstime,* 40–43.

Maslow, A. H. (1954). *Motivation and personality.* New York: Harper & Row.

Mauro, J. (1980). Application of census data for circulation sales. In P. Hirt (Ed.), *Census applications in newspaper management and marketing* (pp. 11–17). Reston, VA: International Newspaper Promotion Association.

Mauro, T. (1997). Internet feels court's embrace. *Quill, 85*(7), 30–32.

Mayo, E. (1945). *The social problems of an industrial civilization.* Boston: Graduate School of Business Administration, Harvard University.

McCavitt, W., & Pringle, P. (1986). *Electronic media management.* Boston: Focal Press.

McClelland, D. (1961). *The achieving society.* Princeton, NJ: Van Nostrand.

McEwan, E. K. (1997). *Leading your team to excellence.* Thousand Oaks, CA: Corwin Press, Inc.

McGregor, D. (1960). *The human side of enterprise.* New York: McGraw–Hill.

McKean, R. N. (1975). Cost–benefit analysis. In E. Mansfield (Ed.), *Managerial economics and operational research* (3rd ed., pp. 549–561). New York: Norton.

McQuarrie, F. A. E. (1992). Dancing on a minefield: Developing a management style in media organizations. In S. Lacy, A. B. Sohn, & R. H. Giles (Eds.), *Readings in media management* (pp. 229–239). Columbia, SC: Media Management & Economic Division of the Association for Education in Journalism and Mass Communication.

Meade, R. D. (1967). An experimental study of leadership in India. *Journal of Social Psychology, 72,* 35–43.

Media Perspektiven. (1994). Media perspektiven basisdaten: Daten zur mediensituation in Deutschland 1994 [Media Perspektiven base data: Data on the media situation in Germany 1994.] Frankfurt, Germany: Author.

Merskin, D. (1996, August). *The daily newspaper and audiotext personals: A case study of organizational adoption of innovation.* Paper presented to the Association for Education in Journalism and Mass Communication, Anaheim, CA.

Miller, P. & Miller, R. (1995). The invisible women: Female sports journalists in the workplace. *Journalism and Mass Communication Quarterly, 72,* 883–889.

Millman, C. (1996, November 17). Holiday TV ads may have a kick. *Chicago Tribune,* D1.

Mintzberg, H. (1979). *The structuring of organizations.* Englewood Cliffs, NJ: Prentice–Hall.

Miracle, G., & Nevett, T. (1987). *Voluntary regulation of advertising.* Lexington, MA: Heath.

Misumi, J. (1985). *The behavioral science of leadership.* Ann Arbor: University of Michigan Press.

Moriarty, S. (1986). *Creative Advertising: Theory and Practice.* Englewood Cliffs, NJ: Prentice–Hall.

Mueller, J. E. (1997). Delivery system disaster: Circulation problems of *The St. Louis Sun.* In C. Warner (Ed.), *Media management review* (pp. 115–125). Mahwah, NJ: Lawrence Erlbaum Associates.

NAB legal guide to FCC broadcast regulations. (1984). (2nd ed.). Washington, DC: National Association of Broadcasters.

Nadler, D. A., & Lawler, E. E. III. (1977). Motivation: A diagnostic approach. In J. R. Hackman, E. E. Lawler III, & L. W. Porter (Eds.), *Perspectives on behavior in organizations* (pp. 26–38). New York: McGraw–Hill.

Napoli, P. (1997). The media trade press as technology forecaster: A case study of the VCR<2146>s impact on broadcast. *Journalism and Mass Communication Quarterly, 74*(2), 417–430.

N.Y. Post fights Jewell lawsuit. (1997, September 6). *Editor & Publisher,* 40.

Noon, M. (1994). From apathy to alacrity: Managers and new technology in provincial newspaper. *Journal of Management Studies, 31*(1), 19–32.

Ouchi, W. (1981). *Theory Z.* New York: Avon Books.

Pease, T. (1992). *Race, gender, and job satisfaction in newspaper newsrooms.* In S. Lacy, A.B. Sohn, & R. H. Giles (Eds.), Readings in media management (pp. 97–122). Columbia, SC: Media management & Economics Division of the Association for Education in Journalism and mass Communication.

Petersen, B. K. (1992). The managerial benefits of understanding organizational culture. In S. Lacy, A. B. Sohn, & R. H. Giles (Eds.), *Readings in media management* (pp. 123–152). Columbia, SC: Media Management & Economics Division of the Association for Education in Journalism and Mass Communication.

Phillips, C. L. (1991). Evaluating and valuing newsroom diversity. *Newspaper Research Journal,* 12(2), 28–37.

Phillips, D. (1976). *A systematic study of the leadership process at the corporate level of two television group owners.* Unpublished doctoral dissertation, Ohio University, Athens.

Picard, R. G. (1988). Pricing behavior of newspapers. In R. G. Picard, J. P. Winter, M. E. McCombs, & S. Lacy (Eds.), *Press concentration and monopoly* (pp. 55–69). Norwood, NJ: Ablex.

Pilenzo, R. C. (1990, February). Managing for survival in the 1990s. *Modern Office Technology,* pp. 25–37.

Polansky, S. H., & Hughes, D. W. (1986). Managerial innovation in newspaper organizations. *Newspaper Research Journal, 8,* 1–12.

Policy regarding character qualifications in broadcast licensing, 102 FCC 2d 1179 (1986).

Policy statement on deception (1983). Letter from then Federal Trade Commission Chairman James C. Miller III to Congressman John D. Dingell, 14 October 1983. Reprinted as an appendix to Cliffdale, 103 FTC 110 at 174 (1984).

Policy statement regarding advertising substantiation program, 49 Federal Register 30999 (1984).

Porter, M. (1980). *Competitive strategy: Techniques for analyzing industries and competitors.* New York: Free Press.

Powers, A. (1990). The changing market structure of local television news. *Journal of Media Economics, 3*(1), 37–55.

Powers, A., & Lacy, S. (1992). A model of job satisfaction in local television news. In S. Lacy, A. Sohn, & R. Giles (Eds.), *Readings in Media Management* (pp. 5–20). Columbia, SC: Association for Education in Journalism and Mass Communication.

Preston, I. (1994). *The tangled web they weave: Truth, falsity and advertisers.* Madison, WI: University of Wisconsin Press.

Preston, I. (1996). *The great American blow-up: Puffery in advertising and selling.* (Rev. ed.). Madison, WI: University of Wisconsin Press.

Primer on Ascertainment of Community Problems by Broadcast Applicants, 27 FCC 2d 650 (1971).

Pruzan, T. (1996, June 17). Spirits spots could proliferate. *Advertising Age,* 8.

Public Service Responsibility of Broadcast Licensees (1946, July 2). Public Notice 95462, pp. 45–47. (Commonly known as the "Blue Book").

Puritz, J. (1996). *Making headlines on the Internet: Online newspapers and the challenge of cyberspace.* Paper presented to the Association for Education in Journalism and Mass Communication, Anaheim, CA.

Rauch, H. (1991, January). Editors beware! Improperly handled complaints mean trouble. *Folio,* pp. 108, 110–112.

Report on benefits for domestic partners. (1997, October 4). *Editor & Publisher,* 16.

Report and Statement of Policy re: Commission en banc Programming Inquiry, 44 FCC 2303 (1960).

Revision of Programming and Commercialization Policies, Ascertainment Requirements, and Program Log Requirements for Commercial Television Stations, 98 FCC 2d 1076 (1984).

Reynolds, P. D. (1971). *A primer in theory construction*. Indianapolis: Educational Publishing.

Rich, O., & Martin, E. (1981). Qualitative data: The why of Broadcast Research. In J. Fletcher (Ed.), *Handbook of radio and TV broadcasting* (117–136). New York: Van Nostrand Reinhold.

Richards, J. (1990). *Deceptive advertising: Behavioral study of a legal concept*. Hillsdale, NJ: Lawrence Erlbaum Associates.

Robins, M.J. (1997). Bad news for TV is good campaign. *TV Guide, 45*(4), 43–44.

Rogers, E. (1983). *Diffusion of innovation* (3rd ed.). New York: Free Press.

Rogers, E. (1986). *Communication technology: The new media in society*. New York: Free Press.

Rosener, J. (1990). Ways women lead. *Harvard Business Review,* 68, 119–125.

Ross, C. (1996, December 23). Anheuser–Busch pulls beer ads off MTV network. *Advertising Age,* 1, 27.

Rotfeld, H., Abernethy, A., & Parsons, P. (1990). Self–regulation and television advertising. *Journal of Advertising, 19*(4), 18–26.

Rudder, G. (1997, October). Newsprint '98. *Presstime,* 33–39.

Russial, J. T. (1997). Topic–team performance: A content study. *Newspaper Research Journal, 18*(1-2), 126–144.

Schein, E. H. (1985). *Organizational culture and leadership: A dynamic view*. San Francisco: Jossey–Bass.

Schiffman, L. G., & Kanuk, L .L. (1997). *Consumer behavior.* (6th ed.) Englewood Cliffs, NJ: Prentice–Hall.

Schumacher, L. (1997). Driver records still in jeopardy. *Quill, 85*(7), 23–25.

Schriesheim, J., & Schriesheim, C. (1980). Test of the path–goal theory of leadership and some suggested directions for further research. *Personnel Psychology, 33*(2), 349–371.

Severin, W. J., & Tankard, J. W., Jr. (1992). *Communication theories: Origins, methods, and uses in mass media* (3rd ed.). New York: Longman.

Shaver, M. (1995). *Making the sale: How to sell media with marketing*. Chicago, IL: Copy Workshop.

Sheppard, D. L. (1989). Organizations, power and sexuality: The image and self-image of women managers. In J. Hern, D. Shappard, P. Tancred–Sheriff, & G. Burell (Eds.), *The sexuality of organization* (pp. 139-157). London: Sage.

Sherif, M. (1962). *Intergroup relations and leadership*. New York: Wiley.

Shoemaker, P. (1987). Building a theory of news content. *Journalism Monographs,* 103.

Silvesti, G. (1997, December 29). Employment projections, table 4b, *BLS Home Page,* http://stats.bls.gov/ecopro.table6.htm.

Simmons Market Research Bureau (1989). *Simmons 1989 study of media markets: Total audiences*. New York: Simmons Market Research Bureau.

Simon, H. (1957). *Models of man*. New York: Wiley.

Simon, H. (1960). *New science of management decisions*. New York: Harper & Row.

Sissors, J., & Surmanek, J. (1982). *Advertising media planning* (2nd ed.). Chicago: Crain.

Skinner, B. F. (1972). *Beyond freedom and dignity*. New York: Knopf.

Smith, G. D., Arnold, D. R., & Bizzell B. G. (1985). *Strategy and business policy*. Boston, Houghton Mifflin.

Smith, P. B., & Peterson, M. F. (1988). *Leadership, organization and culture*. London: Sage.

Sohn, A. B., & Chusmir, L. (1985). The motivational perspectives of newspaper managers. *Journalism Quarterly, 62,* 492–496.

Sohn, A., Ogan, C., & Polich, J. (1986). *Newspaper leadership*. Englewood Cliffs, NJ: Prentice–Hall.

Solomon, D. (1989, December). *Media research tool box.* Marketing & Media Decisions, 24, 122, 124–125.

Stein, M. (1997a, July 5). First Amendment advice. *Editor & Publisher,* 19, 31.

Stein, M. (1997b, October 4). Advice on freelance rights. *Editor & Publisher*, 24.

Stern, C. (1996, February 5). New law of the land. *Broadcasting & Cable*, 8, 12.

Stigler, G. J. (1952). *The theory of price* (rev. ed.). New York: Macmillan.

Stoneman, P. (1983). *The economic analysis of technological change.* New York: Oxford University Press.

Strassmann, P. (1976). Stages of growth. *Danamation, 22*(10), 46–50.

Straub, J. T. (1984). *Managing: An introduction.* Boston: Kent Publishing.

Sukosd, M. (1992, October). *No title.* Paper presented at the Battelle–Mershon conference on technology and democracy, Columbus, OH.

Sullivan, D., & Goldberg, H. (1997). Public speaking out on privacy concerns. *Quill, 85*(7), 17–19.

Sundar, S. S., Narayan, S., Obregon, R., & Uppal, C. (1997, August). *Does Web advertising work? Memory for print versus online media.* Paper presented to the Association for Education in Journalism and Mass Communication, Chicago.

Supreme court overturns anti–trust rule that prohibited publishers from establishing the maximum resale price of newspapers. (1997). NAA Public Policy/Legal Affairs Page. *State Oil v. Khan.* U.S. Supreme Court case decided November 4, 1997. http://www.naa.org/ppolicy/legal/resale.html.

Sylvie, G. (1995). Editors and pagination: A case study of management. *Journal of Mediated Communication, 10*(1), 1–20.

Sylvie, G. (1996). Departmental influences on interdepartmental cooperation in daily newspapers. *Journalism and Mass Communication Quarterly, 73*, 230–241.

Sylvie, G., & Danielson, W. (1989, May). *Editors and hardware: Three case studies in technology and newspaper management.* Austin, TX: The University of Texas at Austin.

Syracuse Peace Council v. Television Station WTVH, 2 FCC Rcd 5043 (1987); Order Requesting Comment, 2 FCC Rcd 794 (1987).

Tannenbaum, R., & Schmidt, W. H. (1973, May/June). How to choose a leadership pattern. Harvard Business Review, pp. 162–180.

Tausky, C. (1980). Theories of organization. In J. A. Litterer (Ed.), *Organizations: Structure and behavior* (3rd ed., pp. 11–33). New York: Wiley.

Taylor, F. (1947). *Scientific management.* New York: Harper.

Taylor, R. N. (1984). *Behavioral decision making.* Glenview, IL: Scott, Foresman.

Terry, C. (1997a, September). Times group begins drug policy. *Presstime*, 54.

Terry, C. (1997b, October) AAJA trains would–be leaders. *Presstime*, 44.

Time settles Jewell claim (1997, September 20). *Editor & Publisher*, 39.

Tip on the Telcom. (1996, February 5). *Broadcasting & Cable*, 9.

Tobenkin, D. (1997, October 6). Univision vs. Telemundo. *Broadcasting & Cable*, 34–42.

Toner, M. (1997a, May). 1997: Another billion–dollar year. *Presstime*, 76–77

Toner, M. (1997b, July). Duplicating pre-press savings. *Presstime*, 78.

Truitt, R. (1997a, July). "No benefits": Get it in writing. *Presstime*, 35.

Truitt, R. (1997b, October). Round two in cyberight fight. *Presstime*, 24.

Turow, J. (1992). The organizational underpinning of contemporary media conglomerates. *Communication Research, 19*(6), 682–704.

TV ad for contraceptive wins FDA approval. (1997, July 9). *Advertising Age*, 11.

Two network affiliates accept TV ads for lifestyle condoms. (1996). *Supermarket Business, 51*(11), 49.

U.S. Department of Commerce National Telecommunications and Information Administration. (1993). *The globalization of the mass media.* NTIA Special Publication 93–290. Washington, DC: Government Printing Office.

U.S. House of Representatives Committee on Government Operations. (1980). International information flow: Forging a new framework. Washington, DC: U.S. Government Printing Office.

U.S. House of Representatives Committee on Government Operations. (1981). *International Communications Reorganization Act of 1981*. Washington, DC: U.S. Government Printing Office.

U.S. House of Representatives Subcommittee on Telecommunications, Consumer Protection, and Finance of the Committee on Energy and Commerce. (1981). *Telecommunications and information products and services in international trade*, serial No. 97–59. Washington, DC: U.S. Government Printing Office.

Van Maanen, J., & Barley, S. R. (1984). Occupational communities: Culture and control in organizations, In B. M. Staw, & L. L. Cummings (Eds.), *Research in organizational behavior* (pp. 287–365). Greenwich, CT: JAI Press.

Veronis, C. (1990, March). Moving minorities up instead of out. *Presstime*, pp. 23–25.

Vroom, V. H. (1964). *Work and motivation*. New York: Wiley.

Vroom, V. H., & Yetton, P. W. (1973). *Leadership and decision making*. Pittsburgh: University of Pittsburgh Press.

Walley, W. (1990, September 24). Nets force Nielsen showdown. *Advertising Age*, pp. 3, 60.

Warner, C. (1997). Compensating broadcast salespeople: Some recommendations. In C. Warner (Ed.), *Media management review* (pp. 157–176). Mahwah, NJ: Lawrence Erlbaum Associates.

Weaver, D. H., & Wilhoit, G. C. (1996). *The American journalist in the 1990s: U.S. news people at the end of an era*. Mahwah, NJ: Lawrence Erlbaum Associates.

Weber, M. (1947). *The theory of economic and social organization*. (A. M. Henderson & T. Parsons, Trans.). New York: Free Press. (Original work published 1921.)

Webster's new world dictionary (2nd College ed.). New York: Simon and Schuster.

Whiting, C. S. (1995, October). Operational techniques and creative thinking. *Advanced Management*, pp. 24–30.

Wickham, P. (Ed.). (1988). *The insider's guide to demographic know–how*. Ithaca, NY: American Demographics Press.

Wicks, J. L. (1991a). An exploratory study of television advertising practices: Do profitability and organization size affect clearance formality? *Journal of Advertising, 20*(3), 1–12.

Wicks, J. L. (1991b). Varying commercialization and clutter to enhance airtime attractiveness in early fringe: How TV sales managers may be responding to deregulatory freedoms. *Journal of Media Economics, 4*, 3–18.

Wicks, J. L. (1994). Does infomercial clearance vary by managerial, organizational and market factors? *Journal of Broadcasting Electronic Media, 38*(2), 229–239.

Wicks, J. L., & Abernethy, A. (1997). *Do employee ethical beliefs affect advertising clearance decisions at commercial television stations?* Paper presented to the Association for Education in Journalism and Mass Communication, Chicago.

Williamson, O. E. (1964). *The economics of discretionary behavior: Managerial objectives in a theory of the firm*. Englewood Cliffs, NJ: Prentice–Hall.

Willis, J. (1988). *Surviving in the newspaper business: Newspaper management in turbulent times*. New York: Praeger.

Wimmer, R., & Dominick, J. (1991). *Mass media research* (3rd ed.). Belmont, CA: Wadsworth.

Wirth, M. (1977). *The effects of crossmedia ownership on television and newspaper prices*. Unpublished doctoral dissertation, Michigan State University, East Lansing, MI.

Witcover, J. (1971, September/October). Two weeks that shook the press. *Columbia Journalism Review*, pp. 7–15.

Zanot, E. (1985). Unseen but effective advertising regulation: The clearance process. *Journal of Advertising, 14*, 44–51, 59, 68.

AUTHOR INDEX

SUBJECT INDEX